The Narrative Function of the Holy Spirit as a Character in Luke-Acts

SOCIETY
OF BIBLICAL
LITERATURE

DISSERTATION SERIES

David L. Petersen, Old Testament Editor
Pheme Perkins, New Testament Editor

Number 147

THE NARRATIVE FUNCTION OF THE HOLY SPIRIT
AS A CHARACTER IN LUKE-ACTS

by
William H. Shepherd, Jr.

William H. Shepherd, Jr.

THE NARRATIVE FUNCTION OF THE HOLY SPIRIT AS A CHARACTER IN LUKE-ACTS

Scholars Press
Atlanta, Georgia

THE NARRATIVE FUNCTION OF THE HOLY SPIRIT AS A CHARACTER IN LUKE-ACTS

William H. Shepherd, Jr.

Ph.D., 1993
Emory University

Advisor:
Fred B. Craddock

Library of Congress Cataloging in Publication Data
Shepherd, William H. (William Henry), 1947-
    The narrative function of the Holy Spirit as a character in Luke
-Acts / William H. Shepherd, Jr.
        p.   cm. — (Dissertation series / Society of Biblical
Literature ; no. 147)
    Originally presented as the author's thesis (Ph.D.)—Emory
University, 1993.
    Includes bibliographical references.
    ISBN 0-7885-0019-8 (alk. paper). — ISBN 0-7885-0020-1 (pbk. :
alk. paper)
    1. Holy Spirit—Biblical teaching. 2. Bible. N.T. Luke—
Criticism, interpretation, etc. 3. Bible. N.T. Acts—Criticism,
interpretation, etc. I. Title. II. Series: Dissertation series
(Society of Biblical Literature) ; no. 147.
BS2545.H62S544   1994
231'.3—dc20   94-29596
                                                    CIP

Printed in the United States of America
on acid-free paper

Table of Contents

Chapter 1

Introduction

The Holy Spirit, of course, figures greatly in the book of Acts—so much so that Luke's second volume has been referred to as "the gospel of the Holy Spirit." Scholars attempt to discern how Luke's view of the Holy Spirit fits in with his overall theology.[1]

Mark Allan Powell correctly notes the prominence of the Holy Spirit in Acts (as in the Gospel of Luke), but his summary of scholarship suggests the inadequacy of such studies: they look for a "view" which is part of a "theology." Scholars have tried to delineate a "conception" of the Spirit—either Luke's own theological conception, or that of the early church. While this approach has produced many laudable insights, in the end it fails to take into account that Luke wrote neither a personal theological treatise nor a theology of the early church, but a narrative. The quest for Luke's theology (or that of the Lukan community) falls short because it seeks conceptions where one actually finds story.

---

[1]Mark Allan Powell, *What Are They Saying about Acts?* (New York: Paulist Press, 1991), 50.

A more adequate approach would do full justice to the form of Luke's work. The purpose of this study is to determine the narrative function of the Holy Spirit in Luke-Acts. Working in narrative rather than doctrinal categories, I will make explicit use of a broad spectrum of literary and narrative theories. Such theories provide a category useful for this study; that category is "character." My thesis is that the Holy Spirit in Luke-Acts is best understood as a character in the narrative.

No effort in biblical studies, however, stands in isolation; therefore the present chapter will examine previous scholarship on the Holy Spirit in Luke-Acts, in order to profit from its accomplishments as well as clarify its limitations. Chapter Two will lay the theoretical foundation for the rest of this study: what do we mean when we speak of "character" in a literary work? It will first be necessary to determine exactly what words such as "literary" and "narrative" mean, and to question whether such categories are appropriately applied to biblical documents. I will then discuss and evaluate theories of character and characterization in current narrative studies, and show that the Spirit can be said to be a "character" in Luke-Acts. The two following chapters (one on Luke and one on Acts) will be exegetical; using categories presented in Chapter Two, I will analyze in order and in detail the narrative sections in which the character of the Holy Spirit appears, in order to ascertain the role of this character in Luke's narrative. I will show that this character functions to ensure the reliability of the narrative and thus serves Luke's avowed literary purpose of providing the reader with "certainty" (ἀσφάλεια, Luke 1:4).[2]

Until recently, studies of the Holy Spirit in Luke-Acts have concentrated on two major questions: (1) What (or who) is the Holy

---

[2]On the translation "certainty" (rather than NRSV "truth"), see *Greek-English Lexicon of the New Testament Based on Semantic Domains,* ed., Johannes P. Louw and Eugene A. Nida (New York: United Bible Societies, 1988), 1:371 (§ 31.41), and Luke Timothy Johnson, *The Gospel of Luke,* Sacra Pagina Series, vol. 3 (Collegeville, Minn.: The Liturgical Press, 1991), 28. See below, chap. 3, on Luke 1:1-4.

Spirit according to Luke? and (2) What does the Holy Spirit do?[3] Both of these questions are at heart theological. The first question asks whether some seeds of later Trinitarian theology can be found in Luke. The second attempts to place Luke within the developing pneumatology of the early church. These questions have been discussed at length, yet have produced little in the way of a consensus. In this chapter, I will review the many ways in which scholars have answered these two questions, critique the methods used, and examine the tentative steps scholarship has taken in a new direction that holds great promise and is the basis for my own proposal.

What (or Who) Is the Holy Spirit?

Should the Holy Spirit, as depicted in Luke-Acts, be thought of as a personal being (a Who) or an impersonal force (a What)? Modern New Testament scholars have disagreed on this point; representative of those who lean toward the latter option is G. H. W. Lampe:

> St. Luke follows the Old Testament in his conception of the nature of the divine Spirit. In his writings the Spirit is still, generally speaking, non-

---

[3]For reviews of research see François Bovon, *Luke the Theologian: Thirty-Three Years of Research (1950-1983)*, trans. Ken McKinney, Princeton Theological Monograph Series, no. 12 (Allison Park, Penn.: Pickwick Publications, 1987), 198-238; Robert P. Menzies, *The Development of Early Christian Pneumatology with Special Reference to Luke-Acts*, Journal for the Study of the New Testament Supplement Series, no. 54 (Sheffield: JSOT Press, 1991), 18-47; Powell, *Acts*, 50-56; idem, *What Are They Saying about Luke?* (New York: Paulist Press, 1989), 108-11; M. M. B. Turner, "Jesus and the Spirit in Lucan Perspective," *Tyndale Bulletin* 32, (1981): 3-42; idem, "Luke and the Spirit. Studies in the Significance of Receiving the Spirit in Luke-Acts," Ph.D. diss., Cambridge University, 1980, 1-41.

On my twofold division of the issues, cf. J. Patout Burns and Gerald M. Fagin, *The Holy Spirit*, Message of the Fathers of the Church, vol. 3 (Wilmington: Michael Glazier, 1984), 14-15; Powell, *Acts*, follows a similar format, adding a separate section on the reception of the Spirit.

personal; it is the mode of God's activity in dealing with man and the
power in which he is active among his people.[4]

On the other hand, J. H. E. Hull attributes to Luke an almost
Trinitarian view:

> We have found ample evidence in Acts to show that the Church is not
> represented as being driven by Something but led by Some One.[5]

While there are those who side with either Lampe[6] or Hull[7] on this
issue, the disagreement is nothing new. Lampe draws on a tradition

---

[4]G. W. H. Lampe, "The Holy Spirit in the Writings of St. Luke," in *Studies
in the Gospels: Essays in Memory of R. H. Lightfoot*, ed. D. E. Nineham (Oxford:
Basil Blackwell, 1955), 163.

[5]J. H. E. Hull, *The Holy Spirit in the Acts of the Apostles* (London: Lutterworth Press, 1967), 172.

[6]Herman Gunkel, *The Influence of the Holy Spirit: the Popular View of the
Apostolic Age and the Teaching of the Apostle Paul* (1888), trans. Roy A. Harris-
ville and Philip A. Quanbeck, II (Philadelphia: Fortress Press, 1979), 6-7; Hans
Leisegang, *Pneuma Hagion: Der Ursprung des Geistbegriffs der synoptischen
Evangelien aus der griechischen Mystik* (Leipzig: Hinrichs, 1922), 22ff; Ernest
F. Scott, *The Spirit in the New Testament* (New York: George H. Doran Co.,
[1923]), 87. Eduard Schweizer speaks of the Spirit as "a fluid which fills man"
(*Theological Dictionary of the New Testament*, 6:406)—definitely a "what"!

[7]N. Adler, *Das erste christliche Pfingstfest. Sinn und Bedeutung des
Pfingstberichtes Apg. 2: 1-13* (Münster, Aschendorff'sche Verlagsbuchhandlung,
1938); idem, *Taufe und Handauflegung. Eine exegetisch-theologische
Untersuchung von Apg. 8, 14-17* (Münster, Aschendorff'sche Verlagsbuchhand-
lung, 1951); Heinrich von Baer, *Der Heilige Geist in den Lukasschriften*, Beiträge
zur Wissenschaft vom Alten und Neuen Testament: Ditte Folge Heft 3 (Stuttgart:
W. Kohlhammer, 1926); Bovon, *Luke the Theologian*, 219; F. F. Bruce, "The
Holy Spirit in the Acts of the Apostles," *Interpretation* 27 (1973): 173; Robert
Koch, "Spirit," *Encyclopedia of Biblical Theology*, originally published as
Bibeltheologisches Wörterbuch, ed. Johannes B. Bauer, 3rd ed., 1967 (London:
Sheed and Ward, 1970) 3:869-89; Henry Barclay Swete, *The Holy Spirit in the
New Testament: A Study of Primitive Christian Teaching* (London: Macmillan and
Co., Ltd., 1921), 291; Arthur W. Wainwright, *The Trinity in the New Testament*
(London: SPCK, 1962), 200-201.

Yves M. J. Congar (*I Believe in the Holy Spirit*, trans. David Smith (New
York: Seabury Press, 1983), 1:47) cites in support of this view Gonzalo Haya-
Prats (*L'Esprit, force de l'Eglise. Sa nature et son activité d'apres les Actes des*

at least as old as Hermann Gunkel's influential *Die Wirkungen des heiligen Geistes nach der populären Anschauung der apostolischen Zeit und der Lehre des Apostels Paulus*[8] in seeing something "indeterminate, impalpable, and impersonal"[9] in Luke's depiction of the Spirit. Hull follows a tradition far more ancient, as patristic writers cited Acts 10:19-20 as proof that the Holy Spirit was the Third Person of the Trinity.[10]

Yet the question "Who or What?" is thoroughly modern in both form and content: that it *asks* about the personality of the Spirit, and that it asks about *Luke's view* of the Spirit, distinguishes it from precritical biblical scholarship. There was little debate in the early church over the personality of the Holy Spirit; the debate, when there was one (mainly in the fourth century C.E.), was over the Spirit's place in the Godhead. References to the Spirit in the Apostolic Fathers were rare and never dealt with the issue of the Spirit's nature. By the time of the Apologists (mid-second century C.E.), however, the Spirit was clearly attributed a personality (e.g., Athenagoras, *Plea Regarding Christians*, 10) and placed within a "triad" including the Father and the Son (Theophilus, *To Autolycus* 2.10). Irenaeus at the end of the second century fleshed out the Trinitarian model in reaction to the Montanist controversy, and established a consensus that held through the next century (Irenaeus, *Against Heresies*, 3.1.1; 3.4.1-2; 3.17.1-3; 3.24.1; 4.20.1, 6-8; 5.9.1-3). Thereafter, the personality of the Spirit was not in ques-

---

apôtres (Paris: Éditions de Cerf, 1975), 82-90) though Haya-Prats notes (p. 82) that the distinction between personal and impersonal would not have occurred to Luke.

[8]Göttingen: Vandenhoeck & Ruprecht, 1888; citations are from the English translation (see n. 6).

[9]Gunkel, *Influence of the Holy Spirit*, 6.

[10]Bovon, *Luke the Theologian*, 218. See also idem, *De Vocatione Gentium: histoire de l'interprétation d'Act 10, 1 - 11, 18 dans les six premiers siècles*, Beiträge zur Geschichte der biblischen Exegese, vol. 8 (Tübingen: J. C. B. Mohr (Paul Siebeck), 1967), 195-98.

tion.[11] By the time the issue of pneumatology was raised once again, in the fourth century, the debate was not whether the Spirit had a personality, but what sort of personality it was. The full divinity of the Spirit and its existence as distinct hypostasis in the Trinity was affirmed at the Council of Constantinople (381) and the Council of Rome (382), having been championed by many, especially the Cappadocian Fathers, Basil of Caesarea, Gregory of Nazianzus, and Gregory of Nyssa.[12] The place of the Spirit as the Third Person of the Trinity having been established, the personality of the Spirit was hardly questioned in the church, apart from some fringe groups, until the rise of modern biblical criticism.[13]

Further, the idea that Luke's view of the Spirit would have been any different from Paul's or Jesus' or Amos's would have seemed strange before historical criticism. The early church did not treat Luke as a separate, independent thinker. Indeed, patristic writers made their cases primarily on the basis of the more complete pneumatologies of Paul and John; where they cited Luke-Acts, they

---

[11]An exception might be Lactantius (c. 240-320 C.E.), who was said by Jerome to deny the personality of the Spirit; this is not certain, however. See Henry Barclay Swete, *The Holy Spirit in the Ancient Church: A Study of Christian Teaching in the Age of the Fathers* (London: Macmillan and Co., 1912), 150-51; also 373-76.

[12]Basil of Caesarea, *Letter 125,* and *On the Holy Spirit;* Gregory of Nazianzus, *Fifth Theological Oration* and *Sermon on Pentecost;* Gregory of Nyssa, *On the Holy Spirit Against the Followers of Macedonius, On the Holy Trinity, That We Should Not Think of Saying There are Three Gods,* and *Third Sermon on the Lord's Prayer.* Other important authors include Cyril of Jerusalem, *Catechetical Lectures;* Athanasius, *To Serapion;* Hilary of Poitiers, *On the Trinity;* Didymus the Blind, *On the Holy Spirit;* Epiphanius, *Ancoratus;* Ambrose of Milan, *On the Holy Spirit.* See Burns and Fagin, *Holy Spirit,* 90-154.

[13]On the personality of the Spirit in post-patristic periods, see Howard Watkin-Jones, *The Holy Spirit in the Mediaeval Church: A Study of Christian Teaching Concerning the Holy Spirit and His Place in the Trinity from the Post-Patristic Age to the Counter-Reformation* (London: Epworth, 1922), 329-31; idem, *Holy Spirit from Arminius to Wesley: A Study of the Christian Teaching Concerning the Holy Spirit and His Place in the Trinity in the Seventeenth and Eighteenth Centuries* (London: Epworth, 1929), 131-47.

read it in light of the others.[14] To question "Who or What?" and to ask the question solely of Luke is by and large a modern phenomenon.[15] However, modern scholarship continues to cast the issue in theological terms. In this sense, it hearkens to the theological tradition of the church. Those who are concerned for the theological continuity of church tradition may see Luke as in full harmony with later tradition, as does Hull: the Spirit is a Person in Luke-Acts, says Hull, attributed implicit if not explicit divinity—Hull in effect continues the reading of the early church, where the pneumatology of Luke is read in light of fuller and more specific theologies.[16] Scholars such as Lampe, who see the Spirit as an impersonal force, tend to stretch continuity in the other direction; Luke, they would

---

[14]E.g., the blending of John and Acts in John Chrysostom: "The Gospels, then, are a history of what Christ did and said; but the Acts, of what that 'other Comforter' said and did" (*First Homily on Acts*, 5, cited in Burns and Fagin, *Holy Spirit*, 156-57). The index to Swete, *Holy Spirit in Ancient Church*, a book which contains extensive excerpts from patristic literature, has ten references to Luke (many of which refer to passages shared with Mark and Matthew), only four to Acts, but thirty-two to John and twenty-one to the Pauline epistles.

[15]On the Spirit in patristic thought, see A. Benoit, "Le Saint-Esprit et l'église, dans la théologie patristique greque des quatre premiers siècles," in *L'Esprit Saint et L'Eglise*, ed. S. Dockx (Paris, Fayard, 1969), 125-41; J. H. S. Burleigh, "The Doctrine of the Holy Spirit in the Latin Fathers," *Scottish Journal of Theology* 7 (1954): 113-32; Burns and Fagin, *Holy Spirit*; G. W. H. Lampe, *The Seal of the Spirit: A Study in the Doctrine of Baptism and Confirmation in the New Testament and the Fathers* (London: Longmans, Green and Co., 1951); John McIntyre, "The Holy Spirit in Greek Patristic Thought," *Scottish Journal of Theology* 7 (1954): 353-75; Paul D. Opsahl, ed. *The Holy Spirit in the Life of the Church from Biblical Times to the Present* (Minneapolis: Augsburg Publishing House, 1978); Swete, *Holy Spirit in Ancient Church*. On later periods, see Opsahl, *Holy Spirit in Life of Church;* Watkin-Jones, *Holy Spirit in Mediaeval Church;* idem, *Holy Spirit from Arminius to Wesley.*

[16]Hull's argument even resembles patristic exegesis at times—as, e.g., when he argues that the masculine participle used of the Holy Spirit in Acts 28:25-26 proves that Luke "thought of the Holy Spirit in 'personal' terms" (Hull, *Holy Spirit in Acts*, 155). For examples of Hull's harmonization of Luke with John and Paul, see pp. 156-67; for his appropriation of patristic thought, see p. 174, where he cites Augustine, *On the Trinity.*

hold, stands in the tradition of the Hebrew scriptures, where
Trinitarian thought is unknown, and the Spirit could rarely be construed as anything other than a mysterious, impersonal power.[17] The
dichotomy between the two attempts to establish Luke's theological
lineage spills over into the second question usually asked of the
Spirit: what does the Spirit do? Those who read Luke as standing in
line with earlier tradition tend to limit the Spirit's work to inspiration of prophetic speech,[18] while those who read Luke in light of
Paul, John, and the early church will attribute additional functions,
involving salvation and sanctification, to Luke's Spirit.[19] In both
cases, the issue is theological: where does Luke stand in relation to
theological thought before and after him?

The theological impetus behind the modern question "Who or
What?" can be illustrated by the mediating position of Rudolf Bultmann. Bultmann gives classic expression to a middle way, a position
between the two extremes of "Who" and "What."[20] According to

---

[17]See Lampe, "Holy Spirit in Writings of Luke," 160-63. "St. Luke follows
the Old Testament in his conception of the nature of the divine spirit....It is in
terms of the Old Testament view of the Spirit...that St. Luke interprets the events
which it is the purpose of his two books to record" (163).

[18]A prime example is the thoroughgoing attempt of Menzies (*Development of
Early Christian Pneumatology*) to limit the Spirit's work in Luke-Acts to inspired
speech; Menzies sees Luke as indebted entirely to Old Testament pneumatology
and only partially in continuity with that of Paul (see esp. pp. 1-48 for his review
and critique of scholarship on this question). See also Lampe, ("Holy Spirit in
Writings of Luke," 193) who explicitly contrasts Luke's pneumatological view of
preaching to the pneumatologies of John and Paul.

[19]See, e.g., Hull, *Holy Spirit in Acts,* 143-68. See below, pp. 17-20.

[20]Other representatives of the mediating position include Henry J. Cadbury,
The Making of Luke-Acts (New York: Macmillan Co., 1927), 270; Joseph A.
Fitzmyer, *The Gospel According to Luke,* Anchor Bible, vol. 28 (Garden City:
Doubleday & Co., Inc., 1981), 1:228; Marie E. Isaacs, *The Concept of Spirit: A
Study of Pneuma in Hellenistic Judaism and its Bearing on the New Testament,*
Heythrop Monographs, vol. 1 (London: Heythrop College (University of
London), 1976), 89; Wilfred L. Knox, *The Acts of the Apostles* (Cambridge:
Cambridge University Press, 1948), 92; Gerhard Krodel, "The Functions of the
Spirit in the Old Testament, the Synoptic Tradition, and the Book of Acts," in
Holy Spirit in Life of Church, ed. Opsahl, 36-37; Edward William Winstanley,
Spirit in the New Testament: An Enquiry into the Use of the Word ΠΝΕΥΜΑ *in*

Bultmann, both conclusions, though mutually incompatible, are understandable, for they reflect two very different conceptions of πνεῦμα, both of which are found in Luke-Acts. These two conceptions Bultmann calls "animistic" and "dynamistic":

> In *animistic thinking pneuma* is conceived as an independent agent, a personal power which like a demon can fall upon a man and take possession of him, enabling him or compelling him to perform manifestations of power. In *dynamistic thinking*, on the contrary, *pneuma* appears as an impersonal force which fills a man like a fluid, so to say. One or the other of these ways of thinking may be distinctly present in a given passage; but in general little emphasis is placed upon the distinction, and the two conceptions can intertwine in the same author.[21]

According to Bultmann, both conceptions can be traced to the Old Testament, and both were common in early Christianity.[22] Thus Luke followed a somewhat confused tradition which conceived of πνεῦμα as both personal and impersonal. While Bultmann maintains that the authors of the New Testament saw little difference between the two ways of thinking, the conceptual clash has plagued other scholars, who seem loath to let this potential contradiction go unresolved.[23]

All Passages, and a Survey of the Evidence Concerning the Holy Spirit (Cambridge: Cambridge University Press, 1908), 133. Many would agree that "On ne peut donc dire que Luc voie nettement l'Esprit Saint comme une personne divine semblable et égale au Père et au Fils, mais sa présentation de l'Esprit est ouverte sur les développements ultérieurs" (A. George, "L'Esprit Saint dans l'oeuvre de Luc," *Revue biblique* 85 (1978): 533).

[21] Rudolf Bultmann, *Theology of the New Testament*, trans. Kendrick Grobel, Scribner Studies in Contemporary Theology (New York: Scribner's, 1951), 1:155. Emphasis his.

[22] Ibid., 155-57.

[23] Cf. the contention of Eduard Schweizer (in *Theological Dictionary of the New Testament*, 6:406) that Luke is attempting to overcome the (Jewish) animistic view of the Spirit with the (Hellenistic) dynamistic view, in the interest of a more holistic anthropology: "This view is better adapted to define the Spirit as that which moulds the whole existence of man." Yet Luke retains some animistic language, "for it emphasizes the fact that the Spirit is fundamentally the Spirit of God, alien to man." Schweizer thus harmonizes the two "views" by positing a

Note that for Bultmann, as for most modern scholars, it is a matter of Luke's "conception" of the Spirit. But is this really the right question? M. M. B. Turner has criticized Bultmann on this point:

> Whereas in the oldest strata of the OT these different types of language *may* have corresponded to animistic and dynamistic *conceptions* of the Spirit, by the time *Luke* wrote such language can no longer be considered a sure indication of the way men *thought;* it could merely have been a *way of speaking.*[24]

Turner believes that Luke's use of both types of expressions reflect either a self-conscious metaphor, or a "dead" metaphor—a metaphor in use long after its users ceased to be aware of the origin of the expression.[25] In either instance, the issue is not Luke's conception of the Spirit, but his use of language. What Bultmann has observed in Luke-Acts is not that there are two conceptions of the Spirit, but that there are two ways of speaking of the Spirit.

Turner's criticism of Bultmann is linguistically naive, as it posits too great a dichotomy between language and reality; metaphors, even supposedly "dead metaphors," participate in and help create the reality of which they speak.[26] But Turner does begin to ask the right question: the question of language. Modern scholarship has shown more interest in the theological conceptions lying behind Luke's language than in the language itself. But Luke's language is

---

conceptual evolution.

[24]M. M. B. Turner, "Spirit Endowment in Luke-Acts: Some Linguistic Considerations," *Vox Evangelica* 12 (1981): 50. Emphasis his.

[25]Turner owes the expression "dead metaphor" to G. B. Caird, *The Language and Imagery of the Bible* (London: Duckworth, 1981), 66.

[26]See Max Black, *Models and Metaphors: Studies in Language and Philosophy* (Ithaca: Cornell University Press, 1962); Paul Ricoeur, *The Rule of Metaphor: Multi-disciplinary Studies of the Creation of Meaning in Language,* trans. Robert Czerny, Kathleen McLaughlin, and John Costello (Toronto: University of Toronto Press, 1977); S. Sacks, ed, *On Metaphor* (Chicago: University of Chicago Press, 1979).

that of narrative, not systematic theological discourse. "Conception" is not an adequate category by which to analyze a narrative and its components. The shortcomings of this theologically-laden approach become more evident when we turn to the second question usually asked in discussions of the role of the Holy Spirit in Luke-Acts: what does the Holy Spirit do?

What Does the Holy Spirit Do?

While there is no firm consensus on whether the Holy Spirit is a Who or a What, there is broad agreement that for Luke, the Spirit is the Spirit of prophecy. As Lampe says, "To Luke the Spirit means primarily the Spirit of prophecy," and the function of Spirit is "to witness to Christ by empowering and inspiring the preaching of the gospel and by reproducing Jesus' own works of power."[27] Thus

---

[27]G. W. H. Lampe, *God as Spirit*, The Bampton Lectures, 1976 (Oxford: Clarendon Press, 1977), 65. This was established by Baer, *Heilige Geist in den Lukasschriften*, and popularized by Hans Conzelmann, *The Theology of St. Luke*, trans. Geoffrey Buswell (New York: Harper & Row, 1961). Other studies include David E. Aune, *Prophecy in Early Christianity and the Ancient Mediterranean World* (Grand Rapids: Eerdmans, 1983); Darrell L. Bock, *Proclamation from Prophecy and Pattern: Lucan Old Testament Christology*, Journal for the Study of the New Testament Supplement Series, vol. 12 (Sheffield: Sheffield Academic Press, 1987); M. Eugene Boring, *The Continuing Voice of Jesus: Christian Prophecy and the Gospel Tradition* (Louisville: Westminster/John Knox Press, 1991); Max-Alain Chevallier, "Luc et l'Esprit Saint," *Revue des Sciences Religieuses* 56 (1982): 10-11; idem, *Souffle de Dieu. Le Saint-Esprit dans le Nouveau Testament*, Le Point Théologique, no. 26 (Paris: Editions Beauchesne, 1978) 1:160-225; Nils Alstrup Dahl, "The Purpose of Luke-Acts," in *Jesus in the Memory of the Early Church* (Minneapolis: Augsburg Publishing House, 1976), 87-98, 1976; idem, "The Story of Abraham in Luke-Acts," in *Jesus in the Memory of the Early Church* (Minneapolis: Augsburg Publishing House, 1976), 66-86; Fitzmyer, *Luke*, 1:228-30; George, "L'Esprit Saint"; Haya-Prats, *L'Esprit*; David Hill, *New Testament Prophecy* (London: Marshall, Morgan & Scott, 1979); Jacob Jervell, "Sons of the Prophets: The Holy Spirit in the Acts of the Apostles," in *The Unknown Paul: Essays on Luke-Acts and Early Christian History* (Minneapolis: Augsburg Publishing House, 1984), 96-121; idem, "The Center of Scripture," in *The Unknown Paul: Essays on Luke-Acts and Early Christian History* (Minneapolis: Augsburg Publishing House, 1984), 122-37; Luke T. Johnson, *The Literary Function of Possessions in Luke-Acts*, Society of Biblical Literature Dissertation Series, no. 39 (Missoula, Mont.: Scholars Press,

Luke stands in continuity with the Old Testament scriptures, which connect the Spirit with the divine empowerment received by the prophets.[28] The Spirit spoke through the prophets of the Old Testament (Acts 1:16; 4:25; 28:25). The same Spirit of prophecy was at work in Jesus (Luke 3:22; 4:1, 14, 18; 10:21; 24:49; Acts 1:2; 10:38), who as a prophet spoke "the word of God" (Luke 5:1; 8:11;

1977); idem, *Luke;* Knox, *Acts,* 89; Menzies, *Development of Early Christian Pneumatology;* David P. Moessner, "Luke 9:1-50: Luke's Preview of the Journey of the Prophet like Moses of Deuteronomy," *Journal of Biblical Literature* 102 (1983): 575-605; Gottfried Nebe, *Prophetische Züge im Bilde Jesu bei Lukas, Beiträge zur Wissenschaft vom Alten und Neuen Testament,* vol. 127 (Stuttgart: Verlag W. Kohlhammer, 1989); Leo O'Reilly, *Word and Sign in the Acts of the Apostles: A Study in Lucan Theology* (Rome: Editrice Pontificia Università Gregorriana, 1987); James B. Shelton, *Mighty in Word and Deed: The Role of the Holy Spirit in Luke-Acts* (Peabody, Mass.: Hendrickson Publishers, 1991); Roger Stronstad, *The Charismatic Theology of St. Luke* (Peabody Mass.: Hendrickson Publishers, 1984); David L. Tiede, *Prophecy and History in Luke-Acts* (Philadelphia: Fortress Press, 1980); M. M. B. Turner, "Luke and the Spirit. Studies in the Significance of Receiving the Spirit in Luke-Acts," Ph.D. diss., Cambridge University, 1980; Stephen G. Wilson, *The Gentiles and the Gentile Mission in Luke-Acts* (Cambridge: Cambridge University Press, 1973), 29-55.

[28]On the Spirit in the Old Testament, see Charles A. Briggs, "The Use of רוח in the Old Testament," *Journal of Biblical Literature* 19 (1900): 132-45; Ernest DeWitt Burton, *Spirit, Soul, and Flesh: The Usage of* Πνεῦμα, Ψυχή, *and* Σάρξ *in Greek Writings and Translated Works from the Earliest Period to 180 A.D.; And of Their Equivalents* רוּחַ, נֶפֶשׁ, *and* בָּשָׂר *in the Hebrew Old Testament,* reprinted, with additions and revisions, from the *American Journal of Theology,* 1913-1916, Historical and Linguistic Studies, second series, vol. 3 (Chicago: University of Chicago Press, 1918); J. Köberle, *Natur und Geist nach dem Auffassung des Alten Testaments* (München: C. H. Beck, 1901); Robert Koch, *Geist und Messias: Beitrag zur biblischen Theologie des Alten Testaments* (Vienna: Verlag Herder, 1950); Daniel Lys, *"RUACH": Le Souffle dans l'Ancien Testament: enquête anthropologie a travers l'histoire theologique d'Israel* (Paris: Presses Universitaires de France, 1962); Menzies, *Development of Early Christian Pneumatology,* 52-67; Lloyd Neve, *The Spirit of God in the Old Testament* (Tokyo: Seibunsha, 1972); William Ross Shoemaker, "The Use of רוח in the Old Testament and of πνεῦμα in the New Testament: A Lexicographical Study," *Journal of Biblical Literature* 23 (1904): 13-67; Paul Volz, *Der Geist Gottes und die verwandten Erscheinungen im Alten Testament und im anschliessenden Judentum* (Tübingen: J. C. B. Mohr (Paul Siebeck), 1910).

11:28; 21:33; 24:19); he was in fact the promised "prophet like Moses" (Deut 18:15-19; 34:10-12, cf. Acts 2:22-24).[29] And among the early Christians, the Spirit was still at work through prophets (Acts 11:28; 13:1-4; 19:6; 21:10-11). The Spirit of prophecy is a unifying force throughout Luke's narrative—what was foretold by the prophets was fulfilled in Jesus, and the disciples carry on the work of Jesus:

> Witness is rooted in prophecy, and therefore the latter, though necessarily transformed by the coming of the Christ and the fullness of time, did not disappear but in a new form remained at the centre of the life of God's Israel, the disciples of Jesus. Our Lord's possession of the Spirit, his prayer, and his gift of prophecy were all passed on in full measure to the Christian community.[30]

Most scholars agree that the prophetic Spirit is at work in the inspired speech of the disciples—the Spirit inspires them as they carry out their witness:

> It is above all else as the power granted for the church's preaching that the gift [of the Spirit] is portrayed in Lucan theology. Hence, the Spirit is primarily the prophetic spirit which we find so prominent in the writings of Hellenistic Judaism.[31]

---

[29]Adrian Hastings, *Prophet and Witness in Jerusalem: A Study of the Teaching of St. Luke* (London: Longmans, Green, 1958), 50-75; Johnson, *Luke,* 18-20; Lampe, "Holy Spirit in Writings of Luke," 172-76; Paul S. Minear, *To Heal and to Reveal: The Prophetic Vocation According to Luke* (New York: The Seabury Press, 1976), 102-9; David P. Moessner, *Lord of the Banquet: The Literary and Theological Significance of the Lukan Travel Narrative* (Minneapolis: Fortress Press, 1989), 45-69; idem, "Luke 9:1-50," 582-605; Tiede, *Prophecy and History,* 17, 39-55; Turner, "Luke and the Spirit," 73-95.

[30]Hastings, *Prophet and Witness,* 97.

[31]Isaacs, *Concept of Spirit,* 89. Other scholars who connect the prophetic Spirit and witness are Chevallier, "Luc et l'Esprit Saint," 10; Congar, *I Believe in the Holy Spirit,* 19; Hastings, *Prophet and Witness;* Haya-Prats, *L'Esprit;* I. Howard Marshall, "The Significance of Pentecost," *Scottish Journal of Theology* 30 (1977): 365; Menzies, *Development of Early Christian Pneumatology,* 245; and Schweizer, *Theological Dictionary of the New Testament,* 6:407-9.

M. M. B. Turner ("The Significance of Receiving the Spirit in Luke-Acts: A Survey of Modern Scholarship" *Trinity Journal,* n.s. 2 (1981): 157) argues that it is wrong to identify the Spirit of prophecy with either preaching or prophecy

While not usually called "prophets," the disciples are described in stereotypically prophetic terms, language familiar to readers of the Greek Old Testament: they are "filled with the Spirit" (πίμπλημι, Acts 2:4; 4:8, 31; 9:17; 13:9) or "full of the Spirit" (πλήρης, 6:3, 5, 8; 7:55; 11:24)[32] and so speak with "boldness" (2:29; 4:13, 29, 31; 9:27-28; 13:46; 14:3; 19:8; 26:26; 28:31)[33] as "witnesses" (1:8; 2:32; 3:15; 5:32; 10:39, 41; 13:31; 22:15, 20; 26:16)[34] "to the people" of Israel (3:12; 4:1, 10, 17; 5:20, 25; 10:42; 13:15, 31; 21:39; 28:26).[35] The disciples speak, as did Jesus and the prophets of old, the "word of God" (Luke 1:2; Acts 2:41; 4:4, 29; 6:2, 4, 7; 8:4, 14, 25; 10:36, 44; 11:1, 19; 12:24; 13:5, 7, 44, 46, 49; 14:3, 25; 15:7, 35, 36; 16:6, 32; 17:11, 13; 18:11; 19:10, 20; 20:32).[36]

That Luke connects "the Spirit" (rather than "God" or "Jesus") with prophecy is significant, in that it points to his appropriation of his literary forebears. Luke writes while breathing the rich air of the

---

itself, but rather the Spirit is the divine-human organ of communication. It is difficult, however, to see how this communication can take place in the abstract, apart from preaching and/or prophecy.

[32]Cf. Exod 31:3; 35:31; Mic 3:8; Wisd 1:7; Sir 48:12 LXX (Codex A)). For the connection between the Spirit and prophecy, see e.g., Gen 41:38; Num 11:24-30; 23:7 LXX; 24:2; 27:18; 1 Sam 10:6, 10; Isa 61:1; Ezek 2:2; Joel 2:28.

[33]Boldness was frequently demonstrated by Old Testament prophets, e.g. Moses before Pharaoh, Nathan before David, Elijah before Ahab.

[34]Cf. Isa 43:10, 12; 44:8

[35]Cf. e.g., LXX Exod 4:16, 30; 11:2; 13:3; 14:13; Num 11:24; Amos 7:15.

[36]Cf. Deut 18:19-20; Amos 1:1; 3:1; 4:1; 5:1; 7:16; Mic 1:1; Joel 1:1; Jonah 1:1; 3:1; Zeph 1:1; 2:5; Zech 1:1-7; 4:6, 8; 6:9; 7:1-12; 8:1; 9:1; Isa 1:10; 2:3; 28:14, 23; Jer 1:2-13; 2:4, 31; 7:2; 10:1; 14:1; 17:15, 20; 22:1 and often in Jeremiah; Ezek 1:3; 2:7; 3:4, 16 and often in Ezekiel.

Johnson (*Luke*, 17) notes other language which is reminiscent of Old Testament prophets: "Good news," "signs and wonders." "Taken together," says Johnson, "these characteristics point unmistakably to one image in the biblical tradition, that of the prophet" (p. 18).

Septuagint; his portrait of Jesus and the disciples is indebted to the biblical portrait of the Spirit-empowered prophet. For Luke to speak of the prophetic Spirit is to place his writing within the biblical literary tradition; further, it is to appropriate and reinterpret that tradition. Luke gives the prophetic Spirit a new context while asserting connections between old and new; as many have noted, the prophetic Spirit in Luke-Acts provides continuity among Jesus, the church, and their biblical predecessors.[37] Luke's church can claim to embody Israel, because the same Spirit which was at work in Moses, Elijah, and Elisha is at work in Jesus, Peter, and Paul. The "word of God" preached by Jesus and the disciples is like that given to the Old Testament prophets. The rhetorical function of the depiction of the Spirit as prophetic is to establish continuity between Israel and the church.

That the Lukan Spirit is the Spirit of prophecy is the one point on which there is broad consensus among scholars. But what, exactly, does this Spirit do? When one tries to move beyond this point, a wide variety of positions emerges. Is the Spirit in Luke-Acts responsible solely for inspired, prophetic speech, or does the Spirit enable salvation and sanctification (as in Paul)? And what relationship does Luke posit among human reception of the Spirit, rites such as baptism and laying-on-of-hands, and overt manifestations of the Spirit such as healing power and glossolalia? One finds myriad answers to these questions.

Most scholars agree that the Spirit in Luke-Acts is primarily the source of inspired speech. There is disagreement, however, on whether Luke limits the Spirit to this function. For example, what is the role of the Spirit in the miracles performed by Jesus and the disciples? Eduard Schweizer holds that Luke does not connect healing miracles with the Spirit:

> Though miracles are important for Luke, they are never ascribed to the Spirit. Healing power is associated with the name of Jesus, with faith in Jesus, with Jesus himself, with prayer, with bodily contact through the dis-

---

[37]This idea was fundamental to the threefold salvation-history scheme developed by Baer and Conzelmann; it persists even among those who reject the threefold scheme. See e.g., Johnson, *Luke*, 17-21.

ciple, his shadow or his handkerchief, or more simply with the δύναμις of Jesus.[38]

While his observations are true, most scholars agree that Schweizer's construal of the Lukan rhetoric is too narrow. Schweizer himself notes the close connection of πνεῦμα and δύναμις (Luke 1:17, 35; 4:14, 18-19; 5:17, 24:49; Acts 1:8; 6:5, 8; 10:38); some think that this is proof enough that the Spirit is behind the healing miracles.[39] Further, Leo O'Reilly notes the connection Luke makes between miracles and preaching: the miracles are in fact part of the preaching.[40] Jesus is "a man attested to you by God with deeds of power, wonders, and signs" (Acts 2:22). Preaching and healing are frequently linked by Luke (Luke 4:14, 23, 36; 5:15; 7:21-22; 9:1-2; Acts 3:1-4:22; 10:38; 14:3, 8-10; 16:16-18; 20:7-12).

> The miracles authenticate the word, attest to its divine origin, and make it possible for the disciples to speak more boldly. In addition, the miracles themselves are interpreted as signs of the glory that Jesus has received from God and so they too are proclamations that Jesus is Lord.[41]

As we shall see, miracle-working is part of the prophetic profile: the prophetic figures of Luke-Acts, like those of the Old Testament, work "signs and wonders" (Acts 2:19).[42] And certainly Luke does

---

[38]Schweizer, *Theological Dictionary of the New Testament*, 6:408. Cf. Haya-Prats, *L'Esprit*, 38-43; Menzies, *Development of Early Christian Pneumatology*, 124-26; Eduard Schweizer, *The Holy Spirit*, trans. Reginald H. Fuller and Ilse Fuller (Philadelphia: Fortress Press, 1980), 58-59.

[39]Hull, *Holy Spirit in Acts*, 137-42. Cf. C. K. Barrett, *The Holy Spirit and the Gospel Tradition* (London: SPCK, 1947), 69-78, esp. p. 76.

[40]O'Reilly, *Word and Sign*.

[41]Powell, *Acts*, 53. Cf. Jervell, "The Signs of an Apostle: Paul's Miracles," in *Unknown Paul*, 79-90; Lampe, "Holy Spirit in Writings of Luke," 184; Shelton, *Mighty in Word and Deed*, 78; Turner, "Significance of Receiving the Spirit," 155; and idem, "Jesus and the Spirit in Lucan Perspective," 16-17.

[42]Johnson, *Luke*, 17-18.

not limit the scope of the miraculous to healing; the disciples' sudden ability to speak in foreign tongues is certainly miraculous, certainly of the Spirit, and certainly a means of proclaiming the word of God (Acts 2).[43] For Luke, the Spirit is "the *miraculous* power behind bold and effective witness."[44]

Is the Spirit connected to salvation? Does Luke see the Spirit as a sanctifying force? That is, is the Spirit of Paul also the Spirit of Luke? If so, the Spirit would certainly influence not only inspired speech and action, but the moral and spiritual growth of the disciples. J. H. E. Hull argues that the superiority of baptism in the Spirit over the water baptism of John (Acts 1:4) consists in provision of

> the power to rise to nobler heights of living. Jesus Himself had been full of the Holy Spirit and it was this fact which had accounted for His life. When men were baptized with the Spirit, they in their turn would be Spirit-saturated men. The Holy Spirit would make them holy too.[45]

But surely this is to "read Luke's pneumatology with Pauline-colored spectacles";[46] the contrast between John's baptism and Spirit-baptism is not enough evidence to justify Hull's contention. Heinrich von Baer argues more convincingly that there is a strong connection between the Spirit and the inner lives of the disciples: the Spirit was responsible for "boldness," (Acts 4:31), "joy" (13:52), "fear of God" (9:31) and the formation of the community (Acts 2:43-47, 4:32-33).[47] Luke can even speak of "the comfort of the Spirit" (9:31). Yet one could argue that all of these passages have to

---

[43]Shelton, *Mighty in Word and Deed*, 74-78.

[44]Ibid., x. Emphasis mine.

[45]Hull, *Holy Spirit in Acts*, 44.

[46]Shelton, *Mighty in Word and Deed*, 135.

[47]Baer, *Heilige Geist in den Lukasschriften*, 188-90.

do with mission, not sanctification.[48]

Some scholars see the Lukan Holy Spirit at work in the conversion of new believers. James D. G. Dunn's influential work, *Baptism in the Holy Spirit,* holds that

> the baptism in or gift of the Spirit was part of the event (or process) of becoming a Christian, together with the effective proclamation of the Gospel, belief in (εἰς) Jesus as Lord, and water-baptism in the name of the Lord Jesus; that it was the chief element in conversion-initiation so that only those who had thus received the Spirit could be called Christians; that the reception of the Spirit was a very definite and often dramatic *experience,* the decisive and climactic experience in conversion-initiation, to which the Christian was usually recalled when reminded of the beginning of his Christian faith and experience.[49]

Dunn tries to show that the New Testament writers are unified in these beliefs, but his interpretation of Luke-Acts becomes quite strained in the process. For example, he argues that the disciples had no faith before Pentecost.[50] Dunn is generally thought to have

---

[48]Menzies (*Development of Early Christian Pneumatology,* 39) points out an inconsistency in Baer's views:

> On the one hand Baer insists that the Spirit's activity is distinctive in each of the various epochs, but on the other hand he emphasizes the fundamental continuity which binds Luke's pneumatology and scheme of salvation history together. Similarly, Baer asserts that the Spirit is the source of the moral-religious life of the believer, yet he acknowledges that it is fundamentally the power to proclaim the gospel. One is left with a sense of ambiguity.

Turner makes the same observation ("Jesus and the Spirit in Lucan Perspective," 3-7; "Luke and the Spirit," 10-15; "Significance of Receiving the Spirit," 138-41).

[49]James D. G. Dunn, *Baptism in the Holy Spirit: A Re-Examination of the New Testament Teaching on the Gift of the Spirit in Relation to Pentecostalism Today,* Studies in Biblical Theology: Second Series, no. 15 (London: SCM Press Ltd., 1970), 4. Emphasis his.

[50]Ibid., 52. This view founders on Luke 17:5 and 22:32.

assimilated Luke and Paul too readily.[51]

Thus some scholars have questioned whether Luke depicts the Holy Spirit effecting conversion. Many would agree with Roger Stronstad in excluding the work of the Spirit in Luke-Acts from the realm of salvation or sanctification:

> for Luke, the Holy Spirit is not brought into relation to salvation or to sanctification, as is commonly asserted, but is exclusively brought into relation to a third dimension of Christian life—service....Luke is found to have a charismatic rather than a soteriological theology of the Holy Spirit.[52]

As James Shelton has noted, however, the question depends on how one connects "salvation" with the mission of proclaiming "the Word of God"; if inspired speech produces conversion, then the Spirit certainly has a soteriological function. Shelton believes that the connection Luke seems to make between the Spirit and conversion is due to the close relationship between witness and conversion:

---

[51]See the sharp criticism by Turner ("Jesus and the Spirit in Lucan Perspective," 29-31; "Luke and the Spirit," 25-28 and passim; "Significance of Receiving the Spirit," 149-53); and Menzies (*Development of Early Christian Pneumatology,* 31-34 and passim).

[52]Stronstad, *Charismatic Theology of Luke,* 12. Cf. Bruce, "Holy Spirit," 178; Gunkel, *Influence of the Holy Spirit,* 43; Haya-Prats, *L'Esprit,* 118-62; Lampe, "Holy Spirit in Writings of Luke," 193-200; Marshall, *Luke, Historian and Theologian,* 199-202; Menzies, *Development of Early Christian Pneumatology,* 47-49; Schweizer, *Theological Dictionary of the New Testament,* 6:407-13; idem, *The Holy Spirit,* 126.
M. M. B. Turner has proposed a mediating view. He argues against Dunn that Luke sees the Spirit as the matrix of Christian life in the Pentecost story, yet he agrees with Dunn that the Spirit mediates salvation—Jesus is empowered by the Spirit to bring salvation, and so the Spirit brings salvation through Jesus ("Jesus and the Spirit in Lucan Perspective," 33; "Significance of Receiving the Spirit," 157-58). The Spirit is essential to Christian existence as the mode of communication between God and humanity ("Luke and the Spirit," 185). But it is hard to see how the Spirit can be responsible for such communication apart from the actual message communicated; see the critique of Menzies, *Development of Early Christian Pneumatology,* 43-47 and passim.

Luke does not clearly delineate between the Spirit's role in conversion and empowerment for mission. This is especially true in Acts 5:29-32 where the preaching of repentance, witness of believers, and witness of the Holy Spirit are mentioned in close proximity. Why is Luke not clearer? It is primarily because the role of the Holy Spirit in conversion is not his major interest. His fundamental concern is to show how the witness concerning Jesus spread.[53]

And if, as I shall argue later, the Spirit is at work building a community which will spread this Word of God, the Spirit's activity cannot be limited to inspired speech (cf. Acts 1:15-26; 2:37-47; 4:23-31; 4:32-5:11; 6:1-7; 8:4-25; 10:1-48; 13:1-3; 15:1-35; 18:24-19:7).[54]

There is little consensus on the frequently-discussed question of the connection of the reception of the Spirit, baptism, laying-on-of-hands, and glossolalia. As Powell notes, many scholars attribute a normative function to Acts 2:38, but other sections of Acts do not cohere to such a norm:

At the conclusion of his sermon on the day of Pentecost, Peter tells the crowd that has gathered, "Repent and be baptized every one of you in the name of Jesus Christ...and you will receive the gift of the Holy Spirit" (Acts 2:38). At first, this may appear to offer a divine order for the life of faith: 1) repentance, 2) baptism, 3) gift of the Spirit. But actually, the situation is more complex....The Spirit may also come after baptism and the laying on of hands (with some lapse of time between these two); after baptism accompanied immediately by the laying on of hands; or before baptism as the divine response to inward faith (Acts 8:14-17; 19:1-7; 10:44-48).[55]

Repentance and baptism are frequently held to be Luke's normal conditions for reception of the Spirit.[56] But one could easily argue

---

[53]Shelton, *Mighty in Word and Deed*, 135.

[54]See below, chap. 4.

[55]Powell, *Acts*, 55.

[56]Chevallier, "Luke et L'Esprit Saint," 7; Congar, *I Believe in the Holy Spirit*, 45; J. Giblet, "Baptism in the Spirit in the Acts of the Apostles," *One in Christ* 10 (1974) 162-71; Hull, *Holy Spirit in Acts*, 119-20; Kirsopp Lake, "The Holy Spirit," in *The Beginnings of Christianity: Part I, The Acts of the Apostles*,

that Acts 2:38 represents the exception, and the norm is found else-where. Dunn, for example, pointing to passages where the reception of the Spirit is not linked to baptism, sees faith and not baptism as the normative prerequisite for the reception of the Spirit.[57] Talbert holds that it is not faith *per se* but prayer which brings the Spirit, and cites Luke 11:13; Acts 1:14; 2:1-4; 2:21; 2:39; 4:23-31; 8:15-18; and 22:16.[58] Baer holds that the reception of the Spirit was con-nected to laying-on-of-hands; here he is followed by Adler, Käsemann, and Bovon.[59] Whichever view one holds, one must

---

ed. Kirsopp Lake and Henry J. Cadbury (London: Macmillan and Co., Ltd., 1933) 5:109-10; Lampe, "Holy Spirit in Writings of Luke," 199-200; Marshall, *Luke: Historian and Theologian*, 181; Menzies, *Development of Early Christian Pneumatology*, 247 (with reservations); George T. Montague, *The Holy Spirit: Growth of a Biblical Tradition* (New York: Paulist Press, 1976), 287; Opsahl, *Holy Spirit in Life of Church*, 32-36; Schweizer, *Theological Dictionary of the New Testament*, 6:414; Shelton, *Mighty in Word and Deed*, 11.

[57]Dunn, *Baptism in the Holy Spirit*, 55-68, following Gunkel, *Influence of the Holy Spirit*, 16-17.

[58]Charles H. Talbert, *Reading Luke: A Literary and Theological Commentary on the Third Gospel* (New York: Crossroad, 1982), 41. Lampe ("Holy Spirit in the Writings of Luke," 167-70) and Schweizer (*Theological Dictionary of the New Testament*, 6:414) make similar observations about the importance of prayer for the reception of the Spirit.

[59]Baer, *Heilige Geist in den Lukasschriften*, 169-82; Adler, *Taufe und Hand-auflegung;* Ernst Käsemann, "The Disciples of John the Baptist in Ephesus," in *Essays on New Testament Themes* (Philadelphia: Fortress Press, 1982), 136-48; Bovon, *Luke the Theologian*, 234.
    G. B. Caird (*The Apostolic Age* (London: Gerald Duckworth & Co., 1955), 70) sees laying-on-of-hands as part of the baptismal rite; cf. Bruce, "Holy Spirit in Acts," 176; Opsahl, *Holy Spirit in Life of Church*, 35, and Swete, *The Holy Spirit in New Testament*, 90-92. Frederick Harm ("Structural Elements Related to the Gift of the Holy Spirit in Acts," *Concordia Journal* 14 (1988): 28-41) and J. E. L. Oulton ("The Holy Spirit, Baptism and Laying on of Hands in Acts, *Expository Times* 66 (1954-1955): 236-40) see laying-on-of-hands as a special granting of extra power from the Spirit for specific work. Schuyler Brown, ("'Water-Baptism' and 'Spirit-Baptism' in Luke-Acts," *Anglican Theological Review* 59 (1977): 144) attributes the reception of the Spirit either to laying-on-of-hands or "direct divine intervention."

argue that passages which say otherwise are somehow exceptions to the rule. If baptism or laying-on-of-hands are seen as a requirement for reception of the Spirit, the Cornelius episode (Acts 10:44) becomes an embarrassment. If faith or prayer are taken as normative prerequisites, one must explain what happened to the Samaritans (Acts 8:15). As we will see below (p. 24-25), it is difficult to attribute to Luke's narrative a coherent and normative doctrine of baptism, laying-on-of-hands, and the reception of the Spirit.

In the end, many would throw up their hands in light of these difficulties. "In the final analysis," Powell notes, "Jesus can and does give the Spirit to whomever he chooses."[60] Others speak of the freedom of the Spirit and may even cite John 3:8, τὸ πνεῦμα ὅπου θέλει πνεῖ.[61] Even some of those who believe that Luke did present a normative relationship among faith, baptism, and the Holy Spirit admit that he is not quite consistent.[62] Some simply see Luke as theologically capricious.[63] "St. Luke cannot always make his theology entirely clear," says Lampe.[64] Scholarship here meets an impasse; there is no clear reason to prefer one position over another, nor is there a convincing mediating position.

In summary, there is wide consensus that Luke stands in continuity with the Old Testament in portraying the Holy Spirit as the Spirit of prophecy, responsible for inspired human speech. This is the major contribution of scholarship to date, and I will base much

---

[60]Powell, *Acts,* 56.

[61]Kevin Giles, "Present-Future Eschatology in the Book of Acts (II)," *The Reformed Theological Review* 41 (1982): 13-14; Geoffrey F. Nuttall, *The Moment of Recognition: Luke as Storyteller* (London: Athlone Press, 1978), 28; cf. Schweizer, *Theological Dictionary of the New Testament,* 6:414.

[62]Cf. Nuttall, *Moment of Recognition,* 28. Michael Quesnell (*Baptisés dans L'Esprit: Baptême et Esprit dans les Actes des Apôtres,* Lectio Divina, vol. 120 (Paris: Éditions du Cerf, 1985)) attributes Luke's lack of uniformity to the variety of ecclesiastical and cultural practices known to Luke.

[63]Isaacs, *Concept of Spirit,* 91.

[64]Lampe, "Holy Spirit in Writings of Luke," 200.

of my subsequent argument on this foundation. It is remarkable, however, that there is so little agreement beyond this consensus. While there are many who would limit the work of the Spirit to inspired speech, there are good reasons to argue (as I shall argue later) that this is too restrictive. There is little agreement about what the normative mode of receiving the Spirit might have been in Luke's view, had Luke held such a norm, and there are no sure grounds for preferring one position over another. Likewise, whether the Spirit is properly a Who or a What is also a question that finds very little consensus.

The long tradition of theologically-based scholarship ends with mixed results; many have expressed frustration that Luke was not a more systematic theologian. I believe that the problem lies not with Luke as theologian, but with the concept of Luke as theologian. One cannot treat Luke-Acts as if it were a highly allusive treatise on systematic theology. These studies try either to determine Luke's theology, or to determine the history of theological thought that influenced Luke. But is this theological focus adequate for a full understanding of Luke's narrative? Or do these methodologies obscure important aspects of the text? Perhaps the problem is not with Luke, but with the way Luke has been read. It is to this problem that I now turn.

The Search for a Lukan Theology

Many would agree with Ernst Haenchen that while "Luke is no systematic theologian....Nevertheless he has a theology of his own; he sets out from definite theological premises and treats the immediate theological questions of his age."[65] Haenchen himself

---

[65]Ernst Haenchen, *The Acts of the Apostles: A Commentary*, trans. Bernard Noble, Gerald Shinn, Hugh Anderson, and R. McL. Wilson (Philadelphia: Westminster Press, 1971), 91. Even those who see Luke primarily as a historian believe that he was "driven by fundamental theological concerns" (W. Ward Gasque, *A History of the Interpretation of the Acts of the Apostles* (Peabody, Mass.: Hendrickson Publishers, 1989), 352). Cf. Marshall, *Luke: Historian and Theologian*.

was influential, along with Martin Dibelius,[66] Philip Vielhauer,[67] Ernst Käsemann,[68] and above all Hans Conzelmann,[69] in establishing the issue of Luke's theology as the main line of debate—thus the English translation of Conzelmann's *Die Mitte der Zeit* was retitled *The Theology of St. Luke.* While Conzelmann's interpretation fell under severe criticism, his focus was by and large accepted. The question became not so much "Was Luke a theologian?" but "What kind of theologian was he?" Redaction criticism of Luke-Acts was born.

The difficulties of this redactional-theological approach when it comes to the study of the Holy Spirit in Luke-Acts can be illustrated by reference to a scholar who agrees with Conzelmann's outline of Lukan theology, Joseph Fitzmyer.[70] Fitzmyer tackles the thorny problem of the reception of the Spirit, and attempts to attribute theological consistency to Luke. He claims that "it becomes plain in Acts that the Spirit is given only when the Twelve are present or a member or delegate of the Twelve is on the scene."[71] He holds that the Spirit is always connected to the Twelve, and thus Luke portrays a Christian community which is Spirit-led, top to bottom. But note

---

[66]Martin Dibelius, *Studies in the Acts of the Apostles,* trans. M. Ling, ed. H. Greeven (London: SCM Press, 1956).

[67]Philipp Vielhauer, "Zum 'Paulinismus' der Apostelgeschichte," *Evangelische Theologie* 10 (1950-51): 1-15.

[68]Ernst Käsemann, "Das Problem des historischen Jesus," *Zeitschrift für Theologie und Kirche* 51 (1951): 123-53.

[69]Hans Conzelmann, *The Theology of St. Luke.* It is strange that Conzelmann never acknowledged his debt to Heinrich von Baer, *Heilige Geist in den Lukasschriften.* Baer first suggested that Luke worked with a three-fold scheme of salvation history, unified by the work of the Holy Spirit in effecting salvation; Conzelmann's scheme is much the same, unified by one particular aspect of the work of the Spirit, prophecy. See M. M. B. Turner, "Jesus and the Spirit in Lucan Perspective," 4-7, and idem, "The Significance of Receiving the Spirit," 138-42.

[70]Fitzmyer, *Luke,* 1:227-31.

[71]Ibid., 1:231.

that he must qualify this claim from the start: a delegate of the Twelve may suffice. He allows one exception to the rule, the case of Saul himself in Acts 9. He goes on to say that Paul is an indirect representative of the Twelve in Acts 19. However, the evidence he cites (Acts 11:22, 25-26; 13:2-4) connects Paul through Barnabas to the Jerusalem church, but not specifically the Twelve—it certainly does not make him a "delegate" of the Twelve. The only other example he cites is Acts 8, where the Samaritans must wait for the presence of Peter and John to receive the Spirit. But he does not address the perplexing question of why Philip, who had a more direct connection than Paul, did not suffice as a representative of the Twelve. Thus two of his three examples prove to be exceptions to the rule, and the third raises even more questions. The text does not fit into this theological Procrustean bed. Luke-Acts simply resists this kind of systematization.

The redaction critic is faced with competing methods for determining the theology of Luke; the problem of the inconsistencies in the text is compounded by disagreement over method. Beverly Gaventa has identified four different methods commonly used to determine the theology of Luke; all four have their problems.[72] First, some redaction critics seek to determine Luke's views by isolating the additions made to his sources; the difficulties inherent in this procedure, which works from the dubious assumption that he modified sources only because he disagreed with their theology, includes the challenge of determining exactly what his sources were (difficult at best, especially in Acts). Second, some seek Luke's theology in the speeches of Luke-Acts; this position follows the questionable supposition that while Luke's narrative sections were constrained by both his sources and the putative inability of story to bear theological weight, Luke composed speeches from scratch and thus was able to express freely his own views in them, and them alone. Third, some isolate key texts as central to the narrative, and attempt to fit the entire complex narrative into a simplified frame-work. Finally, some isolate one or another theological theme in

---

[72]Beverly Roberts Gaventa, "Toward a Theology of Acts: Reading and Rereading," *Interpretation* 42 (1988): 148-49.

Luke and treat it as essential to the theology of Luke, without consideration of how other themes may relate to this theme and to each other. All these methods, says Gaventa, share the assumption that Luke operated with a theological conception, which he then tried to express in narrative form:

> What is missing from all of these methods is some attempt to deal seriously with the character of Acts as a narrative. Each of them treats Acts as if it were a theological argument somehow encased—or even imprisoned—in a narrative. The assumption seems to be that Luke has a thesis or main point to demonstrate, and he creates his story in order to bear the thesis.[73]

Gaventa goes on to say that "the many unsuccessful efforts to separate Luke's theology from its narrative home should convince us that that enterprise is doomed."[74]

Certainly the impossibility of explaining Luke's depiction of the Holy Spirit in systematic, doctrinal terms leads to this conclusion. It is not just that such systematic synthesis minimizes the inherent contradictions within the text, but that it violates the very nature of the text. Whatever Luke's theology was, he wrote a narrative. If we are to understand the place of the Holy Spirit in Luke-Acts, we must understand the text as a narrative.

The Search for a Pre-Lukan Theology

The same critique may be leveled against those who appear to emphasize the narrative form of Luke's text, but prove to be concerned with the history of doctrine which underlies the text rather than the shape of Luke's narrative. Traditionally, of course, Luke-

---

[73]Ibid., 149-50. Cf. Stephen D. Moore's complaint that "naive Platonism" underlies much New Testament scholarship, even among those who espouse literary methods: "Hypostatized Content, invariant and discoverable, is the enabling fiction of our exegetical practice. Today, it is not our biblical texts that need demythologizing so much as our ways of reading them" (*Literary Criticism and the Gospels: The Theoretical Challenge* (New Haven: Yale University Press, 1989), 66).

[74]Ibid., 150.

Acts has been understood to be a narrative, and a particular kind of narrative at that: a historical narrative. And yet among those who embrace Luke-Acts as historical narrative, the emphasis has been on "historical" rather than "narrative." The dominant concern has been: how well does Luke-Acts reflect history? This question has not been construed narrowly, as if it concerned only historical events. The concern for historical accuracy has extended also to the beliefs of the early church. In this respect, the search for history does not escape the problems of the search for theology; it merely pushes them back to another level. The question is no longer only, "What did Luke believe?" but "How accurately does Luke transmit the beliefs of his predecessors?" It is still a question of conception—no longer Luke's conception alone, but also that of the first generation of Christians.

An example of the search for a pre-Lukan theology of the Holy Spirit in Luke-Acts, and the kinds of problems it generates, can be found in the work of James D. G. Dunn.[75] Dunn believes that what Jesus experienced in his baptism was initiation into the messianic age and anointing as Messiah. Luke-Acts, according to Dunn, depicts Jesus as a charismatic—endowed with divine gifts by the Spirit—much as the apostolic church was charismatic. But during his ministry, Jesus was the sole possessor of the Spirit. The net effect is to picture Jesus as a proleptic Christian; his experience becomes the archetype for his followers. Thus the Spirit provides continuity between the experience of Jesus and that of the early church.

There are two things to note about Dunn's approach. First, it has an overriding conceptual concern: despite Dunn's appeal to "experience," the question is whether Luke is accurate in couching the experience of Jesus in a particular conceptual framework (the experience of the Spirit as "charismatic"). Second, Dunn's work ultimately has theological concern. He wants to find a theological connection between the religion of Jesus and that of the early church. To find this connection, he must stretch the text of Luke-Acts; to call the Jesus of Luke a "charismatic" is problematic, as

---

[75]Dunn, *Baptism in the Holy Spirit;* idem., *Jesus and the Spirit: A Study of the Religious and Charismatic Experience of Jesus and the First Christians as Reflected in the New Testament* (Philadelphia: Westminster Press, 1975).

Jesus' experience of the Spirit as Messiah seems fundamentally different from that of the apostles in Acts, and Jesus himself lacks the most prominent feature of the later Christian charismatic, glossolalia.[76]

An even more problematic example of the historical approach is found in the work of J. H. E. Hull, *The Holy Spirit in the Acts of the Apostles.* Hull's reconstruction of the theology of the Holy Spirit in the early church depends on harmonizing constructions that obscure the Lukan text.[77] For example, Hull asserts that Acts 2:38 provides the "norm" for receiving the Spirit: repentance, faith in Jesus, and the readiness to be baptized.[78] However, "faith in Jesus" is not mentioned in Acts 2:38; Hull assumes that it is implied by the other two. In fact, Hull must assume that whenever the text speaks of the reception of the Spirit, these three norms are implied, no matter what the text says. Curiously, he appeals to literary stylistics for this lack of consistency in Luke:

> The literary value of Acts would have been sadly diminished if its author had mentioned repentance, faith in Jesus, baptism in His name and the gift of the Spirit on each and every occasion that strict accuracy required their presence.[79]

However, Hull is determined to find in Acts not literary appeal but theological consistency. He faces the historical counterparts of the problems faced by scholars such as Fitzmyer; to posit a consistent conceptual framework, he must harmonize and systematize beyond the evidence. He has simply pushed the question of the conception of the Spirit away from Luke and back to the early church. But the problems remain; indeed, they seem greater.

---

[76]Cf. the critique by Turner, "Jesus and the Spirit," 7-9; idem., "The Significance of Receiving the Spirit," 149-53; and Menzies, *Development of Early Christian Pneumatology.*

[77]Cf. the critique of Bovon, *Luke the Theologian,* 215-18.

[78]Hull, *Holy Spirit in Acts,* 95.

[79]Ibid., 99.

A variation on the historical approach is source-critical analysis. A common criterion for distinguishing sources is the perception that a text contains differing theological conceptions. For example, the usual source analysis of Acts 8 sees two differing theological traditions at work—one which held Philip to be the instrument of the Spirit in the conversion of the Samaritans, and another which reserved the gift of the Spirit to the twelve.[80] The apparent discrepancies among theological conceptions of the Spirit—in this case, between the idea that the Spirit comes with faith and baptism, and the idea that it comes only with the apostolic laying on of hands—are attributed to the clumsy combination of two sources. Thus the source-critical method, like the historical approach of Dunn and Hull, shares with the theological approach a conceptual concern. For the theologian, it is the theological concern of Luke; for the historian, that of the early church; and for the source-critic, it is the theological concern of one or more anonymous representatives of that early church.

Towards a Literary Approach

To chide exegetes for being concerned with theological concepts is in one sense unreasonable: to ask about the Holy Spirit is to ask a theological question. But the issue is the way in which the theological question is posed. Theologians and historians alike act as if theology could be distilled from narrative, without taking into account the peculiar nature of narrative itself. As Gaventa says,

> Lukan theology is intricately and irreversibly bound up with the story he tells and cannot be separated from it. An attempt to do justice to the theology of Acts must struggle to reclaim the character of Acts as a narrative.[81]

---

[80]Dibelius, *Studies,* 17; Haenchen, *Acts,* 263-65; Hans Conzelmann, *Acts of the Apostles,* trans. James Limburg, A. Thomas Kraabel, and Donald H. Juel; ed. Eldon Jay Epp and Christopher R. Matthews, Hermeneia (Philadelphia: Fortress Press, 1987), 62.

[81]Gaventa, "Toward a Theology of Acts," 150.

There is, of course, a rich tradition of scholarship concerning the literary aspects of Luke. Adolph Harnack, in *Luke the Physician,* focused attention on Luke's literary style in his search for the sources of Acts.[82] Henry Cadbury furthered this work with his careful attention to Luke's literary style, placing Luke-Acts in the literary world of Hellenistic historians.[83]

In the last two decades, literary scholars have given greater attention to the overall structure of Luke's narrative. This research was stimulated by Charles Talbert, who finds parallel patterns of structure and content which give unity to Luke-Acts.[84] Talbert is indebted to previous theological as well as literary scholarship; though their conclusions differed, he shares with Cadbury the concern for placing Luke-Acts stylistically and generically within Hellenistic literature, but he also draws on Conzelmann's insight that a unified purpose is at work in Luke-Acts—with attention now no longer on the distillation of the redactor's theological themes, but the discerning of overall literary patterns.[85] Similar literary studies

---

[82]Adolph von Harnack, *Luke the Physician: The Author of the Third Gospel and the Acts of the Apostles,* trans. J. R. Wilkinson (New York: G. P. Putnam's Sons, 1907).

[83]Cadbury, *The Making of Luke-Acts;* see also idem, *The Style and Literary Method of Luke,* Harvard Theological Studies, vol. 6 (Cambridge: Harvard University Press, 1920) and *The Book of Acts in History* (New York: Harper and Brothers, 1955). For a cautious examination of the legacy of Cadbury to literary studies of Luke-Acts, see Beverly Gaventa, "The Peril of Modernizing Henry Joel Cadbury," in *Cadbury, Knox and Talbert: American Contributions to the Study of Acts,* ed. Mikeal C. Parsons and Joseph B. Tyson, Biblical Scholarship in North America (Atlanta: Scholars Press, 1992), 7-26, with responses by Donald L. Jones and Richard Pervo (27-44).

[84]Charles H. Talbert, *Literary Patterns, Theological Themes and the Genre of Luke-Acts,* Society of Biblical Literature Monograph Series (Missoula, Mont.: Scholars Press, 1974). See also his *Reading Luke.*

[85]For an evaluation of Talbert, see Parsons and Tyson, *Cadbury, Knox and Talbert,* 133-240.

have been carried out by John Drury,[86] who pictures Luke as a creative writer in Jewish midrashic style, and Luke T. Johnson, who traces the literary patterns concerning one theme in Luke-Acts, the use of possessions.[87]

More recently, literary studies of the New Testament have become more methodologically self-conscious, drawing on the work of non-biblical literary criticism. Thus Robert Tannehill traces literary patterns in a way similar to that of Talbert, but with more methodological sophistication.[88] James Dawsey draws on the theories of Wayne Booth in order to study point of view in Luke-Acts and the role of the Lukan narrator.[89] Several scholars, most notably John Darr and David Gowler, have employed literary-critical categories in the study of various aspects of Lukan character-

---

[86]John Drury, *Tradition and Design in Luke's Gospel: A Study in Early Christian Historiography* (Atlanta: John Knox Press, 1977).

[87]Johnson, *The Literary Function Of Possessions in Luke-Acts.*

[88]Robert C. Tannehill, *The Narrative Unity of Luke-Acts: A Literary Interpretation,* Vol. 1: The Gospel According to Luke (Philadelphia: Fortress Press, 1986); idem, *The Narrative Unity of Luke-Acts: A Literary Interpretation,* Vol. 2: The Acts of the Apostles (Minneapolis: Fortress Press, 1990).

[89]James Marshall Dawsey, "The Literary Function of Point of View in Controlling Confusion And Irony in the Gospel of Luke" (Ph.D. diss., Emory University, 1983); idem, *The Lukan Voice: Confusion and Irony in the Gospel of Luke* (Macon: Mercer University Press, 1986). See Wayne Booth, *The Rhetoric of Fiction,* 2nd ed. (Chicago: University of Chicago Press, 1983); idem, *A Rhetoric of Irony* (Chicago: University of Chicago Press, 1974).

Also on point of view and the Lukan narrator: James L. Resseguie, "Point of View in the Central Section of Luke (9:51-19:44)," *Journal of the Evangelical Theological Society* 25 (1982): 41-47; Steven M. Sheeley, "Narrative Asides and Narrative Authority in Luke-Acts," *Biblical Theology Bulletin* 18 (1988): 102-7; idem, *Narrative Asides in Luke-Acts,* Journal for the Study of the New Testament Supplement Series, no. 72 (Sheffield: JSOT Press, 1992); Allen James Walworth, "The Narrator of Acts" (Ph.D. diss., Southern Baptist Theological Seminary, 1984).

ization.[90] Robert Brawley has analyzed Luke-Acts in light of the
critical theories presented in Roland Barthes's influential *S/Z*.[91]
Structuralists, including Barthes himself, have examined the text,[92]
as have post-structuralists.[93] Scholarship has seen a blooming of
what Gaventa calls the struggle to reclaim the character of Luke-
Acts as narrative.[94]

---

[90]John A. Darr, *On Character Building: The Reader and the Rhetoric of Char-
acterization in Luke-Acts,* Literary Currents in Biblical Interpretation (Louisville:
Westminster/John Knox Press, 1992); James Dawsey, "What's in a Name? Characterization in Luke," *Biblical Theology Bulletin* 16 (1986): 143-47; David B.
Gowler, "Characterization in Luke: A Socio-Narratological Approach," *Biblical
Theology Bulletin* 19 (1989): 54-62; idem, *Host, Guest, Enemy and Friend:
Portraits of the Pharisees in Luke and Acts,* Emory Studies in Early Christianity,
vol. 2 (New York: Peter Lang, 1991); Mark Allen Powell, "The Religious Leaders in Luke: A Literary-Critical Study," *Journal of Biblical Literature* 109 (1990):
93-110.

[91]Robert L. Brawley, *Centering on God: Method and Message in Luke-Acts,*
Literary Currents in Biblical Interpretation (Louisville: Westminster/John Knox
Press, 1990); Roland Barthes, *S/Z,* trans. Richard Miller (New York: Hill and
Wang, 1974).

[92]Roland Barthes, "L'Analyse structurale du récit a propos d'Actes X-XI,"
Recherches de Science Religieuse 58 (1970): 17-37; Edgar Haulotte, "Fondation
d'une communauté de type universel: Acts 10, 1 - 11, 18. Etude critique sur la
rédaction la «structure» et la «tradition» du récit," *Recherches de Science
Religieuse* 58 (1970): 63-100; Louis Marin, "Essai d'analyse structurale d'Actes
10, 1 - 11, 18," *Recherches de Science Religieuse* 58 (1970): 39-61.

[93]Stephen D. Moore, *Mark and Luke in Poststructural Perspectives: Jesus
Begins to Write* (New Haven: Yale University Press, 1992); idem, "Narrative
Homiletics: Lucan Rhetoric and the Making of the Reader" (Ph.D. diss.,
University of Dublin (Trinity College), 1986).

[94]Other recent studies include John I. Ades, "Literary Aspects of Luke,"
Papers on Language and Literature 15 (1979): 193-99; James Dawsey, "The
Literary Unity of Luke-Acts: Questions of Style—A Task for Literary Critics *New
Testament Studies* 35 (1989): 48-66; Robert J. Karris, "Windows and Mirrors:
Literary Criticism and Luke's Sitz im Leben," *Society of Biblical Literature 1979
Seminar Papers,* ed. Paul J. Achtemeier, Society of Biblical Literature Seminar
Papers Series, no. 16 (Missoula, Mont.: Scholars Press, 1979), 1:47-58; William
S. Kurz, "Narrative Approaches to Luke-Acts," *Biblica* 68 (1987): 195-220;
Edwin S. Nelson, "Paul's First Missionary Journey as Paradigm: A Literary-
Critical Assessment of Acts 13-14" (Ph.D. diss., Boston University, 1982); Nut-

Narrative and Theology: A Test Case

How might these new literary studies contribute to our understanding of a theological issue, such as the role of the Holy Spirit in Luke's narrative? The answer is that literary studies, precisely because they approach the text from a different direction, can find things that slip through the cracks of traditional doctrinal categories. They open one's eyes to the subtle and non-systematic ways a narrative can make a statement—theological or otherwise.

For example, it has long been held by scholars of Luke-Acts that Luke draws no "direct soteriological significance...from Jesus' suffering or death. There is no suggestion of a connection with the forgiveness of sins."[95] And it is true that Luke makes no explicit statement connecting Jesus' death and the forgiveness of sin. But is an explicit, dogmatic statement the only way to make a point? Narrative can speak in indirect ways.

So in the narration of Jesus death, a subtle and ironic connection is made between that death and the forgiveness of sin. The vocabulary of salvation lies not in the words of the narrator or Jesus, but ironically on the lips of Jesus' opponents: "If you are the King of the Jews, save yourself!" (Luke 23:37, cf. 23:35, 39); the narrative hints at the salvific effect of this event by putting the words in the mouths of those who, the reader easily perceives, do not know what they are talking about—they do not understand that Jesus does not need to save himself, but is instead saving others. And there is indeed one who is saved in Luke's narrative: a "criminal" who confesses his sin and acknowledges Jesus as the one without blame: "We indeed have been condemned justly, for we are getting what we deserve for our deeds, but this man has done nothing wrong" (23:41). He appeals to Jesus for salvation: "Jesus, remember me when you come into your kingdom" (23:42). And Jesus promises salvation: "Truly I tell you, today you will be with me in Paradise" (23:43); as Jesus is dying, he is saving. The words spoken ironically by his opponents stand in sharp relief to what is actually happening

---

tall, *Moment of Recognition;* Mikeal C. Parsons, *The Departure of Jesus in Luke-Acts: The Ascension Narratives in Context,* Journal for the Study of the New Testament Supplement Series, vol. 21 (Sheffield: Sheffield Academic Press, 1987); Jan Wojcik, *The Road to Emmaus: Reading Luke's Gospel* (West Lafayette, Ind.: Purdue University Press, 1989).

in the narrative: Jesus saves not himself, but another, who repents of his sin and is forgiven. Jesus, as he dies, forgives (cf. 23:34).

The reader familiar with how Luke tells a story will gain a further insight into Jesus' death, salvation, and the forgiveness of sin. Luke Johnson has shown that "literary prophecy" is a common Lukan feature: statements of characters within the narrative, especially Jesus, find fulfillment in the story.[96] Jesus is the ultimate source of reliable information.[97] So one expects Jesus' statement about the criminal's salvation to be fulfilled in the narrative, and surely it is no accident that when Jesus dies the centurion reiterates the criminal's confession of Jesus' innocence, providing a literary link between the two scenes (23:47). Further, it is tempting to see Jesus' prayer in 23:34 ("Father, forgive them")[98] as another example of literary prophecy; it would be an ironic prophecy of the salvation of those sinners who in their ignorance mock the very salvation being accomplished before their eyes.

Thus the language of salvation is used in the crucifixion scene, albeit ironically; Jesus is confessed to be without sin, and at least one criminal is saved, with the subtle suggestion that perhaps many more may receive forgiveness as well.[99] A literary analysis of the crucifixion narrative shows that Luke does give soteriological significance to the death of Jesus. True, the text does not say it in so many words. Rather, Luke shows it.[100] A systematic theologian would not work in so subtle and indirect a way. But Luke's point is

---

[95]Conzelmann, *The Theology of St. Luke,* 201. For a review of recent scholarship on this issue, see Powell, *Luke,* 68-71.

[96]Johnson, *Luke,* 16.

[97]See below, chap. 2, "Character: Presentation and Reception."

[98]Though this verse is textually suspect, being absent from a wide variety of early witnesses, it certainly is in harmony with major Lukan themes. See Johnson, *Luke,* 376; Bruce M. Metzger, *A Textual Commentary on the Greek New Testament* (New York: United Bible Societies, 1971), 180.

[99]This interpretation was suggested to me by Fred B. Craddock, *Luke,* Interpretation (Louisville: John Knox Press, 1990), 274.

[100]On the distinction between showing and telling, see below, chap. 3, on

made with every bit of power any systematician could muster—indeed, perhaps more, as Luke requires that the reader engage the text in a more complex and imaginative way. One who has determined what Luke is saying will not soon forget how it was said. And of course, a reader who misses the point will at least remember the story.

The Holy Spirit and the Literary Critics

Few New Testament scholars have described Luke's portrait of the Spirit with terms drawn from literary criticism. Often such terms have been used only in a general sense, and do not indicate the influence of literary-critical theories or methods. Robert Koch, for example, utilized a literary-critical term when he wrote that "In the Acts of the Apostles the chief *protagonist* is neither Peter nor Paul, but the Holy Spirit, by whose assistance the church grows."[101] The word "protagonist" does not reflect any debt on Koch's part to literary criticism, however—he works out of the older tradition which sees the Spirit as personified in Luke-Acts.[102] David Hill also makes use of the language of literary criticism:

> The Spirit is the main hero of the story. In terms of structuralist analysis of the story, it is not the apostles who are the 'actors', while the Holy Spirit is

---

Luke 1-2.

[101]Robert Koch, "Spirit,"in *Encyclopedia of Biblical Theology*, 3:888. Emphasis mine.

[102]To anticipate the next chapter, the relationship between characters and persons is quite complex, and it is important to distinguish between the literary-critical category of the Holy Spirit as character, and the theological category of the Holy Spirit as "person" or "personified." Older studies do not make this distinction, and thus tend to confuse two separate issues.

Similar observations might be made about the figure of Wisdom in Proverbs 8, Wisdom of Solomon 7, and Ecclesiasticus 28. Since Paul's appropriation of the wisdom tradition is an important stage in the development of Christian pneumatology (see Menzies, *Development of Early Christian Pneumatology*, 52-112, 282-318), and Luke was heavily influenced by Septuagintal language, the portrayal of the figure of Wisdom in these passages had far-reaching consequences for the development of Christian theology.

the 'adjuvant', but rather the opposite. The apostles, the co-workers and successors are energised and directed by the Spirit.[103]

While this is about as close as anyone has come to calling the Spirit a "character," Hill's study still does not make use of literary-critical methods.

Of recent studies which make explicit use of literary-critical categories, few have addressed the question of the Holy Spirit with any thoroughness. Narrative commentaries, such as those produced by Tannehill and Talbert, seem ill-suited to sustained discussion of a particular issue; such commentaries tend to have a dramatic, plot-centered focus.[104] While this kind of focus may spring from a laudable attempt to avoid the problems of older historical-critical approaches, and the danger of abstracting and conceptualizing a narrative which is by nature concrete, specific, and dynamic, such an approach can leave certain pages unturned. Thus Tannehill's commentary contains no extended discussion of the Spirit.

Where the new literary approaches have advanced the study of the Holy Spirit in Luke-Acts, it has been under the rubric, "the characterization of God." It has become common to speak of God as a character in biblical literature. Thus Meir Sternberg can speak of "God's portrait."[105] Robert Tannehill speaks of "the character-

---

[103]David Hill, "The Spirit and the Church's Witness: Observations on Acts 1:6-8," *Irish Biblical Studies* 6 (1984): 23. "Adjuvant" refers to a secondary character (perhaps Greimas's "helper"?).

[104]Cf. the critique of Moore, *Literary Criticism and the Gospels*, 35-40.

[105]Meir Sternberg, *The Poetics of Biblical Literature: Ideological Literature and the Drama of Reading*, Indiana Literary Biblical Series (Bloomington: Indiana University Press, 1985), 322. Robert Alter's caution about this kind of language is well-taken (*The World of Biblical Literature* (New York: Basic Books, 1992), 22-23):

> There is little to be gained, I think, by conceiving of the biblical God, as Harold Bloom does, as a human character—petulant, headstrong, arbitrary, impulsive, or whatever. The repeated point of the biblical writers is that we cannot make sense of God in human terms.

But certainly "God" as a literary construct does function in the same ways other characters, both biblical and extra-biblical, function.

ization of God" in Luke-Acts: "God functions as a character in the plot, though hidden from human view." But Tannehill does not explicitly extend this language to the Holy Spirit.[106] However, two recent monographs by Robert L. Brawley and John Darr contain brief examinations of the literary function of the Spirit in connection with the characterization of God.

Robert L. Brawley, in *Centering on God,* has analyzed Luke-Acts using the methodology of the literary critic Roland Barthes. Brawley deals with the Holy Spirit while examining the characterization of God. He analyzes characterization under the rubric of Barthes's "voice of semes"; "semes" are words, phrases, or images in texts which the reader takes as clues about what a character is like, and then constructs into coherent, whole characters:

> Texts beget characters when semes such as emotions, personal traits, thoughts, and actions repeatedly unite under a proper name. The combination of semes makes the character a signifier, a carrier of meaning. Ultimately, however, the character is the signified, that is, the meaning the reader constructs.[107]

One of the characters that must be constructed by the reader of Luke-Acts is God. Brawley justifies his treatment of God as a character by saying that "in Luke-Acts God does have a biography and street address....God does have a past, present, and future."[108]

---

[106]Robert Tannehill, *Narrative Unity of Luke-Acts,* 1:29. Tannehill does sometimes speak of the Spirit as an actor who can "initiate," "inspire," "teach," or "prompt" (2:26, 44, 70, 129), and this might be taken as an indication that the Spirit is understood by him as a character. See below, chap. 2, on "The Spirit as Actor."

[107]Brawley, *Centering on God,* 107. On the construction of characters by the reader, see below, chap. 2, "Character: Presentation and Reception."

[108]Brawley, *Centering on God,* 110.

God is a character because semes repeatedly traverse the same proper name or cluster of names....God is a character whom the reader constructs out of the intersection of information, action, traits, and evaluation.[109]

Brawley thus uses literary-critical categories to establish that one of the major characters of Luke-Acts is in fact God.

One of the semes that "repeatedly traverse the same proper name" of God is "the Holy Spirit." "Although the divine appellation 'Holy Spirit' may serve as nothing more than a convenient designation of God, it frequently occurs in situations where God is particularly related to human beings."[110] The Spirit provides divine revelation to the human characters in the narrative. Jesus, too, has a special relationship with the Spirit.[111] But in Brawley's view the phrase "the Holy Spirit" simply signifies the presence of God among these human characters, not an independent character. For Brawley, the "Holy Spirit" is just another epithet for "God."

Brawley has correctly noted that characters must be constituted and reconstituted by the reader, and that the close relationship between the Spirit and God is a crucial element in constructing both characters. But why then does Luke make a distinction between the two? And does the invocation of Barthes's "semes" really advance our understanding of the phrase "Holy Spirit"? The word "God" is, after all, nothing but an epithet. While Brawley is correct in connecting the Spirit closely with God, and has done a service by defending the notion of "God" as a literary character, he has not explained the role of the phrase "Holy Spirit" in Luke's narrative. Why is this particular phrase connected with "God"? And can this "seme" itself be construed as a separate character? Brawley does not address these questions, and so his analysis does not go far enough.

John Darr has made a major contribution to the study of Lukan characterization in *On Character Building*. Darr, like Brawley, sees God as an important, though offstage, literary persona in Luke-Acts.

---

[109]Ibid., 111.

[110]Ibid., 115.

[111]Ibid., 116.

Since God does not appear onstage, the divine will must be expressed in other ways. One way is through the narrator, who

> provides readers with reliable commentary on persons, events, settings, and objects in the story, and mediates the crucial "inside" views of characters' thoughts, emotions, and intentions....The reader's evaluation of and identification with (or sympathy for) various characters is largely controlled by the narrator.[112]

But this god-like narrator is

> complemented and authenticated by a carefully and tightly constructed "*divine*" frame of reference. In essence, this frame constitutes the point of view of a persona who, although not dramatized in the narrative, actually initiates and largely controls the action![113]

How then does the reader perceive this divine frame of reference? "The answer, of course, is that readers are provided with carefully-authenticated oracles which explicate how the divine impinges on personages, events, and natural forces."[114] According to Darr, this is accomplished in part through the omniscient narrator or through authoritative statements by Jesus, but especially through the Holy Spirit.[115]

> In this narrative, the divine point of view is invariably expressed or authenticated through the auspices of the Holy Spirit. Each protagonist is confirmed as such by an overt action of the Holy Spirit. Even the Lukan Jesus is validated in this manner.[116]

Every speech, every saying is authorized by reference to the Spirit. Even the promises of Scripture bear the Spirit's stamp of approval;

---

[112]Darr, *On Character Building*, 51.

[113]Ibid. Emphasis his.

[114]Ibid.

[115]Ibid., 51; also 180 n. 9.

[116]Ibid., 52.

Darr calls this a "pneumatic hermeneutic": "Readers of Luke-Acts soon recognize that the divine impinges on this narrative world in certain carefully designated ways."[117] For Darr, since God does not act directly in the narrative to ensure that all goes according to plan, the Spirit must do so. Thus the Spirit becomes for the reader a sign that the narrative reliably depicts the work of God, for the Spirit is the onstage representative of the offstage God. To paraphrase Darr in the language I will use in this study, the Spirit is a discursive manifestation of the deity who ultimately directs, guides, and dominates the story.[118]

Darr has gone a long way toward providing a basis for understanding the narrative role of the Holy Spirit in Luke-Acts. He correctly notes not only the close relation between God and the Spirit, but also the crucial role of the Spirit in providing narrative reliability for the reader. "Holy Spirit" serves as a sign that God is at work here. My own work is heavily indebted to the seminal work of Darr. In my opinion, however, Darr does not go far enough, since he does not connect this function of the Spirit with Luke's intent to provide "certainty" (Luke 1:4), as I intend to do in this study.[119] Further, with Brawley, he fails to distinguish adequately between "God" and the "Spirit"; he does not see that in addition to giving confirmation to the words and actions of other protagonists, the Spirit functions as a protagonist as well. "God" may well be offstage; the "Spirit" is certainly not.

Conclusion

That Luke presents the Holy Spirit as the Spirit of prophecy is the thread of continuity stretching across the reams scholars have written on the subject, and the starting point of this study; in what fol-

---

[117]Ibid., 52-53.

[118]"Discursive" refers to the way Luke has told the story, rather than the story itself, which may be told any number of ways; see below, chap. 2, "What is Character?" and chap. 3, on Luke 1:1-4.

[119]See below, chap. 3, on Luke 1:1-4.

lows, I will concentrate on the Spirit's function as the guarantor of the prophetic word. But traditional theological categories do not provide an adequate basis for understanding exactly how the Spirit functions in Luke's narrative. Fortunately, the recent rise of literary-critical work can move the discussion along.

The literary-critical studies of Brawley and Darr have laid important groundwork for a new appreciation of the role of the Holy Spirit in Luke-Acts. Both have seen the important literary connection between God and the Spirit: Luke draws God and Spirit into close correlation, so that the Spirit becomes the onstage representative of the God who directs everything from the wings. Further, Darr has seen the important role of the Spirit in providing narrative reliability. What has been lacking in these studies is the recognition that there is a literary-critical category which would throw light on the role of the Spirit in the narrative. Such a category has firm roots in literary criticism, and is easily applicable to the text of Luke-Acts. One need not look far for this category: it is "character."

Chapter 2

Characterization in Narrative Theory

Before one can ask whether it might make sense to think of the Holy Spirit in Luke-Acts as a "character," one must determine what it means to speak of "character" in narrative. Narrative critics have given a good deal of attention to this question in recent years. In this chapter I will review critical theories on character and characterization in narrative in order to show how these theories might be applied to the study of the Holy Spirit in Luke-Acts.[1] But first, I must address some potential objections to this project.

Some may protest from the outset that the application of modern literary theory to an ancient document is illegitimate—how much

---

[1] For a review of scholarship on character in modern literary theory see David Gowler, *Host, Guest, Enemy and Friend,* 29-75. See also Robert Alter, *The Pleasures of Reading in an Ideological Age* (New York: Simon and Schuster, 1989), 49-76; Seymour Chatman, *Story and Discourse: Narrative Structure in Function and Film* (Ithaca: Cornell University Press, 1978), 107-38; Baruch Hochman, *Character in Literature* (Ithaca: Cornell University Press, 1985), 7-58; Wallace Martin, *Recent Theories of Narrative* (Ithaca: Cornell University Press, 1986), 116-22; Shlomith Rimmon-Kenan, *Narrative Fiction: Contemporary Poetics* (New York: Methuen, 1983), 29-42.

more so when methods drawn from fiction are used to study documents that deal with historical matters? These are certainly important questions and deserve consideration at this point. Can the methods of literary criticism be applied to biblical documents? And are modern theories of narrative applicable to the study of ancient writings? I will deal with each of these questions in turn.

First, some will object that the methods of literary criticism, thought to be based on the study of modern fiction, are not applicable to texts that purport to deal with historical matters. The assumptions of this objection are clearly mistaken; it overlooks the influence of the international, interdisciplinary work done on narrative in recent years. The commonalities of historical and fictional narratives have led both historians and students of literature to similar theories and methods. It would be helpful to look at this trend, which blurs the distinction between fictional and non-fictional narrative, in order to answer the objections of those in biblical studies who question the importation of literary methods into their field. We will see that recent theories of narrative are not limited to modern fictional works, but encompass non-fiction along with fiction, ancient works as well as modern.

The literary critic Northrup Frye began to break down the artificial barriers among narrative genres in the influential *Anatomy of Criticism* (1957).[2] In creating an elaborate typological scheme for classifying different kinds of literature, Frye shows that narrative is a mode of writing that transcends traditional distinctions between fiction and non-fiction. Dissatisfied with the impressionistic categories used to describe literature over the ages, he proposes a more coherent scheme by classifying literature under three categories: "modes" of literature judged by subject matter, "radical of presentation" judged by whether acted, sung/spoken, or written, and "species" judged by authorial perspective. It is this last category which has important implications for the present study. Frye defines an author's perspective in two respects: directed either inward or outward ("introverted" or "extroverted"), and apprehended in either

---

[2]Northrup Frye, *Anatomy of Criticism: Four Essays* (Princeton: Princeton University Press, 1957). On Frye, see Martin, *Recent Theories of Narrative*, 31-35.

personal or intellectual terms. Literary works can be categorized by "species" according to where they fit on a grid which uses these two dichotomies: a novel is personal and extroverted, a romance is personal but introverted, and so on. Thus Frye is able to include "encyclopedic" forms such as the Bible and non-fictional forms such as the confession (e.g., Augustine, Rousseau) in his scheme, alongside fictional forms such as the novel and the romance. As Martin notes, Frye's categories are inevitably successful:

> Like the four elements of medieval science, defined by reference to the dichotomies hot/cold and wet/dry, Frye's four species defined by two dichotomies cannot help but include all prose fiction, either as a "pure" type or as an intermediate mixture. In fact they can include all literature, which cannot escape being introverted or extroverted, personal or intellectual, and much writing not considered literary.[3]

Despite the obvious artificiality of much of Frye's categorization, his work is significant in that it indicates the beginnings of a break in the barrier between fictional and non-fictional narrative.

Frye's work was extended into a unified theory and history of narrative, both fictional and historical, by Robert Scholes and Robert Kellogg in *The Nature of Narrative* (1966).[4] Scholes and Kellogg replace Frye's categories of modes and species with a theory of the history of narrative that relates all forms of narrative throughout the ages. A map of the relationships among the various kinds of narrative depicts a tree-like structure, with ancient epic as the trunk, branches to include empirical narrative (history, biography, autobiography, social and psychological subjects) and fictional narrative (romance, fable, satire, allegory), and ultimately the reunion of the various empirical and fictional branches in the modern novel. While this scheme is, like Frye's, a little artificial, it can be helpful in understanding the relationships among many different types of literature. And like Frye's work, it has helped break

---

[3]Martin, *Recent Theories of Narrative,* 35.

[4]Robert Scholes and Robert Kellogg, *The Nature of Narrative* (London: Oxford University Press, 1966). See Martin, *Recent Theories of Narrative,* 35-39.

down the distinctions between fictional and non-fictional genres, enabling scholars to apply similar methods of study to both.

The rise of structuralism led to further links among the historian, the anthropologist, the psychologist, and the literary critic. Structuralism, an interdisciplinary movement usually associated with the French anthropologist Claude Lévi-Strauss, owes literary-critical debts to the linguistic theories of Ferdinand de Saussure and Charles S. Pierce on the one hand, and to literary formalism, especially the Russian variety as represented by Viktor Shklovsky, Vladimir Propp and Tzvetan Todorov, on the other.[5] Shklovsky holds that all aspects of narrative are formal elements, and that the apparent realism of fiction was a product of technique. It follows that the realism of any narrative is simply a matter of technique. Propp's influential *Morphology of the Folk Tale* (1928) categorizes the formal elements in the Russian folk-tale, reducing the many tales to various combinations of thirty-one different "functions" and seven

---

[5]The literature on structuralism is immense; see Jonathan Culler, *Structuralist Poetics: Structuralism, Linguistics and the Study of Literature* (Ithaca: Cornell University Press, 1976); Terry Eagleton, *Literary Theory: An Introduction* (Minneapolis: University of Minnesota Press, 1983), 91-126; Terence Hawkes, *Structuralism and Semiotics* (Berkeley: University of California Press, 1977); Frank Lentricchia, *After the New Criticism* (Chicago: University of Chicago Press, 1980); Claude Lévi-Strauss, *Structural Anthropology* trans. Claire Jacobsson; Brooke Grundfest Schoepf, and Monique Layton (Chicago: University of Chicago Press, 1967-1976); Martin, *Recent Theories of Narrative*, 90-106; Charles S. Peirce, *Collected Papers*, ed. Charles Hartshorne and Paul Weiss (Cambridge: Harvard University Press, 1958-1960); Vladímir Propp, *The Morphology of the Folktale*, 2nd ed., trans. Laurence Scott, introductions by Svatava Pirkova-Jakobson and Alan Dundes, edited and with a preface by Louis A. Wagner, Publications of the American Folklore Society, Bibliographical and Special Series, vol. 9, Publication of the Indiana University Research Center in Anthropology, Folklore, and Linguistics, vol. 10 (Austin: University of Texas Press, 1968); Ferdinand de Saussure, *Course in General Linguistics*, ed. Charles Bally, Albert Sechehaye and Albert Riedlinger, trans. Roy Harris, (LaSalle, Ill.: Open Court, 1983); Viktor Shklovsky, "Art as Technique," (1917) in *Contemporary Literary Criticism*, Robert Con Davis (New York: Longman, 1986), 51-63, repr. from *Russian Formalist Criticism: Four Essays*, ed. by Lee T. Lemon and Marion J. Reis (Lincoln: University of Nebraska Press, 1965), 5-24; Tzvetan Todorov, *The Fantastic: A Structural Approach to a Literary Genre*, trans. Richard Howard, foreword by Robert Scholes (Ithaca: Cornell University Press, 1975).

"spheres of action." Structuralism combines this kind of formalism with the linguistic insight of Saussure and Pierce that language is made up of "signs" which are arbitrarily related to things, concepts or meanings. Structuralists such as Lévi-Strauss, Roland Barthes (in his early work), Gérard Genette, and A. J. Greimas have applied this linguistic theory outside language itself, and everything is fair game:

> You can view a myth, wrestling match, system of tribal kinship, restaurant menu or oil painting as a system of signs, and structuralist analysis will try to isolate the underlying set of laws by which these signs are combined into meanings. It will largely ignore what the signs actually "say," and concentrate instead on their internal relations to one another.[6]

Lévi-Strauss, for example, applied structuralism to the anthropological study of myth. He found that any particular myth could be broken down into language-like structures, which he believes reflect the structures of the human mind itself. It is clear that in structuralism, traditional distinctions between fiction and non-fiction are useless; indeed, structuralism blurs the distinctions between the study of literature and the social sciences. The collapse of the barriers between fictional and non-fictional narrative has resulted in a new, amorphous body of scholarship called "narratology."[7] And though structuralism has largely fallen out of favor, due to its many limitations,[8] it does mark an important stop on the literary-critical journey from the study of "fiction" to the study of "narrative."

---

[6]Eagleton, *Literary Theory*, 97.

[7]Representative narratologists include Mieke Bal, *Narratology: Introduction to the Theory of Narrative*, trans. Christine von Boheemen (Toronto: University of Toronto Press, 1985); Gérard Genette, *Narrative Discourse: An Essay in Method*, trans. Jane E. Lewin (Ithaca: Cornell University Press, 1980); Gerald Prince, *Narratology: The Form and Functioning of Narrative* (New York: Mouton, 1982).

[8]See the critiques by Eagleton, *Literary Theory*, 106-26, and Martin, *Recent Theories of Narrative*, 102-6.

Historians also have dealt with the issue of the nature of narrative.[9] The pioneer of this trend among historians is Hayden White, who speaks of the dissolution of the distinction between realistic and fictional discourses:

> Recent theories of discourse, however, dissolve the distinction between realistic and fictional discourses based on the presumption of an ontological difference between their respective referents, real and imaginary, in favor of stressing their common aspect as semiological apparatuses that produce meanings by the systematic substitution of signifieds (conceptual contents) for the extra-discursive entities that serve as their referents.[10]

Obviously, White shows the influence of linguistic structuralism when he speaks of "referents," "signifieds," and "semiological apparatuses"; such is the pervasive cross-disciplinary influence of these theories. The traditional view, that the distinction between fiction and non-fiction was based on whether a text's referents were thought to be real and imaginary, is in the opinion of White and others faulty; these historians now hold that both history and literature share a common aspect as texts which use words to describe things outside the texts themselves. Further, non-fictional narrative tells more than just a story:

> Narrative is not merely a neutral discursive form that may or may not be used to represent real events in their aspect as developmental processes but

---

[9]Hayden White, *The Content of the Form: Narrative Discourse and Historical Representation* (Baltimore: Johns Hopkins University Press, 1987), x. White's review of scholarship on narrative history, "The Question of Narrative in Contemporary Historical Theory," is found in the same volume, 27-57. See also Arthur C. Danto, *Narration and Knowledge (Including the Integral Text of "Analytical Philosophy of History")* (New York: Columbia University Press, 1985; *Metahistory: Six Critiques,* vol. 19 of *History and Theory* (1980); Paul Ricoeur, *Time and Narrative,* trans. Kathleen McLaughlin and David Pellauer (Chicago: University of Chicago Press, 1984-1988), esp. 1:121-208; Hayden White, *Metahistory: the Historical Imagination in Nineteenth-Century Europe* (Baltimore: Johns Hopkins University Press, 1973).

[10]White, *Content of Form,* x.

rather entails ontological and epistemic choices with distinct ideological and even specifically political implications.[11]

For White, historical narrative is not a value-neutral accounting of the facts. Like fiction, historical narratives (and their readers) are shaped by the way the story is told. And in this, the distinction between history and fiction is blurred.

Since narrative has displaced the novel as the central concern of literary critics, and historians and social scientists have also entered the theoretical fray, one can conclude with Stephen Moore that "the literary study of the Gospels and Acts, in consequence, need by no means be chained to the novel."[12] Theories of character and characterization can appropriately be applied to biblical texts. One need not worry that the theories and methods of narrative criticism are unsuited to biblical studies.

Second, in answer to the objection that ancient documents cannot be read through modern theories, I must again point to the depth and breadth of work in narratology. Frye's work extends back to ancient forms, as part of his purpose is to develop a historical theory about the changes in literature over the years; one of his "modes" of literature is "myth," which includes the Bible and ancient epics, and one of his "radicals of presentation" is spoken literature such as the Homeric poems. Scholes and Kellogg likewise account for ancient epic, ancient historical and biographical forms, ancient romance, and other forms, all within one theory of historical development. Other theorists of narrative have dealt with ancient literature. Mikail Bakhtin's influential work *The Dialogic Imagination,* for example,

---

[11]Ibid., ix.

[12]Moore, *Literary Criticism and the Gospels,* xviii. Martin, *Recent Theories of Narrative,* 7-56, details the turn in literary theory from novel to narrative. For a thoughtful critique and defense of the application of literary methods to the Hebrew Bible, see Meir Sternberg, *Poetics of Biblical Narrative,* 1-29. A critique and defense of the application of literary theories to Luke-Acts is found in William S. Kurz, "Narrative Approaches to Luke-Acts," 195-200.

deals with the Greco-Roman romance at great length.[13] Studies of characterization in ancient narrative in particular have shown the great commonalities that all narratives share in their depiction of character; contrary to common opinion, ancient characters were not necessarily shallow and unchanging.[14] Beyond this, it is hard to see how we can read as other than moderns. No one would object that form or redaction criticism employ strictly modern points of view and are therefore inappropriate for the study of ancient documents, yet both methods are distinctly modern creations. While as moderns we cannot fully understand the cultural context that spawned ancient literature, we have gained critical acumen by virtue of the long tradition of interpretation which stands before us. So we are in some respects better readers because we are moderns and therefore have more experience. "Though it may sound odd, we are in fact better readers of biblical narrative because we are lucky enough to come after Flaubert and Joyce, Dante and Shakespeare."[15] As the narratologist Gerald Prince has said,

> Learning how to read is—among other things—learning how to ask more and more relevant questions. An ingenious reader is not only one who can find new answers to old questions but also one who can think of new questions.[16]

---

[13]M. M. Bakhtin, *The Dialogic Imagination: Four Essays,* ed. Michael Holquist, trans. Michael Holquist and Caryl Emerson, University of Texas Press Slavic Series, vol. 1 (Austin: University of Texas, 1981).

[14]Gowler, *Host, Guest, Enemy and Friend,* 77-176, and 327-76. Hochman, *Character in Literature,* deals with a number of characters from ancient literature. See also Edward Burns, *Character: Acting and Being on the Pre-Modern Stage* (New York: St. Martin's Press, 1990); Christopher Pelling, ed., *Characterization and Individuality in Greek Literature* (Oxford: Clarendon Press, 1990).

[15]Robert Alter, *World of Biblical Literature,* 20.

[16]Prince, *Narratology,* 105.

Insofar as it teaches us to think of new questions, modern narrative theory can enhance our understanding of the world evoked by the ancient writers.[17]

Having provided a rationale for using narrative theories in the study of biblical texts, I turn to recent theories of character and characterization in narrative. First, one must define what one means by the word "character." Inevitably this leads into the debate over the relationship between characters in written narratives and real-life, flesh and blood people; there is a related debate over the complex relationship between character and plot in narratives, and these discussions will prove important for an understanding of what it means to say that the Holy Spirit is a "character." Second, recent narrative theorists have developed paradigms for classifying characters, and it will be necessary to review this work in order to lay a foundation for classifying the Holy Spirit as a character in Luke-Acts. Third, scholarship has addressed the issue of how characters are presented by authors and received by readers, and this too is essential to our understanding of the Spirit in Luke-Acts. Finally, I will show that narrative theories do allow one to speak of the Holy Spirit in Luke-Acts as a "character." This chapter will provide the theoretical underpinnings for the following chapters, which will examine the role this character plays in the narrative.

What is Character? Characters, People, and Plots

What do we mean when we say "character"? That depends on the context in which we speak. Dictionaries list twenty or so different

---

[17]Often those who object to the use of literary theory in studying biblical texts are reacting to efforts to exclude historical judgments from literary criticism along the lines of the New Criticism (early efforts in applying literary criticism to biblical studies were frequently of this type; see Lynn M. Poland, *Literary Criticism and Biblical Hermeneutics: A Critique of Formalist Approaches* (Chico: Scholars Press, 1985)). Again, literary criticism has become more diverse and interdisciplinary in recent years, and the study of ancient history and culture continues to inform literary readings of the Bible. No document can be read intelligently apart from its historical and cultural context.

definitions of the word. Joel Weinsheimer cites fifteen distinct uses of "character" and its cognates, not all of them literary:

1. The inscription was engraved in Runic characters.
2. He thought he could read everybody's character.
3. Lydgate is a character in *Middlemarch*.
4. He dismissed his dishonest butler without a character.
5. Abraham Lincoln was a man of character.
6. My Uncle Iggy is a real character.
7. After the affair became public, her character was lost.
8. He acted out of character when he shouted at his friend.
9. She was of a deeply passionate character.
10. Extension is a characteristic of all matter.
11. Such self-aggrandizement is characteristic of him.
12. Her most prominent characteristic is intelligence.
13. "Handsome, clever, and rich" is a characterization of "Emma."
14. Fielding's characterization of Tom is performed with loving attention.
15. Newton characterizes time as independent of space.[18]

There is no readily apparent unity among these homonyms. "The inscription was engraved in Runic characters" refers to writing, but not in the sense of "Lydgate is a character in *Middlemarch*," and "Abraham Lincoln was a man of character" has no apparent relation to the written word at all. Certainly the usage in "Fielding's characterization of Tom is performed with loving attention" is similar to but differs from "Newton characterizes time as independent of space." Yet Weinsheimer, while noting this "semantic abyss," holds that all of these meanings spring from one basic concept: "Characters are marks."[19]

Weinsheimer's definition points to a great debate in recent works on characterization: Are characters in literary works in any way like

---

[18]Joel Weinsheimer, "Theory of Character: *Emma*," *Poetics Today*, 1, no. 1-2 (1979): 189-90. One might add to Weinsheimer's list the literary genre modelled on Theophrastus' *Characters*; see J. W. Smeed, *The Theophrastan "Character": The History of a Literary Genre* (Oxford: Clarendon Press, 1985).

[19]Weinsheimer, "Theory of Character: *Emma*," 190. Weinsheimer is inspired by etymology: the Greek word χαρακτήρ was used of an engraver, then of stamps or dies, and finally applied to the images or marks which were cast. See Warren Ginsberg, *The Cast of Character: The Representation of Personality in Ancient and Medieval Literature* (Toronto: University of Toronto Press, 1983), 14.

real people, or are they mere marks on paper? In what sense does a character "exist"? Is it fair to say that character is merely a function of plot? On one end of this debate stand the structuralists, who contend that character is nothing but plot. This may be called a "semiotic" view of character: characters are no more than signs which have certain functions in the text. On the other end stand some older critical theorists who fantasized about the private, extratextual lives of literary characters. This may be called the "mimetic" view: art imitates life, and characters are much like real people. There are good reasons for believing that the truth lies somewhere in between.

On one side of the debate, it is obvious that characters in written literature are composed of marks on paper. As Weinsheimer notes, characters can be considered as "patterns of recurrence, motifs which are continually recontextualized in other motifs."[20] In other words, characters are no more than signs. In Weinsheimer's thirteenth example, "Emma" is enclosed in quotation marks. This is because a character can be considered to be no more than a segment of text: "Emma Woodhouse is not a woman nor need be described as if it were."[21] The neuter pronoun "it" in Weinsheimer's sentence refers to the text segment "Emma," which as a text segment cannot be a "she." Even the denizens of historical works can be considered to be "characters" rather than "people": "No character in a book is a real person. Not even if he is in a history book and is called Ulysses S. Grant."[22]

On the other hand, characters in texts may certainly seem to be real people (witness the letters sent to Sherlock Holmes at 221B Baker Street, or the people who search for Lake Wobegon on maps

---

[20]Weinsheimer, "Theory of Character: *Emma*," 195.

[21]Ibid., 187.

[22]Robert Scholes, *Elements of Fiction* (New York: Oxford University Press, 1968), 17, cited in Gowler, *Host, Guest, Enemy and Friend*, 37. Throughout this study, for reasons detailed below, I will distinguish between "characters" found in narrative works, and real-life, flesh-and-blood "people" who inhabit the extratextual world.

of Minnesota). The realism with which a character may be portrayed in a fictional work is what can touch a reader so deeply: here, indeed, is life as we know it. And characters can be analyzed in political, sociological, or psychological terms, just as flesh-and-blood people may be. One may even be tempted to imagine what will happen to the characters after the book is over; the classic literary treatment in this vein is A. C. Bradley's *Shakespearean Tragedy,* which speculates on the personal lives of characters in ways that go far beyond the texts.[23]

Bradley represents the "mimetic" tradition of literary scholarship. Indeed, the traditional treatment of characterization in literature was mimetic: characters were thought to be imitations of real people, and thus could be understood in the same ways we understand people. Samuel Butler reflected the mimetic perception of character when he said, "The great characters live as truly as the memory of dead men. For the life after death, it is not necessary that a man or woman have lived."[24]

The assault on the mimetic interpretation of character began with the rise of New Criticism.[25] New Criticism, an American literary-critical movement influential from the 1920s to 1950s, was a purely formalist criticism; that is, it held that a literary work could be read objectively and accurately solely on the basis of its structure. The text could be understood completely on the basis of its formal features (particularly paradox and irony), apart from any outside fac-

---

[23]The famous reply to Bradley is L. C. Knights, "How Many Children had Lady Macbeth?" in *Explorations* (New York: New York University Press, 1933, reprint 1964), 15-54.

[24]Samuel Butler, *Notebooks,* quoted in Hochman, *Character in Literature,* 16, who cites as his source the title page of Claude C. H. Williamson, ed., *Readings in the Character of Hamlet* (1974).

[25]On New Criticism, see Eagleton, *Literary Theory,* 45-53. Representative New Critics are Cleanth Brooks, *The Well Wrought Urn: Studies in the Structure of Poetry* (New York: Harcourt Brace and World, 1947); John Crowe Ransom, *The New Criticism* (New York: New Directions, 1941); René Wellek and Austin Warren, *Theory of Literature,* 3rd ed. (New York: Harcourt, Brace and World, 1957); Wimsatt, *The Verbal Icon.*

tors. The most significant factors excluded were the author's intention and the reader's response—neither the reasons the author wrote, nor the emotions of the reader, were relevant to the meaning of a literary work.[26] Rather than seeking to recreate the author's original mental condition, New Critics rejoiced in tightly-woven structures, balanced parallelism, deft use of paradox and irony; as Eagleton notes, they favored poetry over other genres, perhaps because poems are more easily seen as isolated, tightly-balanced forms.[27] The emphasis was on close reading of a reified, isolated text: "A poem should not mean/But be."[28] New Criticism peered at the literary text as through a jeweler's glass, noting every intricate facet of the sparkling gem, oblivious to everything outside of the range of its lens.

Baruch Hochman has argued that the New Critical tendency towards autonomous texts led to a devaluation of both characters and people:

> The prejudice was for literature and against life; for literariness and against personality. It was in effect a prejudice against the self, the soul, the individual—against character as a relatively autonomous component of the literary text.[29]

---

[26]See W. K. Wimsatt, Jr. and Monroe C. Beardsley, "The Intentional Fallacy" and "The Affective Fallacy" in W. K. Wimsatt, Jr., *The Verbal Icon: Studies in the Meaning of Poetry* (Lexington: University of Kentucky Press, 1954), 3-18, 21-39.

[27]Eagleton, *Literary Theory*, 50-51.

[28]Archibald MacLeish, "Ars Poetica," reprinted in John Ciardi, *How Does a Poem Mean?* Part 3 of *An Introduction to Literature* by Herbert Barrows, Hubert Heffner, John Ciardi, and Wallace Douglas (Boston: Houghton Mifflin Co., 1959), 909.

[29]Hochman, *Character in Literature*, 17. For a very different view, see Eagleton, *Literary Theory*, 46-49, who holds that the New Critics isolated texts from history in order to provide transcendent models of human existence.

Eagleton puts it more caustically:

> New Criticism's view of the poem as a delicate equipoise of contending
> attitudes, a disinterested reconciliation of opposing impulses, proved
> deeply attractive to sceptical liberal intellectuals disoriented by the clashing
> dogmas of the Cold War. Reading poetry in the New Critical way meant
> committing yourself to nothing: all that poetry taught you was
> "disinterestedness," a serene, speculative, impeccably even-handed
> rejection of anything in particular.[30]

New Criticism, in rejecting the mimeticism of older criticism, in
effect lost any connection between life outside the text and life
inside the text—and that included any connection between characters
and people. Thus New Critics, when they thought about character at
all (the concept does not figure greatly in short poems), tended to
believe that "'character' is merely the term by which the reader
alludes to the pseudo-objective image he composes of his response
to an author's verbal arrangements."[31] The New Critic wanted to
study the marks on the page, not the "pseudo-objective image"
found only in the reader's mind. Thus "character" was not a particularly relevant concept for New Critics. It is noteworthy that the
standard New Critical textbook, Wellek and Warren's *Theory of Literature,* contains barely two pages on characterization.[32] In a
thoroughgoing formalism, the critic has no business moving outside
the text, not even to a picture formed in the mind of a reader.

So it is no surprise that the other major challenge to mimetic
theory sprang from yet another variety of formalist criticism, structuralism. Propp's *Morphology of the Folk Tale* set the terms of the
structuralist view of character. Propp holds that in the Russian folk-
tale, character is merely a function of the plot. What is important is
the role of a particular character, and in the end it makes no dif-

---

[30]Eagleton, *Literary Theory,* 50.

[31]C. H. Rickword, "A Note on Fiction," in *Towards Standards of Criticism:
Selections from "The Calendar of Modern Letters," 1925-7,* ed. F. R. Leavis
(London: Lawrence and Wishart, 1933, reprint 1976), 31, cited with slight
inaccuracies in Hochman, *Character in Literature,* 18.

[32]Wellek and Warren, *Theory of Literature,* 219-20).

ference who or what the character is. Characters thus become inter-changeable plot functionaries: it matters only that the character is a hero or an enemy, not that the hero is young or old, male or female, or the enemy a warrior, witch, or animal. The characters hold no interest in and of themselves; what is central is the plot, within which the characters have certain definable functions. Though Propp concerned himself with only one folk genre, his theory was at heart "semiotic"; that is, it viewed character as a sign within a system of signs, like a word within a language. Propp's theory therefore proved to be the buttress of the structuralist notion of character.[33]

On the linguistic side of this movement, semiologists such as Algirdas Greimas and Claude Bremond took the functional view of character to its logical extreme. For Greimas, the notion of "character" is inadequate to describe what takes place in narrative. Greimas invokes Saussure's distinction between *langue* and *parole*—that is, between language, a structure of differing symbols, and indi-vidual speech-acts. Structuralism carries this distinction to the literary level by contrasting discourse and story, the surface level of a particular story that speaks of people, places and things versus the underlying "deep structure" which deals only with functions and relations.[34] Greimas thus distinguishes between *actants,* part of the deeper syntax and independent of particular discourses, and *acteurs,* seen in a specific discourse. *Actants* perform a limited number of logical functions—sender, object, receiver, helper, opponent, sub-ject—within a basic logical framework that can be illustrated on graph paper. The *acteur* takes on specific characteristics as the place where narrative and discursive structures meet: it is a figure with a function. An *acteur* can thus represent several *actants,* and vice-versa. As with Propp, characters are interchangeable; only a charac-

---

[33]Chatman, *Character in Literature,* 20-21; Gowler, *Host, Guest, Enemy and Friend,* 44.

[34]The distinction between story and discourse (or similar distinctions between *fabula* and *syuzhet, histoire* and *discours* or *récit*) is basic to all structuralist analy-sis. An extensive examination of the relation between the two is found in Genette, *Narrative Discourse.* See also Chatman, *Story and Discourse,* 19-22; Martin, *Recent Theories of Narrative,* 107-11; and below, chap. 3, on Luke 1:1-4.

ter's function has importance. Character is reduced to action; characterization, to plot.[35]

The logic of structuralism works to deny any relationship between characters and human beings, thus invalidating a mimetic understanding of character. It is further to reduce character to plot, leaving only a series of actions; characters are merely "the sequence of all the subjects of all the verbs in a story."[36] As Hugh Bredin has shown, the dissolution of mimetic character is inevitable when narrative is thought to be a kind of language. If the units of a story are, like a language, repeatable, one cannot introduce individual motive as an explanation for action. Further, if the basic units are determined only by relations with each other, the units are deprived of any innate features:

> None of the items which constitute character, however—intellectual and emotional disposition, moral beliefs, personal qualities—can be regarded as

---

[35]A. -J. Greimas, "Les actants, les acteurs, et les figures," in *Sémiotique narrative et textuelle*, ed. Claude Chabrol, (Paris: Librairie Larousse, 1973), 161-76. Cf. Claude Bremond, *Logique du récit* (Paris: Seuil, 1973). On semiological views of character see Gowler, *Host, Guest, Enemy and Friend*, 45-46; Hochman, *Characterization in Literature*, 23-24. The view that characterization is subordinate to plot goes back to Aristotle (e.g., *Poetics* 6.19-20); see T. S. Dorsch, *Classical Literary Criticism* (New York: Penguin Books, 1965), 19, also Chatman, *Story and Discourse*, 108-10, and Gowler, *Host, Guest, Enemy and Friend*, 35-36.

[36]Hochman, *Character in Literature*, 23, citing Todorov. Cf. Prince's definition of character as a "topic" (*Narratology*, 71):

> What we usually call a character is a topic (or 'logical participant') common to a set of propositions predicating of it at least some characteristics generally associated with human beings: the logical participant may be endowed with certain human physical attributes, for instance, and think, will, speak, laugh, etc. The nature of the logical participant is clearly not all important, though it is usually identified as a person, but should a horse be portrayed as philosophizing and should a table be described as thinking and speaking, they would both constitute characters.

relations. So in a semiological conception of story, character has no obvious part to play.[37]

If the dissolution of mimetic character follows from treating narrative as a language, the application of structuralist methods to the world at large leaves humanity in an equal flux. As Hochman notes, the structuralist view of character, part of an anti-mimetic critique of literature as a "constructed unreality,"[38] stems from the structuralist view of life itself. Life is simply a system of signs. The notion of meaning, progress, and value are human impositions on the semiotic interrelations that take place in any structure. As Shlomith Rimmon-Kenan notes, "Structuralists can hardly accommodate character within their theories, because of their commitment to an ideology which 'decentres' man and runs counter to the notions of individuality and psychological depth."[39] In the end, structuralism cannot really believe in characters, because it barely believes in people. Among certain descendents of the structuralists, real life has become a "text" as artificial and fictive as any novel—so much so that "Jacques Derrida and his followers go further and come close to denying the existence even of people in life as anything but fictions constructed in our minds."[40] At this point the anti-mimetic logic of structuralism turns on itself with a vengeance: if people are no more than signs within a system of signs, how can structuralists object to a mimetic understanding of character? Characters would function exactly as people function—both merely move the action along. At

---

[37]Hugh Bredin, "The Displacement of Character in Narrative Theory," *British Journal of Aesthetics*, 22 (1982): 299. Cf. Culler, *Structural Poetics*, 230-38.

[38]Hochman, *Character in Literature*, 25.

[39]Rimmon-Kenan, *Narrative Fiction*, 30. See also Culler, *Structuralist Poetics*, 230, and the extensive critique of formalist approaches by Alter, *The Pleasures of Reading*, 49-76.

[40]Hochman, *Character in Literature*, 27. It can be argued that a non-mimetic theory of character and characterization is necessary to study literary narratives produced under the influence of "postmodernism"; see Thomas Docherty, *Reading (Absent) Character: Towards a Theory of Characterization in Fiction* (Oxford: Clarendon Press, 1983).

this point, the ideology behind structuralism leads to an inescapable contradiction, where mimeticism is not really mimetic, but semiotic, while semioticism is really mimetic.

Given the inherent problems of this position, not all structuralists have been content to abandon mimeticism totally. Roland Barthes at first insisted that character must be subservient to plot, but later modified his views and introduced a separate semiotic "code" for dealing with character.[41] Seymour Chatman has been the structuralist who has expressed the most dissatisfaction with the reduction of character to function.[42] For Chatman, the reduction of characters to "mere words" is patently false:

> Too many mimes, too many captionless silent films, too many ballets have shown the folly of such a restriction. Too often do we recall fictional characters vividly, yet not a single word of the text in which they came alive; indeed, I venture to say that readers generally remember characters that way.[43]

Chatman holds that while character can be seen as the sum of all the subjects of all the verbs, the linear, temporal dimension of narrative must be taken into account. As we read, we develop what Chatman calls a "paradigm of traits," an image and conceptualization of the character based on the attributes contained in the narrative. We revise this paradigm as new information about the character is introduced. And we revise on the basis of what we know real people to be like; whether the personage is real or literary, we know them by extrapolating a distinguishing paradigm of traits—in the end, the

---

[41]Hochman, *Character in Literature,* 22-23. See Roland Barthes, *S/Z,* and above, chap. 1, "The Holy Spirit and the Literary Critics."

[42]Chatman, *Story and Discourse,* 107-26. Cf. Rimmon-Kenan, *Narrative Fiction,* 29-42.

[43]Chatman, *Story and Discourse,* 118. He says elsewhere (137), "It is absurd to describe characters as 'abstractions' or 'precipitates' from words; it is like saying that a statue is a 'precipitate' from marble." Cf. Martin, *Recent Theories of Narrative,* 230: "Our sense that fictional characters are uncannily similar to people is therefore not something to be dismissed or ridiculed but a crucial feature of narration that requires explanation."

way we get to know a fictional character such as Sherlock Holmes is little different from the way we get to know our next-door neighbor. Thus characters are "open" and to some extent autonomous beings.[44]

For some, Chatman's theory does not go far enough. Baruch Hochman contends that Chatman's system sticks too tightly to the verbal text, and ignores the great similarity between the ways we construct literary characters and real people:

> What links characters in literature to people in life, as we fabricate them in our consciousness, is the integral unity of our conception of people and of how they operate. I, indeed, want to go further than Chatman by holding that there is a profound congruity between the ways in which we apprehend characters in literature, documented figures in history, and people of whom we have what we think of as direct knowledge in life. In my view, even the clues that we take in and use to construct an image of a person are virtually identical in literature and in life.[45]

Hochman shows that the distinctions often made concerning the ways we apprehend fictional, historical, and living people are spurious. Do we know literary personages "intrinsically," with special knowledge of their inner feelings and thoughts, and living ones only "extrinsically," as W. J. Harvey held?[46] Only if the writing opens up intrinsic knowledge of the character, and our friends do not talk about their feelings. Must our subjective impressions of ourselves be rich and well-rounded, and our perception of others reductive and shallow, as implied in E. M. Forster's distinction between "flat" and "round" characters?[47] Only if we never succumb to self-hatred and self-caricature, and treat our closest loved ones no differently from the checker at the convenience store. And are charac-

---

[44]Chatman, *Story and Discourse,* 119-26.

[45]Hochman, *Character in Literature,* 36.

[46]W. J. Harvey, *Character and the Novel* (Ithaca: Cornell University Press, 1965), 31-32.

[47]See below, pp. 67-70.

ters in narrative mere types, as Northrop Frye held,[48] but real persons always highly individualized? Hochman argues that this distinction ignores the role typology and stereotyping plays in our everyday perceptions of others; indeed, it is the rare acquaintance who breaks out of the bonds of classification—male/female, young/old, rich/poor, black/white—to become a unique individual for us.[49] Hochman concludes that an adequate theory of characterization must take into account the great similarities between our appraisal of the lettered and the living:

> In effect, our retrieval, or reading out, of character is guided by our consciousness of what people are and how people work. To read character adequately we must heighten our consciousness of the reciprocity between character in literature and people in life—between Homo Fictus and Homo Sapiens.[50]

For example, characters and people are subject to the same kinds of conflicts:[51]

> The changing formal psychologies and the schemes for talking about character in literature share the assumption that people are subject to conflict and therefore undergo processes of development, psychic and social....Any adequate conception of character must include some conceptualization of the kinds of conflict that are experienced by people in life and by their analogues in literature.[52]

Hochman notes that an understanding of the world and people in terms of conflict is deeply rooted in Western thought; he cites Plato,

---

[48]Frye, *Anatomy of Criticism,* 171-72.

[49]Hochman, *Character in Literature,* 36-58.

[50]Ibid., 59.

[51]Ibid., 49-58.

[52]Ibid., 49-50.

Aristotle, Moses, Jesus, Hegel, and Freud as examples.[53] The Freudian view that personality traits spring from conflict provides in Hochman's view the most comprehensive view of character, but he notes that one need not be a Freudian to see conflict as an essential aspect of character. Conflict also goes beyond individuals; thus Lukács has argued that the conflicts within an individual epitomize the contradictions in society.[54] Hochman shows that conflict among and within characters need not be articulate or conscious, and is found in and among the most stereotyped of characters. Since conflict is unavoidable in daily human life and underlies much of what we consider as "characterization," our understanding of conflict becomes the point of contact between characters and people:

> In literature we are engaged in the dynamic life of the characters....What makes them meaningful for us is the kinds of conflict they embody and experience and the way those conflicts are articulated in the work.[55]

Hochman concludes that the similarities between these two spheres of existence are mimetic: human life is "the source of the whole spectrum of characters."[56]

Yet Hochman cautions that any effective comparison between characters and real people must take into account the very different worlds in which the two live:

> To deal with people in literature, we must remember that they are not alive, even as we must bear in mind that people in life must not be treated like characters in literature. For Homo Fictus and Homo Sapiens are far

---

[53]The pervasiveness of the idea that conflict is essential to life and literature is one reason Hochman argues that characters in older literature can be retrieved in terms of modern perceptions (Ibid., 54-58).

[54]Georg Lukács, *Studies in European Realism* (New York: Grosset and Dunlap, 1964), cited in Hochman, *Character in Literature*, 53.

[55]Hochman, *Character in Literature*, 50.

[56]Ibid., 58.

from identical. To deal adequately with either, we must distinguish between them, both in themselves and as they take form in our minds.[57]

Obviously, characters as imaginary beings are not people—they do not exist in space-time, they do not breathe, they cannot touch our hands or faces. We cannot interact with them. It is often noted that characters are more like the dead than the living:

> The characters in literature, once they are "written," are finished like the dead. We can manipulate them only to the extent that we respond to the signs that generate them and allow them to inhabit our thoughts, our fantasies, and our dreams.[58]

Not only are characters in this sense finished, but they often offer us only meager information about themselves, and sometimes seem to lack a complete life history. Yet, because real life is so chaotic, literature can seem to offer us more coherent and stable images of humanity than that which we perceive in real life. This is because a character comes to us within a certain structure—the overall structure of a literary work; what characters "mean" is dependent on the larger imaginary world in which they exist, a world created by text and reader. Characters are, in short, language. They are also the complex critical acts that extricate character from language—combining to form what Hochman calls "the paradox of utter embeddedness and radical detachability."[59] What kind of character is generated—whether realistic, stereotyped, clichéd, or psychologically complex—depends on the kind of text which generates it, and the role of that character in that text.[60]

---

[57]Ibid., 59. Cf. Robert Higbie, *Character and Structure in the English Novel* (Gainesville: University of Florida Press, 1984), 3: "All characters must be conventional to some extent, not merely imitations of reality."

[58]Hochman, *Character in Literature,* 60.

[59]Ibid., 71.

[60]Ibid., 59-85. For another comparison of the similarities and differences between people and characters, see E. M. Forster, *Aspects of the Novel,* (New York: Harcourt, Brace & World, 1927), 43-63.

Hochman summarizes the commonalities and differences between characters and people:

> What they have in common is the model, which we carry in our heads, of what a person is. Both characters and people are apprehended in someone's consciousness, and they are apprehended in approximately the same terms. Yet they are clearly not identical. To equate them is to overlook the peculiarities of their habitation—which for characters in literature is the world of language—and to erode the salient qualities of both characters themselves and the texts that generate them.[61]

Hochman's formulation finds wide consensus among literary critics. Weinsheimer, for example, agrees that characters are both people and words—to some extent both semiotic and mimetic theories are correct. The critic must be "Janus-faced" and take both into account.[62] This dual-natured view of character as both illusion and reality, both vivid and delusive, led Rawdon Wilson to call it a "bright chimera."[63] The answer to the question of whether characters are people or words is "Yes."[64]

Similarly, the relation of character and plot requires a Janus-faced view. Here the balanced view of Hochman provides great advantages over the one-sided, self-contradictory view of the structuralists and their heirs. The frequently quoted words of Henry James aptly express the tension: "What is character but the determination of incident? What is incident but the illustration of character?"[65] Character cannot be reduced to or considered independently of plot:

---

[61]Hochman, *Character in Literature*, 7.

[62]Weinsheimer, "Theory of Character: *Emma*," 208-10.

[63]Rawdon Wilson, "The Bright Chimera: Character as a Literary Term," *Critical Inquiry*, 5 (1979): 725-49.

[64]Cf. Gowler, *Host, Guest, Enemy and Friend*, 43.

[65]Henry James, "The Art of Fiction," in *The Art of Criticism: Henry James on the Theory and Practice of Fiction*, ed. William Veeder and Susan Griffin (Chicago: University of Chicago Press, 1986), 174.

> Plot and character are inseparably bound up in the reading experience, if not always in critical thought. Each works to produce the other. Characters are defined in and through plot, by what they do and by what they say. The plot in turn comes into view as characters act and interact.[66]

A true understanding of character in narrative demands that it not be treated in isolation.[67]

To sum up the discussion so far, the definition of character has proved to be complex and elusive. Character can be seen as no more than marks on a page, a function of the plot, the sum of all the verbs of all the sentence in a text. Yet this structuralist, semiotic view has severe limitations, and some structuralists themselves have introduced mimetic elements into their theories. Hochman's synthesis proves to be most adequate: characters cannot be treated in isolation from their actions, but must also be seen in relation to their human counterparts outside the text. Characters and people are different, because they inhabit different worlds. But the way we come to know characters is similar to the way we come to know people. In both cases, a model is generated as we interact with the other, and that model changes and develops as time, life, and text move on. Life and literature are interconnected but not identical; this is why we can learn from life how to read, and from reading, how to live.

This discussion has important implications for our present study. First, it provides two categories essential for the argument I will present in the final section of this chapter: that Luke-Acts portrays the Holy Spirit as a character. These categories are action and conflict. Insofar as Luke presents the Holy Spirit as an actor in the plot, Luke presents the Spirit as a character. And inasmuch as Luke presents the Spirit in conflict with other characters, again, the Spirit can be considered a character.

Second, the complex interrelation between characters and real people throws new light on the question of whether the Holy Spirit

---

[66]Moore, *Literary Criticism of the Gospels,* 15.

[67]Cf. the warning of Gowler, *Host, Guest, Enemy and Friend,* 48 n., citing Henry James, that the various components of a narrative not be treated "as if they were merely parts of an engine."

is personal or impersonal, a Who or a What. Quite simply, this question proves to be misstated. It is important not to confuse characters and people, and so to say that the Holy Spirit is a "character" is to make no claims whatsoever about any entity outside of Luke's text—least of all to imply that Luke presents the Holy Spirit as a divine "person" in the manner of later theology. At the same time, one must recognize the close relationship between textual characters and the figures which inhabit the extra-textual world. Darr and Brawley have already shown the close ties Luke draws between the Holy Spirit and God. And certainly Luke-Acts would not be extant if a community had not believed that it provided insight into a living, extra-textual God. The question one must ask is not whether Luke's conception was personal or impersonal, but what the character of the Holy Spirit within the text can teach the reader about the God of Luke's proclamation, and the proclamation of the church which preserved and read Luke's text.

Types of Characters

Given that we acknowledge the complexity of the relations among characters, people, and plot, how might we further advance our understanding of narrative characterization by distinguishing different types of characters? E. M. Forster, in a groundbreaking work entitled *Aspects of the Novel,* divides characters into two types, flat and round.[68] Flat characters

> are constructed round a single idea or quality....The really flat character can be expressed in one sentence such as "I never will desert Mr. Micawber." There is Mrs. Micawber—she says she won't desert Mr. Micawber, she doesn't, and there she is.[69]

---

[68]E. M. Forster, *Aspects of the Novel* (New York: Harcourt, Brace & World, 1927), 67-78.

[69]Ibid., 67.

Flat characters—sometimes little more than caricatures—are easily recognized and remembered, are often comic, and serve to set off the main, "round" characters. A round character is

> capable of surprising in a convincing way. If it never surprises, it is flat. If it does not convince, it is a flat pretending to be round. It has the incalculability of life about it—life within the pages of a book.[70]

For Forster, the round character is the great achievement of the greatest authors, and "cannot be summed up in a single phrase," but "waxes and wanes and has facets like a human being."[71]

Forster has been subjected to a great deal of criticism, though his categories are still sometimes used.[72] As Rimmon-Kenan notes, these categories are highly reductive; at best one could say that characters run along a continuum between flat and round.[73] But Forster also confuses two criteria when he says that flat characters are simple and undeveloping while round characters are complex and developing, for complex characters need not develop (Rimmon-Kenan cites Joyce's Bloom as an example) while simple characters may develop (the allegorical Everyman).[74] Certainly these criteria must be distinguished, and a greater spectrum of possibilities must be taken into account.[75]

W. J. Harvey attempts to move beyond Forster's simple categories.[76] For Harvey, the spectrum of characters from flat to

---

[70]Ibid., 78.

[71]Ibid., 69.

[72]E.g., Powell, "The Religious Leaders in Luke." Chatman, *Story and Discourse,* 131-34, builds his theory of "open-ended" characterization on Forster's distinction.

[73]As Forster himself acknowledges when he speaks of "the curve towards the round" (E. M. Forster, *Aspects of the Novel,* 67).

[74]Rimmon-Kenan, *Narrative Fiction,* 40-41.

[75]Cf. Hochman, *Character in Literature,* 88.

[76]Harvey, *Character and the Novel,* 52-73.

round can be divided into three groups—protagonists, background characters (who function mainly in terms of plot), and intermediate characters (who fall between the other two categories). Harvey's "protagonist" is in essence equivalent to Forster's "round" character—protagonists are central, multifaceted figures, seen from many vantage points,

> whose motivation and history are most fully established, who conflict and change as the story progresses, who engage our responses more fully and steadily, in a way more complex though not necessarily more vivid than other characters.[77]

The protagonist's life and struggles are for Harvey the central focus of a literary work. In place of Forster's "flat" character, Harvey speaks of "background" characters. Background characters are purely functional in that they merely define an environment, social setting, or theme. These characters, like those in the intermediate group, serve to illuminate the protagonist by contrast. Though one could find in novels a wide variety of intermediate figures, Harvey enumerated but two: the card and the ficelle. The card is a highly-animated or caricatured figure, often odd or outrageous (a hyperbolic form of Forster's "flat" character). The ficelle (a term drawn from the work of Henry James) acts as a foil to the protagonist. The ficelle,

> the character who while more fully delineated and individualized than any background character, exists in the novel primarily to serve some function. Unlike the protagonist he is ultimately a means to an end rather than an end in himself.[78]

As Hochman notes, Harvey's categories are not helpful in studying genres less mimetic than the classic novel, where characterization stands at the center of the work. Nor do his functional descriptions of the minor characters tell us much about their substance or modes of being. A more adequate account of the various types of

---

[77]Ibid., 56.

[78]Ibid., 58.

characters would define ways characters exist both in themselves and within texts. Further, it would provide a wider range of qualities to be found in characters, a spectrum wide enough to encompass many different times of narrative.[79] A greater range of descriptive categories is called for.[80]

Yosef Ewen takes a different approach. Ewen agrees with Harvey that characters are best classified as points along a continuum, but goes further in proposing multiple continua or axes, those of "complexity," "development," and "penetration" into inner life.[81] On the axis of complexity, Ewen places characters of only one trait—allegorical characters, types, and caricatures—at one end. Complex characters, such as Dostoevsky's Raskolnikov, are placed at the other. Between the two extremes stand an infinite number of degrees of complexity. The second axis, development, describes a range between static and dynamic characters. Here Ewen is concerned with the degree to which a character develops as the work proceeds. The third axis, penetration into inner life (or the "mimetic and symbolic axis") refers to the range of consciousness, thoughts, and emotions presented to the reader. Texts in the Hebrew Bible, for example, usually present little in the way of a character's inner thoughts and feelings, while many modern novels would fall on the other end of the axis. As with the other two axes, one can distinguish an infinite number of degrees of difference between the two poles.

While Ewen has taken a step in the right direction, in that more than one quality is used to describe a character, his system is not quite complete. Why limit oneself to only three categories? Are there not other factors that must be taken into account when describ-

---

[79]Hochman, *Character in Literature*, 88.

[80]Cf. Gowler, *Host, Guest, Enemy and Friend*, 51-52.

[81]Yosef Ewen, "The Theory of Character in Narrative Fiction" (in Hebrew with English synopsis) *Hasifrut* 3 (1971): 1-30, and *Character in Narrative* (in Hebrew) (Tel Aviv: Sifriyat Hapoalim, 1980). Cf. the summaries in Rimmon-Kenan, *Narrative Fiction*, 41-42, and Gowler, *Host, Guest, Enemy and Friend*, 52-53.

ing the whole range of possible characterization?[82] These questions lead Baruch Hochman to propose a more comprehensive scheme.

Hochman proposes a classification system of eight categories which he called "aspects and modes" of "characters' existence both in themselves and within the texts that generate them."[83] The categories "allow us to conceptualize the images we form of such characters as we 'liberate' them from the texts within which they figure."[84] Each category embraces its polar opposite:

Stylization	Naturalism
Coherence	Incoherence
Wholeness	Fragmentariness
Literalness	Symbolism
Complexity	Simplicity
Transparency	Opacity
Dynamism	Staticism
Closure	Openness[85]

These categories and their opposites represent poles on a continuum, and while not all of them are relevant for every character, as a whole they provide a thorough description of the qualities we find in characters. Hochman defines these eight categories as follows:[86]

Stylization/Naturalism. Stylization is the comprehensive, umbrella category. It refers to the degree of realism or naturalism used in the representation of characters. Since all characters are to some degree stylized, it is more appropriate to speak of "maximal" and "minimal" stylization. Minimally stylized characters approximate the normal self-presentation of real people. Forster's "round" characters would be an example of minimally stylized characters,

---

[82]Cf. Gowler, *Host, Guest, Enemy and Friend*, 53.

[83]Hochman, *Character in Literature*, 88.

[84]Ibid., 88.

[85]Ibid., 89.

[86]Ibid., 89-140. A summary and application to ancient literature is found in Gowler, *Host, Guest, Enemy and Friend*, 332.

while Harvey's "card" would be a maximally stylized character. Hochman gives many examples as he expounds his categories, usually but not always from modern fiction,[87] in order to clarify what he means by his terms; as for "stylization" and "naturalism,"

> I think we know exactly what is meant when we are told that Anna Karenina is less stylized in presentation than Catherine Earnshaw and that Catherine Earnshaw is less stylized than Estella in *Great Expectations,* while Estella is still less stylized than Miss Havisham....Stylization has to do with some model or norm from which stylized characterizations deviate. The norm...is clearly resemblance to real people, which means some form of realism or naturalism of representation.[88]

Hochman acknowledges the problem inherent in this category: "What do we mean when we speak of the 'originals' or 'models' of the figures presented in literature?"[89] His answer is that "we share quite a clear notion of what we mean by an unstylized image of a person";[90] that is, the reader has a cultural expectation of what a person, and therefore a character, should be like.

As Gowler notes, Hochman's definition of the minimally stylized character invokes the modern standards of individualization and psychological conflict, standards that may not be relevant in dealing with characters in ancient literature.[91] One may not expect the same degree of introspection in literature from a culture that did not place as high a value on this attribute. Gowler has studied ancient characterization in light of Hochman's distinction between stylization and naturalism, and concluded that "taking into account the cultural environment of the ancient world, the whole range of stylization is

---

[87]Gowler has studied ancient characterization in light of Hochman's categories, as noted below. Gowler, *Host, Guest, Enemy and Friend,* 327-32; see also his extensive examples of characterization in ancient narratives, 77-176.

[88]Hochman, *Character in Literature,* 90.

[89]Ibid.

[90]Ibid.

[91]Gowler, *Host, Guest, Enemy and Friend,* 321-22, 327-28.

evident in ancient literature."[92] He cites as examples of maximal stylization, the characters in *The Golden Ass,* of minimal stylization, Chariton's Callirhoe.

Of importance to this study is Hochman's acknowledgment that

> Minimal and maximal stylization of character involves manipulation of conventional norms for characterization. The norms include a considerable range of possibilities, many of which are related to genre. Thus, although caricature and the grotesque dictate one extreme mode of stylization, pastoral and romantic conventions dictate another, milder kind of distortion of the post-Renaissance norm for character.[93]

Thus the degree of realism or lack thereof in the portrayal of a character depends on the literary forbears of that character, and genre in which the character appears. "Stylization" or "naturalism" are judged in part by what kind of text is being read, and what kind of expectations a reader brings to that kind of text. A character can be said to be more or less stylized as it conforms to or breaks from those expectations. This will prove to have important consequences for the study of the characterization of the Holy Spirit in Luke-Acts. One could hardly say that a divine figure could be portrayed "naturally," if "naturalism" is defined solely as "approximating the normal self-presentation of a real person." Since God is not normally encountered in the way people are, this definition of "stylization/naturalism" is not useful. But if stylization is defined in light of literary precedent, it can be and is an important category to apply to a divine character. The question becomes: what body of literature sets the precedents by which the reader understands the divine character, what are those precedents, and how does the present text follow or break those precedents? The literary precedent which sets the expectations of Luke's reader is the Greek Old Testament, and the prophetic literature there which speaks of the Spirit. In what follows, the character of the Holy Spirit will be said to be more or less stylized to the degree to which it follows or breaks from the precedents set by the Septuagint.

---

[92]Ibid., 328.

[93]Hochman, *Character in Literature,* 95.

Coherence/Incoherence. Characters in texts need not present themselves as unified or coherent. Some characters seem to be built on a contradictory and conflicting structure with no decisive unifying principle, such as Shakespeare's Autolychus or Homer's Odysseus, according to Hochman. Others, such as most allegorical characters, or Jaggers in *Great Expectations,* are solidly consistent. Complex characters can be difficult to place on this axis, as the foundation of a character's coherency could be highly conflictual and contradictory, as with Heathcliff or Othello. A judgment about the coherency of these characters will require a great deal of puzzling on the part of the reader. This issue differs from stylization, as both maximally and minimally stylized characters can be quite coherent, or incoherent, as the case may be. The stipulation that a character has a certain degree of coherence or incoherence does not involve a value judgment, as either coherency or incoherency can be a virtue, depending on the text.

Again, Gowler has noted the modern, Western bias implied in the term "consistent."[94] As with stylization, coherence must be judged according to cultural norms. Coherence was valued in ancient literary criticism; Aristotle insisted on character consistency in Greek Tragedy, and a good example of a coherent character is Jason in Euripides' *Medea.* Yet the stringent demands of plot sometimes interfered with character coherence; Gowler cites Chaereas in *Chaereas and Callirhoe* as an example.[95]

Wholeness/Fragmentariness. Wholeness, according to Hochman, refers to the degree to which we sense a text presents us with a complete picture of a character, analogous to the whole of a real person. The characterization seems to give us an complete account of this imaginary person, as with Jane Austen's Elizabeth Bennett or Tolstoy's Anna Karenina. It differs from coherence in that we may (and quite frequently do) know the whole of a contradictory and incoherent personality. And it differs from stylization in that a minimal stylized character can be quite fragmentary, as with the Fool in *King Lear,* who fades from the scene once he has stimulated Lear's

---

[94]Gowler, *Host, Guest, Enemy and Friend,* 323.

[95]Ibid., 328-29.

process of self-discovery. Total wholeness can of course never be achieved, but maximal wholeness in characterization often leads us to speculate about what a character might do, say, and be beyond the text. A high degree of fragmentation, on the other hand, often results in characters so easily typified that they seem to be no more than a synecdochic nose, finger, or purse. Fragmentary characters often lean to being typological and paradigmatic. To the degree a character has a narrower range of actions in a text, it will be seen as more fragmentary.

Gowler believes that Hochman's requirement that wholeness be determined by the reader's awareness of a character's life experiences and hypothetical motives needed to be revised with respect to ancient societies, which had much less individualistic ways of thinking about people. He cites Aeschylus' Clytemnestra as an example of a whole character—one does not know everything about her, but what is there presents a convincing picture.[96]

Literalism/Symbolism. Since all elements of communication are symbolic, says Hochman, complete literalness within a literary work can never be achieved. Characters are never real people. But there is a tension between the character in and of itself, and the qualities or ideas it represents within the work as a whole. The character may signify something outside itself, it may simply represent itself, or it may in some ways do both. Anna Karenina, for example, is apprehended primarily literally as herself, and only secondarily as an adulteress, an inadequate mother, or a narcissist; Emma Bovary is also literally herself, but much more symbolic than Anna—of a certain kind of person who lives in a fantasy world. It would be a mistake to posit a sharp polarity along the continuum between literalness and symbolism, as the line between the individual and the type is often faint. Hochman cites the distinction between Oedipus and Everyman—while Oedipus may seem to be an Everyman, he remains irrevocably himself, whereas Everyman is purely symbolic.[97]

---

[96]Ibid., 329.

[97]Hochman, *Character in Literature,* 118.

Gowler notes that in ancient literature as in modern, characters who are literally themselves are more likely to be perceived as individuals than characters who are primarily representatives of a class. For the former, see Euripides' Medea, for the latter, the Theophrastan characters.[98]

Complexity/Simplicity. Complexity for Hochman is often a function of the number of traits which adhere to a character; the more traits, the more complex the characterization. This distinction is largely defined by the difference between central and secondary characters; flanking characters tend to be simpler than protagonists. But complexity may also be enhanced by the contradictions and tensions between traits, as with Mrs. Bennett in *Pride and Prejudice.* Even subordinate characters can demonstrate more than one trait, sometimes with a high degree of tension between traits.

Gowler holds that modern introspection produces a complexity that could never have been matched by the characters of ancient literature. Still, highly complex characters exist in ancient texts. Odysseus and Medea are examples. In the Hebrew Bible, David would be an example of a complex character; Abishag an example of a simple one.[99]

Transparency/Opacity. Characters can be more or less open to the reader—we can know varying degrees of their inner lives. Hochman cites the example of *Great Expectations:* Jaggers's motives are more transparent than Miss Havisham's, Miss Havisham's than Wemmick's, and Wemmick's than Pip's.[100] Again, these terms do not express value judgments—transparency is no more a virtue than opacity. Simple characters, for example, may be completely transparent, so that the readers knows exactly why they are acting, or completely opaque, because their motives are unimportant. With more complex characters, transparency clarifies characterization for the reader, while opacity introduces a literary "gap" which invites the reader to speculate on the motives and intentions of a character.

---

[98]Gowler, *Host, Guest, Enemy and Friend*, 329-30.

[99]Ibid., 330-31.

[100]Hochman, *Character in Literature*, 126.

Opacity in major characters can result in intriguing characterization, as it helps create verisimilitude and drama.

Gowler cites several transparent characters in ancient narrative: for example, the inward thoughts of characters are almost always open to the reader in *Chaereas and Callirhoe*. The Hebrew Bible, while usually somewhat opaque, does sometimes open up the inner life of its characters.[101] According to Gowler, ancient cultures did not place a high value on individualistic, inward motivation, and so there is less attention to such motivation in ancient characterization.[102]

Dynamism/Staticism. Dynamic characters are those which develop in the course of a work (like Forster's "round" characters). Elizabeth Bennett, King Lear, and Macbeth are notable examples of dynamic characters who shift and change as the story develops. The fixed, static characters of melodrama and fairy tale form the other end of this spectrum, says Hochman.

Many scholars have held that all ancient characters are static and do not change. Scholes and Kellogg, for example, believed that

> Characters in primitive stories are invariably "flat," "static," and quite "opaque." The very recurring epithets of formulaic narrative are signs of flatness in characterization. Odysseus is the man never at a loss—always, whenever we see him....He does not change, he does not age, except to play a role and fool his enemies....Like Achilles, he is a monolith.[103]

Gowler, however, has shown that this view of ancient characters is one-sided and incomplete. Ancient characters can change and grow—they can be dynamic.[104] Gowler cites as examples Homer's Telemachus, Jacob in the Hebrew Bible, and Artaxerxes in

---

[101]See M. Niehoff, "Do Biblical Characters Talk to Themselves? Narrative Modes of Representing Inner Speech in Early Biblical Fiction," *Journal of Biblical Literature* 111 (1992): 577-95.

[102]Gowler, *Host, Guest, Enemy and Friend*, 331.

[103]Scholes and Kellogg, *Nature of Narrative*, 164.

[104]Gowler, *Host, Guest, Enemy and Friend*, 80-84.

Chaereas and Callirhoe. Gowler admits, however, that the majority of characters in ancient literature cluster at the static end of the spectrum.[105]

Closure/Openness. When we wonder about what happens to a character once a book is finished, that character has a high degree of what Hochman calls openness—the character seems to transcend the text (and perhaps invite a sequel). Characters given an open-ended presentation, such as Scarlet O'Hara or Sherlock Holmes, invite speculation on their future actions. On the other hand, a character may seem to be complete and whole (or even dead) by the end; thus there is little room for speculation about the future of Oedipus or Hamlet. The issue is the degree to which the character's conflicts and ambiguities are resolved within the work. Gowler notes open-ended characters in ancient literature: for example, Uriah dies, but how much he knew about David and Bathsheba is still a matter of debate.

With Hochman's scheme, we have a highly detailed, nuanced system for describing the many facets of a character. This scheme will prove useful as a model for describing the character of the Holy Spirit in Luke-Acts. It remains to examine the process by which reader and text work together to produce a character.

Character: Presentation and Reception

James Garvey lists five aspects essential to a complete description of a character:[106]

---

[105]Ibid., 331-32. See also Burns, *Character: Being and Acting*; Stephen Halliwell, "Traditional Greek Conceptions of Character," in Pelling, *Characterization and Individuality*, 32-59.

[106]James Garvey, "Characterization in Narrative," *Poetics* 7 (1978): 63-78.

(1) An identification or name, e.g., "the man," "Emma."

(2) A set of structural attributes (textual roles such as narrator or symbol).

(3) A set of non-structural attributes (attributive characteristics such as "red hair" or "wears a hat").

(4) A time orientation indicating changes in attributes.

(5) A set of norms used in understanding the attributes. Norms can be:

   (a) Logical: X is pregnant means X is female

   (b) Cultural: X belched, X is rude (in western culture)

   (c) Generic: X wears black hat, X is a bad guy (movie westerns)

   (d) Co-textual: X respected his mother, Mrs. Y reminds him of her, therefore X respects Mrs. Y.

It is not always clear, however, whether the text or the reader supplies this information. For example, the structural role of the character may be left ambiguous by the text. Cultural logic may be implied but not supplied; that a belch indicates rudeness may simply be assumed in a text—the reader must supply this information in order to understand the characterization. The relation between reader and text in the creation of character may be quite complex.

On the one hand, certainly the text brings us the character. We have no character if we have no book, actor, or film before us. On the other hand, the character, being an imaginary construct, has no existence apart from our imagination. If there is no one to read the book or watch the actor, the words and actions that form the character have no place to form. This tension, inherent in the act of reading, led Joel Weinsheimer to say that:

All texts are both prior and posterior to their interpreter....The critic's find-
ings are governed by the questions he asks of the text, and his questions are
in turn governed by the cultural gestalt he inherits in part from the text
itself. Thus the text may be both origin and answer of the critic's questions....In short, if the text were not prior, the critic would have no questions to ask; if it were not posterior, he would have nothing to address
them to.[107]

So in some sense a character is both in and after the text, created by
both text and reader. The character is both generated by the text and
constructed by the reader.

The explanation of the relationship between readers and texts is
one of the more enduring legacies of "reader-response criticism," a
designation which embraces the work of critics as diverse as
Wolfgang Iser and Stanley Fish.[108] Reader-response critics agree
that whatever a text may contribute to its own interpretation, the
reader[109] does a substantial amount of the work.[110] In Iser's terms,

---

[107]Weinsheimer, "Theory of Character: *Emma*," 209.

[108]Wolfgang Iser, *The Act of Reading: A Theory of Aesthetic Response*
(Baltimore: Johns Hopkins University Press, 1978); Stanley Fish, *Is There a Text
in This Class? The Authority of Interpretive Communities* (Cambridge: Harvard
University Press, 1980).

[109]The word "reader" requires attention here. Wayne Booth notes the many
different kinds of readers the reading process entails; the flesh-and-blood reader is
not the reader envisioned by the author, who could not have envisioned who
would pick up the book. Nor are either of these readers the reader assumed by the
written text and brought into being by the read text. Further, a critical reader differs from a naive reader, yet the same flesh-and-blood reader can be both critical
and naive (Booth, *Rhetoric of Fiction*, 420-31). These various readers are intertwined. As Darr says, "The reader cannot be found by looking only to the critic,
the text, or the extratext, for readers are in fact the products of a complex interaction among all three factors" (Darr, *On Character Building*, 25). It is difficult to
deny this, especially when the reader posited by biblical scholars so often looks
suspiciously like a biblical scholar; as Darr notes, "We tend to create readers in
our own image." See further Robert M. Fowler, "Who Is 'The Reader' in Reader
Response Criticism?" *Semeia* 31 (1985): 5-23; Moore, *Literary Criticism and the
Gospels*, 71-107; and below, chap. 3, on Luke 1:1-4.

[110]On reader-response criticism, see Eagleton, *Literary Theory*, 74-90;
Elizabeth Freund, *The Return of the Reader: Reader-Response Criticism* (New
York: Methuen, 1987); Roman Ingarden, *The Literary Work of Art: An Investiga-*

the texts contains "gaps" which the reader must fill with the necessary literary, social, cultural, psychological, historical, or other kind of information in order to understand the text. Reading becomes a process of forming and revising expectations as readers fill in the ambiguities of the text:

> Whenever the reader bridges the gaps, communication begins. The gaps function as a kind of pivot on which the whole text-reader relationship revolves. Hence the structured blanks of the text stimulate the process of ideation to be performed by the reader on terms set by the text.[111]

In short, a reader tries to bring coherence to a sometimes incoherent or partially-coherent text. The reader does this by correlating the various elements of the text into a coherent whole, forming opinions and revising them as necessary along the way. When necessary, the reader will add extra-textual information, such as cultural or historical background, to fill in the blank.

John Darr notes the two distinct processes of gap-filling: anticipation/retrospection, and consistency-building. Reading is a temporal process of making and revising meaning—the reader develops expectations along the way, and finds them fulfilled, disappointed, or revised as reading continues. Thus reading is re-reading, forming and revising expectations.[112] Darr calls this process "anticipation and retrospection":

---

tion on the Borderlines of Ontology, Logic, and Theory of Literature, Northwestern University Studies in Phenomenology and Existential Philosophy (Evanston: Northwestern University Press, 1973); Susan R. Suleiman and Inge Crosman, eds., *The Reader in the Text: Essays on Audience and Interpretation* (Princeton: Princeton University Press, 1980); Jane P. Tompkins, ed., *Reader-Response Criticism* (Baltimore: Johns Hopkins University Press, 1980). Robert Fowler has been the most vocal advocate of this method in New Testament studies (*Let the Reader Understand: Reader-Response Criticism and the Gospel of Mark* (Minneapolis: Fortress Press, 1991); see Moore, *Literary Criticism and the Gospels*, 71-107.

[111]Iser, *Act of Reading*, 169.

[112]Darr rightly makes this point in his review of Gowler (in *Journal of Biblical Literature* 112 (1993): 153):

> The interpreter must take *the process of character formation* (e.g., identifi-

Anticipation and retrospection are continuous, complementary activities. Moving through the text, a reader begins to formulate expectations and opinions which then become the basis upon which subsequent data is processed. In turn, one reassesses previously-formed expectations and opinions in light of new information and insights.[113]

What is so remarkable about the process of reading is not that texts contain gaps, but that readers are so persistent at filling them in order to create coherence. Darr calls this "consistency-building":

Readers fully *expect* texts to provide them with sufficient data and guidance....All texts have gaps, tensions, inconsistencies, and ambiguities. And, although some of these will never be completely resolved, the reader can and does process the majority of them.[114]

The reader can and does enjoy the process as well. Puzzling over gaps and ambiguities is part of what Robert Alter once called "the high fun of the act of communication."[115]

Terry Eagleton provides an example of the kind of gap-filling a reader goes through in order to construct a coherent view of a text.[116] "'What did you make of the new couple?' The Hanemas,

---

cation, retrospection and anticipation, consistency building, etc.), and not simply textual imformation, into account....Gowler fails consistently to monitor *accumulation* of character as reading progresses (emphasis his).

Any theory of characterization must take into account the temporal processes of reading.

[113]Darr, *On Character Building*, 30.

[114]Darr, *On Character Building*, 31; emphasis his. See also Iser, *Act of Reading*, 118-29. Darr (31-32) notes two other processes which take place in reading: identification, in which the reader develops various degrees of intimacy and distance with a character, and defamiliarization, in which the familiar is placed in an unfamiliar setting.

[115]Alter, *Pleasures of Reading*, 30.

[116]See Eagleton, *Literary Theory*, 74-77.

Piet and Angela, were undressing." The opening of John Updike's *Couples* requires a great deal of complex, largely unconscious labor on the part of the reader. The apparent lack of connection between the two sentences is only briefly if at all puzzling; one readily recognizes the literary convention here—the speech must be attributed to one of the two characters. A picture of the scene forms; the couple undressing is probably alone in a bedroom, if the usual social conventions are followed. The reader assumes that the two characters are human, that they are married, their last name is Hanema, and so on. If one continues to read this story, one will confirm or revise our opinions as the story progresses, and probably determine the identities of the "new couple." There is no inherent or necessary reason that the reader's conjectures about the first two sentences will be correct; but based on the reader's experience with reading novels, and with undressing couples, there is little reason to suppose otherwise. Only time, and continued reading, will tell for sure. Eagleton concludes that "the text itself is really no more than a series of 'cues' to the reader, invitations to construct a piece of language into meaning."[117]

There is still debate among reader-response critics over how much meaning is brought to the text by the reader. Iser holds that texts tend to maneuver readers in certain ways and thus preserve authoritative readings: the reader must be "manipulated by the text if his viewpoint is to be properly guided."[118] Fish, on the other hand, holds that any constraint on the reader is provided by the "interpretive communities" in which the reader lives and works. In Fish's famous example, a reading list on the blackboard can be construed as a religious poem, if the reading community is so

---

[117]Ibid., 76.

[118]Iser, *Act of Reading*, 152. Meir Sternberg (*Poetics of Biblical Narrative*) presents an extreme version of Iser's theory in his literary interpretation of the Hebrew Bible; Sternberg holds that the Bible uses "foolproof composition" to determine the reader's understanding (48-56). Among the many difficulties with this theory, it is hard to understand how differences in interpretation can arise if the composition is foolproof.

inclined.[119] The questions the reader asks of the text ultimately determine what the reader thinks the text says; the text is a product of interpretation. What keeps Fish's position from total nihilism is the recognition that readers live within interpretive communities which share interpretive strategies. So readers are restrained from idiosyncratic interpretation by communal pressure.

On the whole I lean toward Fish's position, as interpretation cannot take place apart from the training a reader receives from those who have read before. The text provides gaps for the reader to fill, but the text does not dictate how gaps are filled—this is learned behavior for the reader, part of the conventions of reading practiced by a particular interpretive community. I would add that every flesh-and-blood reader lives within a variety of communities, some of which overlap. To some extent, one is free to move about between communities, and so for example, if one finds the pressures of a particular community too much of a constraint, one can change; if spiritual allegories on biblical texts are not acceptable in the seminary, one can always join the monastery or the cult. Or one is free to attempt to change the interpretive standards of the community (that is, after all, the function of a dissertation). There are, however, some communities one would seem to have little opportunity to transcend, perhaps only in the imagination: e.g., the community of English speakers, or of those born in twentieth-century America. A variety of (often conflicting) social standards influence any interpretation.

On either Iser's or Fish's account, however, the relationship between the meaning supplied by the text and the meaning supplied by the reader is complex and dynamic, and recent theories of characters and characterization have been greatly influenced by reader-response criticism. Characters inevitably display the kind of gaps and ambiguities posed by Iser. For Iser, the reader confronted with a character fills in the gaps with an complex imaginary picture, so that in the end the character created by the reader becomes a near-human entity:

---

[119]Fish, "How to Recognize a Poem When You See One," in *Is There a Text?* 323-37.

In imagining a character, we do not try to seize upon one particular aspect, but we are made to view him as a synthesis in all aspects....Now this process has two consequences: first, it enables us to produce an image of the imaginary object, which otherwise has no existence of its own; second, precisely because it has no existence of its own and because we are imagining and producing it, we are actually in its presence and it is in ours.[120]

Thomas Docherty took a similar position when he said that the description of a character in a literary work "positions" and "moves" the reader.

In the process of "character development," it is the reader who changes. The "meaning" of a character is understood in terms of evaluations located in the reader; the reader then of course confers these evaluative judgments back upon the character in terms of sense, significance, or meaning.[121]

Reader and character meet, and in some sense merge. "The meaning of a character is located in our response to or interrelations with the described character."[122] For reader-response critics, what we perceive as a character is actually a change in ourselves; when we confront a character, we are to some extent confronting ourselves. The text changes us even as we assimilate it.

While the reader does a good deal of the work in creating character, there are certain elements in texts that provide the raw materials. Rimmon-Kenan has catalogued these elements.[123] The basic textual indicators are of two types: direct definition, which names a trait, and indirect presentation, which displays it. Direct definition is a form of generalization and conceptualization; to say that Emma Woodhouse is "handsome, clever, and rich" is to make a general statement which asks the reader's assent. Indirect present-

---

[120]Iser, *Act of Reading*, 138-39. Note the similarities to Hochman's view: characters are constructed on the model of human beings, and have some independent existence from texts and plots.

[121]Docherty, *Reading (Absent) Character*, 10.

[122]Ibid.

[123]Rimmon-Kenan, *Narrative Fiction*, 59-70.

ation leads the reader in an inductive process, and takes many forms. The text may present an action, speech, or describe appearances or environments. Thus, in *David Copperfield,* while Uriah Heep's speech would present him as "'umble," his actions show him to be anything but; Heep is indirectly characterized by this combination of speech and action as not only ambitious but deceitful. Also, analogy or metaphor may be used to reinforce characterization: when Holmes refers to Moriarty as "the Napoleon of crime," it is clear that he is speaking of a master criminal.[124] Meir Sternberg adds to this list the use of literary patterns and sequential order.[125] All these factors are taken into account when a reader builds an image of a character.

Yet these elements cannot be taken at face value. Direct definition provided in the Gospels by Jesus, for example, is obviously more authoritative than that provided by the Pharisees. Robert Alter

---

[124]The example is from Gowler, *Host, Guest, Enemy and Friend,* 60.

[125]Sternberg (*Poetics of Biblical Narrative,* 476-80) posits fifteen rhetorical devices that produce characterization (note that he mixes direct and indirect categories):

1. Narratorial evaluation of an agent or an action through a series of epithets (or their equivalent).
2. Through a single epithet.
3. Through a choice of loaded language.
4. Explicit judgment left ambiguous between narrator and characters.
5. As in (1), (2), and (3), except that the judgment is delegated to characters.
6. Judgment through a nonverbal objective correlative.
7. Charged dramatization, lingering over and thus foregrounding the plot elements designed for judgment.
8. Informational redundancy.
9. Direct inside view of characters.
10. The play of perspectives.
11. Order of presentation.
12. Order of presentation involving the .displacement of conventional patterns.
13. Analogical patterning.
14. Recurrence of key words along the sequence.
15. Neutral or pseudo-objective narration.

notes that the reliability of the presentation must be ascertained by the reader:

> Although a character's own statements might seem a straightforward enough revelation of who he is and what he makes of things, in fact the biblical writers are quite as aware as any James or Proust that speech may reflect the occasion more than the speaker, may be more a drawn shutter than an open window.[126]

For Alter, the reliability of the various means of presenting character depends not only on the text's explicitness but also on its certainty—while actions and appearances leave us in the realm of inference, a statement from a reliable narrator gives us a solid foundation for character-building.[127] So when Holmes characterizes Moriarty as the "Napoleon of crime," the reader will accept the hero as a reliable source of information on the villain. The actions of Uriah Heep prove his confessions of humility to be unreliable. Both direct and indirect presentation of character must be judged in terms of the reliability of presentation.

David Gowler has neatly summarized the textual elements a reader must factor into characterization.[128] For Gowler, characters are to be evaluated along two scales, one a scale of reliability and the other a scale of explicitness. Direct definition is the most explicit, but needs to be further evaluated in light of reliability, the degree to which a speaker can be trusted; an omniscient, reliable narrative would have the highest possible authority, a demonstrably unreliable, first-person narrator much less authority.[129] A character

---

[126]Robert Alter, *The Art of Biblical Narrative,* (New York: Basic Books, 1981), 117.

[127]Ibid., 116-17.

[128]Gowler, *Host, Guest, Enemy and Friend,* 55-75.

[129]An omniscient narrator usually stands outside the narrative itself and seems to know everything, while a first-person narrative is part of the story and usually has limited knowledge. Narrators may be reliable or unreliable—that is, their viewpoints may truly reflect those of the implied author, or ironically depart from them. See Wayne Booth, *Rhetoric of Fiction.*

like Jesus or Holmes is obviously more reliable than a Pharisee or a Heep. Indirect presentation, while less explicit than direct definition, can also have varying degrees of reliability. Actions reported by a reliable narrator would have more authority than the same actions reported by an unreliable narrator. The inward speech of a character would be more reliable than outward speech (which may be intended to deceive other characters), unless the inward speech is ironic, or the reader determines that the character is self-deceived. Obviously the possibilities are quite complex.

So for Gowler, the various possibilities of explicitness and reliability in a text's presentation of character are:[130]

Direct Definition. Most explicit, with varying degrees of reliability. Narrators most frequently define characters directly. Characters can also directly define themselves and other characters, and must be evaluated in light of their trustworthiness and consistency.

Indirect Presentation. Less explicit than direct definition, and therefore inherently less reliable. But reliability may further vary depending on the trustworthiness and consistency of the presentation, just as with direct definition.

Types of Indirect Presentation:

(a) Speech—of the narrator, the character, or other characters. Less explicit than direct definition; reliability must be determined.

(b) Action of the character. Much less explicit and therefore less reliable.

(c) External appearance of the character; still less explicit.

(d) Environment of the character.

(e) Comparison and contrast with other characters. One might add in this category the various literary patterns cited by

---

[130]See Gowler, *Host, Guest, Enemy and Friend,* 72.

Rimmon-Kenan and Sternberg. Here we reach the lowest rungs of explicitness and reliability.

As Gowler notes, cultural norms, as well as the other kinds of norms that Garvey specified, must always be taken into account when filling in the gaps to form a character, especially when explicitness and reliability are low. Garvey's syllogism, "X belched, X is rude," assumes the western cultural premise that belching after a meal is rude. It is conceivable that another culture may have the opposite conviction.[131]

The theoretical discussion of literary critics on the presentation and reception of characters has practical consequences for this study. It will first of all be possible to examine and categorize the ways Luke-Acts presents the character of the Holy Spirit, using the typology summarized by Gowler. We will see that the Spirit is usually characterized indirectly, and usually in ways that provide a high degree of reliability. Indeed, the issue of reliability is central to the characterization of the Spirit.

Second, the issue of the interpretive community and the reader of Luke-Acts will prove to be quite complex. What sort of interpretive competency is supposed by the text of Luke-Acts? What kind of reader does this text seem to expect? Where there are gaps, how best to fill them in? This study, working within the interpretive community called "New Testament Studies," assumes that there are at least certain kinds of answers which are appropriate to these questions, even if there is debate over what exactly the answer may be. So, for example, one may assume that the text presupposes a Jewish or a Gentile reader, a Christian or a non-Christian, but not a fourth-century monk. The question of how the reader will fill the gaps in the characterization of the Holy Spirit will become crucial; it is my contention that those gaps are meant to be filled with the reader's knowledge of Luke's literary forebears in the Septuagint.

Third, the issue of the "gaps" left in the characterization of the Spirit is quite intriguing in light of the close relationship of the Spirit and God. What do the ambiguities and inconsistencies of the

---

[131]Ibid., 73-74, and n. 131.

portrait of the Spirit tell the reader about the God of Luke's proclamation? And if, as Iser contended, when a reader is "imagining and producing" a character, the reader ends up "actually in its presence,"[132] does Luke's reader in some way come into the presence of God while reading the text of Luke-Acts?

The Holy Spirit as Character

It is not entirely evident at first glance that one may legitimately speak of the Holy Spirit in Luke-Acts as a "character." As we have seen in Chapter One, there is minimal precedent for using the language of characterization to describe the Spirit. But there has not been a thorough analysis of the Spirit in this vein. Is the description "character" appropriate in reference to the Holy Spirit in Luke-Acts?

In this section, I will establish a basic rationale for using the literary categories "character" and "characterization" to refer to the Holy Spirit, based on two features of Luke's text: it presents the Spirit as an actor in the story, and it involves the Spirit in interaction and even conflict with other characters. In the following chapters, I intend to develop a more detailed analysis of the portrait and role of the Spirit in light of the literary-critical theories of character and characterization already presented. The issues raised here must and will be addressed with more thoroughness. My goal in this section is simply to establish that what I am doing makes sense. While this may entail anticipating conclusions based on evidence not yet presented, it seems best to establish the legitimacy of this project before going further.

The Spirit as Actor

The insight that characters and action go hand in hand is fundamental to understanding the role of the Holy Spirit in Luke-Acts. The language which Bultmann saw as demonstrating an "animistic"

---

[132]Iser, *Act of Reading,* 139.

conception of the Spirit[133] can be understood in literary terms as depicting the Spirit as an actor. The Holy Spirit "reveals" (Luke 2:26), "teaches" (Luke 12:12), and "testifies" (Acts 20:23). The Spirit "leads" (Luke 4:1) and even "forbids" (Acts 16:6-7). It travels in space ("descends," Luke 3:22; transports Philip, Acts 8:39-40; "came on," Acts 19:6). It appoints leaders (Acts 13:4; 20:28). Frequently the Spirit "speaks," in Scripture (Acts 1:16; 4:25; 28:25) and independently (Acts 8:29; 10:19-20; 11:12; 13:2; 21:11). Luke-Acts shows the Spirit acting deliberately and independently. Though the structuralist definition of characterization as the sum total of all the subjects of all the verbs is simplistic, the Holy Spirit would qualify as a character on this count, as it is the subject of a number of verbs.

One may object that in Luke-Acts, the Holy Spirit appears frequently as an actor, but it is at best a minor figure, involved in unusual actions, often acting only as an agent of others. The Spirit is described as acting through mundane intermediaries: thus people are "filled with" or "full of" the Spirit (Luke 1:15, 41, 67; 4:1; Acts 2:4; 4:8, 31; 6:3, 5, 8; 7:55; 9:17; 11:24; 13:9; 13:52), and are thus empowered for extraordinary actions, usually prophetic speech. The Spirit speaks through a prophet (Acts 11:28; 21:11), a community (Acts 15:28; 21:4), or the Scripture (Acts 1:16; 4:25; 28:25); the Spirit also prompts glossolalia (2:4; 10:46; 19:6). The Spirit acts through the casting of lots (Acts 1:26). As Brawley and Darr have shown, Luke's language suggests that the Spirit's actions are actions of God—the Spirit itself is an agent, an intermediary, a gift from God (Luke 11:13; Acts 2:17, 33, 38; 5:32; 8:18; 10:45; 11:17; 15:18).

One might be tempted to think of the Holy Spirit as only a minor character in Luke-Acts, a shadowy figure, which acts on special occasions at the behest of another. But the frequency and duration of this activity should give one pause. Further, the Spirit acts explicitly and extraordinarily: unusual children come to birth (Luke 1:13-17, 35, 41-45), Jesus is led into an unusual fast (Luke 4:1-13), disciples speak in unknown languages at the behest of the Spirit (Acts 2:4), and Philip is whisked away through the air (8:39-40).

---

[133]See above, chap. 1, "What (or Who) is the Holy Spirit?"

One of the more striking features of Luke-Acts is that it depicts the Spirit as an explicit, independent participant in the story. The language is subtle at first: the Spirit is the agent of passive constructions ("It had been revealed to him by the Holy Spirit," Luke 2:26; "Jesus was led by the Spirit," Luke 4:1). Then there is a promise of direct action: when the disciples come before the authorities, "the Holy Spirit will teach you in that very hour what you ought to say" (Luke 12:12), a prophecy fulfilled in the book of Acts (Acts 4:8, 31). The full force of this language becomes clear in Acts, where Luke uses active constructions: at Pentecost the Spirit "gave them utterance" (Acts 2:4) as a witness to the gospel (Acts 5:32); the Spirit speaks directly to Philip (Acts 8:29), just as it had to the Old Testament prophets (Acts 1:16; 4:25; 28:25) and will again to New Testament prophets (Acts 13:1-2; 21:11), to Peter (Acts 10:19; 11:12) to Paul (Acts 20:23), and to other members of the community (Acts 13:1; 21:4); Saul and Barnabas are sent out by the Spirit (Acts 13:4), just as Jesus (Luke 4:14) and Philip (Acts 8:39) had been; the Spirit intervenes directly in Paul's plans (Acts 16:6-7; 19:21; 20:22); and the Spirit is directly responsible for congregational leadership (Acts 20:28). When James says "It has seemed good to the Holy Spirit and to us" (Acts 15:28), one can almost picture the Spirit sitting in an easy chair among the disciples and joining in the conversation as if it were the most ordinary thing in the world.[134]

To be sure, there is a tension throughout Luke-Acts between the portrait of the Spirit as an agent and the portrait of the Spirit as an independent actor. Sometimes Luke depicts explicit action of the Spirit, while the context implies another agency: thus the Spirit is described as speaking directly in Acts 13:2, but prophets are certainly present, probably as intermediaries (Acts 13:1; cf. 21:11); the Spirit makes leaders (Acts 20:28), but Paul appoints them (Acts 14:23); and the Spirit sometimes requires apostolic dispensation (Acts 8:14-17; 19:1-6). In all these instances, it is remarkable that

---

[134]For detailed analysis of these passages, see below, chaps. 3-4. The purpose of this chapter is simply to demonstrate the rationale for referring to the Spirit as a "character."

Luke speaks of the Spirit acting explicitly in conjunction with the explicit or implicit actions of the Spirit's agents. It is not human action, but like the human characters, the Spirit acts.[135]

Luke draws heavily on Greek Old Testament precedent in his portrait of the Spirit as an actor. It is quite common in the Septuagint for the Spirit to speak (e.g., 2 Sam 23:2; 1 Kgs 22:24; Zech 7:12; Ezek 2:2). The Spirit also is pictured as a guide or teacher (Neh 9:20; Ps 143:10; Isa 63:10, 14). The image of the Spirit seizing Philip and whisking him away (Acts 8:29, 39) clearly draws on Ezekiel (e.g., Ezek 2:2; 3:24) There is ample evidence in intertestamental and rabbinic Judaism that testifies to the continuation of the portrait of the Spirit as an actor (cf. Wisd 7:7, 22; 9:17; 1QS 3:6-7; 4:6; 1QH 9:32; 12:11-12; Philo, *de Gig.* 24-28, 47, 53, 55; *de Somn.* 2:252).[136] The literary precedent which Luke draws on is the portrait of the prophetic Spirit found in the Septuagint, and this sets the boundaries by which the reader can judge Luke's stylization of the Spirit.[137] Luke does not invent this way of speaking of the Spirit; rather, he draws from a well-worn manual of style.

Luke's depiction of the Holy Spirit as an explicit actor justifies my description of the Spirit as "character" in the narrative. Further evidence that this designation is appropriate can be found in that there are conflicts between the Spirit and other characters in the narrative.

---

[135]Again, these passages will be discussed in detail in chaps. 3-4.

[136]See Peter Schäfer, *Die Vorstellung vom Heiligen Geist in der rabbinischen Literatur,* Studien zum Alten und Neuen Testament, vol. 28 (Munich, Kösel-Verlag, 1972), 151-62; Turner, "Luke and the Spirit," 197-98; idem, "Spirit Endowment in Luke-Acts," 56.

[137]For the definition of "stylization," see above on "Types of Characters." We will return to the issue of stylization frequently in chaps. 3-4.

The Spirit, Character, and Conflict

Character goes with plot, and plot implies conflict. That characters are in conflict follows naturally from the fact that characters act. In its simplest form, one character, the hero, fights against another character, the villain; the power of both characters is seen in the conflict between the two. More often, the conflicts, and thus the characters, are more complex: the philandering husband pulled by professional ambition on the one side, family duty on another, mid-life sexual crisis on a third; the high-school student involved with drugs because of peer pressure, rebellion, and boredom. These complex and varied influences seem plausible to readers who know such conflicts themselves, and thus the reader applauds the author on her skillful characterization. Conflict among and within characters is one feature which characters share with their human, non-literary counterparts. For the reader knows that in real life, people are not static entities—they move and change as time goes by. Characters, while inhabiting a different world, a textual world, are much like real people, in that we "know" both people and characters as mental constructs drawn from our "reading"—in one case, the reading of a text, in the other, our reading of our experiences in the world. So characters, too, also move and change as story-time goes by. And change usually brings with it conflict (and vice-versa). "In the end, we tend to think of character—of people, to begin with—in terms of conflict, which may be moral, social, or psychological in nature."[138] Indeed, one of the categories in Hochman's classification system is devoted to the resolution of conflict ("Closure").[139]

So if we are to speak of the Holy Spirit as a "character," we should expect to find some indication of conflict between the Spirit and other characters (and perhaps even within the Spirit itself). And certainly we find evidence of such conflict in Luke's narrative.

On the most fundamental level, the Spirit is involved in the cosmic conflict between God and Satan. Indeed, much of the conflict in which the Spirit participates is a manifestation of this basic conflict.

---

[138]Hochman, *Character in Literature*, 51.

[139]Ibid., 138-40.

The conflict is clearly sketched in the temptation narrative (Luke 4:1-15), where the Spirit-empowered Jesus does battle with Satan. Jesus alludes to this conflict again when in the joy of the Spirit he speaks apocalyptically of Satan's fall (Luke 10:21). In Acts, the episode of Ananias and Sapphira symbolizes this conflict when Peter asks, "Why has Satan filled your heart to lie to the Holy Spirit?" (Acts 5:3, cf. v. 9). The conflicts in Acts between the apostles and the magicians also represent the underlying battle between the Spirit and the devil (Acts 8:4-25; 13:4-12).[140] A good deal of the drama in Luke-Acts derives from the struggles, setbacks, and victories of God, the Spirit, Jesus, and the disciples over Satan and his forces.

The conflict between the Spirit and the devil manifests itself in a fundamental division within Israel over the person of Jesus, foreshadowed in the Spirit-inspired prophecy of Simeon that "this child is set for the fall and rising of many in Israel" (Luke 2:34; cf. 2:25, 26, 27). The Spirit has testified to Jesus through the prophets (Acts 4:25; 28:25), has come upon and led Jesus (Luke 3:22; 4:1, 14, 18; 10:21; Acts 1:2; 10:38) as well as the disciples (Acts 1:8; 2:4; etc.). Yet many of the Jews, whom Stephen calls a "stiff-necked people, uncircumcised in heart and ears," have rejected Jesus and thus resisted the Spirit (Acts 6:10-11; 7:51; 28:25-28). The conflict defines the Spirit, on the one hand, as the bearer of the true tradition of Israel (by means of Jesus and his followers), and the resistant Jews, on the other, as disobedient to both God and tradition.[141]

There is conflict with the Spirit within the Christian community as well. Peter accuses Ananias of lying to the Spirit by withholding part of the proceeds of his land (Acts 5:3), and later tells Sapphira that she has tempted the Spirit (Acts 5:9). In both cases, their dishonesty and greed is said to have put them in conflict with not just the community, but the Spirit. The consequence of their resistance is severe.[142]

---

[140]Detailed analysis of these passages may be found in chaps. 3-4.

[141]Again, my purpose here is merely to establish that the Holy Spirit is involved in conflict, and thus can be analyzed in terms of "characterization." Detailed analysis of these passages may be found in chaps. 3-4.

[142]For detailed analysis of this passage, see below, chap. 4.

Less dramatic consequences ensue when Paul, Silas, and Timothy attempt to expand their traveling mission. They are forbidden by the Spirit to preach in Asia, and when they attempt to enter Bithynia, the Spirit prevents them (Acts 16:6-7). Luke gives this unusual scene no explanation; certainly, however, it does indicate a conflict between human and divine characters.[143]

There is a much more nuanced inter-community conflict involving Paul in the later chapters of Acts. At Ephesus, Paul resolves "in the Spirit" (Acts 19:21) to go to Jerusalem, and then on to Rome. He describes himself to the elders as "bound in the Spirit"; he must go to Jerusalem without knowing what will happen, only that the Spirit has confirmed that suffering waits behind every door—a grim foreshadow of Paul's fate (Acts 20:22-23). But along his journey, Paul receives contrary exhortations from disciples who are equally inspired. The disciples in Tyre "through the Spirit" warn Paul not to go to Jerusalem (Acts 21:4). Agabus in a striking prophetic act ironically echoes Paul's rhetoric: Paul will be indeed "bound"—not in the Spirit but in the chains of the Gentiles; hearing this, the disciples beg him not to go on (Acts 21:11-12). The issue is resolved when Paul appeals to the prophetic pattern Luke sets forth so often in Luke-Acts: the prophet must go to Jerusalem to suffer. In the end, Paul does arrive where he says he will, in Rome. But his journey has been one "through the Spirit," which means by way of hardship (Acts 20:23). Here two Spirit-filled parties find themselves in conflict—or do we have here conflict and ambivalence within the Spirit itself? This conflict illustrates the difficulty of pinning down precisely the leading of the Spirit as it is pictured in Luke-Acts. Presumably Paul was right, but the possibility lingers—he might have been spared for other work.[144]

The Spirit is involved in multi-faceted conflict. It is possible for other characters to resist the Spirit, bump up against it, or even to disagree while being inspired by it. Indeed, conflict follows natu-

---

[143]See below, chap. 4.

[144]See below, chap. 4.

rally from action—one who acts independently inevitably falls into conflict with another. The Spirit is involved in conflict, and can be said to be a "character."

Conclusion

New multi-disciplinary theories of narrative have left the once-formidable barriers between fiction and non-fiction teetering, and at some points in ruins. One result is that we can now speak of "characters" in genres outside the realm of literary fiction. The complex relationship between characters in narrative and real people is evident if sometimes murky—while there are great similarities between the two, especially in the criteria by which we come to know each of them, characters and people live in very different worlds, and the literary world of characters must be taken into account. It will prove important to this study to note that the literary world of Luke-Acts in which the Holy Spirit lives is heavily indebted to biblical precedents found in the Greek Old Testament.

This discussion has not left the interpreter without some practical tools. Hochman has given us a valuable system for classifying the various aspects of characters. Gowler has shown the rhetorical features which texts use to produce characters. But texts do not function in and of themselves—reader-response theory has clarified the complex interaction between text and reader that produces character. These three elements of the critical discussion—Hochman's classification scheme, Gowler's scheme of the presentation of character, and the reader-response theory of "gaps"—will together figure greatly in the exegetical chapters of this study.

Luke-Acts presents the Holy Spirit as an actor in the story who has definite rhetorical features: the Spirit acts in ordinary as well as extraordinary ways, independently and through agents. Further, Luke-Acts shows the Spirit as being involved in conflict with other characters. On these two basic levels, action and interaction, the Spirit proves to be a character in the narrative. We can now ask in greater detail what the various features of this character are, and how the reader and text work together to produce this character. And most importantly, we can determine what narrative function this character plays. How does the Holy Spirit as character contribute to the purpose of Luke-Acts? As we shall see, the entanglement between plot and character is nowhere more evident than in the Lukan characterization of the Spirit. The plot of Luke-Acts and the character of the Spirit are inextricably intertwined.

Chapter 3

The Characterization of the Holy Spirit in Luke-Acts (I)
The Gospel of Luke

To summarize my argument so far, I have shown that there is wide consensus among New Testament scholars that Luke sees the Holy Spirit as the ancient Spirit of prophecy. There is less consensus that Luke limits the work of the Spirit to inspired prophetic speech, and little agreement over whether Luke posits a normative reception of the Spirit. The question of the personality or personification of the Spirit prompts no little dissent among those who use traditional theological and historical methodologies.

I have proposed that new light can be shed on the role of the Holy Spirit in Luke-Acts by making use of recent multi-disciplinary theories of character and characterization in narrative. These theories allow us to speak of "characters" in genres outside the realm of modern fiction. They elucidate the complex relationship between characters in narrative and real people, which have great similarities yet live in very different worlds. Narrative theorists have given us helpful categories for understanding how characters work. In particular, Baruch Hochman has given us a valuable system for classifying the various aspects of characters, David Gowler has shown the rhetorical features which texts and readers use to produce characters, and reader-response criticism has elucidated the temporal processes by which readers accumulate a notion of character.

I have shown that Luke-Acts presents the Holy Spirit as an actor in the story; further, the Spirit is involved in conflict with other characters. Thus the Spirit can be understood as a character in the narrative. On occasion (more often in Luke's Gospel than in Acts), this character acts only indirectly, in the background, implicitly rather than explicitly. But the Spirit takes center stage in Luke's narrative more than once, especially at important junctures in Acts. Since one of the activities involved in reading is the reader's constant attempt to create consistency—to read, reread and unread, to revise previous readings in light of what comes later—the reader may be justified in seeing the Holy Spirit functioning as a character even where this character operates only implicitly.[1] Looking back on the Gospel from Acts, the reader may be inclined to see the actions of the Spirit in a new light: here is a character who has been active, both explicitly and implicitly, from the beginning of the story.

In this chapter and the next I intend to show in detail the narrative function this character plays in Luke-Acts. The effect of Luke's characterization of the Spirit is cumulative, pieced together by the reader as the story moves along. My method, therefore, will be to move sequentially through the portions of Luke-Acts which mention the Spirit, to examine it in light of what we have learned from narrative theorists of characterization. Since a character cannot be studied in isolation, but is inextricably linked to plot, my focus will be not only the verses which speak of the Spirit explicitly, but the larger sections of narrative in which Luke develops his portrait of

---

[1]On the reading as the attempt to create consistency, see Darr, *On Character Building*, 30-31; Iser, *Act of Reading*, 118-25. See above, chap. 2, "Character: Presentation and Reception." The requirement that characters be consistent stems from Aristotle, *Poetics* 15; cf. Chatman, *Story and Discourse*, 110. Hochman's category of "coherence" addresses this issue (*Characterization in Literature*, 97-103).

the Spirit.[2] In what follows, I will discuss the segments of Luke's text which mention the Holy Spirit along with their literary contexts.

My method provides a thorough survey of the relevant material, but it is not perfect. Dealing with discrete sections of a narrative by necessity involves forsaking the continuity provided by the narrative as a whole. It will not be possible to discuss every aspect of Luke's plot; the following commentary deals only with those passages which speak of the Holy Spirit (with one exception: Luke's all-important prologue). Further, since characterization is developed only in the course of reading, not every mention of the Spirit will lend itself to a full elaboration of Luke's characterization; it is not necessary, for example, to analyze every passage in light of all eight of Hochman's categories, because not every passage sheds new light on every category. So to compensate for lost narrative transitions and the sometimes sketchy nature of Luke's characterization of the Holy Spirit, I will pause periodically to pay special attention to Luke's plot, the kind of portrait he paints of the Spirit (with reference to Hochman's eightfold classification) and the textual rhetoric which produces this portrait (with reference to Gowler's model of presentation and reception).

My goal in making use of these literary theorists is to determine how the character of the Holy Spirit functions in the narrative—how it works, what it represents, and why. I will finally be asking, in light of the close correlation between characters and people, what Luke's characterization of the Holy Spirit implies for the God of Luke's proclamation. My thesis is that in Luke-Acts, the character of the Holy Spirit signals narrative reliability, and that ultimately the Spirit's presence and action is that of God. For I believe that what is at stake for Luke in his portrayal of the Spirit—and indeed his entire narrative—is the very reliability of God. So I will begin by looking at a section of Luke's Gospel which does not mention the Holy Spirit, but is important for understanding the role of the Spirit in Luke's proclamation: the prologue.

---

[2]A complete list of these passages may be found in the Table of Contents. I have omitted from consideration the many instances of $\pi\nu\varepsilon\hat{\upsilon}\mu\alpha$ in Luke-Acts which obviously do not refer to the Holy Spirit, but to human or demonic spirits (Luke 1:47, 80; 4:33, 36; 6:18; 7:21; 8:2, 29, 55; 9:39, 42; 10:20; 11:24, 26; 13:11; 23:46; 24:37, 39; Acts 5:16; 8:7; 16:16, 18; 17:16 19:12, 13, 15, 16, 21).

Luke's Literary Purpose (Luke 1:1-4)

Luke[3] begins his two-volume work with a common Hellenistic literary device—a prologue.[4] The second volume will also begin

---

[3]Throughout this study, by "Luke" I mean "the implied author of Luke-Acts" who as reconstructed by the reader establishes the narrative norms. The implied author is a construct created by the reader from the text, and thus differs from the real-life author who sat down and penned the words. The implied author may also be distinguished from the narrator, who may be a participant in the story and at odds with the implied author. See Booth, *Rhetoric of Fiction*, 67-77, 425-35; Chatman, *Story and Discourse*, 147-51; Martin, *Recent Theories of Narrative*, 135.

In much the same way, I will distinguish between the "implied reader" and real-life, flesh-and-blood persons who may read Luke's text. The implied reader is, like the implied author, a construct of the text: an ideal reader posited by a text and the reading process. It is ultimately one of the roles a flesh-and-blood reader must take on in order to understand a text fully. See Booth, *Rhetoric of Fiction*, 425-35; Chatman, *Story and Discourse*, 147-51; Fowler, *Let the Reader Understand*, 25-40; idem, "Who is 'The Reader'?"; Martin, *Recent Theories of Narrative*, 156-61. When I say "reader" in this study, I am referring to the implied reader.

[4]Luke's prologue is unique to the New Testament, and stands out stylistically from the Septuagintal mode of expression which follows in the infancy narratives. On the prologue see Loveday Alexander, *The Preface to Luke's Gospel: Literary Conventions and Social Context in Luke 1.1-4 and Acts 1.1*, Society for New Testament Studies Monograph Series (Cambridge: Cambridge University Press, 1993); idem, "Luke's Preface in the Context of Greek Preface-Writing," *Novum Testamentum* 28 (1986): 48-74; François Bovon, *Das Evangelium nach Lukas*, Evangelisch-Katholischer Kommentar zum Neuen Testament Band 3 (Zürich: Benziger Verlag, 1989), 29-43; Brawley, *Centering on God*, 38-44; Schuyler Brown, "The Role of the Prologues in Determining the Purpose of Luke-Acts," in *Perspectives on Luke-Acts*, ed. Charles H. Talbert (Danville, Va.: Association of Baptist Professors of Religion, 1978), 99-111; Henry J. Cadbury, "Commentary on the Preface of Luke," in *Beginnings*, 2:489-510; Craddock, *Luke*, 15-19; Fitzmyer, *Luke*, 287-89; Richard J. Dillon, "Previewing Luke's Project from his Prologue (Luke 1:1-4)," *Catholic Biblical Quarterly* 43 (1981): 205-27; Johnson, *Luke*, 27-30; Günter Klein, "Lukas 1, 1-4 als theologisches Programm," in *Zeit und Geschichte: Dankesgabe an Rudolf Bultmann zum 80. Geburtstag*, ed. Erich Dinkler (Tübingen: J. C. B. Mohr (Paul Siebeck), 1964), 193-216; Kurz, "Narrative Approaches to Luke-Acts," 204-9; I. Howard Marshall, *The Gospel of Luke: A Commentary on the Greek Text*, New International Greek Testament Commentary (Grand Rapids: Eerdmans, 1978), 39-44; David P. Moessner, "The Meaning of ΚΑΘΕΞΗΣ in the Lukan Prologue as a Key to the Distinctive Contribution of

with a prologue, referring back to the previous volume (Acts 1:1-2; cf. Josephus, *Against Apion* 1.1 and 2.1). The prologues, dedicated to one Theophilus (Luke 1:3, Acts 1:1),[5] have a programmatic function, in that they foreshadow the major directions Luke's work will take; to examine Luke's stated literary purpose is in effect to be

---

Luke's Narrative among the 'Many,'" in *The Four Gospels. Festschrift Frans Neirynck*, ed. F. Van Segroeck, C. M. Tuckett, G. Van Belle, J. Verheyden (Leuven: Leuven University Press, 1992), 2:1513-28; Léopold Sabourin, *L'Evangile de Luc: introduction et commentaire* (Rome: Editrice Pontificia Universita Gregoriana, 1987), 51-53; Gerhard Schneider, *Das Evangelium nach Lukas*, Ökumenischer Taschenbuchkommentar zum Neuen Testament, vol. 3 (Gütersloh: Gütersloher Verlagshaus Mohn, 1977), 37-41; idem, "Zur Bedeutung von καθεξῆς im lukanischen Doppelwerk," *Zeitschrift für die neutestamentliche Wissenschaft* 68 (1977): 128-31; Heinz Schürmann, *Das Lukasevangelium: Kommentar zu Kap. 1, 1-9, 50*, vol. 1, Herders Theologischer Kommentar zum Neuen Testament (Freiburg: Herder, 1969), 1-17; Eduard Schweizer, *The Good News According to Luke* (Atlanta: John Knox Press, 1984), 10-14; Tannehill, *Narrative Unity of Luke-Acts*, 1:9-12; W. C. van Unnik, "One More St. Luke's Prologue," in *Essays on the Gospel of Luke and Acts* (*Neotestamentica* 7, New Testament Society of South Africa, 1973): 7-26; Wolfgang Wiefel, *Das Evangelium nach Lukas*, Theologischer Handkommentar zum Neuen Testament, vol. 3 (Berlin: Evangelische Verlagsanstalt, 1988), 38-41.

[5]Θεόφιλος is a common name in papyri and inscriptions, so the reference is generally thought to be to a real but unidentifiable person, Jew or Gentile, probably a Christian (in light of κατηχέω in Luke 1:4), perhaps Luke's literary sponsor (Fitzmyer, *Luke*, 299-300; Johnson, *Luke*, 28-29; Sabourin, *Luc*, 53; but for caveats on what exactly "literary sponsor" would have meant, see Alexander, *Preface*, 187-200). The honorific κράτιστε (Luke 1:3) is equestrian and often thought to indicate that Theophilus was a Roman official, but at most it implies only that he was socially respected (Alexander, *Preface*, 132-33; Cadbury, "Commentary on the Preface," 505-7; Fitzmyer, *Luke*, 300; Marshall, *Luke*, 43; Schweizer, *Luke*, 12-13; contra Sabourin, *Luc*, 53).

The symbolic interpretation that Theophilus refers to any Christian "friend who loves God" dates from Origen; while few modern scholars doubt the reality of Theophilus, certainly in literary terms he functions as the "narratee," an extension of the "implied reader," and thus represents the successive generations of Luke's audience, those Christians who desire assurance of the things they have been taught. In Hochman's terms, he has both literal and symbolic functions. See Kurz, "Narrative Approaches to Luke-Acts," 211-12; Schürmann, *Lukasevangelium*, 13-14; cf. Fitzmyer, *Luke*, 300: "Theophilus stands for the Christian readers of Luke's own day and thereafter."

"previewing Luke's project from his prologue."[6] If, as reader-response critics have insisted, reading is a process of forming and revising expectations, of discerning "gaps" and filling them in from clues left by the author in order to create a consistent picture of the text, then the prologue in Luke 1:1-4 functions as the primary seed of expectation, and the basis on which readers will later fill the interpretive "gaps" in the narrative. Since Luke gives such a clear indication of his intent, a careful study of the prologue is required for proper guidance in reading what follows. The prologue helps the reader understand Luke's rhetoric: why the story is told in this discourse.[7]

---

[6]Dillon, "Previewing Luke's Project," 205-6.

[7]In structuralism, the "story" is the basic action or plot, which can be expressed in a variety of "discourses"—the various retellings of the story in different media (See Chatman, *Story and Discourse*, 19-22; and above, chap. 2, "What is Character? Characters, People, and Plots"). "In simple terms, the story is the *what* in a narrative that is depicted, discourse the *how*" (p. 19). This distinction can be quite useful, even for non-structuralists.

In this study I will use the terms "rhetoric" and "rhetorical" as well as "discourse" and "discursive." This stems in part from an awareness of "the ways in which the language of the narrative attempts to weave its spell over the reader" (Robert Fowler, *Let the Reader Understand*, 2). See also Booth, *Rhetoric of Fiction*, 3-20, and Moore, *Literary Criticism and the Gospels*, 41-45, who points out that the change from "discourse" to "rhetoric" originated with David Rhoads and Donald Michie, *Mark as Story: An Introduction to the Narrative of a Gospel* (Philadelphia: Fortress Press, 1982).

"Rhetoric" is also appropriate due to the rhetorical nature of ancient writing. See Werner H. Kelber, *The Oral and Written Gospel: The Hermeneutics of Speaking and Writing in the Synoptic Tradition, Mark, Paul, and Q* (Philadelphia: Fortress Press, 1983); George A. Kennedy, *New Testament Interpretation through Rhetorical Criticism* (Chapel Hill: University of North Carolina Press, 1984); Kurz, "Narrative Approaches to Luke-Acts," 197-200; Burton Mack, *Rhetoric and the New Testament*, Guides to Biblical Scholarship (Minneapolis: Fortress Press, 1990); Burton L. Mack and Vernon K. Robbins, *Patterns of Persuasion in the Gospels*, Foundations & Facets: Literary facets (Sonoma, Calif.: Polebridge Press, 1989); Moore, *Literary Criticism and the Gospels*, 84-88; Walter J. Ong, *Orality and Literacy: The Technologizing of the Word* (New York: Methuen, 1982); Vernon K. Robbins, *Jesus the Teacher: A Socio-Rhetorical Interpretation of Mark* (Philadelphia: Fortress Press, 1984).

Moore (*Literary Criticism and the Gospels*, 60-62, 66-68) quite rightly points out the artificiality of a rigid separation between "story" and "discourse," since all narrative is rhetorical. But the distinction is useful in dealing with characters

The prologue has a threefold structure: a causal clause (vv. 1-2) states known material as the basis of a subsequent main clause (v. 3), which delineates Luke's action, and leads finally to a purpose clause (v. 4). The structure reflects the context, procedure, and purpose of Luke.[8]

Behind Luke's writing stands the issue of the transmission of tradition. "Many," referring to (but perhaps not limited to) Luke's sources, such as the Gospel of Mark and the hypothetical sayings source called "Q,"[9] "have undertaken to set down an orderly account of the events that have been fulfilled among us" (Luke 1:1). While Luke puts himself in the company of these predecessors (κἀμοί, v. 3), his language may be taken as subtle criticism of them; Johnson suggests that the problem is not so much the content of

---

and characterization, because as we have seen (chap. 2 above), characters tend to transcend their rhetoric, and to exist on a level beyond the words on a page.

[8]Dillon, "Previewing Luke's Project," 218; cf. Schneider, *Lukas,* 37-38; Wiefel, *Lukas,* 38. Fitzmyer (*Luke,* 288), however, sees balance between protasis (vv. 1-2) and apodosis (vv. 3-4), each with three parallel phrases; cf. Alexander, *Preface,* 105-6; Marshall, *Luke,* 40; Sabourin, *Luc,* 52.

[9]While there is still some debate over Luke's sources, the general consensus that Luke made use of the Gospel of Mark and a sayings source (shared with Matthew) stands. The problem of the sources of the Acts of the Apostles is much more complicated, as no parallel documents or possible sources are extant, so there is no standard for comparison; the "we"-sections (Acts 16:10-17; 20:5-15; 21:1-18; 27:1-28:16) provide the clearest indication that Luke used earlier material. The problem is complicated by Luke's tendency to completely recast traditional material in a distinctive style. See Fitzmyer, *Luke,* 63-106; Haenchen, *Acts,* 81-90; Johnson, *Luke,* 6-7; idem, *Acts,* 3-5. Alexander (*Preface,* 114-15) notes that scholarly preoccupation with written sources has diverted attention from the plain meaning of Luke's statement about the "many" who "tried to put together an account": they may well have included unwritten, oral traditions.

While I agree with the consensus view that Luke made use of Mark and Q, the argument that follows is based on literary criteria and is not, by and large, dependent on source analysis or theories of redaction.

these works, but that "they lacked a convincing sort of order."[10]
That Luke believes in the persuasive power of an "orderly account"
(or "narrative," διήγησις) is shown amply in Luke-Acts (the verbal
form διηγέομαι is used in Luke 8:39; 9:10; Acts 8:33; 9:27;
12:17).[11] Luke foreshadows one of his major themes, prophetic fulfillment, when he speaks of events being "fulfilled," presumably in
divine action (πληροφορέω in passive voice, cf. πληρόω in Luke
1:20; 4:21; 9:31; 24:44; Acts 1:16; 3:18; 13:27).[12] The traditions
about these fulfilled events have surfaced[13] through two previous
layers, that of the "eyewitnesses and servants of the word," and that
of Luke's "many" sources.[14] Luke's concern is with the faithfulness

---

[10]Johnson, *Luke*, 30; cf. Fitzmyer, *Luke*, 291-92. The view that ἐπιχειρέω is
meant perjoratively extends back to Origen, but most commentators see only mild
implicit criticism here, if any at all; see Alexander, *Preface*, 115-16; Cadbury,
"Commentary on the Preface," 493-94; Dillon, "Previewing Luke's Project,"
207-8; Klein, "Lukas 1,1-4," 195-96; Marshall, *Luke*, 40-41; Sabourin, *Luc*, 52;
Schweizer, *Luke*, 11; van Unnik, "Once More St. Luke's Prologue," 15-16.

[11]A διήγησις is a longer narrative composed of several events, as opposed to a
single-event διήγημα (Hermogenes, *Progymnasmata* 2, cited in Tannehill, *Narrative Unity of Luke-Acts*, 1:10). See also Alexander, *Preface*, 111.

Contra Conzelmann (*Theology of St. Luke*, 11), there is no distinction between
"narrating" and "proclaiming" in Luke-Acts, as if narrative could provide only
historical foundation and not kerygma. Luke's use of διηγέομαι, κηρύσσω, and
ἀπαγγέλλω (Luke 8:36, 39; 9:36; Acts 9:27; 12:17) indicates "functional unity"
(Dillon, "Previewing Luke's Project," 208).

[12]Dillon, "Previewing Luke's Project," 209, 211-17; cf. Alexander, *Preface*,
113-14; Klein, "Lukas 1,1-4," 196-99; Marshall, *Luke*, 41; Schweizer, *Luke*, 11.
On the importance of prophecy in Luke's narrative, see Johnson, *Luke*, 15-21.

[13]"Handed down"; παραδίδωμι is a technical term for the transmission of
Christian tradition, cf. 1 Cor 11:2, 15:3; 2 Pet 2:21; Jude 3; Pol. *Phil.* 7:2;
Diogn. 11:1. See Marshall, *Luke*, 41-42. It was also used of the work of Hel-
lenistic historians (van Unnik, "Once More St. Luke's Prologue," 14).

[14]Dillon, "Previewing Luke's Project," 210. The "eyewitnesses" and
"servants" are one group, not two (Fitzmyer, *Luke*, 294; Johnson, *Luke*, 28; Marshall, *Luke*, 42; Schweizer, *Luke*, 11). Dillon (213-15) takes both αὐτόπται and
ὑπηρέται as attributive and translates "those who were eye-witnesses from the
beginning and became servants of the word," which gets at the sense of it—they
were eyewitnesses, then became ministers after Easter (cf. Acts 1:21-22; 26:16).
Fitzmyer (*Luke*, 291) sees Luke as third-generation, but speculates that the

of this testimony (λόγος):[15]

> The biblical author is concerned to establish from the outset how the events transmitted by the tradition relate to the present and future generation of believers. Indeed, the issue turns on the change effected when the oral proclamation of the gospel is set down in narrative, written form by a chain of tradents different from the original eyewitnesses.[16]

That the "events that have been fulfilled" concern and include not just the implied author, the eyewitnesses, or the purveyors of tradition, but also the implied readers, is indicated rhetorically by the inclusive pronoun, "us."[17]

The main clause of Luke's prologue (v. 3) explains the author's decision[18] to initiate a thorough investigation[19] of these traditions,

---

"many" writers may not have been distinct from the "eyewitnesses."

Luke in composing a διήγησις on the authority of αὐτόπται follows Hellenistic historical practice; cf. Lucian, *How To Write History,* 47-48. See Johnson, *Luke,* 28-30; van Unnik, "Once More St. Luke's Prologue," 12-13; contra Alexander, *Preface,* 120-23.

[15]"Word," λόγος, is used programmatically in Luke-Acts of the Christian mission (cf. Luke 4:32; 5:1, 15; 7:17; 8:11-15, 21; Acts 4:4; 6:2, 7; 8:4; 12:24; 13:49; 19:10, 20). Cf. Johnson, *Luke,* 28.

[16]Brevard S. Childs, *The New Testament as Canon: An Introduction* (Philadelphia: Fortress Press, 1984), 104.

[17]"The eschatological nature of these events encompasses the 'we' of Luke's generation along with the original eyewitnesses" (Childs, *New Testament as Canon,* 105; cf. Johnson, *Luke,* 27; Schweizer, *Luke,* 11; Schneider, *Lukas,* 39; Wiefel, *Lukas,* 39-40); Fitzmyer (*Luke,* 294) connects this passage to "we-accounts" of Acts, but Dillon ("Previewing Luke's Project," 210-11) cautions against a facile conclusion about Luke's participation in historical "events." Kurz ("Narrative Approaches to Luke-Acts," 210-11) points out that the "I" and "we" of the prologue are distinguished, which is not the case in the travel section of Acts.

[18]ἔδοξε κἀμοί, "I too decided" (NRSV, cf. Alexander, *Preface,* 127; Fitzmyer, *Luke,* 296; Johnson, *Luke,* 28; van Unnik, "Once More St. Luke's Prologue," 16). Some manuscripts of the Western tradition read "it seemed good to me and to the Holy Spirit" (cf. Acts 15:28); see Johnson, *Luke,* 28; Metzger, *Textual Commentary,* 129.

which resulted in an "orderly account" directed to the implied
reader as represented by the narratee Theophilus.[20] Luke shows
elsewhere that he expects a narrative delivered step-by-step
($\kappa\alpha\theta\varepsilon\xi\hat{\eta}\varsigma$) to have persuasive power; Peter's account delivered
$\kappa\alpha\theta\varepsilon\xi\hat{\eta}\varsigma$ (Acts 11:4) carries the day in his controversy over eating
with Gentile believers.[21] In the same way, Luke's entire narrative
will create a literary "world," enabling the reader to see things in a
new light. The example of Peter's speech indicates the persuasive
power which Luke attaches to this kind of "orderly account."
Luke's own material has been arranged to help the reader connect
"the things fulfilled among us" concerning Jesus to the larger world
of God's action among humanity.[22]

The final clause (v. 4) gives clear indication of Luke's rhetorical
purpose. Luke's narratee Theophilus, and thus his implied reader, is
a Christian, as indicated by the phrase "the things about which you
have been instructed."[23] Luke's narrative tries to secure the faith of

---

[19]Fitzmyer (*Luke*, 296) translates the perfect participle of $\pi\alpha\rho\alpha\kappa\text{o}\lambda\text{ou}\theta\acute{\varepsilon}\omega$
"after tracing everything carefully." (Cf. Alexander, *Preface*, 128-30; Dillon,
"Previewing Luke's Project," 218-19; Johnson, *Luke*, 28; van Unnik, "Once
More St. Luke's Prologue," 16-17). $\ddot{\alpha}\nu\omega\theta\varepsilon\nu$ probably means "from the
beginning," but may refer to the length of Luke's research (Schürmann,
Lukasevangelium, 11; contra Marshall, *Luke*, 43).

[20]See above, n. 5.

[21]Luke T. Johnson, *Decision Making in the Church: A Biblical Model*
(Philadelphia: Fortress Press, 1983), 67-87. Cf. Alexander, *Preface*, 131-32, 134-
36; Brawley, *Centering on God*, 38-39; Dillon, "Previewing Luke's Project,"
219-23; Schneider, "Zur Bedeutung von $\kappa\alpha\theta\varepsilon\xi\hat{\eta}\varsigma$"; Tannehill, *Narrative Unity of
Luke-Acts*, 1:11-12; Moessner, "Meaning of KAΘΕΞΗΣ"; Martin Vökel,
"Exegetische Erwägungen zum Verständnis des Begriffs KAΘΕΞΗΣ im Lukanischen Prolog," *New Testament Studies* 20 (1973-1974): 289-99. See below, chap.
4, on Acts 11:1-18.

[22]Cf. Brawley, *Centering on God*, 38-43.

[23]The verb $\kappa\alpha\tau\eta\chi\acute{\varepsilon}\omega$ is used of formal religious instruction in Acts 18:25;
Rom 2:18; 1 Cor 14:19; Gal 6:6; only in later literature (e.g., *2 Clem.* 17:1) does
it refer to the Christian catechumenate. It could also mean "to hear by rumor"
(Acts 21:21, 24; see van Unnik, "Once More St. Luke's Prologue," 18). But con-
sidering Luke's programmatic use of $\lambda\acute{o}\gamma\text{o}\varsigma$ to refer to the Christian mission (see
above, n. 15), and in light of the whole of Luke's work, it seems best to picture

Christian believers, both for the present time and beyond, by demonstrating the solid grounds of the tradition. He writes to provide "security" (ἀσφάλεια); the word stands in emphatic final position.[24]

Luke Johnson has argued that "security" is the goal of Luke's entire literary effort. Johnson assumes with the majority of scholars that Luke's audience was overwhelmingly Gentile. Few Jewish Christians are left in the churches, and this creates uncertainty—God's promises, after all, were to the Jews:

> If that historical people was not *now* in possession of the promised blessings, and someone else was, what did that signify for God's reliability? Did God keep his word, or did he utterly betray Israel? And what were the implications for *gentile* believers in this God? Could they rely on "the things fulfilled among them" any more than the Jews could? If God's word failed Israel, could it not fail the Gentiles as well?[25]

Johnson holds that Luke is dealing with the problem of theodicy; Luke means to show that "God in fact did *first* fulfill his promises to

---

Luke's narratee and implied reader as having received Christian instruction. See Alexander, *Preface*, 139; Fitzmyer, *Luke*, 300-1; Johnson, *Luke*, 28-29; Marshall, *Luke*, 43-44; Schweizer, *Luke*, 13.

[24]ἀσφάλεια is not, as in NRSV and RSV, "truth" as opposed to "falsehood," but "certainty." It was used as a legal financial term for "written security" (Epictetus 2.13.7 and in several papyrii). Cf. Acts 5:23, where it refers to securely-locked doors; also 1 Thess 5:3 and ἀσφαλής in Phil 3:1 and Heb 6:19. See Alexander, *Preface*, 140-41; Dillon, "Previewing Luke's Project," 223-27; Fitzmyer, *Luke*, 300; Johnson, *Luke*, 28; Louw and Nida, *Greek-English Lexicon*, 1:371 (§ 31.41); Marshall, *Luke*, 44; James Hope Moulton and George Milligan, *The Vocabulary of the Greek Testament Illustrated from the Papyrii and Other Non-Literary Sources* (Grand Rapids: Eerdmans, 1930), 88; Walter Radl, *Das Lukas-Evangelium*, Erträge der Forschung, vol. 261 (Darmstadt: Wissenschaftliche Buchgesellschaft, 1988), 54; Schürmann, *Lukasevangelium*, 14.

[25]Luke T. Johnson, *The Writings of the New Testament* (Philadelphia: Fortress Press, 1986), 203.

Israel and *then* extended the blessings to the gentile world."[26] Thus writing καθεξῆς is of utmost importance; the history of Israel must be told "step-by-step" so that Gentile Christians can understand that God has been faithful to the promises made to Israel, and so will continue in faithfulness. "The saving of Israel was necessary for the security of Gentile faith."[27] Johnson concludes that this places Luke-Acts within the genre of apologetic history—Luke seeks "to defend God's ways in the world."[28]

Johnson's thesis is not without problems. For one, not all scholars would agree that the Jewish presence in the church had become insignificant, or that the mission to the Jews had ended. Contra Johnson, I believe that the open ending of Acts is best seen as an indication that the Jewish mission will continue. True, Paul announces his intention to turn to the Gentiles (Acts 28:28). But twice before he has made this announcement (13:46; 18:6), and in both cases returned to preach to the Jews elsewhere. The reader can expect this pattern to continue—there is no indication that 28:28 is God's final judgment; rather the pattern of "first to the Jews, then to the Gentiles," will continue to "the ends of the earth" (1:8).[29]

---

[26]Ibid., 204; emphasis his. Cf. Tiede, *Prophecy and History in Luke-Acts.*

[27]Johnson, *Luke,* 10. Cf. Tannehill, *Narrative Unity of Luke-Acts,* 1:12.

[28]Ibid. See Johnson, *Luke,* 3-10; idem, *Writings of New Testament,* 200-204. Note that for Johnson, "apologetic" has a wider connotation than it does for older scholarship, which saw Luke-Acts as apologetic directed to outsiders in response to a local and temporary dilemma—a political tract directed toward Roman officials, or written as a defense of Paul. Rather, as with contemporary Jewish apologetic found in *The Letter of Aristeas,* Philo, Josephus, Artapanus, and Eupolemus, Luke-Acts has an important function for insiders: to give "certainty" by showing the value of a tradition within a pluralistic context (*Luke,* 8-9). The apology is not addressed to a passing crisis, but to "the very existence of a messianic sect in the Gentile world" (*Luke,* 10).

[29]On this question see Robert L. Brawley, *Luke-Acts and the Jews: Conflict, Apology, and Conciliation,* Society of Biblical Literature Monograph Series, no. 33 (Atlanta: Scholars Press, 1987); J. Bradley Chance, *Jerusalem, the Temple, and the New Age in Luke-Acts* (Macon: Mercer University Press, 1988); Nils Dahl, "The Purpose of Luke-Acts,"; Jacob Jervell, *Luke and the People of God* (Minneapolis: Augsburg Publishing House, 1972); Luke T. Johnson, "The New Testament's Anti-Jewish Slander and the Conventions of Ancient Polemic,"

Another difficulty facing Johnson's thesis is that the thorny prob-lem of the exact genre of Luke-Acts has found no consensus. My designation of Luke-Acts as "narrative" skirts the question of genre in some ways, due to the conviction (held in common with current narratological studies) that the similarities among narratives allow us to deal with them across traditional generic lines. Nevertheless, genre is a crucial factor in the development of the reader's expecta-tions, so some sort of generic determination must be made.[30] In the end I must agree with Johnson that Luke writes "the continuation of biblical history."[31] Certainly Luke is a selective historian, and there are numerous questions about his accuracy. But I do not find the alternatives convincing. There are analogies between Hellenistic biography and Luke-Acts, but in the end the two look very dif-ferent.[32] And as Johnson points out, Luke extends his vision beyond

---

Journal of Biblical Literature 108 (1989): 419-41; Earl Richard, "The Divine Purpose: the Jews and the Gentile Mission (Acts 15)," *Luke-Acts: New Perspec-tives from the Society of Biblical Literature Seminar,* ed. Charles H. Talbert (New York: Crossroad, 1984), 188-209; Jack T. Sanders, *The Jews in Luke-Acts* (Philadelphia: Fortress Press, 1987); idem, "The Salvation of the Jews in Luke-Acts," in *Luke-Acts: New Perspectives,* 104-28; Jeffrey S. Siker, *Disinheriting the Jews: Abraham in Early Christian Controversy* (Louisville: Westminster/John Knox Press, 1991), 103-27; idem, "'First to the Gentiles': A Literary Analysis of Luke 4:16-30," *Journal of Biblical Literature* 111 (1992): 73-90; Joseph B. Tyson, ed., *Luke-Acts and the Jewish People: Eight Critical Perspectives* (Min-neapolis: Augsburg Publishing House, 1988); idem, *Images of Judaism in Luke-Acts* (Columbia: University of South Carolina, 1992); Laurence M. Wills, "The Depiction of the Jews in Acts" *Journal of Biblical Literature* 110 (1991): 631-54; Stephen G. Wilson, *Gentiles and Gentile Mission;* idem, *Luke and the Law,* Society for New Testament Studies Monograph Series, vol. 50 (Cambridge: Cam-bridge University Press, 1983); and below, chap. 4, on Acts 28:16-31.

[30]On the importance of genre for interpretation, see E. D. Hirsch, Jr., *Validity in Interpretation* (New Haven: Yale University Press, 1967), 68-126.

[31]Following Dahl, "The Story of Abraham in Luke-Acts."

[32]On biography as the generic convention followed by Luke-Acts, see Talbert, *Literary Patterns.* Talbert is refuted by D. L. Barr and J. L. Wentling, "The Con-ventions of Classical Biography and the Genre of Luke-Acts," in *Luke-Acts: New Perspectives,* 63-88.

Jesus and the disciples to "the events that have been fulfilled among us," extending back towards the whole history of God's people, Israel.[33] In the same way, Acts contains elements of Hellenistic romance, but in the end it is hard to believe that its sole purpose is "profit with delight."[34] And to pose a generic split between Luke and Acts, Luke being biography and Acts being romance, does violence to the thematic unity of the two works. Perhaps one could say that Luke-Acts mixes elements from a number of genres, but this is to return to my starting point—the similarities among various kinds of narratives allow us to study them as a group. In the end I believe that Johnson's formulation is the most adequate: Luke-Acts is a historical apologetic which addresses the problem of theodicy.

So in spite of my reservations about his construal of the ending of Acts, I believe that Johnson's thesis goes a long way toward making sense of Luke-Acts as a whole. Johnson correctly sees that the initial expectations of the implied reader are formed by the prologue, which promises "security." The reader will expect to find assurance as the narrative progresses. At issue is reliability—how reliable are the traditions which have been passed down? How sure can we be about what has happened? And ultimately, how reliable is God?

To anticipate the argument that follows, I will attempt to show that on the discursive level, the Holy Spirit plays a crucial function in Luke's quest to give assurance to his readers. Like all implied authors, Luke must convince his readers that he is reliable. "Holy Spirit" serves as one sign of that reliability. The Spirit's primary narrative function is to ensure reliability—formulations like "Zechariah was filled with the Holy Spirit and spoke this prophecy" (Luke 1:67) serve as rhetorical clues that what follows is reliable commentary.[35] Mention of the Spirit operating on a human agent, which

---

[33]Johnson, *Luke*, 8.

[34]See Richard L. Pervo, *Profit with Delight: The Literary Genre of the Acts of the Apostles* (Philadelphia: Fortress Press, 1987).

[35]"Reliable commentary" can refer to a summary provided by a reliable narrator, but also to comments made by characters who are portrayed and perceived as trustworthy. See Booth, *Rhetoric of Fiction*, 169-266; Robert Fowler, *Loaves and Fishes: The Function of the Feeding Stories in the Gospel of Mark*, Society of Biblical Literature Dissertation Series, vol. 54 (Chico, Cal.: Scholars Press,

sometimes seems redundant (e.g., Simeon in Luke 2:25-27; Peter in Acts 2:4; 4:8, 31; Stephen in Acts 6:5, 10; 7:55; Paul in Acts 9:17; 13:9, 52), reminds the implied reader that what we have here is accurate and assured. The importance of the prophetic pattern in Luke's writings in this connection is clear: since the Spirit enables every prophetic utterance that takes place within the story, the fulfillment of those utterances as the story moves along helps establish Luke's credibility with the reader; thus in the argument which follows, my emphasis will be primarily (but not exclusively) on the prophetic aspects of the Spirit's work as they bear on Luke's rhetoric. Further, the Spirit as a independent actor, a character closely related to and in fact an extension of God, enhances Luke's reliability by bringing to bear direct divine authority—when the Spirit descends on Jesus (Luke 3:22) or whisks Philip to Azotus (Acts 8:39-40), there can be doubt as to who is in charge of this story.

Thus my reading of Luke's prologue is an integral part of my subsequent argument. The prologue posits an implied reader with certain expectations, the foremost being a concern with reliability. The reader expects that Luke's narrative will deal with the reliability of the Christian tradition, and (the reader will discover) ultimately with the reliability of God. In what follows, we will see that the narrative function of the Holy Spirit as a character in Luke-Acts is to ensure the reliability of Luke's narrative, lending that narrative the ultimate authority of God.

Infancy Narrative (Luke 1-2)

Luke's style changes markedly between the prologue and the infancy narrative, and the shift is a significant indication of the implied author's concern with reliability.[36] There is a Septuagintal

---

1981), 149-79.

[36]On Luke's infancy narrative, see Bovon, *Lukas,* 43-161; Raymond Brown, *The Birth of the Messiah: A Commentary on the Infancy Narratives in Matthew and Luke* (Garden City: Doubleday & Co., Inc., 1979), 235-495; Craddock, *Luke,* 21-43; Fitzmyer, *Luke,* 303-448; Johnson, *Luke,* 31-62; Rene Laurentin, *Structure et théologie de Luc 1-2* (Paris: Gabalda, 1957); Marshall, *Luke,* 45-130; Menzies,

flavor to this section: here is storytelling with an antique ring—
without a doubt we are dealing with a biblical-style discourse.[37] The
reader learns from the shift between the prologue and the infancy
narrative that the implied author is master of two styles—Hellenistic
Greek as well as the Semitic style. The implication is that this work
will fuse Hellenistic and biblical historiographical styles.[38] Also, the
use of biblical style creates certain expectations in the reader about
reliability; the style of this narrative resonates with texts known and
loved, believed above all to tell the truth. Familiarity and continuity

---

Development of Early Christian Pneumatology, 116-34; Paul Minear, "Luke's
Use of the Birth Stories," in *Studies in Luke-Acts,* ed. Leander E. Keck and J.
Louis Martyn (Philadelphia: Fortress Press, 1966), 111-30; Sabourin, *Luc,* 53-
110; Jane Schaberg, *The Illegitimacy of Jesus: A Feminist Theological Interpreta-
tion of the Infancy Narratives* (San Francisco: Harper & Row, 1987), 78-144;
Schneider, *Lukas,* 42-79; Schürmann, *Lukasevangelium,* 18-146; Schweitzer,
Luke, 15-67; Tannehill, *Narrative Unity,* 1:13-44; Wiefel, *Lukas,* 42-85.

The many attempts to reconstruct Luke's sources for the infancy narrative have
met with limited success. There is general consensus that whatever sources may
have been used, Luke has given them considerable shaping (Brown, *Birth of Messiah,* 245-50; Fitzmyer, *Luke,* 305-16; Marshall, *Luke,* 46-49; Menzies, *Development of Early Christian Pneumatology,* 116-18). The continuity of the themes and
perspectives of the infancy narrative with the rest of Luke-Acts argues against the
thesis of Conzelmann and others that these chapters are clumsy, non-Lukan
editorial additions—they are in fact integral to Luke-Acts. See Conzelman, *Theology of St. Luke;* Craddock, *Luke,* 21-22; Fitzmyer, *Luke,* 310; Minear, "Luke's
Use of the Birth Stories."

[37]I use the term "Septuagintal" to describe the Greek of the infancy narrative,
in recognition that despite a few possible Aramaisms, the many Lukan stylistic
touches make the hypothesis of an underlying Semitic source unlikely. See Brown,
Birth of Messiah, 245-50; Cadbury, *Making of Luke-Acts,* 70-75; Craddock, *Luke,*
22-24; Fitzmyer, *Luke,* 312; Johnson, *Luke,* 34-35; Nigel Turner, "The Relation
of Luke I and II to Hebraic Sources and to the Rest of Luke-Acts," *New Testament
Studies* 2 (1955-56): 100-109.

[38]As noted by Kurz, "Narrative Approaches to Luke-Acts," 207. A further
implication concerns the implied reader posited by this text: the ideal reader will
be familiar with the biblical traditions Luke alludes to. This is further support for
the notion that the implied reader is a Christian, taught by and familiar with Old
Testament scripture.

are significant factors in making what follows in the narrative seem credible and reliable. By switching to biblical-style rhetoric, Luke begins to create the feeling of certainty spoken of in the prologue. Point of view also shifts from "telling" to "showing," as signified by the shift from the first-person narration of the prologue to the omniscient third-person narration used in most of the rest of Luke's discourse.[39] "Showing" is always a more reliable way to get a point across, for several reasons. For one thing, a third-person omniscient narrator's reliability is rarely questioned (especially outside modern literature);[40] a first-person narrator's reliability is much more likely to be questioned—how does this speaker know what is told, and what personal investment might this narrator have? Further, with third-person "showing," the reader is left to fill in the gaps in the narrative, in order to draw conclusions about what the text signifies; in the long run, a conclusion drawn by the reader on the basis of what is shown is more powerful than an assertion accepted on the basis of what is told. The change from "telling" to "showing" thus moves the reader to a position of more certainty, and so the text gains extra reliability. Thus by this one move—the shift from a Hellenistic, first-person prologue to a biblical, third-person omniscient style—Luke greatly increases the perceived reliability of the narrative.[41]

In structure, the section consists of contrasting panels of two annunciations (John, 1:5-25; Jesus, 1:26-38) and two births (John, 1:57-80; Jesus, 2:1-21), connected by the meeting of Mary and

---

[39]Kurz ("Narrative Approaches to Luke-Acts," 204-8) finds biblical precedents for this shift in Ezra, 1 Esdras, Tobit, and 2 Maccabees. "Telling" and "showing" are discussed in Booth, *Rhetoric of Fiction*, 3-20.

[40]See the critique of Dawsey, *Lukan Voice* by Moore, *Literary Criticism and the Gospels*, 30-34: the unreliable narrator which Dawsey posits in Luke would be quite uncharacteristic of ancient literature. See also Darr, *On Character Building*, 181-82; and Sheeley, "Narrative Asides and Narrative Authority."

[41]Sternberg complains that Luke's shift to omniscient narration is inconsistent (*Poetics of Biblical Narrative*, 86). But he misses the significance of the Septuagintal model for Luke; the shift does not mark the narrator as unreliable or inconsistent, but establishes the utmost reliability, akin to that of a biblical author.

Elizabeth (1:39-56), and followed by two stories about Jesus (2:22-40, 2:41-52).[42] The structure serves to place Jesus within, yet superior to, the prophetic tradition as represented by John.[43] The witness to Jesus is supported further by other Spirit-inspired, prophetic figures: Zechariah, Mary, Elizabeth, Simeon, and Anna.

Zechariah (Luke 1:5-25, 57-80)

Luke shifts to a Septuagintal style in his introduction of Zechariah and Elizabeth (ἐγένετο ἐν ταῖς ἡμέραις κτλ; cf. e.g., Gen 26:32; 34:25; Exod 2:11). The scene is familiar to readers of the Old Testament: a righteous but barren woman is given the promise of new life, and the result is the birth of a leader or prophet (cf. Gen 18:1-15; Judg 13:2-7; 1 Sam 1:1-20).[44] There are a number of other allusions to Old Testament texts in the birth announcement.[45]

---

[42]See Craddock, *Luke,* 24. There is little consensus on the exact details of the structure, though the parallelism is clear; see Brown, *Birth of Messiah,* 248-53; Craddock, *Luke,* 24; Fitzmyer, *Luke,* 313-15; Johnson, *Luke,* 34; idem, *Writings,* 211.

[43]Fitzmyer (*Luke,* 315) speaks of the parallels between Jesus and John as "a parallelism with one-upmanship. The Jesus-side always comes off better." Cf. Craddock, *Luke,* 28; Johnson, *Luke,* 38-39; Marshall, *Luke,* 45; Tannehill, *Narrative Unity of Luke-Acts,* 1:15-20.

[44]Fitzmyer (*Luke,* 318) describes the form of the Old Testament birth announcement as five-fold: (1) Appearance of divine figure, (2) Human fear, (3) Heavenly message, (4) Objection, and (5) Sign. Additional examples can be found in Gen 16:7-13 and 17:1-21. Cf. Tannehill, *Narrative Unity of Luke-Acts,* 1:18.

[45]Genealogies (v. 5): 1 Chr 24:10; Neh 12:4, 17; Exod 6:23. Living according to "commandments and regulations" (v. 6): Gen 26:5; Deut 4:40; Ezek 36:27. Old and barren (v. 7): Gen 18:11. Priestly duties (v. 8-9): 2 Chr 31:2; Exod 30:7-8. Angel of the Lord (v. 11): Judg 6:12 and often. Child as an answer to prayer (v. 13): Gen 25:21. Birth announcement (v. 13): Gen 17:19. Child a Nazirite (v. 15): Num 6:2-4; Judg 13:6-7; 1 Sam 1:11. Elijah as forerunner (v. 17): Mal 3:1, 23. "Hearts of parents" (v. 17): Sir 48:10. Objection to announcement (v. 18): Gen 15:8; 17:17 18:12. Cf. Craddock, *Luke,* 26: "God is at work from within, not from outside the institutions, rituals, and practices of Judaism."

The allusions encourage the implied reader to expect that this text will deal with the narrative world of the Old Testament.[46]

The "angel of the Lord" (v. 11) or "Gabriel" (v. 19) is certainly a reliable commentator in biblical literature;[47] the angel's reliability is reinforced by his location "at the right side of the altar of incense."[48] The angel's reliability will be further reinforced by the fulfillment of his predictions within the narrative: Elizabeth does bear a son (vv. 13, 57), Zechariah is mute until John's circumcision (vv. 20-22, 64), and John's mission to Israel meets with the predicted success (vv. 16-18, cf. 3:1-22).[49]

John's birth is cast in prophetic terms, reminiscent of a Nazirite such as Samson or Elijah (vv. 15-17; cf Num 6:2-4; Judg 13:6-7; 1

---

[46]Cf. Tannehill, *Narrative Unity of Luke-Acts,* 1:18: "The Lukan birth narrative is permeated with the Old Testament hope and celebrates its fulfillment."

[47]The "angel of the Lord" appears in Samson's birth announcement (Judg 13:3) and often in the Old Testament as a mouthpiece for God (Gen 16:7-13; 21:17; 22:10-18; 31:11-13; Exod 3:2-6; 14:19-24; Judg 2:1-5; Zech 1:11-14). The angel will reappear in Luke-Acts (Luke 2:9, Acts 5:19; 8:26; 12:7, 23). See Fitzmyer, *Luke,* 324.

"Gabriel" first appears in Dan 8:16 and 9:21, is one of the three angels named in the Old Testament, and one of the seven angels of the presence in Jewish literature. See Fitzmyer, *Luke,* 327-28.

The Lukan angels, like the Holy Spirit, function as stand-ins for God, as they convey reliable proclamation about God's intentions. Indeed, sometimes "the angel of the Lord" and "the Spirit" appear to be interchangeable (cf. Acts 8:26 with 8:29; also 23:9). On the reliability of the Lukan angels, see Tannehill, *Narrative Unity of Luke-Acts,* 1:22.

[48]"The 'right side,' being usually considered the favored side, would convey to Zechariah that the angel's visit to him was not ominous" (Fitzmyer, *Luke,* 324-25).

[49]Tannehill (*Narrative Unity of Luke-Acts,* 1:22) notes, however, that the strong statements of salvation for Israel will be called into question in light of the later narrative; again, reading involves both raising and modifying expectations, and any simple nationalistic expectations regarding the salvation Jesus brings to Israel will be revised in the course of reading Luke-Acts.

Sam 1:11).[50] Of particular interest to this study is the angel's statement that "even before his birth he will be filled with the Holy
Spirit" (v. 15; cf. Jer 1:5; Gal 1:15).[51] The angel, in making a
direct characterization of John, also makes an indirect statement
about the character of the Spirit: as John is explicitly described in
prophetic terms and said to be filled with the prophetic Spirit, the
Spirit is implicitly characterized as being that Spirit which inspired
the Old Testament prophets (e.g., Gen 41:38; Num 11:24-30; 23:7
LXX; 24:2; 27:18; 1 Sam 10:6, 10; Isa 61:1; Ezek 2:2; Joel 2:28;
Mic 3:8).[52] Thus the implied reader is encouraged in certain
expectations—just as the biblical style of the narrative invites the
expectation that the narrative will stand within the prophetic tradition, so the Spirit, being described in terms drawn from that tradition, will be seen as the prophetic Spirit. Luke's phrase "filled with
the Spirit" also points forward to later prophetic figures: Jesus
(Luke 4:1) and the disciples of Jesus (Acts 2:4; 4:8, 31; 7:55; 9:17;
11:24; 13:9).[53]

Zechariah too proves to be one of the prophets (Luke 1:67-79),
as he too is said to be "filled with the Spirit" (1:67). Again, a direct

---

[50]Though the parallels between John the Baptist and the Nazirites are not
exact; see Fitzmyer, *Luke,* 325-26; Johnson, *Luke,* 33; Marshall, *Luke,* 57;
Schweizer, *Luke,* 22; Sabourin, *Luc,* 58-59; Schürmann, *Lukasevangelium,* 33-34.

[51]"John is a prophet 'from the womb,' a fact demonstrated literally by his
leaping in Elizabeth's womb in recognition of Jesus in 1:41" (Johnson, *Luke,* 33);
cf. Tannehill, *Narrative Unity of Luke-Acts,* 1:23.

[52]"The relation of 'Spirit' and 'filling' is not unknown in the OT" (Fitzmyer,
Luke, 319; see Exod 31:3; 35:31; Wisd 1:7; Sir 48:12 LXX (Codex A)). The connection between "filled with the Spirit" and prophecy is explicit in Mic 3:8.

[53]There is no indication that Luke makes any distinction between Zechariah
and the disciples (contra Hull, *Holy Spirit in Acts,* 68). The language suggests a
parallel: both are cast in prophetic terms. Cf. Menzies, *Development of Early
Christian Pneumatology,* 211-12; Shelton, *Mighty in Word and Deed,* 15-16.

The expressions ἐπλήσθη πνεύματος ἁγίου (using πίμπλημι, as in Luke 1:67)
and πλήρης πνεύματος ἁγίου (as in Luke 4:1) are virtually synonymous. See
Marshall, *Luke,* 58; Menzies, *Development of Early Christian Pneumatology,*
155-56; Turner, "Spirit Endowment," 53-58.

characterization of a human character, this time by the narrator, provides indirect characterization of the Spirit, since Luke explicitly connects "filled with the Holy Spirit," and "prophecy" (v. 67).[54] Zechariah's Spirit-inspired song (vv. 68-79)[55] proclaims God's faithfulness to Israel; God will remember the covenant with Israel, and the oath sworn to Abraham (vv. 72-73). John's role as a prophet and forerunner is stipulated (v. 76-77; cf. 3:1-6). That Zechariah's prophecy concerning God's faithfulness to Israel is explicitly said to be inspired by the Spirit gives it an extra degree of narrative authority: here the human character is guaranteed to be a reliable commentator.[56] The Spirit thus functions to insure the reliability of Zechariah's statement that God is faithful.

Mary and Elizabeth (Luke 1:26-56)

The parallel annunciation to Mary draws out the similarities and contrasts between the prophets Jesus and John.[57] The same angel

---

[54]Cf. Fitzmyer, *Luke*, 382; Johnson, *Luke*, 45.

[55]The Song of Zechariah is built from numerous phrases from the Septuagint, and is probably based on a Jewish hymn; see Brown, *Birth of the Messiah*, 346-50, 377-92; Fitzmyer, *Luke*, 374-89

[56]Contra David P. Moessner ("The Ironic Fulfillment of Israel's Glory," in *Luke-Acts and the Jewish People*, ed. Tyson, 35-50), who sees Zechariah, Mary, and Elizabeth as slightly unreliable, and their prophecies as anticipating a political, nationalistic Messiah; such expectations find only ironic fulfillment in suffering servanthood. However, the Spirit assures the reliability of Zechariah's prophecy, not the infallibility of the reader. As Tannehill (*Narrative Unity of Luke-Acts*, 1:34-38) notes, the theme of the salvation of Israel stands in ironic tension with the subsequent story. Readers' expectations, if nationalistic, will be revised as the story proceeds. See Brawley, *Centering on God*, 44-46; Tannehill, *Narrative Unity of Luke-Acts*, 1:22.

[57]See Brown, *Birth of the Messiah*, 292-98; Craddock, *Luke*, 27; Johnson, *Luke*, 39; Marshall, *Luke*, 62-63; Tannehill, *Narrative Unity of Luke-Acts*, 1:15-16.

Gabriel appears, with a similar announcement.[58] There is a human objection (vv. 18, 34), and a divine sign (vv. 20, 36). So the reader will expect to hear of the birth of a new prophet. Yet this prophet has a different, more regal lineage: of the house of David, not Aaron (vv. 5, 27). Like John, "He will be great" (vv. 15, 32), but this prophet "will be called the Son of the Most High, and the Lord God will give to him the throne of his ancestor David. He will reign over the house of Jacob forever, and of his kingdom there will be no end" (vv. 32-33; cf. 2 Sam 7:8-16).[59]

The Holy Spirit also appears in this announcement. But unlike the announcement of the birth of John, who is said to be filled with the Holy Spirit from the womb (v. 15), this announcement designates the mother as the locus of the Spirit: "The Holy Spirit will come upon you" (v. 35). The active construction, with the Spirit as the subject of a future-tense verb, is rhetorically significant: it indicates to the reader the importance of this event. The Spirit is again at work, but not merely as the agent in a passive construction, as with John ("he will be filled with the Holy Spirit," 1:15). Now the Spirit will be a direct actor in the story, a character, a protagonist (cf. 3:22).[60] Here the Spirit is attributed a generative function, as it enables Mary to conceive a divine child, the Son of God.

---

[58]Cf. v. 13 with v. 30-31,

Μὴ φοβοῦ, Ζαχαρία,	Μὴ φοβοῦ, Μαριάμ,
διότι εἰσηκούσθη ἡ δέησίς σου,	εὗρες γὰρ χάριν παρὰ τῷ θεῷ·
καὶ ἡ γυνή σου Ἐλισάβετ	καὶ ἰδοὺ
γεννήσει υἱόν σοι,	συλλήμψῃ ἐν γαστρὶ καὶ τέξῃ υἱόν,
καὶ καλέσεις τὸ ὄνομα αὐτοῦ Ἰωάννην	καὶ καλέσεις τὸ ὄνομα αὐτοῦ Ἰησοῦν.

See Craddock, *Luke*, 27; Johnson, *Luke*, 39; Marshall, *Luke*, 62-63.

[59]Cf. Tannehill, *Narrative Unity of Luke-Acts*, 1:25.

[60]Throughout this study, I will distinguish between the Spirit as a direct and indirect actor. The Spirit is a direct actor when it is the subject of an active verb (as here, "Spirit" is the subject of the verb "come upon") or the agent of a passive construction. The Spirit is an indirect actor when a human intermediary acts under the influence of the Spirit (e.g., Acts 11:28 and 21:4, where prophets work "by" or "through" the Spirit). See above, chap. 2, "The Spirit as Actor."

The announcement not only explains how the virgin Mary can conceive, but also prepares the reader for Mary's proclamation in vv. 46-55: Mary, like Zechariah, speaks under the influence of the prophetic Spirit, and is thus a reliable source of information.[61] Mary, too, is one of the prophets. That Mary is a prophet is reinforced by her self-designation as ἡ δούλη κυρίου (v. 38; cf. Luke 2:29; Jer 7:25; 25:4; Dan 9:6, 10; Amos 3:7; Zech 1:6; Rev 10:7; 11:18; 22:6, 9).

Thus the Song of Mary (Luke 1:46-55), like that of Zechariah, is a prophetic announcement.[62] Under the influence of the Spirit (v. 35), Mary[63] extols God's reversal of her fortunes, anticipating a recurrent Lukan theme (v. 48).[64] Her description of God's action— to scatter the proud, to bring down the powerful, to lift up the lowly, to feed the hungry—will be echoed in Jesus' ministry (vv. 51-53, cf. e.g., 4:18-19). She announces that God will be faithful to the promises made to Abraham and to Israel (vv. 54-55). Mary's

---

[61] As Luke uses the same word (ἐπέρχομαι) for the coming of the Spirit on the disciples in Acts 1:8, it does not seem that "Luke's sole concern" is with "the effect of his creative Spirit on Mary" in producing the Messiah (Fitzmyer, *Luke,* 351; cf. Schweizer, *Luke,* 29. See Menzies, *Development of Early Christian Pneumatology,* 122-28).

[62] Like Zechariah's song, it is a mosaic of Greek Old Testament expressions and allusions (particularly 1 Sam 2:1-10), and may be pre-Lukan. See Brown, *Birth of the Messiah,* 355-65; Fitzmyer, *Luke,* 359-62; Sabourin, *Luc,* 73-77; Schürmann, *Lukasevangelium,* 70-80; Robert C. Tannehill, "The Magnificat as Poem," *Journal of Biblical Literature* 93 (1974): 263-75.

[63] "Mary" (with all Greek manuscripts and most versions), not "Elizabeth" (only in Old Latin and a few patristic quotations), is certainly the best reading. The reading "Elizabeth" arose in a scribal attempt to connect the canticle to the statement that Elizabeth was filled with the Spirit (1:41) and to the remote antecedent "her" in 1:56. Another possible reason for the alternate reading is that Elizabeth more closely parallels Hannah, whose prayer forms a good deal of the basis of this speech (see 1 Sam 2:1-10). See Brown, *Birth of the Messiah,* 334-36; Fitzmyer, *Luke,* 365-66; Johnson, *Luke,* 41; Marshall, *Luke,* 77-78; Metzger, *Textual Commentary,* 130-31.

[64] See Craddock, *Luke,* 30; Johnson, *Luke,* 43; Tannehill, *Narrative Unity of Luke-Acts,* 1:26-32.

speech is prophetic, not only in that it predicts her future fame (Luke 1:48),[65] but in proclaiming her conception as a fulfillment of God's plan to reverse the fortunes of Israel and to make good the promise to Abraham. In lifting up the lowly servant Mary by bringing the Son of God into the world through her, God has "filled the hungry with good things" (v. 53); God's mercy to Mary (vv. 46-49) typifies the blessing to come through her son, Jesus (vv. 50-55).[66] Mary's speech draws out the far-reaching implications of Jesus' birth, and sets forth a number of important Lukan themes: divine reversal, the concern for the poor and the weak, and the importance of God's promise to Israel. Mary's words are implicitly inspired by the Spirit; Luke's statement that the Spirit will "come upon" and "overshadow" Mary (v. 35; cf. Acts 1:8) cannot be limited to the conception of Jesus, but also functions to assure the reader of the reliability of Mary's proclamation.

The character of Elizabeth helps confirm Mary's prophetic speech. Elizabeth also is cast in prophetic terms—doubly so, as the prophet within her confirms her words. In his first prophetic act, John "leaped in her womb" (Luke 1:41; cf. Gen 25:22) at the sound of Mary's voice, expressing joy (v. 44).[67] Elizabeth is explicitly said to be filled with the Spirit (v. 41) as she speaks of Mary's status and faith (vv. 43-45; cf. Judg 5:24; Jdt 13:18). Elizabeth, under the power of the Spirit, confirms Mary's own confession of faith and servanthood (v. 38). Luke explicitly connects the prophetic Spirit with Elizabeth, affirming her reliability along with that of Mary. The reliability of Mary is confirmed by another Spirit-filled character; her declaration of God's faithfulness is thereby assured.

---

[65]Mary's prophecy that she will be blessed is fulfilled in Luke 11:27.

[66]"Mary is here made the representative if not the personification of 'Israel'" (Johnson, *Luke,* 43).

[67]The Spirit is thus indirectly characterized as the source of joy. On the close association of the Spirit and joy in Luke-Acts, see below on Luke 10:1-24.

Simeon and Anna (Luke 2:22-38)

Luke's use of prophetic language to describe Simeon borders on rhetorical overkill—there is no doubt that this man is being portrayed as a prophet.[68] Simeon is directly characterized as "righteous and devout, looking forward to the consolation of Israel" (2:25). That he is filled with the prophetic Spirit is emphasized by threefold repetition—the Spirit is habitually with him (v. 25), has given him a revelation (v. 26), and now guides him into the temple to see Jesus (v. 27). He, like Mary, describes himself as a "servant" (v. 29). And like Zechariah, Elizabeth, and Anna, he is old, having waited long to see the Messiah (2:26, 29; cf. 1:7; 2:36-37).

So Simeon's words and actions possess a high degree of reliability.[69] He speaks of God's "salvation" seen with his own eyes in the person of the baby Jesus now presented "in the presence of all peoples" (vv. 30-31). This salvation is not only for Israel, but for the Gentiles (v. 32)—a Spirit-backed foreshadowing of developments to be found in Acts. Simeon also anticipates the Lukan theme of a division among the people of Israel (v. 34).[70] Simeon's speech creates expectations in the reader as it anticipates the conflict within Israel over Jesus, and the subsequent offering of salvation to the Gentiles; Simeon's reliability is assured by the Spirit. Thus the reader is prepared to interpret the division of Israel and the Gentile mission as God-driven, while the characters within the story come to this understanding only after an arduous discernment process.[71]

Anna, too, is a "prophet" (v. 36), though she is not explicitly said to be filled with the Spirit. She is a pious widow, a constant

---

[68]See Johnson, *Luke,* 55; Marshall, *Luke,* 118; Menzies, *Development of Early Christian Pneumatology,* 120; Tannehill, *Narrative Unity of Luke-Acts,* 1:39.

[69]Cf. Johnson, *Luke,* 56-57; Tannehill, *Narrative Unity of Luke-Acts,* 40-44. On Simeon's song, see Pierre Grelot, "La cantique de Siméon (Luc II, 29-32)," *Revue biblique* 93 (1986): 481-509.

[70]See Johnson, *Luke,* 57; Tannehill, *Narrative Unity of Luke-Acts,* 43-44.

[71]See below, chap. 4, on Acts 10-15.

habitué of the temple, who prays and fasts often (vv. 36-37; cf. 5:33; Acts 9:9; 13:3; 14:23).[72] The parallel with Simeon confirms her prophetic status.[73] Indeed, her message is similar: she "praised God" (v. 38, cf. v. 28) and spoke of Jerusalem's redemption.[74]

As with Zechariah, Elizabeth, and Mary, the words of Simeon are explicitly said to be inspired by the Spirit, while Anna is portrayed in prophetic terms, and is thus implicitly inspired by the Spirit. The presence of the Spirit with these human characters assures their reliability. Once again, Luke's mention of the Spirit, and the characterization of a human being as a prophet, serve to persuade the reader of the reliability of what these human characters are saying. In Simeon's case, the Spirit also clearly functions as an actor in the drama. Thus the character of the Spirit functions to provide narrative reliability.

Conclusion:
The Characterization of the Spirit in the Infancy Narrative

The reader of the infancy narrative is plunged into a semantic world which has an antique ring familiar to readers of the Septuagint. Thus the expectations the reader will form concerning the Spirit are largely those culled from the Old Testament: the Spirit inspires prophetic speech and produces miraculous events. In Hochman's terms, the characterization of the Spirit has a high degree of stylization and symbolism. One might also say that the literary environment of the character helps define it—the Septuagintal language leads us to expect a Septuagintal Spirit. The highly stylized

---

[72]On the combination of prayer and fasting in Jewish and Christian piety, see Jer 14:12; Neh 1:4; Matt 6:5, 16; *Joseph and Aseneth* 10:17-12:12; *Testament of Simeon* 2:12-3:4; Polycarp, *Philippians* 7:2; *2 Clement* 16:4; *Didache* 8:1-2; *Shepherd of Hermas* Vis. 2.2.1; 3.1.2; 3.10.6.

[73]Luke often pairs males and females. See Johnson, *Luke,* 56; Fitzmyer, *Luke,* 423.

[74]Johnson (*Luke,* 56) notes that "Israel" and "Jerusalem" are "symbolically synonymous" for Luke (cf. 2:32, 34).

Lukan language produces a highly stylized characterization of the Spirit.

On the discursive level, the Spirit functions to insure the narrative reliability of the prophetic figures found in these chapters. In effect, the Spirit stands in the background, content to tell us more about God and Jesus than itself. On the level of the story, this feature lends the character of the Spirit a certain degree of what Hochman calls opacity, simply because Luke's focus is elsewhere. The reader can only begin to guess why the Spirit acts in these ways, and to test these guesses against subsequent reading.

In the case of Simeon, however, the reliable narrator provides indirect characterization of the Spirit in the description of the Spirit's actions—actions that confirm Simeon's prophetic status (Luke 2:25-27). In this respect, the character of the Spirit gains a degree of transparency, as the purpose of the Spirit's actions is clearly shown as the narrative unfolds. It is clear that the Spirit leads Simeon to the temple so that Simeon may make prophetic testimony to Jesus. As we shall see, the Lukan characterization of the Spirit will move back and forth along the axis of transparency and opacity; sometimes it is clear what the Spirit is up to, sometimes not.

The apparent single-mindedness of the Spirit gives this character a high degree of coherence and simplicity, as well as a high degree of fragmentariness. The characterization is coherent, as the Spirit would seem to have one primary function: to inspire the speech and action of other characters, to make prophets of them. A secondary function of the Spirit is to announce and assist in the births of new prophets, John and Jesus; the generative function of the Spirit, though it receives only passing notice (Luke 1:35), does modify the apparent simplicity of the Lukan portrait of the Spirit. The limited scope of these functions lend the Spirit a fragmentary characterization, however, as if, in a human character, one were completely defined by an occupation.

The Spirit appears to have a great deal of what Hochman calls "dynamism." Indeed, the Spirit is highly active in these first two chapters, hard at work among the various prophetic figures. Luke shows the reader in these first few pages that this is a book about action—God's action, working through the Spirit.

Hochman's category "closure" is difficult to apply at this early stage of the narrative. However, since the Spirit is a prophetic

Spirit, and inspires prophecies of what is to come, it may be safe to assume that the characterization Luke is developing will be open-ended. The Spirit will continue to work within the narrative, and perhaps beyond narrative time. The reader must wait to see.

In Gowler's terms, the characterization of the Spirit is largely indirect. The Spirit is most often mentioned by the narrator, but what the reader learns is minimal: the Spirit fills, abides with, leads, and inspires the prophetic figures. We learn more about the Spirit from the reliable words of the angel Gabriel—but again indirectly, as what we learn has more to do with Jesus and John than the Spirit itself. We also learn about the Spirit indirectly from the words and actions of the characters it inspires, but once again the focus is not on the Spirit itself but on the message. Again, the nature of the prophetic Spirit is to inspire prophets to witness to God's action, not to draw attention to itself. It will become clear as the narrative proceeds that the Spirit speaks and acts not for itself, but for God.

In terms of plot, the focus in the infancy narrative has been on the birth of the prophetic figures John and Jesus, Jesus being the chief of the two. The Spirit functions to show that both these children are prophets, descended from a lineage of prophets. The narrative will now turn to focus on the prophet Jesus. We will pick up the story where it next mentions the Holy Spirit, at the baptism of Jesus.

Baptism by John (Luke 3:1-22)

Chapter Three of Luke provides a transition between the infancy narrative and the adult ministry of Jesus.[75] The focus is at first on

---

[75]On John the Baptist and Jesus' baptism in Luke 3, see Bovon, *Lukas,* 162-84; Brown, "'Water-Baptism' and 'Spirit-Baptism'"; Craddock, *Luke,* 46-50; Fitzmyer, *Luke,* 449-87; A. Feuillet, "Le Baptême de Jésus," *Revue biblique* 71 (1964): 321-52; Johnson, *Luke,* 63-72; L. E. Keck, "The Spirit and the Dove," *New Testament Studies* 17 (1970-71): 41-67; Marshall, *Luke,* 131-57; Menzies, *Development of Early Christian Pneumatology,* 135-54; Sabourin, *Luc,* 111-23; Schneider, *Lukas,* 80-93; Schürmann, *Lukasevangelium,* 147-98; Schweitzer, *Luke,* 69-81; Tannehill, *Narrative Unity,* 1:47-60; Wiefel, *Lukas,* 86-96; G. O. Williams, "The Baptism in Luke's Gospel," *Journal of Theological Studies* 45 (1944): 31-38; Walter Wink, *John the Baptist in the Gospel Tradition,* Society for New Testament Studies Monograph Series, vol. 7 (London: Cambridge University Press, 1968).

John the Baptist, who is carefully placed in context, both historically (3:1-2) and scripturally (v. 3-6). Again, Luke's language suggests that John is a prophet: the "word of God" comes to him (v. 2).[76] John's narrative reliability as prophet and forerunner of the Messiah is reinforced by Luke's quotation of Isaiah (v. 4-6); again, the use of biblical material assures the reader of reliability of this narrative and this character.[77]

John provides indirect characterization of the Spirit when he says of Jesus, "He will baptize you with the Holy Spirit and fire" (v. 16). This characterization temporarily lends opacity to the character of the Spirit, as it is not clear what John means by this statement until the coming of the Spirit on the disciples at Pentecost (Acts 2:1-4). As in the Pentecost scene, Luke links the "Holy Spirit" with "fire" (cf. Matt 3:11; contrast simply "Holy Spirit" in Mark 1:8). The "fire" symbolizes judgment in Luke 3:9 and 3:17, but Luke clearly connects it to Pentecost as well (Acts 2:3, 19; cf. 1:5 and 11:16).[78] John's use of the term $\beta\alpha\pi\tau\iota\zeta\omega$ here is metaphorical, and while it is more vivid than the other metaphors Luke uses to express the Spirit's agency (e.g., "come upon," "fall upon," "full of,"

---

[76]See Baer, *Heilige Geist in den Lukasschriften*, 46; Brawley, *Centering on God*, 174; Craddock, *Luke*, 46-47; Fitzmyer, *Luke*, 453; Hastings, *Prophet and Witness*, 60-62; Johnson, *Luke*, 67; Lampe, "Holy Spirit in Writings of Luke," 166-67; Marshall, *Luke*, 134-35; Sabourin, *Luc*, 113; Schürmann, *Lukasevangelium*, 149-53; Shelton, *Mighty in Word and Deed*, 38-39; Swete, *Holy Spirit in New Testament*, 12-19; Tannehill, *Narrative Unity of Luke-Acts*, 1:47-48.

[77]Moessner ("Ironic Fulfillment") disputes John's reliability along with that of the prophets of the infancy narrative; again, this view fails to take into account the complexities of the reading process. See above on Luke 1:5-25, 57-80.

[78]See Johnson, *Luke*, 66-67; cf. Brown, "'Water-Baptism' and 'Spirit-Baptism,'" 141-42; Craddock, *Luke*, 49; Fitzmyer, *Luke*, 473-74; Hull, *Holy Spirit in Acts*, 167; Menzies, *Development of Early Christian Pneumatology*, 135-45; Marshall, *Luke*, 146-48; Opsahl, *Holy Spirit in Life of Church*, 24-27; Sabourin, *Luc*, 116-18; Schürmann, *Lukasevangelium*, 171-77.

"anoint" etc.), it does not differ markedly in meaning.[79] The metaphor is particularly appropriate in light of the context: Jesus' baptism and anointing with the Spirit (Luke 3:21-22).[80] Again, the reliability of the prophet is confirmed by the subsequent fulfillment of the prophecy within Luke's narrative. The fulfillment of John's words is not limited to the Pentecost narrative, however. John's prophecy that a stronger one is coming is fulfilled immediately in the narrative by the story of the baptism of Jesus; the connection of Jesus and the Spirit is also affirmed (v. 21-22). Further, the promise of Spirit-baptism extends beyond Pentecost (cf. Acts 11:16; 19:4).[81]

The reliable narrator provides further indirect characterization of the Spirit in the description of Jesus' baptism. Here the Holy Spirit acts—the Spirit "descends" on Jesus from heaven as he prays (v. 21-22).[82] The description of the descent ($\kappa\alpha\tau\alpha\beta\alpha\acute{\iota}\nu\omega$) looks both forward and backward—backward, as the "Holy Spirit" (contrast simply "the Spirit" in Mark 1:10 and "the Spirit of God" in Matt 3:16) has already been active in the narrative, and forward, in reference to the effects of the anointing on Jesus (Luke 4:18; cf. Acts 10:38) and later the similar descent on the disciples (Acts 1:8).[83] The active construction, with the Spirit as the subject of the verb, is a rhetorical indication of the importance of this scene. Here the Spirit is presented as a direct actor, and not merely the subject of a future-tense verb (as in 1:35). The Spirit intervenes directly in the story.

Further, in an instance of indirect presentation of character on the basis of external appearance, the Spirit is described (albeit meta-

---

[79]See Turner, "Spirit Endowment in Luke-Acts."

[80]For the metaphorical use of $\beta\alpha\pi\tau\acute{\iota}\zeta\omega$ to refer to an overwhelming experience in Josephus, Philo, and other Hellenistic writers, see Turner, "Spirit Endowment in Luke-Acts," 50-53.

[81]See Tannehill, *Narrative Unity of Luke-Acts*, 1:51.

[82]The Holy Spirit is often linked with prayer in Luke-Acts; see Luke 10:21; 11:13; Acts 4:31; 8:15; 9:10-18; 10:9, 19; 10:46; 21:4-5.

[83]See Johnson, *Luke*, 69; cf. Tannehill, *Narrative Unity of Luke-Acts*, 1:57.

phorically) as "in bodily form like a dove."[84] Obviously, there is a great deal of opacity, fragmentariness, and symbolism in this description—unfortunately, the significance of a dove-like appearance is unclear.[85] But the whole scene is interpreted by the voice from heaven: it indicates divine approval of the Son of God (v. 22).[86] Once again, while the Spirit is indirectly characterized, the focus is not on the Spirit but on the Son. The descent of the Spirit will prove to be for Luke an empowering, guiding force for Jesus (cf. Luke 4:1, 14, 18). It serves further to confirm the reliability of Jesus, not

---

[84]Luke, in contrast to Mark and Matthew, emphasizes the physical reality of the event with the words σωματικῷ εἴδει (v. 22). On Luke's concern for physical manifestations of the Spirit, see Eduard Schweizer, "The Spirit of Power: The Uniformity and Diversity of the Concept of the Holy Spirit in the New Testament," trans. John Bright and Eugene Debor, *Interpretation* 6 (1952): 265-66.

[85]While the symbolic meaning of the dove cannot be determined precisely, possible Old Testament allusions are Gen 1:2; 8:8; and Deut 32:11; in Hellenistic literature birds are sometimes symbolic heralds of fate. See Craddock, *Luke*, 51; Fitzmyer, 483-84; Stephen Gero, "The Spirit as a Dove at the Baptism of Jesus," *Novum Testamentum* 18 (1976): 17-35; Johnson, *Luke*, 691; Keck, "The Spirit and the Dove"; Marshall, *Luke*, 153-54; Menzies, *Development of Early Christian Pneumatology*, 149-50; Sabourin, *Luc*, 120-22.

Johnson (*Luke*, 71), notes the structural similarities of this scene and the narratives of the annunciation (Luke 1:35) and the angel's song (2:14), and speculates that "the dove is the 'hovering' symbol that enables the reader's imagination to pull these elements into a single focus." The further connection of this baptismal scene to the coming of the Spirit on the disciples at Pentecost could also be noted. At each point the Holy Spirit is the assurance of divine guidance and narrative reliability.

[86]There is little to commend an adoptionistic reading of Luke's Christology here. The descent of the Spirit inaugurates Jesus' ministry, not his messiahship. See Menzies, *Development of Early Christian Pneumatology*, 151-54; cf. Barrett, *Holy Spirit and Gospel Tradition*, 25-45; Lampe, "Holy Spirit in Writings of Luke," 168; Minear, *To Heal and to Reveal*, 46; Sabourin, *Luc*, 122-23; Swete, *Holy Spirit in New Testament*, 40-48; Talbert, *Literary Patterns*, 116-18; idem, *Reading Luke*, 41.

The issue of whether Jesus' baptismal initiation into ministry forms a parallel with the experience of the early Christians is discussed in depth by Turner, "Luke and the Spirit" and "Jesus and the Spirit," in reaction against Dunn, *Baptism in the Holy Spirit*.

just as prophet, but as Son of God.

Luke continues to characterize the Spirit as the Spirit of prophecy. John the Baptist is characterized by the narrator as one to whom the word of God came, and thus as a prophet. Jesus is directly connected to the Holy Spirit by the reliable commentator John. Luke also pictures the Spirit acting directly, bringing prophetic anointing to Jesus. In one of the few instances where Luke attributes an external appearance to the Spirit, the narrator gives a metaphorical description of the Spirit as a "dove"; this is unfortunately also an instance of what Hochman would call "opacity," since it opens a gap which can never be filled with certainty. However uncertain the details here, Luke clearly is still working within the prophetic framework developed in the infancy narrative—the characterization of the Spirit is highly stylized and symbolic, coherent, simple, fragmentary, and dynamic.

The plot now focuses on the beginning of the prophetic ministry of Jesus. His baptism inaugurates the ministry proper. But before he begins his public ministry, he must undergo a test. At every step, he is guided by the Spirit.

Temptation (Luke 4:1-15)

The Temptation narrative is framed by references to the Spirit.[87] Jesus is described as "full of the Holy Spirit" (Luke 4:1), an

---

[87]On the temptation, see Bovon, *Lukas,* 191-204; Craddock, *Luke,* 54-58; Fitzmyer, *Luke,* 506-20; A. Feuillet, "Le récit lucanien de la tentation (Lc 4, 1-13)," *Biblica* 40 (1959): 613-31; Susan R. Garrett, *The Demise of the Devil: Magic and the Demonic in Luke's Writings* (Minneapolis: Fortress Press, 1989), 38-43; Johnson, *Luke,* 73-77; J. Andrew Kirk, "The Messianic Role of Jesus and the Temptation Narrative: A Contemporary Perspective," *Evangelical Quarterly* 44 (1972): 11-29, 91-102; Marshall, *Luke,* 165-74; Menzies, *Development of Early Christian Pneumatology,* 154-61; Petr Pokorný, "The Temptation Stories and Their Intention," *New Testament Studies* 20 (1973-1974): 115-27; Sabourin, *Luc,* 124-29; Schneider, *Lukas,* 98-102; Schürmann, *Lukasevangelium,* 204-20; Schweitzer, *Luke,* 81-84; Hamish Swanston, "The Lukan Temptation Narrative," *Journal of Theological Studies,* n.s. 17 (1966): 71; Tannehill, *Narrative Unity,* 1:59-60; Arch. B. Taylor, Jr., "Decision in the Desert: The Temptation of Jesus in the Light of Deuteronomy," *Interpretation* 14 (1960): 300-309; Wiefel, *Lukas,* 98-102.

expression which reminds the reader of the baptism (Luke 3:22). The phrase connects Jesus both forward and backward with other prophetic figures—forward, as the disciples will be described as πλήρης πνεύματος ἀγίου (Acts 6:5; 7:55; 11:24; cf. Acts 6:3, πλήρεις πνεύματος); backward, as the similar expression ἐπλήσθη πνεύματος ἀγίου has been used of John, Elizabeth, and Zechariah (Luke 1:15, 41, 67).[88] Luke's telling of a story about forty days in the wilderness makes further backward connections to stories of the prophets Moses and Elijah (Exod 34:28; 1 Kgs 19:8).[89] Jesus is being indirectly characterized as a prophet; the Spirit, as a prophetic Spirit. The description sets the tone for the rest of Luke's Gospel, where the focus is on Jesus the Spirit-filled prophet.[90]

Jesus is further described as "led by the Spirit in the wilderness."[91] Again, the description places Jesus within the prophetic tradition.[92] Both Jesus and the Spirit are indirectly characterized by means of the action of a character—the action of the Spirit, here expressed in the passive voice. The focus again is on Jesus (thus the

---

[88]Cf. Johnson, *Luke*, 73; Menzies, *Development of Early Christian Pneumatology*, 155-56.

[89]See Craddock, *Luke*, 54; Johnson, *Luke*, 76; Schürmann, *Lukasevangelium*, 207.

[90]The influential contention of Conzelmann (*Theology of St. Luke*, 179-84, following Baer, *Heilige Geist in den Lukasschriften*, 77-84) that only Jesus is given the Spirit during his ministry is not entirely convincing, as the disciples are characterized as at least prophets-in-waiting (cf. Luke 9:1-6; 10:1-12, 17-20; see Turner, "Jesus and the Spirit," 32-33; idem, "Luke and the Spirit," 98-116). However, Luke's exclusive association of the expression "the Holy Spirit" with "Jesus" is a rhetorical device that helps point the reader to the centrality of Jesus as prophet.

[91]Or, noting the imperfect tense of ἄγω, "was being led by the Spirit in the wilderness," indicating the Spirit's continual guidance during the forty days. See Fitzmyer, *Luke*, 513.

[92]Cf. the Spirit's guidance of Simeon (Luke 2:27), Philip (Acts 8:39), Peter (Acts 10:19-20), and Paul (Acts 16:6-7). See Menzies, *Development of Early Christian Pneumatology*, 157.

passive voice), who is characterized as continually under divine guidance; the expression ἤγετο ἐν τῷ πνεύματι in conjunction with πλήρης πνεύματος ἁγίου gives the reader clues about the eventual outcome of the temptation story. The Spirit is indirectly characterized by its own action as a Spirit of prophetic guidance. The presence of the Spirit on Jesus, so clearly emphasized in this passage, establishes Jesus as the primary source of reliable information in the narrative which follows. No other character will have quite the credibility of Jesus, and no other words—not even those of the narrator—will carry such weight.

This passage also provides an illustration of another method of indirect presentation of character: comparison and contrast with other characters.[93] The Spirit is characterized by contrast with another character, the devil. The Spirit "was leading" Jesus (ἄγω, Luke 4:1). This expression stands in ironic contrast to later statements that the devil "led" Jesus (ἀνάγω, Luke 4:5; ἄγω, v. 9). The devil ultimately leads Jesus nowhere; Luke clearly states that Jesus finished the temptation in the power of the Spirit (Luke 4:14). Similarly, other enemies will attempt to lead him to his death (Luke 4:29; 22:54; 23:1), but their success is limited, because Jesus is led beyond death in the power of the Spirit (cf. Luke 24:44-49).[94] The Spirit is thus characterized as the power that truly leads Jesus, in contrast with the devil and other enemies of Jesus.[95]

At the end of the temptation narrative, the reliable narrator says that "Jesus returned in the power of the Spirit" (Luke 4:14). The reference to the Spirit forms an *inclusio* around the temptation story, and confirms for the reader the positive outcome of the story.[96] It also points ahead to the application of Isaiah 61:1 to Jesus (Luke

---

[93]See Gowler, *Host, Guest, Enemy and Friend*, 73.

[94]On the connection between Jesus' temptation and resurrection as victories over Satan, see Garrett, *Demise of the Devil*.

[95]Cf. Craddock, *Luke*, 55; Tannehill, *Narrative Unity of Luke-Acts*, 1:59.

[96]Note the similar connection of the Holy Spirit, power, and victory over the devil in Acts 10:38.

4:18).[97] "Power," δύναμις, is often associated with the Spirit by Luke, usually in terms of miracles (Luke 4:36; 5:17; 6:19; 8:46; 10:13, 19; 19:37; Acts 2:22; 10:38), but here simply in terms of Jesus' preaching (Luke 4:15; cf. 9:1-2; Acts 1:8; 4:33). The expression helps connect Jesus back to the prophetic figures of the infancy narrative, John and Mary (Luke 1:17, 35). It also points forward to similar power among the disciples (Luke 9:1; 10:19; 24:49; Acts 1:8; 3:12; 4:7-8, 33; 6:8; 8:13; 19:11). Further, δύναμις has eschatological overtones—the power of the Spirit manifested in Jesus signals a new beginning (cf. Luke 21:27; 22:69). Here again, the primary focus on Jesus as the Spirit-empowered prophet serves secondarily to characterize the Spirit who makes that power possible.[98]

To pause and summarize Luke's characterization of the Spirit thus far, up to and including the temptation narrative: the Holy Spirit is clearly portrayed as a character in Luke-Acts. It acts decisively and directly, leading the prophetic figures of the narrative; the primary beneficiary of these actions is Jesus, who himself is characterized by association with the Holy Spirit. The Spirit's actions lead into conflict with the demonic forces that oppose God's plan, as demonstrated by the temptation narrative. Thus, in the first four chapters of Luke, the Spirit is portrayed as an actor in conflict with other actors—in short, the Spirit is portrayed as a character in the narrative.

The Spirit has been in Gowler's terms indirectly characterized by the speech of the reliable narrator and other characters, by its own actions, by description, by (metaphorical) description of appearance, and by comparison with other characters. Also, the Spirit is characterized by its environment—it is at work among the people and prophets of Israel. There has been no hint of what Gowler would

---

[97]Johnson, *Luke,* 78.

[98]On Luke's connection between δύναμις and πνεῦμα, see Barrett, *Holy Spirit and Gospel Tradition,* 76-77; Bruce, "Holy Spirit in Acts," 169; Conzelmann, *Theology of St. Luke,* 182-83; Menzies, *Development of Early Christian Pneumatology,* 125-28; Schweizer, "Spirit of Power"; Shelton, *Mighty in Word and Deed,* 75-77.

call "direct characterization," i.e., a statement by the narrator or another character that "the Holy Spirit is..."; but since Luke's focus is obviously on the prophets who are inspired by the Spirit rather than the Spirit itself, this poses no surprise—indeed, the function of the Spirit for Luke is to inspire testimony about and by Jesus, rather than itself. The character of the Spirit serves primarily to establish the characterization of the primary figure in the narrative, Jesus. The characterization of the Spirit thus stands behind that of Jesus; to characterize the Spirit is ultimately to characterize Jesus. The Spirit-empowerment of Jesus places him within the prophetic tradition and confirms his pre-eminent place in the narrative.

In Hochman's terms, the presentation of the Spirit is highly stylized and symbolic—the Spirit is presented in essentially Old Testament terms, with little development. The portrait of the Spirit may also be said to be fragmentary, in that it is seen almost exclusively in prophetic terms; the Lukan focus on Jesus accounts for this fragmentariness. The Spirit as character is fairly coherent, simple, and transparent, as the function of the Spirit's actions are clear, and will be clarified further in the subsequent narrative. The Spirit as an active force in the narrative can be said to be dynamic. Certainly at this point of the story, Luke's characterization of the Spirit is quite open-ended. Luke has already, in these first few chapters, set the basic outlines of the characterization of the Spirit. The reader can expect to see much of the same as the narrative moves along.

Nazareth (Luke 4:16-30)

Luke's summary statement (Luke 4:14-15) both rounds off the previous section and begins a new one: we now turn to Jesus' ministry proper.[99] The episode in the Nazareth synagogue[100] is program-

---

[99]Craddock, *Luke,* 59-60; Fitzmyer, *Luke,* 521-22; Johnson, *Luke,* 78.

[100]On the Nazareth episode, see Hugh Anderson, "The Rejection at Nazareth Pericope of Luke 4:16-30 in Light of Recent Critical Trends," *Interpretation* 18 (1964): 259-75; J. Bajard, "La structure de la pericope de Nazareth en Lc iv. 16-30," *Ephemerides Theologicae Lovanienses* 45 (1969): 165-71; Bovon, *Lukas,* 204-16; Craddock, *Luke,* 61-64; Fitzmyer, *Luke,* 525-40; F. Gils, *Jésus prophète d'apres les évangiles synoptiques,* Orientalia et Biblica Lovaniensia (Louvain:

matic for Luke; the themes that will characterize Jesus' mission—prophetic anointing, ministry to the lowly, division among the people, rejection—are presented here in a close-knit, dynamic form.[101] Jesus places himself within the prophetic tradition by announcing, in the words of Isaiah, that "the Spirit of the Lord is upon me, because he has anointed me" (Luke 4:18). He proclaims a ministry to the poor, the captive, the blind, and the oppressed (vv. 18-19). The words "proclaim the year of the Lord's favor" (v. 19) echo the ancient traditions about the year of Jubilee, in which all debts are canceled (Luke 4:19; cf. Lev 25:8-12; 11Q Melchizedek).[102] Yet the response to him among his fellow citizens, mixed at first, takes a dark, foreboding turn.

Jesus characterizes himself directly, via his reading of Isaiah 61:1, as a Spirit-anointed prophetic figure (Luke 4:18-19, cf. v. 21).[103] Jesus is not only prophet, but is in fact a literal Christ,

---

Publications Universitaires, 1957); Johnson, *Luke*, 77-82; Marshall, *Luke*, 173-90; Menzies, *Development of Early Christian Pneumatology*, 161-77; Sabourin, *Luc*, 130-36; Schneider, *Lukas*, 103-12; Schürmann, *Lukasevangelium*, 204-16; Schweitzer, *Luke*, 84-96; Siker, "First to the Gentiles"; Tannehill, *Narrative Unity*, 1:60-73; Tiede, *Prophecy and History*, 19-55; Wiefel, *Lukas*, 103-7.

[101]Luke has relocated this episode, which occurs later in Jesus' ministry in Mark and Matthew. The relocation is due to the programmatic nature of the scene for Luke; it sets the stage for all that is to follow: "this event announces who Jesus is, of what his ministry consists, what his church will be and do, and what will be the response to both Jesus and the church" (Craddock, *Luke*, 61).

[102]See Turner, "Jesus and the Spirit," 14-22. Cf. Craddock, *Luke*, 62; Fitzmyer, *Luke*, 533; Johnson, *Luke*, 81; Marshall, *Luke*, 184; Sabourin, *Luc*, 133-34; Schürmann, *Lukasevangelium*, 230-31.

[103]The quotation from Isaiah is not found in Mark or Matthew; clearly Luke is presenting in dramatic form what he believes to be true—that Jesus is a prophetic Messiah, a modern "servant of the Lord" in fulfillment of prophecy. Luke's citation is rather free and contains elements of Isa 61:1, 58:6, and 61:2 LXX. See Fitzmyer, *Luke*, 528; Johnson, *Luke*, 81; Marshall, *Luke*, 182-84; Menzies, *Development of Early Christian Pneumatology*, 163-77; Sabourin, *Luc*, 133-34; Schürmann, *Lukasevangelium*, 229-30.

having been "anointed" ($\chi\rho\iota\omega$) at his baptism (3:21-22).[104] Isaiah's parallel clauses emphasize a mission among the poor and downtrodden, and Jesus' speech gives it an eschatological turn: "Today this scripture has been fulfilled in your hearing."[105] Yet this eschatological Jubilee year is not centered on economic reform; Jesus defines his liberating mission in terms of proclamation and deliverance. The direct self-characterization of Jesus provides indirect characterization of the Spirit as well—the Spirit which anointed Jesus is the kind of Spirit who enables proclamation and deliverance. The coherence and transparency of the character of the Spirit is enhanced in this passage, as it presents a single-minded, clear, and purposeful Jesus who is motivated by the Spirit.

Jesus and the Spirit are also indirectly characterized by contrast with the people of Nazareth. They, unlike Jesus, are double-minded; they "speak well of him"[106] and are "amazed" (Luke 4:22), yet turn against him when he intimates that God's favor is neither limited to nor assured by one's lineage (vv. 23-30).[107] Jesus' speech about the prophets Elijah and Elisha, not found in Mark or Matthew, provides reliable commentary on the significance of the preaching and rejection at Nazareth. Luke presents only the words of Jesus in Luke 4:23-25 as the cause of the peoples' turn to wrath, and in both of the Old Testament stories Jesus cites, the prophets bestow God's favor on non-Jews (the widow of Zarephath, 1 Kgs 17:8-14; Naaman, 2 Kgs 5:1-17) rather than Jews. As the sayings in v. 23 indicate, the message came too close to home. The people are

---

[104]Johnson, *Luke*, 79; Marshall, *Luke*, 183; Schürmann, *Lukasevangelium*, 229; Tannehill, *Narrative Unity of Luke-Acts*, 1:63. Contra Fitzmyer, *Luke*, 529-30, who sees only prophetic and not messianic anointing here.

[105]Cf. Tannehill, *Narrative Unity of Luke-Acts*, 1:64-68.

[106]The irony of Luke's choice of $\mu\alpha\rho\tau\upsilon\rho\epsilon\omega$ here becomes apparent in Acts, where the word is used positively—of the prophet's witness to Jesus in scripture (Acts 10:43), of Paul's witness (Acts 23:11), and of God's witness to Jesus and the apostles (Acts 14:3; 15:8).

[107]See Craddock, *Luke*, 63; Johnson, *Luke*, 81-82; Siker, "First to the Gentiles"; Tannehill, *Narrative Unity of Luke-Acts*, 1:68-73.

enraged by the hint that God will work among foreigners. In stark contrast to the Spirit-led Jesus, their rage leads them not to liberation but to murder (v. 29). The inverse stoning (hurling the person against the stones rather than the stones against the person) parodies Torah, and reinforces the irony of the people who are unable to recognize the predicted prophet and Messiah among them.[108] The division and rejection at Nazareth foreshadows the fate of Jesus and his disciples in the rest of Luke-Acts.[109]

Luke has now established the basic plot-function of the Holy Spirit in the narrative. Having set the stage for Jesus' earthly ministry, Luke omits further mention of the Spirit during most of the rest of the Gospel, for there is little need to remind the reader of the relationship between Jesus and Spirit. There are, however, a few references to the Spirit in the remainder of the Gospel, and they are important, as they cast new light on Luke's characterization of the Spirit.

The Seventy(-Two) (Luke 10:1-24)

Only Luke recounts the mission of the seventy(-two)[110] in hostile Samaria (cf. Luke 9:53), in parallel with the earlier mission of the twelve (Luke 9:1-11; cf. Mark 6:7-13; Matt 10:1-42).[111] Jesus, like

---

[108]Cf. Craddock, *Luke*, 63-64.

[109]See Craddock, *Luke*, 64; Johnson, *Luke*, 81-82.

[110]The text-critical problem of the number of disciples Jesus sends in Luke 10:1 is virtually insoluble; the evidence for the readings "seventy" and "seventy-two" is almost evenly divided. See Johnson, *Luke*, 167; Fitzmyer, *Luke*, 845-46; Marshall, *Luke*, 414-15; Metzger, *Textual Commentary*, 150; idem, "Seventy or Seventy-Two Disciples?" *New Testament Studies* 5 (1958-59): 299-306; Sabourin, *Luc*, 220.

[111]On Luke 10:1-24, see Craddock, *Luke*, 144-48; Fitzmyer, *Luke*, 843-76; Johnson, *Luke*, 166-71; Marshall, *Luke*, 412-39; Menzies, *Development of Early Christian Pneumatology*, 178-80; Sabourin, *Luc*, 218-24; Schneider, *Lukas*, 234-45; Schweitzer, *Luke*, 172-84; Tannehill, *Narrative Unity*, 1:232-37; Wiefel, *Lukas*, 194-206.

Moses (Num 11:16-25),[112] extends his prophetic mission through these disciples, who are commanded to prepare cities for Jesus' arrival by doing as he has done—healing and preaching (Luke 10:9); the mission of the seventy(-two) previews the mission in Acts.[113] When the seventy(-two) return with joy, proclaiming their victory over demonic forces, Jesus speaks apocalyptically of the fall of Satan (10:17-20).[114] By contrast, Jesus clearly works in the power of the Holy Spirit, who is the source of Jesus' own joy (Luke 10:21).[115] Again, as in the temptation narrative, Jesus is indirectly characterized by the contrast between Satan and the Holy Spirit, a contrast central to Luke's story.[116]

The Holy Spirit is indirectly characterized as the source of joy. Luke first associates the Spirit and joy when he describes the Spirit-filled John as leaping for joy (Luke 1:44, cf. 1:15) in the womb,

---

[112]This may be one of many allusive comparisons between Jesus and Moses, who chose seventy (or seventy-two, if one includes Eldad and Medad from Num 11:26) elders to help him; see Garrett, *Demise of the Devil*, 47-48; Johnson, *Luke*, 167. Cf. the allusion to Numbers 11 in Luke 9:49-50. Craddock (*Luke*, 144) and Tannehill (*Narrative Unity of Luke-Acts*, 1:223) see here a reference not to the prophet-like-Moses, but to the seventy(-two) nations of Genesis 10, and thus to the future Gentile mission. Both allusions are possible, however.

[113]See Tannehill, *Narrative Unity of Luke-Acts*, 1:233-37.

[114]See Garrett, *Demise of the Devil*, 46-57.

[115]Some manuscripts omit τῷ ἁγίῳ, implying that the reference may be to Jesus' human spirit (cf. Luke 1:47). But "the Holy Spirit" is better attested and also the more difficult reading, as the strange expression "rejoiced in the Holy Spirit" has no other parallel. The preposition ἐν, absent from many early manuscripts, often follows ἀγαλλιάω in the Septuagint; its absence would not change the meaning. See Fitzmyer, *Luke*, 871; Menzies, *Development of Early Christian Pneumatology*, 178; Marshall, *Luke*, 432-33; Metzger, *Textual Commentary*, 152.

[116]Cf. Garrett, *Demise of the Devil*, 58: "The struggle between Jesus (or the Holy Spirit) and Satan lies at the very heart of Luke's story." For a similar view see Jack Dean Kingsbury, *Conflict in Luke* (Philadelphia: Fortress Press, 1991), 2, 11-14.

prompting Elizabeth to be "filled with the Holy Spirit" (1:41).[117] The Spirit will be associated with the joy of the disciples as well (Acts 13:52). The joy sparked by the Spirit underscores the presence of the Spirit among the seventy(-two) disciples.[118] Here, the connection of the Spirit and joy is much more direct and explicit, since the expression ἐν τῷ πνεύματι τῷ ἁγίῳ means "under the influence of (or guided by) the Holy Spirit," as in Luke 2:27.[119] The words of the reliable narrator imply action on the Spirit's part—the Spirit gives joy to Jesus. The narrator's statement diminishes the fragmentariness and simplicity of Luke's portrait of the Spirit, as the Spirit is given a new dimension of action. Though the expression in Luke 10:21 is unusual, it does not provide a true break from stylization, as the connection of the Spirit and joy is traditional.[120]

In addition, the Spirit is once again connected with prayer.[121] In

---

[117]See Shelton, *Mighty in Word and Deed*, 17-18. One might argue that the Holy Spirit and joy are directly associated in Luke 1:47, ἠγαλλίασεν τὸ πνεῦμά μου, but that reference would seem to be to Mary's human spirit; certainly, however, there is an indirect association, as Mary is a Spirit-inspired prophet.

[118]As Turner ("Luke and the Spirit," 88) notes, contra Baer, *Heilige Geist in den Lukasschriften*, 77-84; Conzelmann, *Theology of St. Luke*, 179-84; Menzies, *Development of Early Christian Pneumatology*, 182; and Tannehill, *Narrative Unity of Luke-Acts*, 1:239; see above, n. 90).

[119]See Fitzmyer, *Luke*, 871; Johnson, *Luke*, 169. The verb ἀγαλλιάω and noun ἀγαλλίασις are characteristic of Luke, and usually are associated with words of praise to God. Cf. Luke 1:14; 44, 47; Acts 2:26, 46; 16:34. See Lampe, "Holy Spirit in Writings of Luke," 165; Menzies, *Development of Early Christian Pneumatology*, 179-80.

[120]Cf. Ps 50:13-14 LXX, and the rabbinic expression, "the Holy Spirit rests only on a joyful man" (*y. Sukk.* 5.55a, 54; cited in Menzies, *Development of Early Christian Pneumatology*, 180).

[121]See Bovon, *Luke the Theologian*, 206-9, 235; Conzelman, *Theology of St. Luke*, 180; Fitzmyer, *Luke*, 868-70; Hastings, *Prophet and Witness*, 76-97; Lampe, "Holy Spirit in Writings of Luke," 169; Menzies, *Development of Early Christian Pneumatology*, 179-80; Stephen S. Smalley, "Spirit, Kingdom and Prayer in Luke-Acts," *Novum Testamentum* 15 (1973): 59-71; Schweizer, *The Holy Spirit*, 76; Talbert, *Reading Luke*, 41.

contrast to the baptismal scene, in which the coming of the Spirit seems to be in response to Jesus' prayer (Luke 3:21-22), here the Spirit is depicted as inspiring prayer.[122] Jesus' joy sparks him to praise the Father in a prayer that elucidates the relationship of Father, Son, and the divine mission. Again the Spirit is given a new locus of action, the inspiration of human prayer—though as a form of inspired speech, this function could be said to be an extension of the Spirit's previous action.[123] Again, this is very much an indirect characterization of the Spirit, as the focus is not on the fact of the Spirit's inspiration, but on how Jesus' inspired and reliable words comment on the narrative. The Spirit will be further related to prayer as Luke's story proceeds.

Luke's characterization of the Spirit continues to move along the same lines as before. The Spirit is indirectly characterized, by association and by contrast. The fragmentariness and simplicity of this characterization has been somewhat diminished by two new connections: the Spirit is the source of joy, and the Spirit prompts yet another form of inspired speech, prayer. The character of the Spirit remains highly stylized, symbolic, coherent, transparent, dynamic, and open-ended.

As in the two following sections, Jesus is on a slow journey to his death in Jerusalem (9:51-19:27). The plot allows him time to dispute with the Jewish leaders, teach the people publicly, and instruct the disciples privately.[124] The reader has been (and will be) given ample hints of what awaits Jesus in Jerusalem (cf. Luke 9:22; 9:57-62; 10:16; 11:14-23, 53-54). Yet the reader also knows that Jesus has been and still is led by the Spirit.

---

[122]Contra Schweizer (in *Theological Dictionary of the New Testament* 6:412), the Spirit often inspires prayer and praise in Luke-Acts. Cf. Luke 1:35, 46, 67; 2:26-28; Acts 2:4, 11, 47; 10:44-46. See Shelton, *Mighty in Word and Deed*, 86.

[123]Menzies, *Development of Early Christian Pneumatology*, 179-80, sees Jesus' prayer as a facet of prophetic activity (cf. Mary in Luke 1:35, 47, and David in Acts 2:25, 30).

[124]See Johnson, *Luke*, 164-65.

Teaching on Prayer (Luke 11:1-13)

While Jesus is praying, his disciples ask that he teach them to pray.[125] Jesus responds with the Lord's Prayer, a parable, and a series of sayings on prayer; the teaching on prayer, with the appropriate setting, is one of a number of didactic sections woven into the Lukan travel narrative (9:51-19:27).[126] The final saying in this section concerns the Holy Spirit: "If you then, who are evil, know how to give good gifts to your children, how much more will the heavenly Father give the Holy Spirit to those who ask him?" (Luke 11:13).[127] This is the first of several sayings of Jesus con-

---

[125]On Luke 11:1-13, see Raymond E. Brown, "The Pater Noster as Eschatological Prayer," in *New Testament Essays* (Milwaukee: Bruce, 1965), 217-53; Craddock, *Luke*, 153-54; Peter Edmonds, "The Lucan Our Father: A Summary of Lucan Teaching on Prayer?" *Expository Times* 91 (1979-80): 140-43; Fitzmyer, *Luke*, 896-916; Johnson, *Luke*, 176-80; Marshall, *Luke*, 454-70; Menzies, *Development of Early Christian Pneumatology*, 180-85; Sabourin, *Luc*, 229-33; Schneider, *Lukas*, 255-64; Schweitzer, *Luke*, 190-93; Tannehill, *Narrative Unity*, 1:237-40; Wiefel, *Lukas*, 213-18.

[126]See Johnson, *Luke*, 179. There is little doubt that the variant in 11:2, ἐλθέτω τὸ πνεῦμα σου τὸ ἅγιον ἐφ᾽ ἡμᾶς καὶ καθαρισάτω ἡμᾶς, is secondary, as the manuscript evidence for it is quite weak. See Menzies, *Development of Early Christian Pneumatology*, 180-81; Jean Magne, "La réception de la variante 'Vienne ton esprit sur nous et qu'il nous purifie' (Lc 11, 2) et l'origine des épiclèses, du baptéme et du 'Notre Pere,'" *Ephemerides Liturgicae* 102 (1988): 81-106; Marshall, *Luke*, 458; Metzger, *Textual Commentary*, 156; Gerhard Schneider, "Die Bitte um das Kommen des Geistes im lukanischen Vaterunser (Lk 11, 2 v.l.)," in *Studien zum Text und zur Ethink des Neuen Testaments*, edited by Wolfgang Schrage (Berlin: Walter de Gruyter, 1986), 344-73.

[127]Some manuscripts allow ἐξ οὐρανοῦ to be taken with πνεῦμα ἅγιον rather than ὁ πατήρ, the difference being the absence of the article (ἐξ οὐρανοῦ as opposed to ὁ ἐξ οὐρανοῦ). The evidence is evenly divided between the two readings. See Fitzmyer, *Luke*, 915; Marshall, *Luke*, 469-70; Metzger, *Textual Commentary*, 157-58. Johnson (*Luke*, 178) cites Luke 3:21-22; Acts 1:8; 2:33; and 10:44 as support for the reading "Holy Spirit from heaven," contra NRSV, Fitzmyer.

Matt 7:11 also reads ἀγαθά rather than πνεῦμα ἅγιον, and this is reflected in the transmission of Luke's text. Luke's emphasis on the Holy Spirit accounts for his original reading πνεῦμα ἅγιον, which is strongly attested. See Fitzmyer, *Luke*, 913-16; Johnson, *Luke*, 178-79; Menzies, *Development of Early Christian Pneumatology*, 181; Metzger, *Textual Commentary*, 158.

cerning the Holy Spirit;[128] it introduces new dimensions to the characterization of the Holy Spirit, as now Jesus, a reliable commentator in Luke's narrative, offers his own teaching about the Spirit. Yet this is still indirect characterization of the Spirit, albeit with great specificity and a high degree of reliability; there is no direct characterization here (Jesus does not say, "The Holy Spirit is like this..."). Further, the main focus is still elsewhere: Jesus' lesser-to-greater argument primarily (though again indirectly) characterizes a caring, providential Father.

Jesus indirectly characterizes the Spirit as the promised gift of the Father. That God gives the Spirit is a common Lukan theme (cf. Luke 24:49; Acts 1:4, 5, 8; 2:38; 8:20; 10:45; 11:17; 15:8).[129] Jesus' teaching makes explicit what the reader has already seen in the baptism narrative: the Spirit descends from heaven (Luke 3:21-22). The ability to give the Spirit will later extend to the apostles (Acts 8:18). Luke continues to characterize the Spirit along traditional lines—the Holy Spirit is a gift from God (Cf. Num 11:24-30; 24:2; Ps 51:11 (50:13 LXX); Isa 63:10f; Sir 48:12 (Codex A); Sus 45 (Theod.)).[130]

---

[128]As Tannehill (*Narrative Unity of Luke-Acts,* 1:238) notes, "There is an unusual concentration of references to God as Father and to the Holy Spirit in 10:21-12:32." Tannehill sees this as a way of emphasizing "the special relation of the disciples to God as Father through Jesus."

[129]John Borremans, "The Holy Spirit in Luke's Evangelical Catechesis. A Guide to Proclaiming Jesus Christ in a Secular World," *Lumen Vitae* 25 (1970): 284; Thomas Marsh, "Holy Spirit in Early Christian Teaching," *Irish Theological Quarterly* 45 (1978): 103-5; Marshall, "Significance of Pentecost," 365; Schweizer, *The Holy Spirit,* 75; idem in *Theological Dictionary of New Testament,* 6:410; Turner, "Luke and the Spirit," 35.

Luke often uses the verbs δίδωμι, λαμβάνω and the noun δωρεά in connection with the Holy Spirit (Acts 2:33, 38; 5:32; 8:15-20; 10:45; 11:17). He also speaks of it coming or falling on people (Luke 1:35; 3:22; 24:49; Acts 1:8; 10:44; 19:6). See Turner, "Luke and the Spirit," 35.

[130]Kirsopp Lake, "The Holy Spirit," 96-98; cf. Haya-Prats, *L'Esprit,* 22-23; Schweizer, *Holy Spirit,* 126.

Jesus also indirectly characterizes the Spirit as one given in response to prayer. Again, this view of the Spirit draws on Old Testament precedents (Num 11:29; Ps 51:11). The reader has already seen that Jesus' own reception of the Spirit at baptism came during prayer (3:21-22). This will prove to be the case for others as well (Acts 1:14 with 2:1-4; 2:21 with 2:38; 4:31; 8:15; 9:11, 17; 22:16).[131] Here again is an example of literary prophecy within Luke's narrative—what a reliable commentator says will happen, will happen.[132]

Courage (Luke 12:1-12)

After a series of controversies with scribes and Pharisees, Jesus addresses the disciples on the issue of opposition.[133] With danger of

---

[131]Talbert, *Reading Luke*, 41; cf. C. K. Barrett, "Light on the Holy Spirit from Simon Magus (Acts 8, 4-25)," in *Les Actes des Apôtres: traditions, rédaction, théologie*, ed. J. Kremer, Bibliotheca Ephemeridum Theologicarum Lovaniensium, vol. 48 (Gembloux: Leuven University Press, 1979), 295; Bovon, *Luke the Theologian*, 235; Dunn, *Baptism in the Holy Spirit*, 33; Menzies, *Development of Early Christian Pneumatology*, 185; Schweizer in *Theological Dictionary of New Testament*, 6:414; Shelton, *Mighty in Word and Deed*, 93; Smalley, "Spirit, Kingdom and Prayer," 61-62; Tannehill, *Narrative Unity of Luke-Acts*, 1:239-40.

As Tannehill (*Narrative Unity of Luke-Acts*, 1:239) notes, there is also here a subtle anticipation of what becomes clear in the next saying on the Holy Spirit: the Spirit gives strength against opposition when needed (Luke 12:11-12). The Spirit thus is an answer to the petition concerning testing (11:4).

[132]Cf. Menzies, *Development of Early Christian Pneumatology*, 182: "the saying anticipates the post-resurrection experience of the church."

[133]On Luke 12:1-12, see M. Eugene Boring, "The Unforgivable Sin Logion, Mark III 28-29/Matt XII 31-32/Luke XII 10: Formal Analysis and History of the Tradition," *Novum Testamentum* 18 (1976): 258-79; Craddock, *Luke*, 160-62; Fitzmyer, *Luke*, 953-67; Johnson, *Luke*, 193-97; Marshall, *Luke*, 508-21; Menzies, *Development of Early Christian Pneumatology*, 190-98; Sabourin, *Luc*, 244-47; Schneider, *Lukas*, 276-80; Schweitzer, *Luke*, 202-6; Tannehill, *Narrative Unity*, 1:240-46; Wiefel, *Lukas*, 230-35; Hans-Theo Wrege, "Zur Rolle des Geisteswortes in frühchristlichen Traditionen (LC 12, 10 parr.)," in *Logia: les paroles de Jésus—The Sayings of Jesus*, ed. Joël Delobel, Bibliotheca Ephemeridum Theologicarum Lovaniensium, vol. 59 (Leuven: Leuven University

his own lurking in the background (Luke 11:53), Jesus speaks of the "leaven of the Pharisees" (Luke 12:1-3) and tells the disciples neither to fear human authority (12:4-7) nor to be anxious before them when they defend themselves (12:11). In this context come the sayings about acknowledging the Son of Man (12:8-9), the blasphemy against the Holy Spirit (12:10), and the teaching by the Holy Spirit in times of trial (12:11-12).

Luke places the saying concerning blasphemy against the Holy Spirit in the context of persecution, trial, and confession of faith, and leaves it to the reader to discern the implicit connection—here is a gap that cries out to be filled with information gleaned from the literary context. The saying about the blasphemy against the Holy Spirit and the words concerning acknowledgment of the Son of Man stand in parallelism.[134] Acknowledgment of the Son of Man is contrasted with denial (vv. 8-9; cf. 9:26); the parallel saying moves it a step further, as speaking against the Son of Man can be forgiven, but not blasphemy against the Holy Spirit (v. 10). To deny the Son is in fact to blaspheme the Spirit, as the final saying makes clear (vv. 11-12). Since the Holy Spirit will provide the words, there is no reason for a disciple to deny the Son; indeed, such a denial would be clear indication that the Holy Spirit is not present. The subsequent narrative lends credence to this interpretation. Peter's denial was so serious that it required the special intervention of Jesus (Luke 22:32); the consequences for disciples of resisting the Holy Spirit are made quite clear in the story of Ananias and Sapphira (Acts 5:1-11). Here is another instance of literary prophecy fulfilled within the narrative: Peter denies Jesus and is forgiven; Ananias and Sapphira lie to the Spirit, and are not so lucky.[135] Of course, in Luke's story it is not usually disciples who deny the Son; the saying

---

Press, 1982) 373-77.

[134]Cf. v. 8, πᾶς ὃς ἂν ὁμολογήσῃ κτλ with v. 11, πᾶς ὃς ἐρεῖ κτλ. Note also that both sayings have parallel adversative clauses (with δέ). Cf. Fitzmyer (*Luke*, 962), who underestimates the signficance of the parallelism; there is more that "catchword bonding" and a "common topic" at work here, for the sayings serve to interpret each other.

[135]As Tannehill (*Narrative Unity of Luke-Acts*, 1:245) notes.

foreshadows events in Acts, where the leaders will "resist the Holy Spirit" (Acts 7:51). The implicit contrast foreshadowed in this saying is between the disciples of Jesus, who witness to him, and those who blaspheme the prophetic Spirit by refusing to acknowledge the prophetic Messiah.[136]

The final saying provides another example of literary prophecy within Luke-Acts; the words point forward to what happens later in the story.[137] The apostles will in fact be brought before "the synagogues, the rulers, and the authorities" in Acts (cf. Acts 4:1-22; 5:12-42; 6:8-8:2; 13:13-52; 17:1-9; 21:27-26:32).[138] Luke will give the Spirit an explicit role in the these stories; before recounting a speech, Luke reminds the reader that the apostles are "filled with

---

[136]Cf. Brown, "'Water-Baptism' and 'Spirit-Baptism,'" 146; Johnson, *Luke*, 197. Some scholars hold that the passage refers only to Christians who fail to bear witness to Jesus when persecuted (Craddock, *Luke*, 162; Hull, *Holy Spirit in Acts*, 20; Lampe, "Holy Spirit in Writings of Luke" 190-91; Menzies, *Development of Early Christian Pneumatology*, 193; Schweizer in *Theological Dictionary of New Testament*, 6:407; Shelton, *Mighty in Word and Deed*, 102; Baer, *Heilige Geist in den Lukasschriften*, 138). The subsequent narrative, however, depicts no such apostasy (Acts 5:1-11, which does not deal with persecution, comes closest), while it does depict a great deal of resistance on the part of outsiders.

Johnson (*Luke*, 197) carries the parallelism in this passage too far when he proposes that the saying characterizes the division between the Gospel and Acts:

The denial of Jesus as the prophet in the Gospel can be reversed by conversion to the proclamation by his successors in Acts. But the rejection of *their* proclamation in the Holy Spirit leads to a final rejection from the people.

As we have seen above (on Luke 1:1-4), Luke's ending is more open-ended than Johnson supposes. (Johnson seems to have modified his position in *Acts*, 18: "Acts does not even end with a total abandonment of the Jews").

[137]Cf. Craddock, *Luke*, 160-61.

[138]Cf. Johnson, *Luke*, 195. Fitzmyer (*Luke*, 963) notes that the reference to synagogues, rulers, and authorities is unique to Luke's version of the saying (cf. Matt 10:19-20).

the Holy Spirit" (Acts 4:8; cf. 4:31; 6:5; 7:55). The Spirit "teaches" the disciples what to say (Luke 12:12).[139]

In saying the Spirit "will teach" the disciples, Jesus presents the Spirit as a direct actor in the story (using a future verb, cf. Luke 1:35). This is a break from the more common rhetoric, in which the Spirit is spoken of passively ("the Father gives the Spirit," Luke 11:13) or as the agent of a passive construction ("it had been revealed by the Holy Spirit," 2:26; cf. 4:1; or the common "filled with the Spirit"). The effect is rhetorical emphasis; the reader is being prepared for the important role the Spirit will play in witnessing to Jesus through the disciples (cf. Acts 2:44; 5:32).

Luke continues to characterize the Spirit indirectly in stylized terms as the reliable source of inspired speech. The Spirit will give the appropriate words at the right moment. Even more indirectly, the Spirit is implicitly characterized as a source of courage in the face of fear (cf. Luke 12:4). Since the inspiration of courage in the face of persecution is a new attribute of the Spirit, the fragmentariness of the characterization is further diminished. Otherwise, this characterization moves along previously established lines—stylized, symbolic, coherent, transparent, dynamic.

These sayings of Jesus provide the most explicit and reliable statement of the function of the Spirit in Luke-Acts: the Spirit will inspire trustworthy speech in other characters. The sayings foreshadow the subsequent narrative, and so provide the reader with a high degree of certainty about what transpires—Jesus himself, the most reliable of Luke's characters, guarantees the trustworthiness of the story as it will be carried on in Acts. The Spirit will insure the

---

[139]Contrast Mark 13:11 and Matt 10:20, where the Spirit actually does the speaking. For Luke, the Spirit is the teacher of inspired prophetic speech. See Johnson, *Luke,* 195.

The parallel saying in Luke 21:15 has Jesus himself teaching the disciples what to say in times of persecution. This foreshadows the close connection in Acts between the risen Jesus and the Spirit (cf. Luke 24:49; Acts 2:33; 4:7-10, 29-31; 9:17; 16:7; 20:22-24; 21:11-14). See Marshall, *Luke,* 768-69; R. F. O'Toole, "Activity of the Risen Jesus in Luke-Acts," *Biblica* 62 (1981): 484-86; G. Stählin, "Τὸ πνεῦμα Ἰησοῦ (Apostelgeschichte 16:7)," in *Christ and Spirit in the New Testament* ed. Barnabas Lindars and Stephen S. Smalley (Cambridge: Cambridge University Press, 1973), 229-52.

reliability of the speaker who "makes a defense" (ἀπολογέομαι, Luke 12:11; cf. 21:14; Acts 19:33; 24:10; 25:8; 26:1-2, 24); to say otherwise is unpardonable (Luke 12:10). The explicit message of Jesus is that the Spirit ensures the reliability of the disciples' speech in times of trial. The implicit message to the reader is that all which transpires as the story proceeds is indeed reliable; the Spirit will function symbolically in the narrative to remind the reader of the "certainty" of what has been taught (Luke 1:4).

In terms of Luke's plot, the Holy Spirit will not be mentioned again until the denouement of the Gospel. Jesus the righteous prophet will be put to death by those who reject his leadership, but will be vindicated by God when he is raised from the dead. This message is to be carried to the ends of the earth by those who acknowledge God's work in Jesus. The end of Luke's Gospel prepares the reader for the beginning of the book of Acts, and so the Spirit will appear once more, and will be clearly characterized at the power of the proclamation that is to come.

The Promise of the Father (Luke 24:36-53)

In the final, climactic scene of Luke's Gospel, Jesus appears to the startled disciples and gives proof positive of his resurrection.[140] Jesus' farewell speech summarizes the entire Gospel story, as it

---

[140]On the final scene of Luke's Gospel, see Craddock, *Luke*, 288-95; Richard J. Dillon, *From Eye-witnesses to Ministers of the Word: Tradition and Composition in Luke 24*, Analecta Biblica: Investigationes Scientificae in Res Biblicas, vol. 82 (Rome: Biblical Institute Press, 1978); Joseph A. Fitzmyer, "The Ascension of Christ and Pentecost," *Theological Studies* 45 (1984): 409-40; idem, *Luke*, 1572-93; Johnson, *Luke*, 400-6; Gerhard Lohfink, *Die Himmelfahrt Jesu: Untersuchungen zu den Himmelfahrts- und Erhöhungstexten bei Lukas* (München: Kösel-Verlag, 1971), 147-76; Marshall, *Luke*, 900-10; Menzies, *Development of Early Christian Pneumatology*, 198-204; Parsons, *The Departure of Jesus;* Sabourin, *Luc*, 382-86; Schneider, *Lukas*, 500-7; Schweitzer, *Luke*, 374-80; John H. Sieber, "The Spirit as the 'Promise of My Father' in Luke 24:49," in *Sin, Salvation, and the Spirit*, ed. Daniel Durken (Collegeville, Minn.: Liturgical Press, 1979) 271-78; Tannehill, *Narrative Unity*, 1:293-301; P. A. Van Stempvoort, "The Interpretation of the Ascension in Luke and Acts," *New Testament Studies* 5 (1958-59): 30-42; Wiefel, *Lukas*, 412-18.

reiterates the Lukan theme that all has taken place according to prophecy (Luke 24:44).[141] The disciples, as witnesses, will carry forth this message in the power of the Spirit to all nations (24:48-49); Jesus thus points the way for the narrative of Acts.[142]

Jesus speaks of the Holy Spirit as the "promise of the Father" (Luke 24:49; cf. Acts 1:4; 2:33, 39). This is the first instance of direct definition of the character of the Holy Spirit in Luke-Acts.[143] The force of this definition is slightly obscured by the allusive quality of the text, which does not name the Spirit. The rhetorical effect is to emphasize the importance of this attribute (through direct definition by Jesus) while allowing for a bit of mystery (through allusion)—after all, neither the disciples within the story, nor the one who reads it for the first time, know what will happen when the promise is fulfilled.

Jesus has already made this promise to the disciples: the Father will give the Holy Spirit to those who ask (Luke 11:13), and the Spirit will teach them what to say in times of trouble (12:12). Another reliable commentator, John the Baptist, has also promised that the Spirit will come upon them (3:16). For Luke, the promise is from the Father because it is part of the prophetic witness (Joel 3:1-5 LXX; cf. Acts 2:17-21; also Isa 32:15).[144] So Luke continues to present the Holy Spirit in stylized, biblical terms.

---

[141]Cf. Craddock, *Luke*, 290-91; Fitzmyer, *Luke*, 1580; Johnson, *Luke*, 402-6; Sabourin, *Luc*, 384-85.

[142]Menzies, *Development of Early Christian Pneumatology*, 198; Talbert, *Literary Patterns*, 60; Tannehill, *Narrative Unity of Luke-Acts*, 1:294-98

[143]It may be helpful to review the distinction between direct definition and indirect presentation of a character. Direct definition occurs, as here, when the narrator or a character within the narrative directly assigns attributes to a character; here the (implicit) definition would be, "The Spirit is the promise of the Father." Indirect presentation occurs when the attributes of a character must be inferred through speech, action, appearance, environment, or contrast with other characters. In other words, direct definition is telling, indirect presentation is showing. See above, chap. 2, "Character: Presentation and Reception."

[144]Cf. Craddock, *Luke*, 290; Hull, *Holy Spirit in Acts*, 15; Marshall, "Significance of Pentecost," 351; Menzies, *Development of Early Christian Pneumatology*, 199-204; Sieber, "The Spirit as the Promise." Luke, like Paul, draws the idea of divine promise from the story of Abraham (Acts 2:39; 3:24-26;

The new facet Luke contributes to this stylized, traditional picture is that Jesus himself sends (ἀποστέλλω) the promise of the Father (Luke 24:48). Once again the Spirit is characterized as closely connected to Jesus—now not only the recipient of the Spirit's anointing (cf. Luke 3:21-22; 4:18), but also the dispenser of this Spirit to others (cf. Luke 3:16; Acts 2:33; 9:17). Luke makes clear connections to his previous narrative; Jesus, one "sent" (ἀποστέλλω) by God (Luke 4:43), who sent others in his steps (9:2; 10:1; cf. 6:13 and Acts 1:2), now will send the ultimate stand-in.[145]

The Spirit is characterized as divine power for witness.[146] Just as the Spirit led Jesus in his mission (Luke 4:1, 14, 18-19), so now the disciples will have access to this power. The Spirit's work among the disciples will not be limited to times of persecution, as in Luke 12:11-12. The necessities of the plot lead Luke to emphasize this aspect of the Spirit's characterization. Luke is preparing the reader for the sequel to the Gospel, the book of Acts, in which the empowered disciples will take the mission from Jerusalem to the ends of the earth (Acts 1:8). The presence of the Spirit as the source of their power insures that their witness will be as reliable as that of Jesus. The promise of "power" (δύναμις) is closely connected to the Spirit in Luke-Acts, and includes not only inspired speech, but the miraculous deeds which substantiate that witness (cf. Luke 5:17; 6:19; Acts 4:8-10).[147]

13:32; 26:6; cf. Gal 3:16-18; Rom 4:13-14; 15:8); see Johnson, *Luke,* 403.

[145]See Johnson, *Luke,* 403.

[146]The expression ἐξ ὕψους δύναμιν reflects the common circumlocution for divine origin and means "God's power" (cf. Luke 1:35). The image of clothing (ἐνδύω) with a quality is also common (e.g., LXX Ps 34:26; 92:1; 108:18; 131:9, 16, 18; Prov 31:25; Wisd 5:18) and is connected with the Spirit in 1 Chr 12:18 LXX.

[147]Fitzmyer, *Luke,* 1580, 1585; Menzies, *Development of Early Christian Pneumatology,* 204; Leo O'Reilly, *Word and Sign in the Acts of the Apostles: A Study in Lucan Theology* (Rome: Editrice Pontificia Università Gregoriana, 1987), 16-17; Shelton, *Mighty in Word and Deed,* 74-84; Turner, "Luke and the Spirit," 139-45.

Luke notes that the witness inspired by the Spirit will be proclaimed "to all nations" (Luke 24:47; cf. Isa 49:6). The expression εἰς πάντα τὰ ἔθνη clearly anticipates the Gentile mission portrayed in Acts.[148] Thus at the end of his Gospel, Luke echoes the Spirit-inspired utterance of Simeon, that Jesus will be "a light for revelation to the Gentiles" (2:32), an idea that the Spirit-anointed Jesus himself affirmed (4:16-30). By connecting the witness to the Gentiles with the expression "power from on high" (24:49), Luke anticipates the decisive role the Holy Spirit will play in initiating and sustaining that mission (cf. Acts 8:26; 10:19, 44-47; 11:12, 15-17; 13:2; 15:8, 28).

By the end of his Gospel, Luke has subtly but clearly set the stage for the major role the Holy Spirit will take on in Acts.[149] The Holy Spirit has been characterized (directly) as the gift of the Father dispensed by Jesus himself and (indirectly) as the source of inspired witness. Plot and characterization are tightly woven: the Spirit promised by the Father will be given by Jesus and become a major force in the action. While the presentation of the Spirit is, in Hochman's terms, highly stylized and symbolic, since it draws heavily on Old Testament themes, Luke has broken the stylization by introducing a strong connection between the Spirit and Jesus. Jesus, the one anointed with the Spirit, will now dispense the Spirit. This connection between Jesus and the Spirit lends a new degree of dynamism to the characterization of the Spirit; here Luke foreshadows a change in the action of the Spirit, which will now focus on the mission of Jesus' disciples. The Spirit will ensure that the message of the prophets—"that the Messiah is to suffer and to rise from the dead on the third day, and that repentance and forgiveness of sins is to be proclaimed in his name to all nations" (Luke 24:46-47)—is accurately and powerfully transmitted. The Spirit of Jesus ensures the reliability of the prophetic message about Jesus; the mention of the Spirit will be for the reader a sign of narrative reliability. To use Hochman's terms, Luke has provided a coherent, simple, transparent, and fragmentary characterization of the Spirit as the source of

---

[148]Cf. Craddock, *Luke*, 291; Johnson, *Luke*, 403.

[149]Cf. Johnson, *Luke*, 405-6.

prophetic, inspired speech. And characterization is open-ended, as Jesus' final words point towards the continuation of the story. The reader will find that Luke will develop this portrait extensively in Acts.

Chapter 4

The Characterization of the Holy Spirit in Luke-Acts (II)
The Acts of the Apostles

Prologue to Acts (Acts 1:1-11)

Luke begins his second volume with a brief reprise of the prologue to Theophilus.[1] This second prologue[2] looks back to "the

---

[1]On Acts 1:1-11, see Otto Bauernfeind, *Kommentar und Studien zur Apostelgeschichte*, Wissenschaftliche Untersuchungen zum Neuen Testament, vol. 22 (Tübingen: J. C. B. Mohr (Paul Siebeck), 1980), 16-24; F. F. Bruce, *The Acts of the Apostles: The Greek Text with Introduction and Commentary*, 3rd ed., (Grand Rapids: Eerdmans, 1990), 97-105; Conzelmann, *Acts*, 3-8; Haenchen, *Acts*, 135-52; Luke T. Johnson, *The Acts of the Apostles*, Sacra Pagina Series, vol. 5 (Collegeville, Minn.: The Liturgical Press, 1992), 23-32; Jacob Kremer, "Die Voraussagen des Pfingstgeschehens in Apg 1, 4-5 und 8: ein Beitrag zur Deutung des Pfingstberichts," in *Die Zeit Jesu*, ed. Günther Bornkamm and Karl Rahner (Freiburg: Herder, 1970), 145-68; Lake and Cadbury, *Beginnings*, 4:1-9; Lohfink, *Die Himmelfahrt*; Menzies, *Development of Early Christian Pneumatology*, 198-204; D. W. Palmer, "The Literary Background of Acts 1:1-14," *New Testament Studies* 33 (1987): 427-38; Parsons, *Departure*; Rudolf Pesch, *Die Apostelgeschichte*, Evangelisch-Katholischer Kommentar zum Neuen Testament, vol. 5 (Zürich: Benziger, 1986), 1:59-77; Gerhard Schneider, *Die Apostelgeschichte*, Herders theologischer Kommentar zum Neuen Testament, vol. 5 (Freiburg: Herder, 1980), 1:187-208; David L. Tiede, "The Exaltation of Jesus and the Restora-

first book," the Gospel of Luke, which contains "all that Jesus began to do and to teach," implying that Jesus will continue his work in the second volume.[3] Indeed, Jesus does make appearances in Acts (1:2-9; 2:33; 7:56; 9:3-6; 18:9-10), but most of the work is carried out in his name by the disciples in the power of the Holy Spirit.

Luke reminds the reader that Jesus himself works in the power of the Spirit: he "gave orders" (ἐντέλλομαι) "through the Holy Spirit" (διὰ πνεύματος ἁγίου) "to the apostles whom he had chosen" (Acts 1:2).[4] Just as Jesus in his earthly ministry was "full of the Holy Spirit" (Luke 4:1), went "in the power of the Spirit" (Luke 4:14), and was "anointed" by the Spirit (Luke 4:18), so now Jesus continues to act in the Spirit. Luke's language is both retrospective and forward-looking—like the prophets before him (David, Acts 4:25), and like the Christian prophets after him (Agabus, 11:28; disciples

---

tion of Israel in Acts 1," *Harvard Theological Review* 79 (1986): 278-86; Tannehill, *Narrative Unity*, 2:9-25.

[2]On the function of the prologues in Luke-Acts, see above, chap. 3, on Luke 1:1-4. As Tannehill (*Narrative Unity of Luke-Acts*, 2:9) notes, Luke makes a smooth (if grammatically awkward) transition from an external, first-person perspective to the speech of Jesus, so that much of the book's preview, which would normally be found in a separate prologue, now appears as part of Jesus' instructions to the disciples.

[3]Cf. Johnson, *Acts*, 27; O'Toole, "Activity of Risen Jesus." The phrase ἤρξατο ὁ Ἰησοῦς ποιεῖν τε καὶ διδάσκειν may simply mean "all that Jesus did and taught" (so NRSV; Haenchen, *Acts*, 137; Lake and Cadbury, *Beginnings*, 4:3; cf. Luke 3:8; 4:21), but ἄρχομαι more likely has an inceptive meaning here; see Bauernfeind, *Apostelgeschichte*, 19; Bruce, *Acts*, 98; Johnson, *Acts*, 24; Pesch, *Apostelgeschichte*, 1:60-61; Schneider, *Apostelgeschichte*, 1:191-92.

[4]The phrase διὰ πνεύματος ἁγίου is awkwardly placed and may modify "gave orders" (so Bruce, *Acts*, 99) or "whom he had chosen" (so Haenchen, *Acts*, 139); it could easily modify both (see Johnson, *Acts*, 24; Lake and Cadbury, *Beginnings*, 4:3). "Gave orders" could also be translated "commissioned" (so Johnson, *Acts*, 24; cf. Tannehill, *Narrative Unity of Luke-Acts*, 2:11) or "instructed" (so NRSV). The Western Text of Acts, which specifies the orders as "to preach the gospel," is "evidently conflate" (Bruce, *Acts*, 99; cf. Johnson, *Acts*, 25; Metzger, *Textual Commentary*, 273-78).

at Tyre, 21:4), Jesus has spoken and still speaks διὰ πνεύματος ἀγίου. The well-chosen phrase serves to reinforce the Lukan emphasis on prophecy and prophets, and to link Jesus to both his Old Testament predecessors and the Christian prophets he will inspire.[5] Since the common bond among all prophets is the Spirit, Luke reinforces his characterization of the Spirit as the Spirit of prophecy.

Jesus again directly characterizes the Spirit as "the promise of the Father" (Acts 1:4). "Promise," ἐπαγγελία, is one of several words which link the first chapter of Acts to the final chapter of the Gospel (cf. Luke 24:49).[6] Luke again identifies the Spirit as that promised by God in the Old Testament prophets, by John the Baptist, and by Jesus himself (Joel 3:1-5 LXX quoted in Acts 2:17-21; Luke 3:16; 11:13; 12:12).[7] Jesus' words are reminiscent of the Baptist's preaching about the coming baptism with the Holy Spirit (Luke 3:16; cf. Acts 11:16), but Jesus adds temporal urgency—the promise will be fulfilled "not many days from now" (cf. Acts 2:33, 39).

Jesus tells the disciples that they will be "baptized with the Holy Spirit" (ὑμεῖς δὲ ἐν πνεύματι βαπτισθήσεσθε ἀγίῳ, 1:5). Jesus echoes the Baptist's metaphorical use of βαπτίζω, and the Lukan context clarifies its meaning: what happens "not many days from now" is the overwhelming immersion in the Spirit on Pentecost Day.[8] Here again is an example of literary prophecy, as Jesus' words anticipate the coming narrative.[9] The fulfillment of this prophecy extends beyond Pentecost, however, as the Spirit will pass

---

[5]Cf. Johnson, *Acts*, 30.

[6]See Tannehill (*Narrative Unity of Luke-Acts*, 1:295-98) for a complete account of what Tannehill calls the "interlacing" of the two chapters. Cf. Johnson, *Acts*, 25; Pesch, *Apostelgeschichte*, 1:65.

[7]Cf. Tannehill, *Narrative Unity of Luke-Acts*, 2:12.

[8]On John the Baptist's saying, see above, chap. 3, on Luke 3:16. Since the Spirit is the "promise of the Father," (Luke 24:49; Acts 1:5) and is given by the Father (Luke 11:13) and by Jesus (Acts 2:33), it seems best to translate ἐν as "with" or "in" rather than "by."

[9]Cf. Johnson, *Acts*, 26.

on to new groups with equal power and much consequence for the narrative. The promise of "baptism with the Spirit" will thus be echoed later (Acts 11:16; 19:1-7).[10]

In Jesus' final saying, the Holy Spirit is again characterized as the power for witness: "You will receive power when the Holy Spirit has come upon you; and you will be my witnesses in Jerusalem, in all Judea and Samaria, and to the ends of the earth" (Acts 1:8). Again, Luke has interlaced this scene with the final scene in the Gospel through the repetition of words such as "power" (δύναμις, cf. Luke 24:49) and "witnesses" (μάρτυρες, cf. Luke 24:48). Jesus calls the disciples μου μάρτυρες, a double entendre: they are witnesses to Jesus as well as his representatives. Indeed, the disciples will designate themselves "witnesses" to Jesus' life, death, and resurrection (Acts 2:32; 3:15; 5:32; 10:39, 41; 13:31; 22:15).[11] As in the ending of the Gospel, Acts mentions a mission beginning in "Jerusalem" (cf. Luke 24:27), and the wording here is often taken as a table of contents for the whole book.[12] The mission of witness does move from Jerusalem in the early chapters of Acts, through Judea and into Samaria (Acts 8), and then into the wider-ranging travels of Paul. It will become clear as the story progresses that the Holy Spirit is guiding the movement across these geographic and social lines.[13]

---

[10]See Schneider, *Apostelgeschichte*, 1:200-201; Tannehill, *Narrative Unity of Luke-Acts*, 2:13.

[11]See Johnson, *Acts*, 30; Pesch, *Apostelgeschichte*, 1:69; Schneider, *Apostelgeschichte*, 1:203.

[12]E.g., Bruce, *Acts*, 103; Haenchen, *Acts*, 143-44; Johnson, *Acts*, 10. The "ends of the earth" may refer to Rome, but more likely refers to the extreme limit of the world (see Daniel R. Schwartz, "The End of the ΓΗ (Acts 1:8): Beginning or End of the Christian Vision?" *Journal of Biblical Literature* 105 (1986): 669-76; T. C. G. Thornton, "To the End of the Earth: Acts 1⁸," *Expository Times* 89 (1978): 374-75; W. C. van Unnik, "Der Ausdruck 'ΕΩΣ 'ΕΣΧΑΤΟΥ ΤΗΣ ΓΗΣ (Apostelgeschichte I 8) und sein alttestamentlicher Hintergrund," in *Sparsa Collecta* (Leiden: E. J. Brill, 1973), 1:386-401). As Tannehill (*Narrative Unity of Luke-Acts*, 2:17) notes, "It is more accurate to say that Jesus outlines the mission, and Acts ends with that mission still incomplete."

[13]Cf. Johnson, *Acts*, 14.

Luke continues to model his characterization of the Spirit along traditional lines. The physical removal of Jesus in the sight of the disciples is reminiscent of the stories about the transition of prophetic power: between Moses and Joshua (Deut 34:9) and especially between Elijah and Elisha (2 Kgs 2:9-12).[14] Luke again draws the connection between the Spirit and the prophetic tradition: Jesus, the prophet-like-Moses, now passes his mantle on to the disciples, who will be portrayed in prophetic terms.

Luke will continue the characterization of the Spirit he has begun in the Gospel. The Spirit is directly and indirectly characterized, the focus being not so much on the Spirit itself but on Jesus, the disciples, and their witness. The Spirit is once more portrayed stylistically and symbolically in Old Testament terms as the Spirit of prophecy, the power for inspired speech and witness. The Spirit's reliability is reaffirmed by the one other character in the story who has equal reliability, Jesus himself. This coherent, simple, transparent, and fragmentary characterization helps the reader anticipate the narrative to come.

The Choosing of Matthias (Acts 1:15-26)

With Jesus gone, Peter takes over the leadership of the community, which proceeds to fill out the number of apostles (a highly symbolic "twelve"—here, for Luke, is the new people of God).[15] After limiting the selection to two who could "witness" to Jesus'

---

[14]Note the symbolism of the cloud, and the two men (perhaps a parallel to the appearance of Moses and Elijah in the transfiguration story (Luke 9:30)). See Johnson, *Acts,* 27.

[15]Luke plays close attention to numbers (note καταριθμέω, Acts 1:17; cf. Luke 22:3) in this passage: the number 120 (1:15) was said to be the population required for a city to have a synagogue (*m. Sanh.* 1:6); twelve symbolizes the twelve tribes of Israel (cf. Luke 22:29). Luke uses the symbolism to imply the reconstitution of the people of God. See Johnson, *Acts,* 34-35, 38-40; Tannehill, *Narrative Unity of Luke-Acts,* 2:21-25.

life, death, and resurrection (Acts 1:21-22), the disciples elect Matthias through prayer and casting lots (1:24-26).[16]

Of importance to this study is Peter's stated conviction that all that has happened is in fulfillment of the divine plan. The Holy Spirit had already witnessed to the fate of Judas through scripture (1:16, 20: cf. LXX Pss 68:26; 108:8). Peter is presented to the reader as a reliable commentator, since he expresses Jesus' view that all the events leading up to this point in the story were in fulfillment of prophecy (cf. Luke 24:44).[17] Peter becomes the most reliable human commentator in the narrative, now that Jesus is gone. He states the conviction that the Spirit directly inspired scripture, which is now finding fulfillment (cf. Acts 4:25; 28:25). The Holy Spirit guarantees the prophetic word; indeed, according to Peter, the Spirit itself was the speaker who "foretold" (προλέγω) these things through the agency of David (διὰ στόματος Δαυὶδ, Acts 1:16; cf. Luke 20:41-42; Acts 2:16; 2:25).[18]

Peter makes explicit what has been implicit in the Gospel: the words of the prophetic scriptures were inspired by the Holy Spirit. Luke reminds the reader that this community of believers stands in continuity with the prophets of Israel, for as the reader will soon see, the same Spirit rests on both groups.

---

[16]On Acts 1:15-26, see Bauernfeind, *Apostelgeschichte*, 24-31; Bruce, *Acts,* 107-12; Conzelmann, *Acts,* 10-12; Haenchen, *Acts,* 157-65; Johnson, *Acts,* 33-41; idem, *Literary Function of Possessions,* 174-82; Lake and Cadbury, *Beginnings,* 4:11-15; Pesch, *Apostelgeschichte,* 1:82-92; Schneider, *Apostelgeschichte,* 1:212-21; Tannehill, *Narrative Unity,* 2:20-25.

[17]"Peter is taking over a major function of the departed Jesus" (Tannehill, *Narrative Unity of Luke-Acts,* 2:20).

[18]Cf. Haenchen, *Acts,* 159 n. 9: "It was really the Spirit that spoke in the psalm, David being merely his human mouthpiece." Luke often speaks of the necessity (δεῖ) of the divine will in general (cf. Luke 9:22; 17:25; 24:7, 26, 44; Acts 3:21; 9:16; 14:22) and in reference to the Old Testament (Luke 22:37; 24:26, 44; Acts 1:21; 17:3). See Charles H. Cosgrove, "The Divine ΔΕΙ in Luke-Acts: Investigations into the Lukan Understanding of God's Providence," *Novum Testamentum* 26 (1984): 168-90; Haenchen, *Acts,* 159; Johnson, *Acts,* 35; John T. Squires, *The Plan of God in Luke-Acts,* Society for New Testament Studies Monograph Series, vol. 76 (Cambridge: Cambridge University Press, 1993).

Pentecost (Acts 2)

Luke now tells the long-anticipated story of Pentecost.[19] From the words of John the Baptist (Luke 3:16), the early promise of

---

[19]On the Pentecost narrative, see J. Abri, "The Theological Meaning of Pentecost," *Kator Shin* 4 (1965): 133-51; N. Adler, *Das erste christliche Pfingstfest;* Bauernfeind, *Apostelgeschichte,* 31-57; Bruce, *Acts,* 113-35; Peter Brunner, "Das Pfingstereignis: eine dogmatische Beleuchtung seiner historischen Problematik," in *Volk Gottes: zum Kirchenverständis der katholischen, evangelischen und anglikanischen Theologie,* ed. Remigius Bäumer and Heimo Dolch (Freiburg: Herder, 1967), 230-42; Conzelmann, *Acts,* 13-24; J. G. Davies, "Pentecost and Glossolalia," *Journal of Theological Studies,* n.s. 3 (1952): 228-31; Dunn, *Baptism in the Holy Spirit,* 39-54; Craig A. Evans, "The Prophetic Setting of the Pentecost Sermon," *Zeitschrift für die Neutestamentliche Wissenschaft* 74 (1983): 148-50; W. Grundmann, "Der Pfingstbericht der Apostelgeschichte in seinem theologischen Sinn," in *Studia Evangelica,* ed. F. L. Cross (Berlin: Akademie-Verlag, 1964), 2:584-94; Klaus Haacker, "Das Pfingstwunder als exegetisches Problem," in *Verborum Veritas,* ed. Otto Böcher and Klaus Haacker (Wuppertal: Theologischer Verlag Rolf Brockhaus, 1970), 125-31; Haenchen, *Acts,* 166-96; Johnson, *Acts,* 41-63; idem, *Literary Function of Possessions,* 183-89; Walter C. Kaiser, Jr., "The Promise of God and the Outpouring of the Holy Spirit: Joel 2:28-32 and Acts 2:16-21," in *The Living and Active Word of God: Studies in Honor of Samuel J. Schultz,* ed. Morris Inch and Ronald Youngblood (Winona Lake, Ind.: Eisenbrauns, 1983), 109-22; Jacob Kremer, *Pfingstbericht und Pfingstgeschehen: eine exegetische Untersuchung zu Apg 2, 1-13* (Stuttgart: KBW Verlag, 1973); Georg Kretschmar, "Himmelfahrt und Pfingsten," *Zeitschrift für Kirchengeschichte* 16 (1954-1955): 209-53; Kirsopp Lake, "The Gift of the Spirit on the Day of Pentecost," in *Beginnings,* 5:111-21; Lake and Cadbury, *Beginnings,* 4:16-30; Eduard Lohse, "Die Bedeutung des Pfingstberichtes im Rahmen des lukanischen Geschichtswerkes," *Evangelische Theologie* 13 (1953): 422-36; Marshall, "The Significance of Pentecost"; Menzies, *Development of Early Christian Pneumatology,* 205-44; B. Noack, "The Day of Pentecost in Jubilees, Qumran and Acts," *Annual of the Swedish Theological Institute* 1 (1962): 73-95; Pesch, *Apostelgeschichte,* 1:97-128; J. Potin, *La fête juive de la Pentecôte* (Paris: Editions du Cerf, 1971); Schneider, *Apostelgeschichte,* 1:239-83; Tannehill, *Narrative Unity,* 2:26-42; Richard F. Zehnle, *Peter's Pentecost Discourse: Tradition and Lukan Reinterpretation in Peter's Speeches of Acts 2 and 3* (Nashville: Abingdon Press, 1971).

Efforts to determine Luke's sources in Acts 2, as in the rest of the book, have been inconclusive. Whatever his sources, the Pentecost account reflects Luke's literary style and was substantially shaped by him. See Haenchen, *Acts,* 185-86; Johnson, *Acts,* 3-5; Menzies, *Development of Early Christian Pneumatology,* 208.

Jesus (Luke 11:13; 12:12), to the words of the risen Jesus (Luke 24:49; Acts 1:5, 8), the reader has long anticipated a massive out-pouring of the prophetic Spirit.[20] The Spirit will now take a more central role in the narrative.

The Pentecost narrative may be divided into three sections: the coming of the gift of the Spirit (Acts 2:1-13); Peter's sermon (2:14-36); and the response of the people (2:37-47).[21] I will consider the last two sections together.

The Gift of the Spirit (Acts 2:1-13)[22]

Luke's highly nuanced language, which makes careful use of synonyms almost to the point of puns, emphasizes the overwhelming power of the coming of the Spirit (Acts 2:1-4); as in the baptism narrative (Luke 3:21-22), the Spirit is characterized indirectly through the metaphorical description of its appearance. The designa-tions of time ("suddenly," ἄφνω) and place ("from heaven," ἐκ τοῦ οὐρανοῦ) highlight divine, not human, control of the Spirit's action (Acts 1:2; cf. Acts 16:26; Luke 3:21-22). The description of a sound "like a strong rushing wind" further emphasizes the powerful,

---

[20]Cf. Johnson, *Acts*, 45.

[21]Cf. ibid., 41, 48, 56.

[22]The question of Luke's dominant literary model for the Pentecost scene is complicated by the dating of sources: in Luke's day, was Pentecost understood as the celebration of the giving of the Torah to Moses at Sinai? Clearly the rabbis understood Pentecost to be a feast celebrating the giving of Torah (*b. Pesaḥ.* 68b), and *Jubilees* (6:17-21) speaks of the Feast of Weeks as a covenant-renewal feast. Philo connects the giving of Torah with flaming speech and speaking flame (*On the Decalogue* 33, 46). Fire is often used as a symbol for Torah (*b. Ta'an.* 7a; *b. B. Bat.* 78B; *Sifre Deut.* Ber. 343). There is little evidence, however, that the con-nection between Pentecost and Sinai was made in Luke's time.

Nevertheless, in light of Luke's parallels between Moses and Jesus, the references in Acts 2:1-4 to sound and fire may be allusions to the Sinai story. As Moses gave the Law, now Jesus gives the Spirit (Acts 2:33). See Haenchen, *Acts*, 174; Johnson, *Acts*, 46; contra Marshall, "Significance of Pentecost," 347-49; Menzies, *Development of Early Christian Pneumatology*, 229-44; Pesch, *Apostel-geschichte*, 1:101-2.

unpredictable nature of the Spirit; the simile is appropriate, since the Greek word meaning "Spirit" (πνεῦμα) can also mean "wind" (here designated by the unambiguous synonym πνοή).[23] The sound "filled the whole house" (πληρόω), just as the disciples will be metaphorically "filled with the Holy Spirit" (πίπλημι, 2:4).[24] The Spirit appears as "divided tongues, as of fire" (2:3); the "tongues" (γλῶσσαι) suggest the miraculous speech about to occur (2:4, 8, 11) and which will twice again accompany a new outpouring of the Spirit (Acts 10:46; 19:6; cf. Mark 16:17; 1 Cor 12-14); as with the description of the house, Luke's language subtly prepares the reader for what is to come. "Fire" (πῦρ) recalls the prophecy of the Baptist (Luke 3:16), partially reiterated by the risen Christ (Acts 1:5).[25] The disciples "began to speak in other tongues" (ἕτεραι γλῶσσαι) given by the Spirit; the word "gave" (δίδωμι) reminds the reader that the Spirit is the promised "gift" (Luke 11:13; 12:12; 24:49; Acts 1:4). Luke makes it clear that this is the promised outpouring of the prophetic Spirit, and the metaphors of "wind," "fire," and "filling" draw a picture of an mighty, overpowering phenomenon (cf. Acts 4:31). The description of the Spirit in this passage characterizes it as the promised gift of the Father, a powerful force, and the source of inspired speech.

Luke again presents the Spirit as a direct actor, the subject of the verbs meaning "gave utterance" (τὸ πνεῦμα ἐδίδου ἀποφθέγγεσθαι αὐτοῖς, v. 4). The rhetoric of direct action in the present tense underlines the importance of this event; the Spirit is not spoken of passively (cf. Luke 11:13), nor as merely the agent of a passive construction (cf. Luke 2:26; 4:1), nor as the subject of past or future

---

[23]Cf. Haenchen, *Acts,* 167, 174. Luke's Old Testament models are the windy experiences of Elijah (1 Kgs 19:11-12; 2 Kgs 2:11). Both these instances are accompanied by fire. Cf. also Ezek 37:9. See Bruce, *Acts,* 114; Johnson, *Acts,* 42.

[24]Noise accompanies the theophany at Sinai (Exod 19:16-19) and is found in conjunction with "fire" in Ps 28:7 LXX. See Johnson, *Acts,* 42.

[25]Fire is a common feature of Old Testament theophanies (cf. Gen 15:17; Exod 3:2; 13:21-22; 14:24; 19:18; 24:17; Deut 4:12; Ps 17:9 LXX. See Johnson, *Acts,* 42. "Fiery tongues" are found in 1 Enoch 14:8-15; 71:5; see Haenchen, *Acts,* 168; Lake and Cadbury, *Beginnings,* 4:17.

actions (cf. Acts 1:16; Luke 1:35). Here the Spirit acts directly in the here-and-now to inspire the disciples. The reader is reminded of Jesus' baptism, where the Spirit was also a direct actor in the narrative (the Spirit "descended" on Jesus, Luke 3:22). The reader is also prepared for the active role the Spirit will take in the narrative to come, in which it will "give utterance" to the disciples many times, as Jesus had promised (Luke 12:12).

Luke does not linger on his description of the outpouring of the Spirit; as in the Gospel, the focus is not on the Spirit but on the prophets inspired by that Spirit. The gift of the Spirit comes at an opportune time, as the Jewish crowd gathered in Jerusalem for the Pentecost festival is cosmopolitan (Acts 2:8-11).[26] The Spirit inspires a miracle of speaking,[27] and all hear in their own language

---

[26]Josephus mentions the large crowds that would gather in Jerusalem at feast time (*Antiquities* 14:337; 17:254; *Jewish War* 1:253); but the word κατοικέω (v. 5) implies that these Jews had permanent residence in Jerusalem (see Haenchen, *Acts*, 175; Johnson, *Acts*, 43; contra Bruce, *Acts*, 115). Luke uses a common literary device, the list of nations (e.g., Gen 10:2-31; *Sibylline Oracles* 3:160-72; 205-9; Ps.-Philo 4:3-17), to symbolize the preaching of the gospel in the presence of Jews from all lands. See Johnson, *Acts*, 43, 47; Menzies, *Development of Early Christian Pneumatology*, 209; Tannehill, *Narrative Unity of Luke-Acts*, 2:27.

Luke, in an unusual lapse of narrative continuity, places the disciples in a "house" (v. 2), but then has a large crowd gather, as if the scene took place outside.

[27]Acts 2:4 suggests that the Spirit gave the disciples the ability to speak in unknown languages. However, the reference to drunkenness v. 13 could be taken to mean that some heard it as gibberish. Glossolalia—ecstatic nonsensical speech—was and is a common religious phenomenon, and in Hellenistic society was associated with mantic prophecy, the result of possession by a deity (Apuleius, *The Golden Ass* 8:27; Cicero, *On Divination* 1, 32, 70-71; Plato, *Phaedrus* 244A-B; *Timaeus* 71E-72B; Plutarch, *On the Obsolescence of Oracles* 14, 40; *The E at Delphi* 6-24; *Testament of Job* 48-52; see Johnson, *Acts*, 42). Ecstatic states were also accompanied by or described as drunkenness (Ovid, *Metamorphoses* 3:528-45; 4:25-30; Philo, *On the Creation* 69-71; Lucian, *Nigrinus* 5; see Johnson, *Acts*, 44). If Luke equates tongues with this kind of ecstatic speech, the miracle would have taken place in the ears of the hearers ("how is it we *hear* them in our own native languages?" Acts 2:8; cf. 1 Cor 14:26-28).

It is more likely that v. 13 refers to the cacophonous sound of many languages spoken at once, since Luke makes it clear that the Spirit came on the disciples, not on the crowd—this is a miracle of speaking, not hearing. The preaching of the gospel in many languages through the Spirit foreshadows the universality of the

"the great acts of God" (2:11).[28] There are some skeptics, however (v. 12),[29] and this provides a smooth narrative transition to Peter's speech.

Peter's Sermon and the People's Response (Acts 2:14-47)

Peter, now the most reliable human commentator in the narrative (having taken this function over from Jesus),[30] gives an authoritative interpretation of what has happened. The disciples are not babbling drunkards; what has happened is the fulfillment of Scripture (Acts 2:14-15). Peter quotes Joel 3:1-5 LXX, which clearly establishes the link between the events of Pentecost and the tradition of the prophetic Spirit.[31] Joel's words, as interpreted by Peter, will

---

coming Christian mission. Luke does not therefore have ecstatic glossolalia in mind (contrast Paul's discussion of tongues in 1 Corinthians 14). Cf. Bruce, *Acts*, 114-15; Haenchen, *Acts*, 168; Luke T. Johnson, "Tongues, Gift of," s.v. in *Anchor Bible Dictionary*, David Noel Freedman, ed., (New York: Doubleday, 1992); Menzies, *Development of Early Christian Pneumatology*, 209-10; Pesch, *Apostelgeschichte*, 1:104; Schneider, *Apostelgeschichte*, 1:250.

[28]"The promised Spirit initiates the action of the plot by initiating the mission that continues through the rest of Acts" (Tannehill, *Narrative Unity of Luke-Acts*, 2:26).

[29]Once again, Luke shows a divided Israel (cf. Luke 2:34) by positing two opposing groups, one sympathetic, one hostile. See Haenchen, *Acts*, 171-72, 175; Menzies, *Development of Early Christian Pneumatology*, 209-10.

[30]See above, p. 158. Luke observed the ancient historian's practice of allowing a character's speech to put events into perspective for the reader: "The speeches in Acts provide authorial commentary on the narrative" (Johnson, *Acts*, 53; cf. Tannehill, *Narrative Unity of Luke-Acts*, 2:28-29).

[31]The passive construction with διά (τοῦτό ἐστιν τὸ εἰρημένον διὰ τοῦ προφήτου, Acts 2:16) "indicates that the Holy Spirit was the real speaker, the prophet but his mouthpiece" (Bruce, *Acts*, 120). Cf. 1:16; see above, p. 158.

become a programmatic prophecy for the rest of Acts, as the newly-empowered disciples continue in the prophetic footsteps of Jesus.[32]

The Spirit is given an eschatological function by the temporal designation "in the last days" (Acts 2:17).[33] The expression prepares Peter's listeners for the sermon to come and signals the beginning of the messianic period. As Acts 2:20 makes clear, this is the beginning, not the end, of the new age. All that is happening comes "before" (πρίν) the day of the Lord; Luke distinguishes between the time of "signs and wonders" and the eschatological climax of the parousia (cf. Luke 21:5-36).[34] The cataclysmic coming of the Spirit, pictured in Acts 2:1-4, has been predicted by the prophet: God will "pour out" the Spirit (v. 17, cf. "filled" in v. 4), and send "fire" (v. 19, cf. v. 3). In this passage the Spirit is being indirectly characterized through the speech of another character; Peter gives it a messianic, eschatological role via his quotation and adaptation of Joel.

The gift of the Spirit is, once again, prophetic. Luke emphasizes the prophetic aspect of the Old Testament by adding "God says" to the Joel citation (Acts 2:17).[35] Those who receive the Spirit act as prophets first of all by prophesying (vv. 17-18); another Lukan addition (καὶ προφητεύσουσιν, v. 18) reiterates this theme.[36] The

---

[32]See Johnson, *Acts,* 54; Menzies, *Development of Early Christian Pneumatology,* 205.

[33]Luke adds ἐν ταῖς ἐσχάταις ἡμέραις to clarify Joel's μέτα ταῦτα (Joel 3:1 LXX). While a few manuscripts conform to the LXX, the preponderance of evidence is in favor of the majority reading; see Johnson, *Acts,* 49; Menzies, *Development of Early Christian Pneumatology,* 213 n. 2; Metzger, *Textual Commentary,* 295; contra Haenchen, *Acts,* 178.

[34]See Johnson, *Acts,* 50; Lampe, "Holy Spirit in Writings of Luke," 193. Menzies (*Development of Early Christian Pneumatology,* 215-17; 229) believes the "last days" in Luke-Acts extend back to the birth of Jesus.

[35]See Johnson, *Acts,* 49; Menzies, *Development of Early Christian Pneumatology,* 217; Pesch, *Apostelgeschichte,* 1:119.

[36]The Western Text omits these words in order to bring the text into conformity with the LXX; see Johnson, *Acts,* 49; Menzies, *Development of Early Christian Pneumatology,* 221; Metzger, *Textual Commentary,* 297-98.

disciples are also characterized as prophets when Peter refers to seeing visions and dreaming dreams (v. 17; cf. 7:55-56; 9:3-10; 10:3, 10-16; 11:5; 16:9-10; 18:9; 27:23).[37] Jesus himself, who received the same gift (v. 33), is described as a prophet who does "deeds of power, wonders, and signs" (δυνάμεσι καὶ τέρασι καὶ σημείοις, vv. 22-23); he stands in the prophetic line of David (vv. 29-30; cf. Luke 24:44; Acts 1:16; 4:25). The expression "signs and wonders" locates Jesus in the tradition of the prophet-like-Moses (Deut 34:10-12; cf. Exod 7:3, 9; 11:9-10; Deut 4:34; 6:22; 7:19; 11:3; 26:8; 29:3; LXX Pss 77:43; 104:27; 134:9).[38] In Luke's summary of the state of the church following Pentecost, the disciples are depicted as prophets in much the same way, since they do "many signs and wonders" (πολλά τε τέρατα καὶ σημεῖα), like Jesus (v. 43; cf. 2:19; 4:16, 22, 30; 5:12; 6:8; 8:6, 13; 14:3; 15:12).[39] It is in fact Jesus himself who is responsible for these signs and wonders, as it is Jesus who has given the gift of the Spirit (Acts 2:33); here is an example of how Luke pictures Jesus continuing to work he "began" among the disciples (cf. Acts 1:1).

The gift is universal.[40] God will pour out the spirit "upon all flesh," including "your sons and your daughters," "young men," "old men" (Acts 2:17; cf. v. 33), and even "slaves, both men and women" (v. 18).[41] God's salvation is open to "everyone who calls

---

[37]Dreams and visions were common among Old Testament prophets. For visions (ὅρασις) in LXX see Num 24:4, 16; 1 Sam 3:1; Ps 88:19; Hos 12:10; Mic 3:6; Obad 1:1; Nah 1:1; Hab 2:2-3; Zech 10:2; Isa 1:1; 13:1; 19:1; Jer 14:14; Lam 2:9; Ezek 1:1; 8:3; 40:2; Dan 4:20; 8:1; for dreams (ἐνύπνιον), Gen 37:5; 41:8; Deut 13:1-5; 1 Sam 28:15; Zech 10:2; Jer 28:25-32; Dan 1:17; 2:1; 4:2. See Johnson, *Acts,* 49; Menzies, *Development of Early Christian Pneumatology,* 224-25.

[38]See Johnson, *Acts,* 50.

[39]See Tannehill, *Narrative Unity of Luke-Acts,* 2:32-33.

[40]Cf. Menzies, *Development of Early Christian Pneumatology,* 227-29.

[41]Luke adds "my" (μου) to the LXX citation to create a nice double-entendre—the Spirit comes even on slaves, both male and female, but also on "my servants," the servants of God (cf. Luke 2:29; Acts 4:29; 16:17). See Johnson, *Acts,* 49.

on the name of the Lord" (v. 21). The gift of the Spirit is promised to all who repent[42] and are baptized[43] (v. 38): "For the promise is for you, for your children, and for all who are far away, everyone whom the Lord our God calls to him" (v. 39).[44] Luke ever so gently foreshadows a major development in his narrative, the Gentile mission.[45] For now, however, the apostles find great success among the Jews (v. 42, 47).[46]

Peter reiterates much of what Luke has already told us about the Spirit, while adding some new elements. As before, it is the promise of the Spirit given to Jesus by the Father (Acts 2:33; cf. Luke 3:21-22; 4:18); Jesus himself gives it to his disciples (cf. Luke 24:49). But now the circle of disciples is opened: all who repent and are baptized can join in receiving the Spirit (Acts 2:38) and many do (vv. 41-47). The Spirit is now characterized as universally available; the implications of this will soon be felt in the narrative. This is a

---

[42]Repentance ($\mu\varepsilon\tau\acute{\alpha}\nu o\iota\alpha$, $\mu\varepsilon\tau\alpha\nu o\acute{\varepsilon}\omega$) is a common Lukan theme; see Luke 3:3, 8; 5:32; 10:13; 11:32; 13:3, 5; 15:7, 10; 16:30; 17:3-4; 24:47; Acts 3:19; 5:31; 8:22; 11:18; 13:24; 17:30; 19:4; 20:21; 26:20. See Bruce, *Acts*, 129; Johnson, *Acts*, 57.

[43]Baptism is taken over from John the Baptist (Luke 3:1-17); the connection between the Baptist's ritual and that of the early church is "repentance" and "forgiveness of sins" ($\ddot{\alpha}\phi\varepsilon\sigma\iota\nu$ $\tau\tilde{\omega}\nu$ $\dot{\alpha}\mu\alpha\rho\tau\iota\tilde{\omega}\nu$, cf. 5:31; 10:43; 13:38; 26:18). Baptism is now done in "the name of Jesus Christ," i.e., in his power and authority (cf. Acts 3:6, 16; 4:10, 12, 17-18, 30; 5:28, 40-41; 8:12, 16; 9:14-16, 21, 27, 28; 10:48; 15:26; 16:18; 19:5, 13, 17; 21:13; 22:16; 26:9). See Bruce, *Acts*, 129; Johnson, *Acts*, 57; Pesch, *Apostelgeschichte*, 1:125.

Here the gift of the Spirit follows baptism, but Luke is not consistent in this regard (cf. 8:15-16; 10:47-48; 19:5-6). See above, chap. 1, "What Does the Holy Spirit Do?"

[44]Here is a clear echo of Joel 3:5b LXX; the language also recalls the promise to Abraham (cf. Acts 3:24-26; 13:32; 26:6; Gal 3:16-18; Rom 4:13-14; 15:8). See Bauernfeind, *Apostelgeschichte*, 53; Johnson, *Acts*, 58, 60; Schneider, *Apostelgeschichte*, 1:278.

[45]See Tannehill, *Narrative Unity of Luke-Acts*, 2:30.

[46]Cf. Johnson, *Acts*, 49.

less stylized characterization of the Spirit, as it breaks from the mainstream of biblical tradition, though it is in line with Joel's prophecy—now all God's people can be prophets.[47]

Further, the Spirit is pictured as initiating a ideal community; Luke says the believers "held all things in common" (v. 44) and pictures them as pious, well-regarded, and prosperous (vv. 46-47).[48] Luke's characterization of the Spirit becomes less fragmentary and more complex as it breaks away from Old Testament stylization— the Spirit is now given, at least implicitly, functions that are outside the range of the traditional, prophetic activities. The Spirit now not only functions within specific prophets, but helps form a community.

The presence of the Spirit establishes the reliability not only of Peter's speech, but of Luke's narrative. God's fidelity is established, because the Messiah has come, has reconstituted the people of God (Acts 1:15-26), has poured out the Spirit of prophecy (2:1-4, 17-18), and has offered salvation to all flesh (2:21, 38-39). And Israel has, in part, responded (2:41, 47). God is faithful, as testified by the Spirit-filled messianic community (2:44-47).[49]

---

[47]Whether all God's people are in fact prophets is another question. Luke seems to imply in Peter's speech that all Christians will receive the Spirit and will prophesy (Acts 2:17-18, 38-39). And indeed, one is hard pressed to find in Luke-Acts an example of a Spirit-filled character who does not function as a prophet. Yet Luke also clearly distinguishes between "prophets" and other members of the community (Acts 11:27; 13:1; 15:32; 21:9-10), so attempts to articulate a Lukan "prophetic ecclesiology" fail—again, Luke cannot be forced into theological consistency.

[48]The phrase εἶχον ἅπαντα κοινά (v. 44) suggests the utopian Hellenistic topos on friendship, "friends hold all things in common" (τοῖς φιλοῖς πάντα κοινά, e.g., in Plato, *Republic* 449C; for further references, see Johnson, *Acts,* 59). The ideal of an original community of possessions is as old as Plato, *Critias* 110C-D, and Ovid *Metamorphoses* 1:88-111. Luke appeals to a powerful societal myth, and connects that myth to the workings of the Spirit: "the gift of the Spirit brought about a community which realized the highest aspirations of human longing: unity, peace, joy, and the praise of God" (Johnson, *Acts,* 62; cf. Haenchen, *Acts,* 232). In light of the placement of this Lukan summary after the bestowal of the Spirit at Pentecost, the function of the Spirit in Luke-Acts cannot be limited solely to inspired speech (contra Menzies, *Development of Early Christian Pneumatology,* 206-7; and Stronstad, *Charismatic Theology of Luke;* see Shelton, *Mighty in Word and Deed*).

Peter and John Arrested (Acts 4:1-31)

The healing of the lame man at the temple (Acts 3:1-10) provides the occasion for Peter's second speech to the crowd (3:11-26), which in turn results in the arrest of Peter and John by "the priests, the captain of the temple, and the Sadducees" (4:1-3).[50] Luke draws a contrast between the "rulers, elders, and scribes" (4:5) and "the people" (v. 1), many of whom believed (v. 4). Israel is divided over this new manifestation of the Spirit.

As Peter begins speaking to the assembly, Luke describes him as "filled with the Holy Spirit" ($\pi\lambda\eta\sigma\theta\epsilon\grave{\iota}\varsigma$ $\pi\nu\epsilon\acute{\upsilon}\mu\alpha\tau\varsigma$ $\acute{\alpha}\gamma\acute{\iota}\upsilon$, v. 8). This is the same expression used in the Pentecost narrative (2:4). The phrase points back to the Pentecost experience to remind the reader of the power working within the apostles, and is a clear signal of the reliability of the speaker. Indeed, "power" ($\delta\acute{\upsilon}\nu\alpha\mu\iota\varsigma$) is one of the issues the Jewish leaders wish to address, along with the "name" ($\acute{o}\nu\omega\mu\alpha$) under which this power is exercised (v. 7); the reader already has learned that the "power" comes from the Holy Spirit, which is given in the "name" of Jesus (Acts 1:8; 2:38)—here is further proof that Jesus is still at work (Acts 1:1). The narrative reminder that a character is "filled with the Spirit" functions to ensure the reliability of the discourse which follows; what Peter says, he says as a Spirit-inspired prophet. Peter is thus characterized by contrast with the "rulers, elders, and scribes"; the issue for Luke is the real leadership of the people, which requires the guidance of the Spirit. Luke continues the theme of a division among the people, as the mission meets with great success (4:4), while incurring the

---

[49]Cf. Johnson, *Acts*, 45, 62-63.

[50]On the arrest and trial of Peter and John in Acts 4, see Bauernfeind, *Apostelgeschichte*, 71-83; Bruce, *Acts*, 147-59; Conzelmann, *Acts*, 31-35; Jacques Dupont, "La prière des apôtres persecutés (Acts 4, 23-31)," in *Etudes sur les Actes des Apôtres*, Lectio Divina, vol. 45 (Paris: Editions du Cerf, 1967), 521-22; Haenchen, *Acts*, 213-29; Johnson, *Acts*, 75-93; Lake and Cadbury, *Beginnings*, 4:39-47; Stanley B. Marrow, "*Parrhēsia* and the New Testament," *Catholic Biblical Quarterly* 44 (1982): 431-46; Pesch, *Apostelgeschichte*, 1:160-79; Schneider, *Apostelgeschichte*, 1:339-62; Tannehill, *Narrative Unity*, 2:59-79.

wrath of the putative leadership.[51]

Following the release of the apostles, the community gathers for prayer (v. 23-24).[52] They find that all that has occurred is in fulfillment of prophecy, inspired through the same Spirit now at work in them (vv. 25-27; cf. 1:16; 2:16, 30). What God and the Spirit said through David[53] about the raging of the Gentiles and rulers came true for Jesus (4:27-28), and is being replicated among the present servants of God (vv. 29-30; cf. 2:18).[54] The community prays for

---

[51]See Johnson, *Acts*, 80-82; Tannehill, *Narrative Unity of Luke-Acts*, 2:59. Johnson notes that Luke employs the literary pattern of the prophet Moses, seen most clearly in Stephen's speech: the prophet comes once and is rejected, and then returns in the power of God to offer a second chance (Acts 7:17-44). Here, the first trial (4:5-22) will be followed by "signs and wonders" (4:23-5:16) and a second trial (5:17-42). The leadership in Jerusalem is given two chances to prove its legitimacy; in both cases they reject the witness of the Spirit (5:32).

[52]Johnson (*Acts*, 90) holds that πρὸς τοὺς ἰδίους in 4:23 refers only to the other apostles, but this is too restrictive (cf. 21:6; 24:23). See Bruce, *Acts*, 156; Haenchen, *Acts*, 226; Lake and Cadbury, *Beginnings*, 4:45; Pesch, *Apostelgeschichte*, 1:175; Schneider, *Apostelgeschichte*, 1:356.

[53]Though its basic intent is clear enough on any reading, the text of Acts 4:25 was hopelessly corrupted at an early stage and is extremely confused. However, the earliest available text (ὁ τοῦ πατρὸς ἡμῶν διὰ πνεύματος ἁγίου στόματος Δαυὶδ παιδός σου εἰπών, p[74] ℵ A B E 33 *al.*) makes explicit what has been implicit in Luke-Acts: the Holy Spirit is the onstage representative of the offstage God, at work in the prophets. So God speaks through the Spirit, who uses human agents. See Metzger, *Textual Commentary*, 321-23; contra Haenchen, *Acts*, 226.

[54]Luke applies Ps 2:1-2 LXX point by point in a fashion resembling the pesher interpretation of the Qumran community. Note the repetition of the key words from the Psalm—ἔθνη, λαοί, συνάγω, χριστός/χρίω, and παῖς—in Peter's speech, with Herod and Pilate as the "kings" and "rulers." See Haenchen, *Acts*, 226-27; Johnson, *Acts*, 84-85.

Tannehill (*Narrative Unity of Luke-Acts*, 2:68-77) notes the many similarities between the crucifixion narrative in the Gospel and this section of Acts, especially in the details of the trial scenes (cf. Acts 4:1 and Luke 22:52; Acts 4:3 and Luke 20:19; Acts 4:5-6 and Luke 22:66; 23:13, 35; 24:20; Acts 4:7 with Luke 20:2; Acts 4:11 with Luke 20:17; etc.). Once again, Luke draws parallels between Jesus and the disciples as prophets.

boldness of speech[55] and power to work "signs and wonders," i.e., for prophetic power (vv. 29-30). God's answer is a second Pentecost; in fulfillment of Jesus' prophecy, the Spirit is given in answer to prayer (Luke 11:13). Once again, the coming of the Spirit is accompanied by physical phenomena; here, the house itself is shaken (v. 31). The community is filled with the Holy Spirit (as was Peter, v. 8) in order to speak the word of God with boldness (v. 31).[56] Again, the phrase "filled with the Holy Spirit" is a narrative reminder and a sign of reliability; the power given at Pentecost is still at work among Jesus' witnesses.

Community of Goods (Acts 4:32-5:11)

As with the Pentecost narrative, Luke follows his account of the influx of the Spirit in Acts 4:31 with an idealistic depiction of the community.[57] Again, the Spirit inspires the community to the ideal

---

[55]"Boldness" (παρρησία, παρρησιάζομαι), associated with the free speech of Cynic philosophers in Hellenistic culture, becomes a characteristic of the Lukan prophet (cf. 2:29; 4:13, 29, 31; 9:27-28; 13:46; 14:3; 18:26; 19:8; 26:26; 28:31). See Johnson, *Acts,* 78, 81; Tannehill, *Narrative Unity of Luke-Acts,* 2:61-62.

For a detailed examination of how Luke combines the philosophical traditions about boldness with Old Testament prophetic traditions, especially in reference to the scene between Jesus and Herod alluded to in Acts 4:27, see Darr, *On Character Building,* 147-68.

[56]To "speak the word of God" (λαλέω τὸν λόγον τοῦ θεοῦ) is another bit of prophetic language Luke draws from the LXX (cf. Deut 18:19-20; Amos 1:1; 3:1; 4:1; 5:1; 7:16; Mic 1:1; Joel 1:1; Jonah 1:1; 3:1; Zeph 1:1; 2:5; Zech 1:1-7; 4:6, 8; 6:9; 7:1-12; 8:1; 9:1; Isa 1:10; 2:3; 28:14, 23; Jer 1:2-13; 2:4, 31; 7:2; 10:1; 14:1; 17:15, 20; 22:1 and often in Jeremiah; Ezek 1:3; 2:7; 3:4, 16 and often in Ezekiel). See Johnson, *Acts,* 85.

[57]On the community of goods, including the Ananias and Sapphira episode, see Bauernfeind, *Apostelgeschichte,* 77-88; Bruce, *Acts,* 159-66; Conzelmann, *Acts,* 36-38; H.-J. Degenhardt, *Lukas Evangelist der Armen* (Stuttgart: Katholisches Bibelwerk, 1965); J. Duncan M. Derrett, "Ananias, Sapphira, and the Right of Property," *Downside Review* 89 (1971): 225-32; Jacques Dupont, "The Community of Goods in the Early Church," in *The Salvation of the Gentiles: Essays on the Acts of the Apostles,* trans. John R. Keating (New York: Paulist Press, 1967), 85-102; Haenchen, *Acts,* 230-41; Johnson, *Acts,* 82-93; idem, *Literary*

of friendship: "friends share all things" (cf. 2:44).[58] The well-being of the community is linked to the work of the prophetic Spirit: in the midst of his report on the community, Luke notes that the apostles gave their "witness" (μαρτύριον) with "great power" (δύναμις, 4:33).[59] Luke pictures a community which lives under the guidance of the Spirit. He goes on to give the positive example of Barnabas, who brought the proceeds of his land sale to the apostles, in contrast to the negative example of Ananias and Sapphira, who held back (4:36-5:2; cf. Josh 7:1-26).[60] Barnabas functions implicitly under the Spirit; Ananias and Sapphira explicitly do not (5:3, 9).

In the story of Ananias and Sapphira, Luke uses Peter's speech to characterize the Spirit indirectly in relation to the church, Jesus, and God. The Spirit is first of all characterized in contrast with another character, Satan, when Peter asks, "Why has Satan filled your heart to lie to the Holy Spirit?" (5:3); later, he asks Sapphira why she "tests" (πειράζω) the Spirit (5:9). As the example of

---

Function of Possessions, 191-210; Lake and Cadbury, *Beginnings*, 4:47-54; Phillipe-H. Menoud, "La mort d'Ananias et de Sapphira (Actes 5:1-11)," in *Aux sources de la tradition chrétienne*, Biblioteque Théologique (Neuchatel: Delachaux & Niestlé, 1950), 146-54; Pesch, *Apostelgeschichte*, 1:179-224; Schneider, *Apostelgeschichte*, 1:352-404; Tannehill, *Narrative Unity*, 2:59-79.

[58]Luke's description of the community in Acts 4:32 as of "one heart and soul" (καρδία καὶ ψυχὴ μία) reflects the Hellenistic *topos* on friendship; cf. Euripides, *Orestes* 1046; Aristotle; *Nichomachean Ethics* 1168B; Plutarch, *On Having Many Friends* 8. See Haenchen, *Acts*, 231, 233; Johnson, *Acts*, 86.

[59]On the prophetic "witness," see above on Acts 1:1-11; on the connection between "Spirit" and "power," see above, chap. 3, on Luke 4:1-15. The combination of witness and power points back to the transition between Luke and Acts (Luke 24:48-49; Acts 1:8).

The text of Acts 4:33 is troubled by awkward word order, but the variants do not substantially affect the meaning. The reading τῆς ἀναστάσεως τοῦ κυρίου Ἰησοῦ (p[8] P Ψ 049 056 0142 and several translations) best accounts for the others. See Bruce, *Acts*, 160; Metzger, *Textual Commentary*, 325-26.

[60]Cf. Johnson, *Acts*, 91. As Johnson (*Acts*, 87) notes, two people conspiring to withhold possessions implies a community of avarice, in contrast with the community of goods. Luke's literary model is the story of Achan in Josh 7:1-26; see Haenchen, *Acts*, 239; Johnson, *Acts*, 92.

Barnabas shows, the Spirit inspires a community of goods, not a community of greed. Luke has made the same contrast before in connection with satanic "testing" (Luke 4:1-14; cf. πειράζω in Luke 4:2) and in Jesus' reaction to the mission of the seventy (Luke 10:18, 21).[61] Second, the Spirit is virtually equated with God; Peter first speaks of lying to the Holy Spirit (v. 3), then of lying to God (v. 4); clearly the Spirit is characterized here as the discursive representative of the God at work behind the narrative.[62] Third, the Spirit is once again closely connected to Jesus when Peter speaks of "the Spirit of the Lord" (Acts 5:9; Acts 2:33; 8:39; 16:6-7).[63] Finally, the Spirit is closely identified with the community, since to lie to the community is to lie to the Spirit and God (Acts 5:3-4).[64]

The Spirit is indirectly characterized by the events of the story as well. The death of Ananias and Sapphira may be counted among the many "signs and wonders" (cf. 5:12) the apostles do through the

---

[61]Similarities between Ananias and Judas, who was also possessed by Satan (Luke 22:3) and whose apostasy was symbolized in a purchase of land (Acts 1:18), serve to characterize by contrast Peter, who was to be tested by Satan (Luke 22:31-32). See Johnson, *Acts,* 88.

[62]Johnson (*Acts,* 88) notes that ψεύδομαι followed by the accusative could be translated "falsify the Spirit," which he understands as "to counterfeit the actions generated by the Spirit" in pretending to share their possessions. But as Bruce (*Acts,* 163) remarks, ψεύδομαι followed by the accusative should be translated "deceive," and thus v. 3 stands in synonymous parallelism with v. 4, where ψεύδομαι is followed by the dative. Also, it is awkward to speak of "falsifying the Spirit"; the construction is used more naturally of oaths or contracts (see Henry George Liddell, Robert Scott, and Henry Stuart Jones, *A Greek-English Lexicon* (New York: Oxford University Press, 1968), s.v. ψεύδω B. II.).

[63]Johnson (*Acts* 89) notes the theme of "testing the Lord" connected with the Exodus story (Exod 17:2, 7; 20:20; Num 14:22; Deut 33:8; LXX Pss 77:41, 56; 94:9; 105:14) and sees here further reinforcement of the image of Jesus as the prophet-like-Moses.

[64]Cf. Lake and Cadbury (*Beginnings,* 4:51): "The apostles, being filled with the Holy Spirit, were not merely the representatives—in a modern sense—of God, but were actually God." Johnson (*Acts,* 92) puts it more precisely: "By testing these apostles they [Ananias and Sapphira] were challenging *prophets*" (emphasis his).

power of the Spirit. The appropriate response of both the believers and all who hear of these things is "great fear" ($\phi \acute{o} \beta o \varsigma \ \mu \acute{e} \gamma \alpha \varsigma$, v. 5, 11). Here the Spirit, now clearly given a punitive function, is characterized as the power of life and death; the symbolic function of the story in Luke's narrative is evident, in that the end of all who test or lie to this Spirit is death, while the prophets inspired by the Spirit offer "all the words of this life" (Acts 5:20). The great contrast set forth in Luke's narrative is the division among the people, which is ultimately a division between truth and falsehood, between the Spirit and the demon, between God and Satan. The great choice offered, both to those within the narrative and the reader without, is between life—life in the Spirit—and death.

While Luke continues to characterize the Spirit as the Spirit of prophecy, he has added some new elements as well. Luke reiterates his new characterization of the Spirit as the power which forms a community. The coming of the Holy Spirit on the assembly at prayer brings the realization of the Hellenistic ideal of friendship and community goods. This dimension adds to the wholeness and complexity of the Spirit's characterization. The opposite side of the Spirit's character is also demonstrated; in a scene that lends a great deal of complexity to the Spirit's character, Luke attributes death-dealing force to the Spirit. Also, the Spirit is clearly depicted in this passage as a divine representative, a stand-in for God, the onstage presence of the offstage deity. To lie to the Spirit is to lie to God; what more indication of the Spirit's trustworthiness could the reader ask for?

Apostles Arrested (Acts 5:12-42)

The apostles continue to meet with great success (Acts 5:12-16), arousing the jealousy[65] of the high priest and Sadducees, who have

---

[65]Luke alludes to another Hellenistic *topos* here. Envy was thought to induce murderous impulses (Wis 2:24; Philo, *On Joseph* 12; Plato, *Laws* 869E-870A; Plutarch, *On Brotherly Love* 17; *Testament of Simeon* 2:7, 11). See Johnson, *Acts*, 96.

them arrested (vv. 17-18).[66] After the first of several miraculous jailbreaks (vv. 19-21; cf. 12:6-11; 16:26-31), they are re-arrested (vv. 21-26; cf. 4:3) and summoned to defend themselves before the council (vv. 27-32; cf. 4:5-8). Hearing the defiance of Christ's faithful witnesses (v. 29; cf. 4:19), the council is enraged to the brink of murder, but the speech of the sage Gamaliel turns aside their wrath (vv. 33-39); Gamaliel's cynical words find ironic fulfillment in the subsequent narrative: the Jewish leadership is not able to overthrow the new movement (5:39).[67] The episode confirms the rejection of the apostolic witnesses by the putative leaders of the people, and the firm establishment of the apostles' leadership.[68]

Of importance to this study are Peter's words, "We are witnesses to these things, and so is the Holy Spirit whom God has given to those who obey him" (Acts 5:32). The Spirit is directly characterized by the speech of another character, with high reliability.[69] Peter reinforces the now familiar characterization of the Spirit as involved in witness and as a gift of God; the Spirit is at work as he

---

[66]On the second trial and arrest scene, see Bauernfeind, *Apostelgeschichte*, 88-97; Bruce, *Acts*, 166-79; Conzelmann, *Acts*, 39-44; Haenchen, *Acts*, 242-58; Johnson, *Acts*, 93-104; Lake and Cadbury, *Beginnings*, 4:54-63; Pesch, *Apostelgeschichte*, 1:204-24; Schneider, *Apostelgeschichte*, 1:378-404; Tannehill, *Narrative Unity*, 2:59-79.

[67]Luke consistently portrays the Pharisees as opponents of Jesus and his disciples, so it is difficult to see anything but irony here. See Darr, *On Character Building*, 42-43; 85-126; esp. 116-20; Johnson, *Acts*, 102-3; contra Gowler, *Host, Guest, Enemy and Friend*, 177-296, esp. 274-80; Haenchen, *Acts*, 256; Tannehill, *Narrative Unity of Luke-Acts*, 2:67. See also Brawley, *Luke-Acts and the Jews;* John T. Carroll, "Luke's Portrayal of the Pharisees," *Catholic Biblical Quarterly* 50 (1988): 604-21; Jack Dean Kingsbury, "The Pharisees in Luke-Acts," in *The Four Gospels*, ed. F. Van Segroeck, C. M. Tuckett, G. Van Belle, and J. Verheyden (Leuven: Leuven University Press, 1992), 2:1497-1512; Sanders, *Jews in Luke-Acts*, esp. 84-130; Joseph Tyson, *Images of Judaism;* idem, *Luke-Acts and the Jewish People;* J. Ziesler, "Luke and the Pharisees," *New Testament Studies* 25 (1978-79): 146-57.

[68]Cf. Johnson, *Acts*, 101-3.

[69]"Peter's statement is provocative: this is said, after all, by one already identified as 'full of the Holy Spirit' (4:8)" (Ibid., 98).

speaks. But in Peter's speech Luke makes two important rhetorical moves.

First, Luke has Peter directly characterize the Spirit itself as a "witness." This is the first direct characterization since the Spirit was said to be "the promise of the Father" (by Jesus in Luke 24:49 and Acts 1:4; repeated by Peter in 2:33). Here again the characterization marks a rhetorical shift. The reader is prepared to expect a significant "witness" from the Spirit, which will occur in the stories about the Gentile mission (esp. Acts 8 and Acts 10-15); the expectation is confirmed when Luke notes that the Holy Spirit has backed the decision to admit Gentiles into the community (Acts 15:28). The Spirit will function as a witness, showing the church the direction it is to take. The direct characterization of the Spirit as a "witness" serves as a yet another literary prophecy of what is to come.

Second, Luke in this characterization portrays the Spirit as a direct actor. The Holy Spirit itself is witnessing to the council. This statement stands side-by-side with the picture of the disciples as agents through whom the Spirit works. As before when Luke has pictured the Spirit as a direct actor (cf. Luke 3:22, Acts 2:4), the rhetoric helps emphasize the importance of the characterization for the narrative to follow. Luke hints that the Spirit will give significant witness in the story to come, and the reader who develops this expectation will not be disappointed.

Stephen and the Hellenists (Acts 6:1-8:3)

A dispute over food distribution introduces Stephen and the Hellenists.[70] Stephen, along with six other Hellenists,[71] is elected to

---

[70]On Stephen and the Hellenists, see Bauernfeind, *Apostelgeschichte*, 97-121; M.-E. Boismard, "Le Martyre d'Etienne (Acts 6, 8-8, 2)," *Recherches de science religieuse* 69 (1981): 181-94; Bruce, *Acts*, 180-215; Henry J. Cadbury, "The Hellenists," in *Beginnings*, 5:59-74; Conzelmann, *Acts*, 44-61; Craig C. Hill, *Hellenists and Hebrews: Reappraising Division within the Earliest Church* (Minneapolis: Fortress Press, 1992); Johnson, *Acts*, 104-44; idem, *Literary Function of Possessions*, 211-12; John Kilgallen, "The Function of Stephen's Speech (Acts 7, 2-53)," *Biblica* 70 (1989): 173-93; idem, *The Stephen Speech: A Literary and Redactional Study of Acts 7, 2-53*, Analecta Biblica, vol. 67 (Rome: Biblical Institute Press, 1976); Haenchen, *Acts*, 259-99; Lake and Cadbury, *Beginnings*, 4:63-88; David P. Moessner, "The Christ Must Suffer: New Light on the Jesus-

wait tables (6:1-7), but functions instead as a prophet, preaching and doing miracles (6:8-9). The criteria for selecting the Seven are prophetic: they are to be πλήρεις πνεύματος καὶ σοφίας (6:3). In addition to Stephen, Philip will also be depicted in the role of prophet (Acts 8:4-40, 21:8). While this may seem incongruous at first—they are chosen to wait tables, but end up preaching the gospel—it is entirely in harmony with the rest of the narrative. Luke sees the distribution of goods as a significant aspect of leadership (cf. Luke 9:3, 12-17; 10:4-9; 12:35-48; 16:1-13; 19:11-27; 22:24-30; Acts 1:15-26; 2:42-47); the transition of prophetic power between the apostles and the Seven is thus symbolized by the author-

---

Peter, Stephen-Paul Parallels in Luke-Acts," *Novum Testamentum* 28 (1986): 220-56; C. F. D. Moule, "Once More, Who Were the Hellenists?" *Expository Times* 70 (1958-59): 100-102; Pesch, *Apostelgeschichte,* 1:224-68; Earl Richard, *Acts 6:1-8:4: The Author's Method of Composition,* Society of Biblical Literature Dissertation Series, no. 41 (Missoula, Mont.: Scholars Press, 1978); Martin H. Scharlemann, *Stephen, A Singular Saint,* Analecta Biblica, vol. 34 (Rome: Pontifical Biblical Institute, 1968); Schneider, *Apostelgeschichte,* 1:405-80; Marcel Simon, *St. Stephen and the Hellenists in the Primitive Church* (London: Longmans, Green and Co., 1958); Tannehill, *Narrative Unity,* 2:80-101; Wilson, *Gentiles and Gentile Mission,* 129-53.

[71]Exactly what Luke means by Ἑλληνιστής is a matter of dispute. It is generally held that a "Hellenist" would be one who spoke Greek or observed Greek customs (from ἑλληνίζω). This is the first occurrence of the term in Greek literature; here it obviously refers to Jewish members of the Christian community. In Acts 9:29 Saul argues with Hellenist enemies; they are obviously Jewish, but not Christian. In Acts 11:20, however, they seem to be Gentiles, since they are contrasted with "Jews" in 11:19 (prompting some scribes to substitute the more familiar Ἑλληνας, "Greeks," for Ἑλληνιστάς; see Metzger, *Textual Commentary,* 386-89; contra Bruce, *Acts,* 272; Haenchen, *Acts,* 365 n. 5; Johnson, *Acts,* 203). It is extremely difficult to harmonize these three distinct usages of the word; there is certainly little basis for positing a liberal, "Hellenist" party in the early church. See Bauernfeind, *Apostelgeschichte,* 101-5; Bruce, *Acts,* 180-81; Cadbury, "The Hellenists"; Haenchen, *Acts,* 260-61; Hill, *Hebrews and Hellenists;* Johnson, *Acts,* 105; Kilgallen, *The Stephen Speech;* Scharlemann, *Stephen, A Singular Saint;* Schneider, *Apostelgeschichte,* 1:406-16; Simon, *St. Stephen.*

ity of the Seven over material goods.[72]

Stephen is described in stereotypically prophetic terms.[73] He is directly characterized by the narrator as "a man full of faith and the Holy Spirit" (6:5; cf. 6:3; 7:55; 11:24) and "full of grace and power" (6:8); the last person to be described as πλήρης πνεύματος ἁγίου was Jesus (Luke 4:1), and the reader will note many similarities between the Stephen story and that of Jesus. Stephen is also indirectly characterized as a prophet when he is depicted as doing "great wonders and signs" (6:8). Stephen engages in argument with opponents, who cannot match his prophetic skills; Luke says "they could not withstand the wisdom and the Spirit with which he spoke" (6:10). "Wisdom" (σοφία) was a characteristic of the prophet Jesus (Luke 2:40, 52; 7:35; 11:31) who promised such wisdom to his disciples (Luke 21:15; cf. Luke 12:12); it was also a characteristic of Jesus' prophetic predecessors, Joseph (Acts 7:10) and Moses (Acts 7:22).[74] Stephen's speech, in particular his portrait of Moses, most clearly establishes the prophetic pattern found throughout Luke-Acts: the prophet comes in wisdom and power, but is rejected and exiled (Acts 7:22-29); he is empowered by God (7:30-35) and returns to do more "signs and wonders" (7:35-38), but again, the response of the people is not faithful (7:39-43) Stephen sees this pattern replicated in the story of Jesus and his disciples (7:51-53). Luke emphasizes the prophetic pattern by painting Stephen with the same brush; the similarities between the death of Stephen and the crucifixion of Jesus are striking.[75] Once again, the Spirit is indirectly characterized here as the source of prophetic power and inspired speech. The strong characterization of Stephen as a prophet signals to the reader that what follows is trustworthy;

---

[72]See Johnson, *Acts,* 110-11.

[73]See ibid., 108; Tannehill, *Narrative Unity of Luke-Acts,* 2:83.

[74]On the connection between the Spirit and wisdom, cf. Deut 34:9; Isa 11:2. See Tannehill, *Narrative Unity of Luke-Acts,* 2:83.

[75]See Haenchen, *Acts,* 274; Johnson, *Acts,* 112, 142-43; Tannehill, *Narrative Unity of Luke-Acts,* 2:91-92.

the mention of the Spirit again functions to ensure reliability—here, the reliability of Stephen's long speech before the council.[76]

The Spirit is clearly characterized by the contrast between Stephen and the council. The council is directly characterized by the reliable, Spirit-filled commentator Stephen as a "stiff-necked people, uncircumcised in heart and ears," in line with their forebears;[77] they continually "resist the Holy Spirit" (7:51; cf. Num 27:14; Isa 63:10 LXX; Luke 12:10; Acts 3:23; 5:1-11). The council will repeat the old pattern: "Which of the prophets did your ancestors not persecute? They killed those who foretold the coming of the Righteous One, and now you have become his betrayers and murderers" (7:52; cf. Luke 6:26; 11:47-50; 13:34; 24:20; Acts 4:10; 5:30). Despite their privileged status, they do not keep Torah (7:53). Stephen's words become a self-fulfilling prophecy: the council kills him (7:57-60) and proceeds on to more widespread persecution of the Christian community (8:1-3).[78] Luke sharpens the contrast between the council and the prophets by reminding the reader that in contrast with the council, which "opposes the Holy Spirit" (7:51), Stephen is "full of the Holy Spirit" (7:55), and as a prophet, is granted a vision of heaven (7:55-56).[79]

Luke is moving the narrative towards a more universal mission, and the Holy Spirit has a definite role in this movement. Stephen, full of the Spirit, sparks a controversy with diaspora Jews (6:9).

---

[76]Cf. Luke's description of Stephen's face immediately before the speech—ὡσεὶ πρόσωπον ἀγγέλου (6:15). Since angels are reliable commentators in the Lukan narrative, this is another indication of Stephen's reliability. Cf. also Jesus' facial glowing at the transfiguration (Luke 9:29). See Johnson, *Acts*, 110.

[77]"Stiff-necked" (σκληροτράχηλος) derives from LXX Exod 33:3, 5; 34:9; Deut 9:6, 13. "Uncircumcised" (ἀπερίτμητος) in "heart" (Lev 26:41; Deut 10:16; Jer 4:4; 9:26; Ezek 44:7, 9) and "ears" (Jer 6:10) deliberately excludes the council from the people of God; cf. 1QS 5:5; 1QpHab 11:13. See Johnson, *Acts*, 133-34.

[78]Cf. Johnson, *Acts*, 142; Tannehill, *Narrative Unity of Luke-Acts*, 2:85-87. Luke hints that the complicity of Saul extends beyond mere sympathy and coat-watching; see Johnson, *Acts*, 140-44.

[79]Cf. Johnson, *Acts*, 139-40.

Stephen's words clearly indicate that God's purpose has been fulfilled: salvation has been announced to the Jewish hierarchy, which rejects it, in keeping with the prophetic pattern.[80] The words that spark Stephen's execution are explicitly said to be inspired by the Spirit; ironically, the persecution sparked by this event serves to spark evangelism in Samaria (Acts 8:5-26) and beyond (8:26-40; 11:19-26), in fulfillment of Jesus' prophecy (Acts 1:8).[81] Stephen and the Seven represent the succession of prophetic authority, necessary to move the mission beyond the confines of Jerusalem.[82] Finally, the Stephen episode introduces Saul (7:58; 8:1-3), soon to become Paul, apostle to the Gentiles.[83] In the narrative which follows, Paul will be the instrument of the Spirit *par excellence*.

The Samaritans (Acts 8:4-25)

The persecution following the death of Stephen sends Philip, one of the Seven (Acts 6:5), to preach to the Samaritans, with great success.[84] Philip is portrayed as a prophet, like Jesus, Peter, and

---

[80]It may be argued that even among the leadership, there is division within the people, for Luke says that many priests joined the community of believers (Acts 6:7). However, there were many thousands of priests in Jerusalem at this time, and they were in some ways marginalized and disaffected from their leadership; cf. Josephus, *Antiquities* 2.181; *Jewish War* 2.409-10. See Johnson, *Acts*, 107-8.

[81]Cf. Johnson, *Acts*, 110; Tannehill, *Narrative Unity of Luke-Acts*, 2:80.

[82]See Johnson, *Acts*, 110-11.

[83]See Haenchen, *Acts*, 297-99; Johnson, *Acts*, 143-44; Tannehill, *Narrative Unity of Luke-Acts*, 2:99-101.

[84]On Philip, the Samaritans, and Simon Magus, see Adler, *Taufe und Handauflegung;* Barrett, "Light on the Holy Spirit"; Bauernfeind, *Apostelgeschichte,* 121-27; Bruce, *Acts,* 216-24; R. P. Casey, "Simon Magus," in *Beginnings,* 5:151-63; Conzelmann, *Acts,* 62-66; J. Coppens, "L'imposition des mains dans les Actes des Apôtres," *Les Acts des Apôtres: traditions, rédaction, théologie,* 405-38; J. Duncan Derrett, "Simon Magus (Act 8[9-24])," *Zeitschrift für die neutestamentliche Wissenschaft* 73 (1982): 52-68; Dunn, *Baptism in the Holy Spirit,* 55-72; Garrett, *Demise of the Devil,* 61-78; Giblet, "Baptism in the Spirit"; Harm, "Structural Elements"; Haenchen, *Acts,* 300-308; Haya-Prats, *L'Esprit,* 134-35; Hull, *Holy Spirit in Acts,* 104-8; Jervell, "The Lost Sheep of

Stephen, preaching and doing "signs and great miracles" (σημεῖα καὶ δυνάμεις μεγάλαι, Acts 8:13, cf. vv. 6-8).[85] Again, "power" (δύναμις) is clear sign of the work of the Spirit.

Philip is characterized as a true prophet by contrast with Simon the magician.[86] While magic was a common feature of Hellenistic religion and a source of general fascination, it held a low place in terms of social respectability.[87] In such a social situation, the miracles of the prophet and the deeds of the magician would look very similar, and this may not lend the prophet a positive public image. Luke capitalizes on the apparent similarities between the "signs and wonders" of Christians and the "magic deeds" of Simon (Acts 8:11) in order to emphasize the critical difference between them—for magic in Luke's view was empowered by satanic

---

the House of Israel. The Understanding of the Samaritans in Luke-Acts," in *Luke and the People of God*, 113-26; Johnson, *Acts*, 144-53; idem, *Literary Function of Possessions*, 213-17; Lake and Cadbury, *Beginnings*, 4:88-95; Lampe, "Holy Spirit in Writings of Luke," 198-200; Wayne A. Meeks, "Simon Magus in Recent Research," *Religious Studies Review* 3 (1977): 137-42; Menzies, *Development of Early Christian Pneumatology*, 248-60; Oulton, "Holy Spirit, Baptism, and Laying on of Hands"; Pesch, *Apostelgeschichte*, 1:268-85; Schneider, *Apostelgeschichte*, 1:481-96; F. Scott Spencer, *The Portrait of Philip in Acts: A Study of Roles and Relations*, Journal for the Study of the New Testament Supplement Series, vol. 67 (Sheffield: JSOT Press, 1992); Tannehill, *Narrative Unity*, 2:102-7.

It may well be that Luke combines two sources here: one a story of Philip, another about Simon Peter and Simon Magus. Certainly Luke has heavily shaped the material. See Barrett, "Light on the Holy Spirit," 283-85; Haenchen, *Acts*, 305-7; Menzies, *Development of Early Christian Pneumatology*, 249-50.

[85]See Johnson, *Acts*, 151; Tannehill, *Narrative Unity of Luke-Acts*, 2:103-4.

[86]Simon Magus appears in later Christian literature as a magician, opponent of Christianity, and founder of gnosticism (Justin Martyr, *Apology* 1.26; Justin, *Dialogue with Trypho* 120.6; *Acts of Peter* 4-32; Pseudo-Clementine *Homilies* 2.22-24; Irenaeus, *Against Heresies* 1.23). See Bauernfeind, *Apostelgeschichte*, 125-26; Johnson, *Acts*, 146.

[87]See Garrett, *Demise of the Devil*, 11-19.

influences (Acts 8:20; 13:6-11; 16:16-18; 19:11-20).[88] Simon's magical "power" (δύναμις, v. 10) is superseded by "the good news of the Kingdom of God" (v. 12). Simon himself is converted, submits to baptism (thus implicitly renouncing magic) and yet remains amazed at the power of the disciples (v. 13, cf. vv. 18-19).[89] The human conflict between the disciple and the magician is indicative of the underlying cosmic conflict between the Spirit which empowers Philip and the demonic forces at work in magic.

While the focus of many commentators has been to unravel Luke's theology of the reception of the Spirit,[90] Luke's concern in the final scene of this story centers on the succession of prophetic power. Luke connects the mission of Philip with the Jerusalem community by narrating the visit of Peter and John (Acts 8:14-23). Though the Samaritans had been baptized, they had not received the Spirit (vv. 15-16), which they now receive through the laying-on-of-hands by Peter and John (v. 17).[91] The presence of the Spirit now indicates not only divine approval of the Samaritan mission, which had been prophesied by Jesus (Acts 1:8), but also continuity with the apostolic mission.[92] The apostolic leadership approves of the

---

[88]See Garrett, *Demise of the Devil;* Johnson, *Acts,* 146-47.

[89]On the contrast between Philip and Simon, see Garrett, *Demise of the Devil,* 63-69; Tannehill, *Narrative Unity of Luke-Acts,* 2:105.

[90]E.g., Adler, *Taufe und Handauflegung;* Barrett, "Light on the Holy Spirit"; Beasley-Murray, *Baptism,* 118-20; Dunn, *Baptism in the Holy Spirit,* 55-72; Giblet, "Baptism in the Spirit"; Harm, "Structural Elements"; Lampe, "Holy Spirit in Writings of Luke," 198-200; idem, *Seal of the Spirit;* Menzies, *Development of Early Christian Pneumatology,* 248-60; Pesch, *Apostelgeschichte,* 1:282-85. See above, chap. 1, "What Does the Holy Spirit Do?"

[91]Note that Luke does not say that the gift of the Spirit was accompanied by glossolalia, though this is inferred by many commentators (e.g., Haenchen, *Acts,* 304). Luke is less concerned with theological consistency than with telling a story.

[92]Is there any hint that the Jerusalem church resisted Philip's foray into Samaria? Luke gives no indication that Philip's new mission excited the kind of negative reaction that accompanied Peter's preaching to the Gentile Cornelius (Acts 11:1-18). Yet the story of the conversion of the Samaritans contains some of the same features found in the later controversy over the opening of the Gentile mission: the direct intervention of the Spirit which leads to the proclamation of the

new mission, and the Spirit comes to Samaria as it had to Jerusalem—through the apostles (cf. 11:1-18, 22-24).[93] The power of the Spirit is not limited to Jerusalem, but is now moving out into the countryside. Once again, the presence of the Spirit assures the reader that the plan of God is working as promised. Even Peter and John now feel free to preach to the Samaritans (8:25).

As with Philip, the apostles are characterized in contrast with Simon, who does not understand that the power to bestow the Holy Spirit, like the Spirit itself, is the free gift of God (v. 20). Simon's offer of money is in keeping with ancient stereotypes about the avarice and venality of magicians; by contrasting Peter and Simon in this regard, Luke clearly distinguishes the early Christians from practitioners of magic.[94] Simon's attempt to buy this power and authority (ἐξουσία, v. 19) is an indication that he does not share in the prophetic ministry (οὐκ ἔστιν σοι μερὶς οὐδὲ κλῆρος ἐν τῷ λόγῳ τούτῳ, v. 21),[95] because his "heart is not right before God" (v. 21,

---

gospel in a new situation, the descent of the Spirit on the new converts, and the careful connection made between the new mission and the Jerusalem church (see below on Acts 10-15). Luke in this passage prepares the reader for the role of the Spirit in the stories to come: the action of the Spirit is taken as the action of God, and is so ratified by the actions of the apostles. The pattern established in the (apparently) non-controversial Samaritan mission will hold in later, more controversial situations.

[93]Cf. Haenchen, *Acts,* 304; Johnson, *Acts,* 151; Tannehill, *Narrative Unity of Luke-Acts,* 2:104. The apostles "become the stabilizing, verifying, unifying element" in the new mission (Tannehill, *Narrative Unity of Luke-Acts,* 2:102).

[94]On magicians and money, see Plato, *Laws* 909A-B; Philo, *Special Laws* 3.100-101; Lucian, *Lover of Lies* 15-16; Origen, *Against Celsus* 1.68; Juvenal, *Satire* 6.546; Philostratus, *Life of Apollonius* 8.7. Cf. Garrett, *Demise of the Devil,* 70.

[95]The λόγος in question (v. 21) is probably apostleship or Christian mission, not Christianity itself (so Schuyler Brown, *Apostasy and Perseverance in the Theology of Luke,* Analecta Biblica, vol. 36 (Rome: Biblical Institute, 1969), 111; Johnson, *Literary Function of Possessions,* 216; contra Garrett, *Demise of the Devil,* 146-47; Haenchen, *Acts,* 305. Cf. Menzies, *Development of Early Christian Pneumatology,* 256; Turner, "Luke and the Spirit," 166). Luke says explicitly that Simon believed (Acts 8:13) and pictures him as repentant at Peter's words (v. 24). The ultimate fate of Simon is left open by Luke (a case of openness in characterization, a gap later generations rushed to fill). That Christians could

cf. 7:51), and he is "in the gall of bitterness and the bonds of wickedness" (8:23; cf. LXX Deut 29:17; Isa 58:6). Luke's use of the language of possessions is subtle: Simon has neither μερὶς οὐδὲ κλῆρος (8:20; cf. Acts 1:17), despite his efforts to acquire a share with money. Simon's use of his wealth is symbolic of the state of his heart;[96] as in other stories about the use of possessions (Acts 2:42-47; 4:31-5:11), the Spirit is indirectly characterized as involved in the moral and spiritual attitudes of the individual. Peter's harsh invocation of judgment (τὸ ἀργύριόν σου σὺν σοὶ εἴη εἰς ἀπώλειαν, v. 20) is a reminder that the Spirit can deal in death as well as life (cf. Acts 5:1-11).

Just as the Spirit was characterized in contrast with Satan in the temptation narrative (Luke 4:1-14) and the story of Ananias and Sapphira (Acts 5:1-11), the contrast between the power of God in the Spirit and the weaker power of magic is clear.[97] Simon, though repentant (8:24), illustrates the bondage that comes with magical powers, in contrast to the freedom of the Spirit.[98] Here Luke involves the Spirit implicitly in human conflicts—between Philip and Simon, then Peter and Simon—which are on a deeper level conflicts between two cosmic characters, Satan and God. That the Holy Spirit can be involved in such a conflict is a fundamental indication that the Spirit can be considered a character in Luke-Acts.

As I have noted before, Luke does not present a consistent picture of the relationship among baptism, laying-on-of-hands, and the reception of the Spirit. Luke's inconsistencies may at one level introduce a certain amount of incoherence into his characterization of the Spirit; it makes it extremely difficult to posit a consistent relation of baptism, laying-on-of-hands, and the reception of the Spirit

---

suffer "destruction" (8:20) is shown by the Ananias and Sapphira episode.

[96]See Johnson, *Literary Function of Possessions,* 213-17.

[97]Cf. Johnson, *Acts,* 152.

[98]Cf. Garrett, *Demise of the Devil,* 72: "the magician wanted to purchase divine authority while himself still trapped under diabolical authority."

in Luke-Acts. On another level, it introduces a new level of complexity and opacity—the Spirit seems to have a mind of its own, not
readily apparent to the reader. Also, the characterization attains a
new measure of dynamism, as the Spirit seems to act in freedom.
These new aspects of Luke's characterization of the Spirit help
prepare the reader for the striking role the Spirit will play in the
next story.

Philip and the Ethiopian Eunuch (Acts 8:26-40)

Philip proceeds at the command of "an angel of the Lord" down
towards Gaza, where he meets and converts an Ethiopian eunuch.[99]
The reliable angelic voice thus directs the mission into new territory.
The eunuch, a financial official of the queen of the Ethiopians, has
been in Jerusalem for worship, but like the Samaritans, he is an outcast there—"No one whose testicles are crushed or whose penis is
cut off shall be admitted to the assembly of the Lord" (Deut 23:1;
cf. Lev 21:20).[100] Luke does not clearly state that the Ethiopian is

---

[99]On Philip and the Ethiopian eunuch, see Bauernfeind, *Apostelgeschichte*,
127-29; Bruce, *Acts*, 224-41; Conzelmann, *Acts*, 67-69; Erich Dinkler, "Philippus
und der ANHP AIΘΙΟΨ (Apg. 8, 26-40)," in *Jesus und Paulus*, ed. E. Earle Ellis
and Erich Grässer (Göttingen: Vandenhoeck & Ruprecht, 1975), 85-95; Beverly
Gaventa, *From Darkness to Light: Aspects of Conversion in the New Testament*
(Philadelphia: Fortress Press, 1986), 98-107; A. George, "L'Esprit Saint dans
l'oeuvre de Luc," *Revue biblique* 85 (1978): 500-542; Haenchen, *Acts*, 309-17;
Johnson, *Acts*, 153-61; Lake and Cadbury, *Beginnings*, 4:95-99; Clarice J.
Martin, "A Chamberlain's Journey and the Challenge of Interpretation for Libera-
tion," *Semeia* 47 (1989): 105-35; R. F. O'Toole, "Philip and the Ethiopian
Eunuch (Acts viii, 25-40)," *Journal for the Study of the New Testament* 17
(1983): 25-34; Pesch, *Apostelgeschichte*, 1:285-96; Schneider, *Apostelgeschichte*,
1:496-509; Spencer, *Portrait of Philip;* Tannehill, *Narrative Unity*, 2:107-12; W.
C. van Unnik, "Der Befehl an Philippus," in *Sparsa Collecta* 1:328-39.

[100]Εὐνοῦχος need not indicate castration but simply high office (Haenchen,
Acts, 310). However, in light of Luke's concern for the downcast and the symbolism of the castrated male in biblical tradition, it seems best to take this expression at face value. Eunuchs were often employed as court officials (Herodotus, *History* 8.105; Plutarch, *Demetrios* 25.5; Philostratus, *Life of Apollonius* 1.33-36).
See Bruce, *Acts*, 225; Johnson, *Acts*, 155; Lake and Cadbury, *Beginnings*, 4:96.

Jewish (Ethiopia would normally be considered Gentile territory), but this is implied by the context—the story of Cornelius is plainly given first place in the account of the Gentile mission.[101] But Ethiopia was considered to be an almost mythic land—a large legendary territory, exotic, distant, and indeterminate, one of the extremities of the inhabited earth. For Philip to preach the gospel to an Ethiopian would indeed be to preach "to the ends of the earth," in fulfillment of Jesus' prophecy (Acts 1:8).[102] Thus, in a gentle foreshadowing of the universal mission to come,[103] Philip preaches not only "to the ends of earth," but also to one who is excluded from the people of Israel, one of the downtrodden and outcast who (in keeping with a characteristic Lukan theme, cf. Luke 1:52-53; 3:5; 14:11; 18:14) can now find acceptance.[104]

---

[101] See Johnson, *Acts,* 159; Haenchen, *Acts,* 314; contra Tannehill, *Narrative Unity of Luke-Acts,* 2:109-10. Luke places Jews from Africa in Jerusalem at Pentecost (Acts 2:10).

[102] T. C. G. Thornton ("To the Ends") argues that "to the ends of the earth" is literally fulfilled when Philip evangelizes the Ethiopian. On the legends about Ethiopia, see Isa 18:2; Homer, *Odyssey* 1.23; Herodotus, *History* 3.25; 3.114; Strabo, *Geography* 1.1.6; 1.2.24; Pliny, *Natural History* 6.180-97; Heliodorus, *The Ethiopians;* Pseudo-Callisthenes, *Life of Alexander of Macedon* 3.18-23; Philostratus, *Life of Apollonius* 3.20; 6.1). See also Bruce, *Acts,* 225; Johnson, *Acts,* 154; Tannehill, *Narrative Unity of Luke-Acts,* 2:108-9; van Unnik, "Der Ausdruck ΄ΕΩΣ ΄ΕΣΧΑΤΟΥ ΤΗΣ ΓΗΣ."

[103] Haenchen's metaphor of "the eunuch's conversion...as a stepping stone between those of the Samaritans and the Gentiles" (*Acts,* 314) is still appropriate, despite the critique of Tannehill (*Narrative Unity of Luke-Acts,* 2:107) that it is instead "a leap to the extreme," i.e., Ethiopia. Luke fulfills the prophesied extension of the gospel to the "ends of the earth" (Acts 1:8) while at the same time anticipating the Cornelius story.

[104] Cf. Isa 56:4-5, where "the eunuchs who keep my sabbath" are promised "an everlasting name that shall not be cut off." See Bruce, *Acts,* 225; Johnson, *Acts,* 155, 160. Note that the passage the eunuch is reading from Isaiah speaks of the "humiliation" of God's servant (Isa 53:7-8 LXX).

Tannehill (*Narrative Unity of Luke-Acts,* 2:109) notes that Ethiopians were generally considered to be black (Herodotus, *History* 2.22; 3.101; Philostratus, *Life of Apollonius* 6.1), and thus this eunuch could be doubly an outsider. See also Dinkler, "Philippus."

Philip's mission has definite divine direction. While it begins at the behest of "the angel of the Lord" (8:26; cf. Luke 1-2; 22:43; Acts 5:19; 10:3-7, 22; 11:13; 12:7-11; 27:23), the direction is taken up by the Spirit (8:29). When the eunuch has been baptized, the Spirit takes Philip on to his new assignment (Acts 8:39-40). As in the infancy narrative of the Gospel (cf. Luke 1:11, 26 with 2:26-27), the "angel of the Lord" and the "Spirit" both function symbolically as indicators of God's presence, and as such they are almost interchangeable;[105] they are the onstage stand-ins for the offstage God.[106]

Given the explicit depiction of divine guidance, the reader is prepared to hear Philip's preaching as reliable and authoritative. As is often the case in Luke-Acts, scripture provides the foundation for the message. The Spirit has already spoken to the eunuch through the prophet Isaiah (8:30-33); he needs only for a modern prophet to open his eyes to the meaning (vv. 34-35). Philip's prophetic stature is enhanced by the obvious similarities between his action and that of the resurrected Jesus, who explained the significance of the prophetic writings to the disciples before he ascended to heaven (cf. Luke 24:27, 45). Like Jesus, Philip as a prophet himself gives authoritative interpretation of the prophetic tradition.

Luke says the Spirit "speaks" to Philip. This is the first time in Luke-Acts that the Spirit speaks in present narrative time.[107] At this crucial point in the story, Luke portrays the Spirit as a direct actor, in order to underscore the divine origin of Philip's mission. Philip acts as a prophet, to whom the Spirit would regularly speak (cf. 1 Kgs 22:24; Ezek 2:24, 27; 11:2, 5).[108] The Spirit's presence is,

---

[105]Cf. Bruce, *Acts*, 230; Johnson, *Acts*, 154-55; Haenchen, *Acts*, 310.

[106]Cf. Brawley, *Centering on God*, 115; Darr, *On Character Building*, 51-53.

[107]For the Spirit speaking in the past through the authors of scripture, see Acts 1:16; 4:25. Cf. also Luke 2:26. Bruce (*Acts*, 226) says that "an inward monition rather than prophetic utterance is indicated," but this is not a distinction that Luke makes (cf. Acts 13:1-2).

[108]Cf. Johnson, *Acts*, 158; Tannehill, *Narrative Unity of Luke-Acts*, 2:108.

once again, a sign of the reliability of the narrative. Now, however, the Spirit itself is the reliable commentator.

The Spirit takes further charge of the mission by snatching Philip away before the very eyes of the eunuch: "Philip found himself at Azotus, and as he was passing through the region, he proclaimed the good news to all the towns until he came to Caesarea" (Acts 8:39-40; cf. 21:8).[109] Luke again draws on prophetic models, those of Elijah (cf. 2 Kgs 2:11-12; 1 Kgs 18:12; 2 Kgs 2:16) and Ezekiel (Ezek 2:2; 3:12, 14, 24; 8:3; 11:1, 5, 24; 37:1; 43:5). Here the Spirit is again characterized as a direct actor, pushing Philip (and the narrative as well) to spread the word of God outward from Jerusalem.[110] Luke's rhetoric serves to assure the reader that God, through the Spirit, is in charge of this story.

The characterization of the Spirit is given a degree of complexity, opacity, and dynamism by the geographical references in this story. Philip begins in Samaria, to the north of Jerusalem. He is then told to head south on the Gaza road, where he meets the eunuch. When he is finished there, he is taken by the Spirit to Azotus, twenty miles north of Gaza along the coast, heading for Caesarea, where the story will find him later (Acts 21:8).[111] There is no logical progression here; the reader may infer that the Spirit takes the prophet where he

---

[109]There is no good reason to think that the longer reading of Acts 8:39 is original (πνεῦμα ἅγιον ἐπέπεσεν ἐπὶ τὸν εὐνοῦχον, ἄγγελος δὲ κυρίου ἥρπασεν τὸν Φίλιππον, read by A, some miniscules, and some western versions). The shorter reading is much better attested. It is likely that these words were added to associate the Holy Spirit with the baptism of the eunuch, and to bring the end of the story into conformity with the beginning (v. 26). See Bruce, *Acts,* 230; Johnson, *Acts,* 157; Metzger, *Textual Commentary,* 360-61; contra Menzies, *Development of Early Christian Pneumatology,* 124.

[110]Cf. Johnson, *Acts,* 157: "Luke again dramatically illustrates how the mission is impelled and directed by the Holy Spirit....Another single incident is expanded by means of geographical references and the imperfect tense to a larger missionary enterprise."

[111]The geographical note also prepares the reader for an important event which will take place later in the plot, as Caesarea is the site of the conversion of Cornelius (chap. 10). Once again, Luke subtly prepares for the narrative to come: as Peter followed Philip into Samaria, so too Peter will follow Philip to Caesarea.

is most needed, and that Philip as one of the Seven is the appropriate prophet for the expanding mission. But the reasoning and motives of the Spirit are not transparent, however clear the overall direction of the mission may be. The obscurity adds an appropriate bit of color to the Lukan portrait—the Spirit does, after all, represent the inscrutable God. And the lack of transparency on this point does not hinder Luke's overall purpose: the mission is moving outward. The Spirit-inspired conversion of the eunuch is an important step in the ongoing story. And the Spirit moves the story along.

Luke's portrait of the Spirit in this passage is in line with Old Testament stylization: the Spirit speaks and provides transport as it did for the prophets, particularly Ezekiel.[112] Luke will continue to use rhetoric which depicts the Holy Spirit as a direct actor in the story—more so as the story moves toward the all-important initiation of the Gentile mission. The Spirit's characterization thus takes on a greater degree of wholeness, transparency, and dynamism as the narrative proceeds; the reader sees more aspects of the Spirit's work when it acts directly, and the direct action gives the reader a sense that something important is developing here. This sense will be enhanced by the story of the conversion of Saul.

Saul's Conversion and Call (Acts 9:1-31)

Saul, who has momentarily become the chief persecutor in Luke's story (Acts 9:1-2; cf. 8:3), now becomes another example of the power of Christ and the purpose of God.[113] Saul's conversion

---

[112]The characterization of Philip is also reminiscent of Elijah; see Bruce, *Acts*, 225; Johnson, *Acts*, 158.

[113]On Saul's conversion, see Bauernfeind, *Apostelgeschichte*, 129-38; Bruce, *Acts*, 232-46; Conzelmann, *Acts*, 70-75; Dunn, *Baptism in the Holy Spirit*, 75-78; Gaventa, *From Darkness to Light*, 52-95; David Gill, "The Structure of Acts 9," *Biblica* 55 (1974): 546-48; Haenchen, *Acts*, 318-36; Charles W. Hedrick, "Paul's Conversion/Call: A Comparative Analysis of the Three Reports in Acts," *Journal of Biblical Literature* 100 (1981): 415-32; Johnson, *Acts*, 161-75; Lake and Cadbury, *Beginnings*, 4:99-107; Gerhard Lohfink, *The Conversion of St. Paul: Narrative and History in Acts*, trans. Bruce Malina (Chicago: Franciscan Herald Press, 1976); Sten Lundgren, "Ananias and the Calling of Paul in Acts," *Studia*

comes on the heels of that of the Ethiopian eunuch and shortly before that of Cornelius; Luke uses the individual conversion stories to establish a wider pattern depicting the gradual but sure rise of a universal mission.[114] Saul's conversion, however, differs from the other two; it is primarily a call.[115] Luke uses his most reliable commentator, the risen Jesus, to explain the significance of the story: "he is an instrument chosen to bring my name before the Gentiles" who "must suffer for the sake of my name" (Acts 9:15-16). Jesus' words to Ananias form a programmatic prophecy of Paul's career, as he will preach before "Gentiles, kings, and the people of Israel" (cf. Acts 13:15-52; 25:12; 26:1-23; 27:24; 28:23-28).[116] The prophecy is fulfilled immediately, as Saul preaches the Lord Jesus and is himself persecuted (vv. 19-30). By relating the conversion

---

Theologica 25 (1971): 117-22; Menzies, *Development of Early Christian Pneumatology*, 260-62; Pesch, *Apostelgeschichte*, 1:296-316; Schneider, *Apostelgeschichte*, 2:18-45; Tannehill, *Narrative Unity*, 2:113-24; Wilson, *Gentiles and Gentile Mission*, 154-70.

The issue of the three differing accounts of Saul's conversion (9:1-22; 22:4-16; 26:9-18) has often been treated as a matter of source analysis, which by any standard proves inconclusive. The differences among the three accounts is better accounted for in literary terms: the differences among them have to do with the function of each account in its context. See Gaventa, *From Darkness to Light;* Haenchen, *Acts*, 325-29; Johnson, *Acts*, 166; Tannehill, *Narrative Unity of Luke-Acts*, 2:115. Since only the first account mentions the Holy Spirit, it is the only one relevant to this study.

[114]Note that Luke does not tell of the establishment of Christianity in Damascus, but after the Philip stories, this does not seem jarring. See Bruce, *Acts*, 237; Johnson, *Acts*, 162, 66.

[115]The question whether the Spirit brings on Paul's conversion or merely provides prophetic endowment has often been asked by commentators (see, e.g., Menzies, *Development of Early Christian Pneumatology*, 260). Certainly it is true that Luke does not consistently and explicitly link the Spirit and conversion (as Paul does, e.g., Rom 8:1-17). However, such a dichotomy between the work of the Spirit in conversion and the work of the Spirit in witness is irrelevant: for Luke, to become a Christian is to join a community which lives and speaks in the Holy Spirit, and so, of course, Christians will receive the Spirit.

[116]See Johnson, *Acts*, 165.

and call of the main protagonist of the last half of Acts, Luke prepares the reader for the work of the Holy Spirit in opening the Gentile mission.

Saul's conversion is marked by his highly symbolic loss of sight; Luke will implicitly tie this symbolism to the character of the Holy Spirit. Luke's subtle use of the language of sight/blindness and light/darkness weaves in and out of the story—what people can and can not see proves significant.[117] The risen Christ appears to Saul in a blinding flash of light from heaven[118] and speaks to him (Acts 9:3, cf. v. 17).[119] Luke recounts the conversion in an ironic nutshell (v. 8): "Though his eyes were opened" (figuratively, to his true state with God, as well as literally) "he could see nothing" (until the Spirit came upon him). Saul's companions in the persecution, blind and mute in their own way ("speechless"..."saw no one," v. 7, cf. Deut 4:12; Dan 10:7; Wis 18:1), lead him by the hand into Damascus.[120] Yet Saul can see the "vision"[121] of how he will

---

[117]Luke's deft irony is not limited to language about vision. Saul begins by "breathing" (ἐμπνέω) threats and murder (Acts 9:1), but ends up filled with the Holy Spirit (πνεῦμα, v. 17).

[118]"From heaven" could be taken literally, but is also a circumlocution for "from God" (cf. Luke 3:22; 11:13; Acts 2:2; 11:9; 22:6). Luke uses a verb connoting the flashing of lightning, ἀστράπτω; see Bruce, *Acts*, 234. Light and lightning are common features of Old Testament theophanies (see Exod 19:16; 2 Sam 22:15; LXX Ps 4:6; 17:14; 35:9; 55:13; 76:18; 77:14; 88:15; 96:4, 11; 103:2; 143:6; Isa 2:5; 60:19; Ezek 1:4, 7, 13; Dan 10:6; cf. Luke 9:29; 10:18; 17:24; 24:4; Acts 22:6; 26:13). Angels with "flashing armor" appear "from heaven" to convert the persecutor Apollonius in 4 Macc 4:1-14. Light also figures in the theophany to Aseneth in a passage that has striking structural parallels to Acts 9 (*Joseph and Aseneth* 14:2-8, 15; 15:2-6). See Johnson, *Acts*, 163, 167-68.

[119]Cf. also the combination of flame and sound in Acts 2:1-4.

[120]Saul/Paul is indirectly characterized by contrast with the magician Bar-Jesus/Elymas, who is blinded by "the hand of the Lord" and must grope "for someone to lead him by the hand" (Acts 13:11). See below on Acts 13:1-12.

The three accounts of Paul's conversion differ markedly in terms of what the companions saw and heard (cf. 22:7, 9; 26:13). In this account, Luke emphasizes the lack of understanding of Saul's companions by noting that they saw nothing.

[121]The words ἐν ὁράματι (v. 12) stand in several different positions in the manuscripts, which may indicate that they are a gloss. On the other hand, the

"regain sight" (v. 12, cf, v. 17, 27). Ananias, too, sees a "vision" of the risen Christ (v. 10), but remains figuratively blind to what he has seen, objecting to God's plan until the Lord opens his eyes by explaining it (vv. 13-16; cf. Luke 24:27, 31).[122] That Saul's eyes are to be opened in more than a literal sense is shown by Jesus' statement that he will "show" ($\upsilon\pi o\delta\epsilon\iota\xi\omega$) him that he is to suffer as a prophet (v. 16; cf. Luke 6:22; 9:22; 17:25; 21:12-19; 24:7, 26). Saul's blindness lingers through a three-day period of fasting (vv. 8-9),[123] and then his sight is restored with the laying-on-of-hands by Ananias and the coming of the Spirit (vv. 17-18); the former persecutor begins to proclaim Jesus in the synagogues (v. 20).

Luke's play on the contrast between seeing and not seeing, between light and darkness, continues after Saul's vision is restored. The Jews who plot to kill him in response to his preaching fail to see him escaping in the darkness, even though they were "watching the gates day and night" ($\pi\alpha\rho\alpha\tau\eta\rho\acute{\epsilon}\omega$, v. 24; cf. Luke 6:7; 14:1; 20:20). The disciples in Jerusalem, like Ananias, are blind to the significance of Saul's conversion until it is explained to them by

---

repetition of the words in v. 10 and the presence of the similar $\grave{o}\nu\acute{o}\mu\alpha\tau\iota$ may account for this confusion. But whether explicitly or implicitly, a vision is indicated. See Bruce, *Acts*, 237; Haenchen, *Acts*, 324 n. 2; Metzger, *Textual Commentary*, 364.

The visions of Paul and Ananias are the first instances of that important Lucan plot device, borrowed from the Old Testament (e.g., Gen 15:1). Cf. Acts 9:10, 12; 10:3, 17, 19; 11:5; 12:9; 16:9-10; 18:9.

[122]Haenchen (*Acts*, 325) notes that the words of Christ exactly counter those of Ananias; rather than inflicting suffering on those who call on the name of Christ, Saul will suffer for that name. Cf. Tannehill, *Narrative Unity of Luke-Acts*, 2:117.

[123]The fasting probably indicates a period of preparation (cf. Exod 34:28; Deut 9:9; Dan 9:3; 10:2-3; *4 Ezra* 5:13, 20; 6:31; *2 Baruch* 9:2; 12:5; 20:5) as well as repentance (Neh 1:4; Jer 14:12; Joel 1:14; Jonah 3:8). The three days evokes the image of Jesus (cf. Luke 22:16, 30). See Haenchen, *Acts*, 323; Johnson, *Acts*, 164.

Barnabas (vv. 26-30).[124] Luke uses the sight/blindness and light/darkness metaphors to establish Saul's character, in contrast with both his enemies, who do not see, and his friends, who only gradually see the importance of what is before them. The story of how the Jewish Christians gradually come to see the plan of God for the Gentiles will continue in Acts 10-15.

That Luke attaches symbolic significance to light/darkness language in relation to Paul is confirmed later in Luke's narrative when Paul applies Isa 49:6 to himself: "For so the Lord has commanded us, saying, 'I have set you to be a light for the Gentiles, so that you may bring salvation to the ends of the earth.'" (Acts 13:47). The quotation looks back to Acts 1:8, and as in Acts 9, draws a link between light and salvation (cf. Luke 1:78-79; 2:30-32; 3:6). Luke will employ this symbolism even more strongly in the final account of Paul's conversion (Acts 26:17-18, 23); Paul's mission from the risen Lord is to "open their eyes," to turn both Jews and Gentiles from "darkness to light," which means "from the power of Satan to God" (v. 18). Since Jesus himself came to proclaim "recovery of sight to the blind" (Luke 2:18; cf. Luke 18:35-43), it is not surprising to find his disciples, once having recovered their own sight, doing the same. Light and sight consistently function in Luke's narrative as metaphors for the understanding that leads to salvation (cf. Luke 10:23-24; 11:34-36).[125]

Luke implies a connection between the Holy Spirit and Saul's recovery of sight, and thus between the Spirit and the symbolism of light and sight. The connection can be seen in the words of Ananias, who is an authoritative commentator in Luke's narrative, since he derives his authority from a message given by the risen Lord and proves himself a willing disciple (Acts 9:10).[126] Ananias tells Saul that he will regain his sight and be filled with the Holy Spirit (Acts

---

[124]"Human disbelief highlights the amazing transformation of Saul....The Lord's work is revealed through events that overthrow human expectations" (Tannehill, *Narrative Unity of Luke-Acts*, 2:116-17).

[125]See Dennis Hamm, "Sight to the Blind: Vision as Metaphor in Luke," *Biblica* 67 (1986): 457-77; Tannehill, *Narrative Unity of Luke-Acts*, 2:121-22.

[126]Cf. Johnson, *Acts*, 169.

9:17). Immediately the prophecy is fulfilled in regard to Saul's blindness, as "something like scales fell from his eyes" (v. 18). The reader is left to infer that the filling with the Spirit also occurred; certainly all the clues are there—Saul is baptized, and in his bold preaching begins to function as a prophet (vv. 20-22), complete with persecutions (vv. 23-25), just as Jesus had said (vv. 15-16).[127] The pattern of preaching/persecution/rescue is repeated in Jerusalem (vv. 28-30).[128] Luke again does not explicitly specify the relationship of the laying-on-of-hands, Saul's healing, his reception of the Spirit, and his baptism, but clearly they are related.[129] The coming of the Spirit and Saul's submission to baptism coincide with the removal of his blindness. The symbolism is not lost on the reader, who knows that Saul's more-than-physical blindness has been healed.[130]

Having wrapped up the story of Saul's conversion and call, Luke punctuates the narrative with one of the periodic summaries that signal all's well with the church (Acts 9:31; cf. 2:42-47; 4:32-35;

---

[127]Cf. ibid., 175.

[128]The historical problem of the relation of Luke's account of Saul's early days in the Christian community to that of Paul in Galatians 1 and 2 Corinthians 11 is quite complex (and beyond the scope of this study). Again, Luke (and Paul as well) construes his account with his literary purposes in mind. See Haenchen, *Acts*, 331-36; Johnson, *Acts*, 173-75.

[129]On the laying-on-of-hands and healing, see Luke 5:13; 13:13; Acts 4:30; 5:12. Laying-on-of-hands enables the reception of the Spirit in Acts 8:17-19 and 19:6. Baptism is related to the reception of the Spirit in various ways; see Luke 3:16; Acts 1:5; 2:38; 10:44-48; 11:15-17, and above, chap. 1, "What Does the Holy Spirit Do?"

[130]The connection between the Holy Spirit and the symbolism of light and sight is often implied Luke-Acts. The message of light from God comes from Spirit-inspired prophets, such as Zechariah (Luke 1:79) and Simeon (2:32). John the Baptist also speaks of "seeing" salvation (3:6); he quotes scripture, which Luke considers to be the words of the Spirit (cf. Acts 1:16, 4:25). Jesus characterizes his own Spirit-anointed mission as involving recovery of sight for the blind (4:18). Paul, too, will characterize his mission as bringing light (Acts 13:47); in support, he, like John the Baptist, quotes scripture.

5:12-16, 42; 6:7; 11:19-21; 12:24; 16:5; 19:20; 28:31). Its persecutor now turned preacher, the church is at peace and is able to
increase its numbers. The Holy Spirit continues to be active in the
church, providing "exhortation," "comfort," "consolation," or
"encouragement" (παρακλήσις). Παρακλήσις has been associated
with the Spirit before, as the prophet Simeon was said to look for
the παρακλήσις of Israel (Luke 2:25), that is, the coming of the
Messiah to bring salvation.[131] Later in Acts, Paul will be asked to
give a "word of παρακλήσις" in the synagogue at Pisidian Antioch
(13:15), and the believers at Syria Antioch will rejoice at the
παρακλήσις they receive in the letter from the Apostolic Council
(15:31).[132] In all of these instances, παρακλήσις is associated with
the proclamation of God's salvation; in light of the context of Acts
9:31, it would seem to have that sense here as well—the church
grew because of "the comfort/exhortation provided by the Holy

---

[131]Contrast the plight of the rich who already have their παρακλήσις (Luke
6:24). The association of the Spirit with παρακλήσις is most clear in the Gospel
of John, which speaks of the Spirit as παρακλήτος (John 14:16, 26; 15:26; 16:7).

[132]The polyvalence of παρακλήσις poses a dilemma for the translator in each
of these passages. Simeon (Luke 2:25) looks for "comfort" or "consolation" (cf.
Isa 40:1; 61:2), as do the rich in Luke 6:24. But Paul in his sermon may be said
to offer "encouragement," as did Barnabas (Acts 9:31). On the other hand, Paul's
sermon may be simply understood as an "exhortation." Similarly, the letter from
the Apostolic Council may be taken as "encouragement," "exhortation," or even
"request" (cf. 2 Cor 8:4, 17). The beauty of the word is in its ambiguity—it may
mean some or all of the above in each passage. (See Walter Bauer, William F.
Arndt, F. Wilbur Gingrich, and Frederick W. Danker, *A Greek-English Lexicon
of the New Testament and Other Early Christian Literature* (Chicago: University
of Chicago Press, 1979), s.v. παρακλήσις; Louw and Nida, *Greek Lexicon*,
§25.150; §36.168).

Thus in Acts 9:31, the expression τῇ παρακλήσει τοῦ ἁγίου πνεύματος may be
taken to mean "the comfort or encouragement provided by the Holy Spirit"
through the ending of the persecution of Saul and the increased spread of the
gospel; or "the exhortation inspired by the Holy Spirit" which resulted in the
growth of the church (cf. Lake and Cadbury, *Beginnings*, 4:107; Schneider,
Apostelgeschichte, 2:41). Or it could mean both.

Spirit"[133] as evidenced in the end of Saul's persecution, the success-ful spread of the gospel, and the church's growing membership.[134]

The conversion of Saul (including his baptism), his vision of Jesus, the ministry of Ananias, and the acceptance of the former persecutor by the Jerusalem church all serve to confirm his position as a prophet and an authoritative figure in Luke's narrative. Saul, soon to be called Paul, will take the place of Peter as the central fig-ure in the narrative.[135] That he is filled with the Holy Spirit (Acts 9:17; cf. 13:9) confirms for the reader Saul's status as a reliable spokesperson for the narrator. Luke's reference to Holy Spirit is, in conjunction with the other elements of the conversion story, a sign of assurance to the reader that all is happening according to God's plan.

To summarize Luke's characterization of the Spirit so far in Acts, Luke continues in much the same vein as in the Gospel. As with the opening chapters of the Gospel, the Spirit is mentioned quite often. Luke clearly establishes the function of the Spirit as inspiring prophetic witness; it is the sure sign of narrative reliability. The apostles and disciples of Jesus are, like Jesus, prophets under the aegis of the Spirit.

Luke continues to make primary use of indirect characterization, though he sometimes has another character make a direct character-

---

[133]The dative τῇ παρακλήσει is instrumental—the church grew because of the παρακλήσις. Contra NRSV, I would take the phrase τῇ παρακλήσει τοῦ ἁγίου πνεύματος with ἐπληθύνετο rather than with the participle πορευομένη; the paral-lelism between τῷ φόβῳ τοῦ κυρίου and τῇ παρακλήσει τοῦ ἁγίου πνεύματος emphasized in NRSV is not exact, as the first clause seems to contain an objective genitive ("they fear the Lord"), while the second is a subjective genitive ("the Spirit gives comfort"). See Bruce, *Acts*, 246; Haenchen, *Acts*, 333; Johnson, *Acts*, 176-77; Lake and Cadbury, *Beginnings*, 4:107; Schneider, *Apostelgeschichte*, 2:41.

[134]There may also be a hint of underlying trouble in this summary. Note that the time of peace is brought on by the removal of Saul from the scene (cf. Johnson, *Acts*, 176). Saul/Paul will continue to spark controversy as the narrative proceeds.

[135]Cf. Tannehill, *Narrative Unity of Luke-Acts*, 2:113.

ization (Acts 1:4; 2:33; 5:32; at no time has the narrator characterized the Spirit directly, however). Indirect characterization is
primarily through speech, whether that of the narrator (Acts 4:8,
31), another character (Acts 2:33, 38), or the Spirit itself (8:29). As
in the Gospel, the Spirit acts directly, inspiring speech, witnessing,
and even snatching Philip bodily (Acts 2:4; 5:32; 8:39). As in the
Gospel, the Spirit is described metaphorically, this time as "fire"
(Acts 2:1-4). The Spirit continues to work in a prophetic environment, now defined as the church. Luke also continues to characterize the Spirit by comparison with prophetic figures, and in contrast
with Satan and the demonic (esp. Acts 5:1-11; 6:1-7:55; 8:4-25).

The heavy Septuagintal stylization of Luke's characterization continues in Acts, though it is broken somewhat by Luke's new emphasis on the role of the Spirit in forming a community (Acts 2:44-46;
4:32-5:11); also, Luke hints at a new universality in the dispensation
of the Spirit (2:38). The coherency of Luke's earlier portrait is
diminished somewhat by the confusing relations among baptism,
laying-on-of-hands, and the reception of the Spirit (Acts 8). But this
theological inconsistency increases the complexity and opacity of the
portrait at the same time (as do the confusing geographical
references in 8:1-40). Further increasing the complexity of this
character is the duality between the Spirit's function as giver of both
life and death; in the episodes of Simon Magus and of Ananias and
Saphhira the Spirit is responsible for inflicting judgment, while to
the faithful church it brings comfort and consolation. Luke's presentation of the Spirit becomes less fragmentary as the Spirit acts
more directly and widely in expanding the mission and forming a
community (2:44-46; 4:32-5:11; 8:1-40). The characterization continues to be highly symbolic, dynamic, and open-ended.

The Spirit remains central to the plot of Luke-Acts. It is given by
God through Jesus to empower proclamation and build the community. Luke clearly establishes the reliability of the apostles, frequently reminding the reader that they are "filled with the Spirit."
But the issue of the proper boundaries of the mission is still to be
resolved, and it will be resolved through the power of the Spirit.

The Gentile Mission Begins (Acts 10-15)

The Holy Spirit plays a prominent role in Luke's account of the development of the Gentile mission.[136] The Spirit directs and participates in a long discernment process in which the church comes to grips with the universalism of Jesus' message. The text provides an extended example of Lukan irony, for Luke has frequently foreshadowed a universal mission (cf. Luke 2:32; 3:6; 4:22-27; 24:47; Acts 1:8; 2:39; 3:25-26). One must not overlook the shape Luke has given the narrative, for it is just as important to see how the story develops as to note that it happens, and to see how the Holy Spirit functions in this development. For as a divine representative in this discourse, the Holy Spirit ensures that the church's decision is in harmony with the plan of God.[137]

I will divide this material into six sections: Cornelius and Peter (Acts 10:1-48); Peter's Defense (11:1-18); the mission in Syrian Antioch (11:19-30); Paul and Barnabas (13:1-12); the mission in Pisidian Antioch (13:13-52); and the Apostolic Council (15:1-35).

Cornelius and Peter (Acts 10:1-48)

Cornelius,[138] the first Gentile convert, is portrayed in terms which Luke has used of the followers of Jesus, and which evoke Old

---

[136]On Acts 10-15 and the rise of the Gentile mission, see Bauernfeind, *Apostelgeschichte*, 140-202; Bruce, *Acts*, 251-328; Conzelmann, *Acts*, 78-123; Dupont, *Salvation of Gentiles;* Haenchen, *Acts*, 343-478; Johnson, *Acts*, 180-281; idem, *Decision Making*, 67-86; Lake and Cadbury, *Beginnings*, 4:112-83; Menzies, *Development of Early Christian Pneumatology*, 264-67; Pesch, *Apostelgeschichte*, 1:326-71; 2:15-90; Schneider, *Apostelgeschichte*, 2:45-193; Tannehill, *Narrative Unity*, 2:128-93; Wilson, *Gentiles and Gentile Mission;* idem, *Luke and the Law*, esp. 69-117.

[137]See Johnson, *Acts*, 186-88; idem, *Decision Making*, 67-86.

[138]On the Cornelius episode, see Barthes, "L'Analyse structurale"; Jouette M. Bassler, "Luke and Paul on Impartiality," *Biblica* 66 (1985): 546-52; François Bovon "Tradition et rédaction en Actes 10, 1-11, 18," *Theologische Zeitschrift* 26 (1970): 22-45; Martin Dibelius, "The Conversion of Cornelius," in *Studies*, 109-22; Gaventa, *From Darkness to Light;* Haulotte, "Fondation d'une communauté"; Kirsopp Lake, "Proselytes and God-fearers" in *Beginnings*, 5:74-96; Karl Loning,

Testament models of piety: Luke directly characterizes him as
"devout" (εὐσεβής, cf. δίκαιος καὶ εὐλαβής of Simeon, Luke 2:25;
also Acts 2:5; 8:2; 22:12), "fearing God" (φοβούμενος τὸν θεόν, cf.
Acts 9:31),[139] "giving much alms" (ποιῶν ἐλεημοσύνας πολλάς,
cf. Luke 7:5; 12:33; Acts 9:36) and "praying constantly" (δεόμενος
τοῦ θεοῦ διὰ παντός, cf. Luke 11:1-13; 18:1; 21:36; Acts 1:24;
4:31; 6:6).[140] Further, the description of Cornelius makes use of
some aspects of the Lukan stereotype of the prophet. For example,
Cornelius' characterization is structurally reminiscent of that of the
first Jews to appear in Luke's story, Zechariah and Elizabeth, in that
it gives a notation of station followed by a description of piety (Luke
1:5-7). And like Zechariah and other prophets, Cornelius has a
vision; he sees "an angel of God" (cf. Luke 1:11, 26-28; 2:9;
22:43; Acts 5:19-20; 7:30, 35, 38; 8:26; 9:10, 12; 10:9-16; 11:5,
13; 12:7-11; 16:9; 18:9; 23:8, 11; 27:23). Again, like these other

---

"Die Korneliustradition," *Biblische Zeitschrift* 18 (1974): 1-19; Marin, "Essai
d'analyse structurale"; Mark A. Plunkett, "Ethnocentricity and Salvation History
in the Cornelius Episode," *Society of Biblical Literature 1985 Seminar Papers,*
ed. Kent Harold Richards (Atlanta: Scholars Press, 1985), 465-79; W. C. van
Unnik, "The Background and Significance of Acts x, 4 and 35," in *Sparsa Collecta,* 1:213-58.

There is little consensus on Luke's sources here. Perhaps Luke had at his dis-
posal a conversion story about Cornelius, and a vision story about Peter (so
Dibelius, "Conversion"; cf. Haenchen, *Acts,* 355-63, who attributes the vision
story to Luke. See Menzies, *Development of Early Christian Pneumatology,* 264
n. 3, for criticism of these views). Clearly, however, Luke has heavily edited
whatever sources he may have used.

[139]Luke frequently speaks of οἱ φοβούμενοι (or σεβόμενοι) τὸν θεὸν (Acts
10:2, 22, 35; 13:16, 26, 43, 50; 16:14; 17:4, 17; 18:7), referring to Gentiles who
practiced Jewish customs but were not full converts (cf. Josephus, *Against Apion*
2.39; 2.282-86; *Antiquities* 14.116-17; Juvenal, *Satires* 14.96-108). See Bruce,
Acts, 252-53, and the extensive bibliography there; also Bauernfeind, *Apostelgeschichte,* 144; Haenchen, *Acts,* 346; Johnson, *Acts,* 182; Kirsopp Lake,
"Proselytes and God-Fearers," in *Beginnings,* 5:74-96; Pesch, *Apostelgeschichte,*
1:336.

[140]Piety as the combination of prayer and almsgiving is traditional, cf. Tob
12:8; Matt 6:2-6; 1 Pet 4:7-8.

characters, Cornelius is not disobedient to the divine vision (Acts 10:8; cf. Luke 1:38, 63; 2:15; Acts 5:21; 7:36; 8:27; 9:17; 10:23; 16:10; 18:11; 26:19). Luke prepares the reader for the conversion of Cornelius by characterizing him in the same terms as the main figures of the book of Acts—Cornelius is described as a pious man[141] and a potential candidate for the corps of prophets, soon to be yet another possessor of the Spirit.

Peter, too, has a vision (Acts 10:9-16). He recognizes the voice speaking to him as the voice of the risen Jesus (v. 14).[142] But later the narrator tells us that the Spirit speaks to Peter (v. 19). Luke freely mixes appearances by different divine representatives in this story; in effect, the entire arsenal of divine figures is brought to bear. The angel, the risen Christ, and the Holy Spirit all serve as representatives of the God who drives the narrative, yet never appears as a character in the discourse. There is no doubt who is at work here—no matter what the form, it is God.[143]

The Spirit again acts directly when it "speaks" to Peter (vv. 19-20). This is the second instance of the Spirit speaking to another character in the narrative (cf. Acts 8:26); Luke records the speech of the Spirit as direct discourse. The quotation gives Peter instruction about what to do. Peter learns of his visitors what the reader already knows—that they are sent by God (again, mediated by a divine rep-

---

[141]Tannehill (*Narrative Unity of Luke-Acts*, 2:133) notes that the particularly Jewish piety of Cornelius helps bind him to Peter and the Jewish Christians: "Everything in the narrative conspires against maintaining the barrier between Jews and this Gentile."

[142]Contra Haenchen (*Acts*, 348) it is not "mysteriously uncertain whose voice resounds." Peter clearly addresses the voice as "Lord" (v. 14), and later attributes the vision to "God" (v. 28)—a clear case of the risen Jesus standing in for the offstage deity. As frequently in Acts, God does not act directly in the discourse, but is attributed the action in a later summary by a human character (cf. Acts 10:34-43; 11:17-18; 15:4, 8, 14). The action of divine representatives (such as angels, Jesus, or the Holy Spirit) are interpreted as actions of God.

Peter's initial reluctance about the divine directive recalls the story of Jonah.

[143]Cf. Bruce, *Acts*, 257.

resentative, the Spirit: "I have sent them," v. 20).[144] The direct discourse also allows the reader to glimpse into the prophetic mindset, and to see that Peter is obeying his instructions to the letter.[145] As before, the Spirit is to be considered a reliable commentator.

The story of Cornelius and Peter previews the way Luke will weave vision-accounts together in order to depict the community's process of discernment.[146] Cornelius reports his dream virtually verbatim (Acts 10:31-32) and piously waits to hear what the messenger of God has to say (v. 33). Peter, however, does not now narrate his vision (he will do so later in the discourse), though he knows and recounts the significance of it: "God shows no partiality" (v. 34-35). The narration of Cornelius' experience has given Peter insight into his own experience; as will happen later (11:1-18; 15:1-21), the transmission of the story has profound persuasive power. Having clarified the meaning of his own vision, Peter sees that it is appropriate to preach the good news of Jesus Christ as Lord (vv. 34-43).[147] Peter's speech briefly sums up the main points of Luke's Gospel narrative, from the baptism of John to the death, resurrection, and exaltation of Jesus, with emphasis on the universality of his work: Jesus "is the one designated by God to be judge of the living and the dead," and "everyone who believes in him receives forgiveness of sins through his name" (v. 43).[148]

---

[144]Here is another instance of direct action by the Holy Spirit. Luke pictures the Spirit as the sender. Cf. Bruce, *Acts*, 257; Haenchen, *Acts*, 358.

[145]Cf. Haenchen, *Acts*, 347.

[146]"The text is concerned not just with what happened but with the transmission of what happened" (Tannehill, *Narrative Unity of Luke-Acts*, 2:130, citing Barthes, "L'analyse structurale," 35-36; see also Johnson, *Decision Making*).

[147]On Peter's speech, see Tannehill, *Narrative Unity of Luke-Acts*, 2:137-42. The text-critical problems of this speech, especially vv. 36-38, are great; however, they are not crucial for the purposes of this study. See Bruce, *Acts*, 261-63; Haenchen, *Acts*, 351-53; Johnson, *Acts*, 191-92; Metzger, *Textual Commentary*, 378-80.

[148]As Peter preaches, he again directly characterizes Jesus as "anointed with the Holy Spirit and power" (v. 38), providing an indirect characterization of the Spirit as well.

While Peter is preaching, the Holy Spirit falls upon Cornelius and his household (v. 44). Again, the Spirit is depicted as a direct actor, this time in a metaphorical "falling upon," which consists, as it did on Pentecost, of inspired speech—glossolalia and praise of God (v. 46; cf. 2:1-4; 4:3; 8:17). By having this event interrupt Peter's speech,[149] Luke allows the reader to experience what the characters in the narrative are experiencing: the unexpected action of God in accepting these Gentiles as equal members of the community, as demonstrated by the same kind of inspired speech which the first Christians experienced.[150] Those "circumcised believers" who came with Peter, witnesses to the Spirit's action, are astounded by this turn of events (v. 47). But Peter clearly sees the significance of what has happened, and moves to baptize the new believers: "Can anyone withhold the water for baptizing these people who have received the Holy Spirit just as we have?" (v. 47). The reader, of course, has been prepared for the coming of the Spirit on all the people (cf. Acts 2:17), and accepts Peter's logic as reliable. Note that Peter draws a conclusion from the action of the Spirit, as

---

[149]The interrupted speech is a common Lukan literary device; cf. 17:32; 22:22; 23:7; 26:24. See Johnson, *Acts*, 193.

[150]Luke mentions glossolalia here (unlike 8:17), since it is crucial to his point: when they heard Cornelius and the others speaking in tongues, the witnesses knew that the Spirit had been given to them, just as it had been to the disciples (2:1-4). Luke does not explicitly mention foreign languages, as in the Pentecost narrative, because it does not help move his story along as it does there; however, foreign languages may be implied when Peter says that the new converts received the Spirit "just as we have" (10:47; contra Haenchen, *Acts*, 354; Menzies, *Development of Early Christian Pneumatology*, 265 n. 3). The Jewish disciples are convinced because they recognize their own experience in what happens to the Gentiles, "a repetition of Pentecost" (Tannehill, *Narrative Unity of Luke-Acts*, 2:142; cf. 129-30; see also Lampe, *God as Spirit*, 68; Earl Richard, "Pentecost as a Recurrent Theme in Luke-Acts,"in *New Views on Luke and Acts*, ed. Earl Richard (Collegeville: The Liturgical Press, 1990), 138-39; Swete, *Holy Spirit in New Testament*, 98).

testified by the inspired speech of the new converts.[151]

Luke continues to characterize the Spirit along the lines he has previously established. Luke's characterization is usually, but not always, indirect. Note that the narrator for the first time directly characterizes the Spirit, repeating Jesus' characterization of the Spirit as a "gift" (Acts 10:45; cf. Luke 11:1-3). The Spirit is a prophetic Spirit, anointing Jesus with power, speaking directly to Peter, inspiring speech among Cornelius and his household. The Spirit again acts directly and works transparently—more so than in the Philip narrative (Acts 8), and more so to the reader than to the characters in the narrative, who are sometimes amazed (and as we will see, even appalled) at what the Spirit is doing (v. 45, cf. 11:2). Luke continues to portray the Spirit as a direct actor in the narrative, increasing the sense of wholeness, complexity, and dynamism established in the Philip narrative.

Peter's Defense (Acts 11:1-18)

When the Jerusalem church hears what Peter has done, he is called to account for his actions.[152] The objection involves table fel-

---

[151]Contra Haenchen (*Acts,* 362-64), Luke does allow for human decision in this story. The divine direction does not leave the humans twitching like puppets; Luke clearly shows that the human characters only gradually came to understand what the divine characters were up to, and only as they experienced God's guidance, and recounted that experience to others. See Johnson, *Decision Making,* 74; Tannehill, *Narrative Unity of Luke-Acts,* 2:128-32.

The oft-discussed issues of whether the Spirit brought about Cornelius' conversion, and the relation between the reception of the Spirit and baptism, are not clearly resolved in Luke. See above, chap. 1, "What Does the Holy Spirit Do?" More important is the role of the Spirit in Luke's story: the visible signs of the Spirit's presence with Cornelius and the others shows the early church the direction God is taking (cf. Menzies, *Development of Early Christian Pneumatology,* 264-67).

[152]On this section, see Haulotte, "Fondation d'une communauté"; Johnson, *Decision Making,* 74-77; John J. Kilgallen, "Did Peter Actually Fail to Get a Word in? (Acts 11, 15)," *Biblica* 71 (1990): 405-10; Marin, "Essai d'analyse structurale"; Schneider, "Zur Bedeutung von καθεξῆς." The scene is similar to trial scenes found in Hellenistic novels (e.g., Achilles Tatius, *Clitophon and Leucippe* 7.7; see Johnson, *Acts,* 199).

lowship: "Why did you go to uncircumcised men and eat with them?" (Acts 11:3);[153] while the narrative did not say that Peter ate with Gentiles, it is implied by Peter's long visit (10:48). The charge is a serious one, for table fellowship implies spiritual fellowship as well, and Peter may thus be guilty of idolatry (cf. Luke 5:30; Dan 1:8, 12-16; 2 Macc 5:27; *b. Ber.* 43b; *b. Sanh.* 104a). Peter's reply is given καθεξῆς (cf. Luke 1:4), which for Luke means that considerable interpretation takes place in the shaping of the story; here is another example of how Luke uses the recounting of a story to give direction to the narrative as a whole.[154] The events have been described already, but now must be retold to a different group; the reader too benefits from the retelling and reshaping. Peter's speech makes it clear that God has not merely modified kitchen and dining room regulations, but has offered "even to the Gentiles the repentance that leads to life" (Acts 11:18).

Peter recounts the direct intervention of the Spirit which told him to go with the representatives of Cornelius. Unlike Luke's original

---

[153]The objectors are οἱ ἐκ περιτομῆς (Acts 11:2), distinguished from οἱ ἀπόστολοι καὶ οἱ ἀδελφοὶ οἱ ὄντες κατὰ τὴν Ἰουδαίαν (v. 1); Luke implies that the leadership and ordinary believers had no problem with Peter's actions in the conversion of Cornelius (see Johnson, *Acts*, 197). In light of this distinction, just who were the οἱ ἐκ περιτομῆς? The narrator has identified Peter's companions in Acts 10:45 as οἱ ἐκ περιτομῆς πιστοὶ, and Peter says explicitly that οἱ ἓξ ἀδελφοὶ accompanied him into Cornelius' house (implicitly clearing himself of the charge of idolatry). The group mentioned here seems to be "especially zealous for the law and sticklers for circumcision" (Bruce, *Acts*, 267; cf. Acts 15:5; 21:20; Gal 2:12), and it particularly ironic that some of their number were included in Peter's party (Johnson, *Acts*, 200-201).

The Western text includes a lengthy secondary addition which may have been intended to avoid putting Peter in a bad light. See Bruce, *Acts*, 266; Johnson, *Acts*, 197; Metzger, *Textual Commentary*, 382-84.

[154]"It is clear that Luke understands a 'recitation in order' as having a peculiarly convincing quality" (Johnson, *Acts*, 197).

Peter's speech contains the standard elements of a Hellenistic defense speech (cf. Plato, *Phaedrus* 266D-E; Aristotle, *Rhetoric* 1354b), omitting the *prooemium* and dominated by the *narratio*, with *probatio* (witnesses and signs, 11:12, 15) and a brief *peroratio* (v. 17). See Johnson, *Acts*, 200.

narrative, in which the words of the Spirit are given by the narrator, Peter summarizes them as indirect discourse: "The Spirit told me to go with them and not to make a distinction between them and us" (Acts 11:12); as before, the Spirit is characterized as a direct actor. That Luke uses διακρίνω in this passage is ironic, due in part to textual variants; Luke pictures Peter as going to the Gentiles either "without hesitation or doubt" (middle voice, as Acts 10:20 and some manuscripts here) or more likely, "without making a distinction" (active voice, as the earliest manuscripts here).[155] Both meanings make sense, however, and both create irony—Peter's objectors in fact are guilty of both doubt and making distinctions (διακρίνομαι, 11:2), while the force of Peter's story is without doubt to eliminate all distinctions between Jew and Gentile. Here again the Spirit functions as a sign of reliability both for the reader and the characters in the story: the coming of the Spirit on the Gentile believers, as witnesses by their prophetic speech, is a reliable sign that there are to be no distinctions between Jew and Gentile—and thus no doubt about Peter's story.

Peter repeats with slight variations the conclusion of the story (cf. Acts 11:15 with 10:44, and 11:17 and 10:44); again, the Spirit is depicted as a direct actor, falling upon the believers (v. 15). Peter interprets the coming of the Spirit by the emphatic observation[156] that it came "just as it had upon us at the beginning" (v. 15). That the experiences are identical will prove to be the grounds for Gentile membership in the church (Acts 15); again Peter makes explicit the comparison to Pentecost (10:46, cf. 2:4, 11; 10:47).[157] Luke adds new material in recounting Peter's recollection of a saying of Jesus (Acts 11:6; cf. 1:5, itself a recasting of John the Baptist's saying in Luke 3:16); the contrast between water and the Spirit further suggests that what is at stake here is community membership, as symbolized by water baptism. Peter's conclusion is restated in light of this situation: "If then God gave them the same gift that he gave us

---

[155]See Johnson, *Acts*, 198; Metzger, *Textual Commentary*, 385.

[156]Note the force of ὥσπερ καὶ in v. 15.

[157]Cf. Bruce, *Acts*, 269.

when we believed in the Lord Jesus Christ, who was I that I could hinder God?" (11:17); note that the actions of the Holy Spirit in the previous discourse are interpreted in Peter's summary as actions of God—God does not act directly in the discourse, but is seen in the story through the eyes of faith. Peter directly characterizes the Spirit as a gift, and the gift here brings fellowship—Peter's action in admitting Gentiles to the church is simply a response to God's gift of the Spirit. The rhetorical question proves effective, as it silences his opposition (v. 18). As before, with Peter himself (10:34), the retelling of a story has profound rhetorical power on the audience.

As in Acts 10, the presence of the Spirit ensures that all is moving according to divine direction; Luke continues to provide coherent and transparent characterization of the Spirit. The opponents within the story are convinced by Peter's narration of the events, and the reader can see that God's will is being discerned by the church, albeit ever so slowly. Ironically, this episode will not settle the question of Gentile membership in the church; it will arise again, and Peter will again be called upon to recount and interpret his experience (Acts 15). Peter's interpretation of the events shows his growing understanding of their significance—what the reader already knows, and Peter and the church are gradually coming to accept, is that the Spirit is moving the mission of the church outward.[158]

Antioch and the Collection (Acts 11:19-30)

Luke has established the connection between Jerusalem and the Gentile mission, and his attention is about to turn more fully on to that mission, centered in Syrian Antioch.[159] Now Luke tells two

---

[158]Cf. Johnson, *Acts*, 201.

[159]Antioch was a large, cosmopolitan city, with a sizable Jewish population, quite suitable for the growth of Christianity. See Bruce, *Acts*, 271, with extensive bibliography; also Bauernfeind, *Apostelgeschichte*, 155-56; Johnson, *Acts*, 203. The city will appear often in Luke's narrative (cf. 13:1-3; 14:26-15:2; 15:35-40; 18:22). See Tannehill, *Narrative Unity of Luke-Acts*, 2:149-50.

Attempts to find an "Antiochian source" behind these stories are generally considered a failure in light of the Lukan stylistic features so abundantly present. See Haenchen, *Acts*, 368-69.

stories which help solidify the ties between Jerusalem and Antioch, and show that the turn to the Gentiles is not just the work of one person.[160] In both cases, the Spirit figures explicitly and prominently.

Luke steps back in narrative time to tell of the scattering of disciples due to persecution in Acts 8:4.[161] The geographical boundaries of the mission is being pushed northward into Syria. Most of the fleeing disciples took the word to Jews only, but some, men of Cyprus and Cyrene (Luke 23:26; Acts 2:10; 6:9; 13:1), spoke also to Gentile Hellenists (Acts 11:19-20).[162] The success of their mission, stated in traditional biblical cadences ("The hand of the Lord was with them," v. 21; cf. 2 Sam 3:12), prompts the church in Jerusalem to send Barnabas as mediator (Acts 11:22-26), a role he has filled well before in the case of Saul (9:27). Barnabas, we are reminded, is a "good man, full of the Holy Spirit and of faith," in other words, a prophet (v. 24, cf. 4:31-37; also Luke 23:50; Acts

---

[160]On this section see Pierre Benoit, "La deuxième visite de Saint Paul à Jérusalem," *Biblica* 40 (1959): 778-92; E. Earle Ellis, "The Role of the Christian Prophet in Acts,"in *Apostolic History and the Gospel,* ed. W. Ward Gasque and Ralph P. Martin (Grand Rapids: Eerdmans, 1970), 129-44; Robert W. Funk, "The Enigma of the Famine Visit," *Journal of Biblical Literature* 75 (1956): 130-36; Oscar Holtzmann, "Die Jerusalemreisen des Paulus und die Kollekte," *Zeitschrift für die neutestamentliche Wissenschaft* 6 (1905): 102-4.

[161]Luke's flashback is indicated rhetorically by verbal repetition, as the opening wording of Acts 8:4 is matched by 11:19: Οἱ μὲν οὖν διασπαρέντες κτλ.

[162]The meaning of Ἑλληνιστάς in Acts 11:20 is once again a matter of great dispute (see above on Acts 6:1-8:3). Here the μέν...δέ construction of vv. 19-20 makes it pretty clear that "Hellenist" is to be distinguished from "Jew." Any other construal reduces these sentences to absurdity. This meaning is so evident that some scribes substituted the more familiar Ἕλληνας, "Greeks," for Ἑλληνιστάς; see Metzger, *Textual Commentary,* 386-89; Bruce, *Acts,* 272; Haenchen, *Acts,* 365 n. 5; Johnson, *Acts,* 203; Pesch, *Apostelgeschichte,* 1:352; Schneider, *Apostelgeschichte,* 2:89; Tannehill, *Narrative Unity of Luke-Acts,* 2:146, n. 1.

6:5).[163] Here Luke gives further evidence that the Gentile mission is divinely-inspired; the approval of the Spirit-filled Barnabas serves as a sign of trustworthiness.[164] Also, Barnabas finds Paul in Tarsus and brings him to Antioch, where they stay and work for a year (11:26);[165] Luke thus prepares the reader for the next major expansion of the Spirit's work (chap. 13).[166]

Luke's second story (11:27-30) binds the churches in Antioch and Jerusalem through the symbolism of possessions. Prophets[167] come from Jerusalem to Antioch (v. 27); one of them, Agabus by name, predicts an empire-wide famine (v. 28).[168] Agabus' words are

---

[163]See Johnson, *Acts,* 204.

[164]Cf. Haenchen, *Acts,* 367; Johnson, *Acts,* 207-8.

[165]The Western text, which is probably secondary, includes a substantial addition which attributes to Paul both greater independence and rabble-rousing capacity: "And having heard that Saul was at Tarsus, he went out to seek him; and when he had found him, he exhorted him to come to Antioch. When they had come, for a whole year a large crowd was stirred up, and then for the first time the disciples in Antioch were called Christians." See Johnson, *Acts,* 204; Metzger, *Textual Commentary,* 390.

[166]Cf. Johnson, *Acts,* 207.

[167]Luke rarely so designates Christians (Acts 11:27; 13:1; 21:10), despite the stereotypical prophetic portraits he gives of the major figures in his narrative. See Johnson, *Acts,* 205.

[168]Luke uses the term οἰκουμένη for "empire" in Luke 2:1; 4:5; Acts 17:6; 24:5; certainly for Antioch to provide relief from a "world-wide" famine (as NRSV) would be self-contradictory. Evidence for famines during the reign of Claudius (41-54 C.E.) can be found in Josephus, *Antiquities* 3.320-21; 20.101; Suetonius, *Life of Claudius* 18.2; Tacitus, *Annals* 12.43; Dio Cassius, *History* 60.11; Orosius, *History* 7.6.17. See Bruce, *Acts,* 276; Haenchen, *Acts,* 376-77; Johnson, *Acts,* 205-6; Peter Garnsey, *Famine and Food Supply in the Graeco-Roman World: Responses to Risk and Crisis* (New York: Cambridge University Press, 1988).

The Western text again provides a substantial addition: "And there was much rejoicing; and when we were gathered together one of them named Agabus spoke, indicating...." There is little evidence that the passage is original, but is of interest as the first "we"-passage in any text of Acts. See Bauernfeind, *Apostelgeschichte,* 157-58; Bruce, *Acts,* 275; Haenchen, *Acts,* 374; Johnson, *Acts,* 205; Metzger, *Textual Commentary,* 391.

explicitly said by the narrator to come from the Holy Spirit (ἐσήμανεν διὰ τοῦ πνεύματος);[169] here is an example of the Spirit as an indirect actor, supplying words to a disciple. Barnabas and Saul are chosen to carry relief funds from Antioch to the church in Jerusalem;[170] possessions again symbolize the true state of the heart—by contributing its material goods, Antioch proves its deep link and indebtedness to Jerusalem.[171]

Luke continues his characterization of the Spirit as the prophetic Spirit. Barnabas is indirectly described as a prophet, and Agabus is directly so characterized and shown acting in the Spirit as well. These stories reinforce Luke's previous characterization and thus help lend coherence to his portrayal of the Spirit. The new direction Luke has taken, which adds complexity to the characterization of the Spirit, is that now these prophets are active among the Gentiles. The connection between the Jewish and Gentile churches is established through the symbolic sharing of possessions as well as the prophetic ethos shared between Antioch and Jerusalem, so pithily depicted by Luke.[172]

---

[169]For the association of σημαίνω with prophetic speech, cf. Dan 2:23; Rev 1:1; Plutarch, *Sayings of the Spartans,* Callicratidas 6; Epictetus, *Discourses* 1, 17, 18; Josephus, *Jewish War* 7.214; 10:241). See Johnson, *Acts,* 205.

[170]Luke's version of the collection is quite different from that found in the Pauline epistles (Rom 15:22-33; 1 Cor 16:1-4; 2 Cor 8-9; Gal 2:10). The details, which are beyond the scope of this study, are irreconcilable in terms of time, motivation, and meaning. Luke has apparently placed the (successful) collection here to affirm the connection between Paul and the Jerusalem church. See Haenchen, *Acts,* 377-79; Johnson, *Acts,* 6-7, 208-9, 377-79.

[171]Cf. Haenchen, *Acts,* 375; Johnson, *Acts,* 208-9. The link between the Jerusalem and Antioch is further indicated rhetorically by *inclusio:* Luke has Barnabas and Saul remain in Jerusalem for another chapter while he tells the story of Herod and the Jerusalem church, bringing them back only at 12:25.

[172]See Johnson, *Acts,* 207.

Paul and Barnabas Sent (Acts 13:1-12)

Luke reiterates what he has already shown to be true: "Now in the church at Antioch there were prophets and teachers" (Acts 13:1; cf. 11:26-27). Luke uses two stories, the commissioning of Saul and Barnabas (13:1-3),[173] and the confrontation with the magician Bar-Jesus/Elymas (13:4-12), to establish the credentials of the prophet he will put in the center stage of the last half of his narrative, Paul.[174]

Barnabas and Saul are part of a corps of prophets at Antioch (the others mentioned are Simeon Niger, Lucius of Cyrene, and Manean, Acts 13:1); after a year spent there, Saul and Barnabas have proved themselves to be thoroughly grounded in the community. As the reader has grown to expect, the Holy Spirit is active among this group; their piety is traditional, demonstrated by prayer and fasting (cf. Luke 2:37; 5:33; Acts 9:9; 14:23), and their authority is passed on in typical Lukan fashion, by laying-on-of-hands (cf. Acts 6:6; 8:17-19; 9:17).[175] Once again, the Spirit appears as a direct actor (cf. Acts 4:31; 8:29, 39; 10:44; 16:6), speaking to the assembled group: "Set apart[176] for me Barnabas and Saul for the work to

---

[173]The commissioning scene in 13:1-3 forms an inclusio with the return of the missionaries in 14:26-27, and thus sets off Acts 13-14 as a separate narrative section with its own introduction and conclusion. See Tannehill, *Narrative Unity of Luke-Acts,* 2:159-60.

[174]On this section see Ernest Best, "Acts XIII. 1-3," *Journal of Theological Studies,* n.s. 11 (1960): 344-48; Garrett, *Demise of the Devil,* 79-87; Arthur Darby Nock, "Paul and the Magus" in *Beginnings,* 5:164-88.

[175]The ritual is reminiscent of the setting apart of Levites in Num 8:5-13; see Best, "Acts XIII. 1-3," 347-48.

[176]"Separate/make holy" (ἀφορίζω) has definite biblical overtones (cf. e.g., LXX Exod 13:12; 29:26-27; Lev 13:4-5; Num 12:14-15; 2 Sam 8:1; Isa 52:11) and reflects Paul's own understanding of his call (Rom 1:1; Gal 1:15). See Johnson, *Acts,* 221.

which I have called them" (v. 2).[177] Luke's rhetoric assures the reader that the Spirit of prophecy is at work in these two, and not any mere human agency (cf. Gal 1:1 for Paul's own statement of this principle). The two missionaries are in fact described in terms reminiscent of Jesus himself: "sent out by the Spirit" (v. 4, cf. Luke 4:1, 14). Luke continues to use language about the Spirit to establish a connection and succession among the various prophets who appear in the narrative.

The story of the journey furthers Luke's portrait of the Saul the prophet by showing him doing signs and wonders (Acts 13:4-12).[178] Luke contrasts Saul (now given the Roman name Paul)[179] with the magician Bar-Jesus (who also has another name, Elymas),[180] again depicting the battle between God and Satan (cf. Luke 4:1-14; Acts 5:1-11; 8:9-13). Bar-Jesus, despite his ironic name, is directly characterized by the reliable narrator as a μάγος and a "Jewish false prophet" (v. 6),[181] who is "opposed" (ἀνθίστημι, cf. Luke 21:15;

---

[177]Though Luke does not say so, one might assume that the words of the Spirit were mediated by one of the assembled prophets; here, then, Luke pictures the Spirit as direct actor, with the prophet acting implicitly. The contrast with other passages, in which the Spirit is the indirect actor while the prophet acts directly (cf. Acts 11:28), underlines the significance of this event. Cf. Bruce, *Acts*, 294; Haenchen, *Acts*, 396; Swete, *Holy Spirit in New Testament*, 103.

[178]Cf. Tannehill, *Narrative Unity of Luke-Acts*, 2:161-62.

[179]For the standard explanations of the dual name, see Bruce, *Acts*, 298; Haenchen, *Acts*, 399 n. 1; Lake and Cadbury, *Beginnings*, 4:145-46.

[180]The problem of the magician's name is complicated by textual and translation problems. The best reading in Acts 13:6 is Βαριησοῦ, an Aramaic name meaning "son of Joshua" (or ironically here, "son of Jesus"); likewise, Ἐλύμας is the best attested reading in v. 8. See Johnson, *Acts*, 222-23; Metzger, *Textual Commentary*, 402-3. Unfortunately, Ἐλύμας does not "translate" Βαριησοῦ nor μάγος; a similar problem with Luke's use of μεθερμηνεύω is found in 4:36. See Bauernfeind, *Apostelgeschichte*, 171; Bruce, *Acts*, 297; Haenchen, *Acts*, 397-98; Johnson, *Acts*, 223; Pesch, *Apostelgeschichte*, 2:24-25; Schneider, *Apostelgeschichte*, 2:122.

[181]For the prevalent association of Judaism and magic, cf. Strabo, *Geography* 16.2.39; 16.2.43; Pliny the Elder, *Natural History* 30.2.11; Apuleius, *Apologia* 90; Josephus, *Jewish War* 6.285-288; *Antiquities* 20:142. See Johnson, *Acts*, 222.

Acts 6:10) to the faith and tries to "turn away" (διαστρέφω, cf.
Luke 23:2, Acts 13:10)[182] others from it, while Paul is said to be
"filled with the Holy Spirit" (v. 9). Again, the mention of the Holy
Spirit reminds the reader of Paul's prophetic lineage as he goes into
battle; it also identifies him to the reader as a reliable commentator.
Paul reinforces the narrator's characterization of the magician when
he calls him "son of the devil" (cf. Acts 5:3), "enemy of righteous-
ness" (cf. Luke 10:19), and "full of all deceit and villainy" (Acts
13:10).[183] Bar-Jesus/Elymas' punishment for "making crooked
(διαστρέφω, cf. v. 8) the straight paths of the Lord" (v. 10; cf.
Luke 3:4-5; Acts 8:21; Isa 40:3-4; Hos 14:10) recapitulates the
experience of Saul/Paul: the magician's blindness leaves him
"groping for someone to lead him by the hand" (Acts 13:11, cf.
Deut 28:28-29; Acts 9:8; 22:11). Once again, the punitive side of
the Spirit's characterization is evident (cf. Acts 5:1-11; 8:20).

The parallels and contrasts between the apostle and the magician
reinforce Paul's status as a prophet. The double name Bar-
Jesus/Elymas contrasts with Saul/Paul, and fits in with the other
parallels between the two: Saul fought "the Way," and was blinded,
in need of a helping hand to the "street called Straight" (Acts 9:2,
8, 11); Elymas, too, "twists straight ways" and is led by the hand,
blind (13:10-11). The symbolism of sight/blindness in connection
with good and evil is reinforced later in the chapter when Paul is
called the "light of the Gentiles" (13:47). The ironically-named
"Bar-Jesus" is called "son of the devil" and identified as "full of
deceit and villainy" (v. 10), in contrast to Paul, who is "full of the
Holy Spirit" (v. 9). Here is a clear example of indirect presentation

---

[182]The word was used frequently in the LXX of false prophets or idols who
misled the people; cf. Num 15:39; Prov 10:9; Isa 59:8; Ezek 13:18, 22; 14:5;
16:34; Mic 3:9. It will be given an ironic twist when Paul uses it of Elymas, who
"twists straight paths," in v. 10. See Johnson, *Acts*, 223.

[183]For δόλος as "fraud, treachery," see LXX Deut 27:24; Ps 23:4; Wis 1:5;
Sir 1:30; 19:26; Jer 5:27. "Villany," "fraud," or "wrongdoing," ῥᾳδιουργία,
appears in Hellenistic moral teaching (Plutarch, *On the Malice of Herodotus* 23;
Philo, *On the Cherubim* 80; cf. ῥᾳδιούργημα, Acts 18:14). See Garrett, *Demise of
the Devil*, 150; Johnson, *Acts*, 224.

of character by contrast; Luke pictures Paul, like Jesus and Peter (cf. esp. Luke 4:1-14; Acts 5:1-11; 8:18-24), as a prophet success-fully engaged in battle with Satan, in the person of the magician.[184] Saul's new status as one invested with authority surpassing that of Satan is symbolized by the new name to be used for him throughout the rest of the narrative, Paul.[185]

Luke uses the language of the Spirit to reinforce his positive pic-ture of Paul. Far from a renegade trouble-maker (cf. Acts 9:26-31; 11:25-26 D), Paul functions like the prophets before him, especially Jesus and Peter,[186] in the power of the Spirit. He is a member of a circle of Christian prophets (13:1), in continuity with the Jerusalem church (11:30), and is selected by the Spirit (13:2) to be commis-sioned by his peers (13:3). His actions are explicitly said to stem from the Spirit (v. 9), and mirror the wonder-working and devil-bashing of Jesus and Peter. From this point on, Paul will be the cen-tral prophetic character in Luke-Acts.

In the wider context of the section we are now considering, Acts 10-15, Luke continues to show the connection between the Jewish believers and the new Gentile church. Further, this first episode shows that Paul is a successful missionary among the Gentiles: not only does he defeat the powers of opposition, he converts the proconsul Sergius Paulus.[187] The miracle Paul works against the magician is taken by the proconsul as the sign of God's power it

---

[184]See Garrett, *Demise of the Devil*, 79-87; Johnson, *Acts*, 227; Tannehill, *Narrative Unity of Luke-Acts*, 2:162-63.

[185]See Garrett, *Demise of the Devil*, 85, who cites Lucian (*The Cock* 14; *Timon* 22) for evidence that a name-change signified a higher status.

[186]See Tannehill, *Narrative Unity of Luke-Acts*, 2:160-61, for the parallels between this passage and the commissioning of Jesus in Luke 3-5 and of Peter in Acts 2.

[187]The conversion of Sergius Paulus presents an unresolvable historical prob-lem, as there is no firm evidence that a Roman official named Sergius Paulus was proconsul of Cyprus at the time Luke places Paul there, and no evidence outside of Acts that Paul converted such an official. This does not diminish Luke's literary thrust: the Roman authorities are open to Paul's preaching, more so than many Jews. See Bruce, *Acts*, 297; Haenchen, *Acts*, 403; Johnson, *Acts*, 222.

truly is; Luke tells us that he "believed" (πιστεύω, Acts 13:12, usually a sign of conversion, cf. 13:48).[188] Paul's success story with the proconsul will later form part of the evidence that establishes the legitimacy of the Gentile mission within the church (cf. Acts 15:12).

Luke continues his characterization of the Spirit as a direct actor, working in, with, and through the Christian prophets. The narrator's threefold reference to the Spirit (a favorite device, cf. Luke 2:25-27; Luke 4:1-14; Acts 1:1-8) leaves no doubt about who is at work here. Once again, the Spirit is characterized by conflict and contrast in yet another confrontation with the devil's minions. Luke's characterization of the Spirit, in its consistency of presentation, continues to demonstrate the qualities of coherence, simplicity, and transparency.

Pisidian Antioch (Acts 13:13-52)

Paul's sermon at Pisidian Antioch[189] presents Luke's view of how Paul's message was delivered and received.[190] Luke presents us in effect with a day in the life of Paul, represented by a sample synagogue sermon (as he will later present a sample sermon to the

---

[188]See Garrett, *Demise of the Devil*, 149 n. 3. As is often noted, here is an example of the positive evaluation of Christianity Luke so often attributes to Roman officials (cf. Acts 26:1-32); see Haenchen, *Acts*, 403; Johnson, *Acts*, 226; Abraham J. Malherbe, "'Not in a Corner': Early Christian Apologetic in Acts 26:26," in *Paul and the Popular Philosophers* (Minneapolis: Fortress Press, 1989), 147-63.

[189]The best reading is the adjectival Ἀντιόχειαν τὴν Πισιδίαν (Acts 13:14), rather than the genitive found in the Western text. This is also most accurate, as the town was actually in Phrygia, near Pisidia. See Bruce, *Acts*, 300-301; Haenchen, *Acts*, 407; Johnson, *Acts*, 229; Metzger, *Textual Commentary*, 404-5.

[190]On this section, see Matthäus Franz-Josef Buss, *Die Missionspredigt des Paulus im Pisidischen Antiochien: Analyse von Apg 13, 16-41 im Hinblick auf die literarische und thematische Einheit der Paulusrede* (Stuttgart: Verlag Katholisches Bibelwerk, 1980).

Gentiles, Acts 17:16-34).[191] The sermon sets the pattern for both Paul's preaching and its response: Paul sketches an outline of the history of Israel, placing Jesus within it as the Davidic prophet, and proclaiming forgiveness of sin to all who believe in his name (Acts 13:16-41). He receives both positive (13:43) and negative (13:45, 50) response from the Jews. Paul then establishes the pattern he will follow throughout Acts: now that the gospel has been preached to the people of Israel, he will announce it to the Gentiles (13:46-52). The sermon fits within the larger Lukan sequence in which Paul's ministry is paralleled with that of Jesus[192] and Peter;[193] as always, the question of prophetic continuity occupies Luke.

Of interest to this study is the summary sentence Luke appends to this account: "And the disciples were filled with joy and with the Holy Spirit" (Acts 13:52). Luke has already shown the "joy" felt by the new converts (v. 48, cf. 8:8, 39; 11:23) and considers joy a proper response to persecution (cf. Acts 5:41). The expression "filled with the Holy Spirit" (cf. Acts 2:4; 4:31; 9:31; 13:9) once again signals to the reader that all is going according to God's plan: Paul has preached to both Jew and Gentile, and met with opposition. That Paul and Barnabas can be said to be filled with joy and the Spirit following the persecution that drove them out of the city (v. 50) testifies to the power of God; that they shake the dust off their feet, in fulfillment of Jesus' words (cf. Luke 9:5; 10:11), indicates the depth of the confidence they hold.

In the wider context of Acts 10-15, Luke continues to characterize the Spirit as active in the spread of the Gentile mission. Paul has

---

[191]Cf. Haenchen, *Acts*, 415-18, who calls the scene "a kind of abridgement of Pauline missionary history" (p. 418). See also Tannehill, *Narrative Unity of Luke-Acts*, 2:164.

[192]Both receive the Holy Spirit (Luke 3:21-22; Acts 9:17); are sent out in the Spirit (Luke 4:1, 14; Acts 13:1-3); confront demonic powers (Luke 4:1-13; Acts 13:4-12); preach in the synagogue (Luke 4:14-21; Acts 13:13-41); meet with response both favorable (Luke 4:22; Acts 13:43, 48) and unfavorable, to the point of persecution (Luke 4:23-30; Acts 13:45, 50). See Johnson, *Acts*, 237.

[193]Paul's speech resembles Peter's Pentecost address (2:15-39), as well as Stephen's speech (7:2-53). See Johnson, *Acts*, 238.

shown in the course of his preaching that the mission to the Gentiles is not an afterthought, but a part of God's plan from the beginning (Acts 13:47).[194] Though Paul will continue to preach to his fellow Jews, increasingly his efforts, and the focus of Luke-Acts, will turn to the Gentiles.[195]

The Apostolic Council (Acts 15:1-35)

Luke now draws the threads of his plot together and brings the first half of Acts to a close.[196] Paul's success among the Gentiles provokes a response from "certain individuals" who "came down from Judea" (Acts 15:1).[197] The issue is Gentile circumcision: "Unless you are circumcised according to the customs of Moses,

---

[194]See Tannehill, *Narrative Unity of Luke-Acts*, 2:172-75.

[195]See Johnson, *Acts*, 244.

[196]On the Apostolic Council in general see Bruce, *Acts*, 329-32; Martin Dibelius, "The Apostolic Council," in *Studies*, 93-101; Haenchen, *Acts*, 455-72; idem, "Judentum Quellenanalyze und Kompositionanalyze in Act 15," in *Judentum, Urchristentum, Kirche*, ed. Walther Eltester (Berlin: A. Töpelmann, 1960), 153-64; Jervell, *Luke and the People of God*, 185-207; Johnson, *Acts*, 6, 269-71; idem, *Decision Making*, 46-58, 67-87; Kirsopp Lake, "The Apostolic Council of Jerusalem," in *Beginnings*, 5:195-212; Richard, "Divine Purpose"; Schneider, *Apostelgeschichte*, 2:189-92; Wilson, *Gentiles and Gentile Mission*, 171-95; idem, *Luke and the Law*.
Paul gives a very different account of the Apostolic Council in Galatians 1-2. While the details are beyond the scope of this study, Luke and Paul differ on matters of chronology, participants, process, and outcome. Luke (like Paul) has shaped his account in accordance with his literary purpose: the promise of God to both Jew and Gentile must be fulfilled.

[197]The Western text identifies these individuals as members of the Pharisaic party (cf. 15:5); it is unclear whether these are the same "circumcised" people who speak to Peter in 11:2. Cf. Gal 2:12, 24. See Bruce, *Acts*, 332-33; Johnson, *Acts*, 259; Metzger, *Textual Commentary*, 426-28.

you cannot be saved."[198] The disagreement is so sharp that Paul, Barnabas, and some others are sent to Jerusalem to clarify the matter (v. 2).[199] There, the testimonies of Peter (vv. 7-11) and Barnabas and Paul (v. 12) prompt James to propose a solution (vv. 13-21): circumcision is not to be required of Gentiles, but they are "to abstain only from things polluted by idols and from fornication and from whatever has been strangled and from blood" (v. 20).[200] Paul

---

[198]The Western text adds an ethical demand, "and walk according to the customs of Moses" (Acts 15:1). See Bruce, *Acts*, 333; Haenchen, *Acts*, 443; Johnson, *Acts*, 259; Metzger, *Textual Commentary*, 426-28.

Luke is not against circumcision (cf. Luke 1:59; 2:21; Acts 7:8; 16:3), but presents it as a Jewish "custom" (ἔθος) rather than a requirement for inclusion into the community (cf. Luke 1:9; 2:42; Acts 6:14; 16:21; 21:21; 26:3; 28:17). See Johnson, *Acts*, 259.

[199]Again, the Western text expands the verse: "For Paul held firmly that they should stay as they were when converted; but those who had come from Jerusalem ordered them, Paul and Barnabas and certain others, to go up to Jerusalem to the apostles and elders that they might be judged by them" (v. 2). This reading has both sides acting more forcefully, and is possibly more sympathetic to the Jerusalem church (though it seems to be dependent on 1 Cor 7:20, 24). See Bruce, *Acts*, 333; Haenchen, *Acts*, 443; Johnson, *Acts*, 259-60; Metzger, *Textual Commentary*, 426-28.

[200]The problems raised by the so-called "Apostolic Decree" are complex; to discuss them in detail would require a separate dissertation. Luke gives differing versions of the decree (Acts 15:20; 15:29; 21:25), and there are substantial textual problems in each version (see Metzger, *Textual Commentary*, 429-43). The terms of the decrees are obscure as well. "Things polluted by idols" (τὰ ἀλισγημάτα τῶν εἰδώλων) seems to refer to meat offered to idols (cf. εἰδωλόθυτα, v. 29 and 21:25). "Sexual immorality" (πορνεία) may refer literally to prostitution, figuratively to idolatry, or both. "Whatever has been strangled" and "blood" may refer to the prohibition of Torah against drinking the blood of animals (Lev 17:10-14). Why these prohibitions have been singled out for Gentile believers is unclear; probably what is at stake is table fellowship between Jews and Gentiles—the two can eat together as Christians if this minimal number of Levitical rules is followed (though this explanation does not sufficiently account for a prohibition against πορνεία). What is clear is that for Luke the decree solved the problems of the Jewish Christians, and the Gentile believers rejoiced (Acts 15:31). See Bauernfeind, *Apostelgeschichte*, 194-201; Craig L. Blomberg, "The Law in Luke-Acts," *Journal for the Study of the New Testament* 22 (1984): 53-80; Bruce, *Acts*, 342-43; idem, "The Apostolic Decree of Acts 15," in *Studien zum Text und zur Ethik*, ed. Schrage, 115-24; Haenchen, *Acts*, 449, 468-72; Johnson, *Acts*, 266-73; Charles Perrot, "Les decisions de l'assemblée de Jérusalem," *Recherches des*

and Barnabas, along with the Jerusalem representatives Judas and Silas,[201] carry this message back to Antioch, where there is great rejoicing (vv. 22-35).

Peter's testimony concerning his conversion of Cornelius is greatly condensed and interpreted (Acts 15:7-11).[202] He does not retell the entire story, as in Acts 11:1-18, but assumes the details are well known; he refers to his experience in a nutshell and draws the implications from it.[203] The essence of his interpretation has not changed from his earlier account: "God, who knows the human heart, testified to them by giving them the Holy Spirit, just as he did to us" (Acts 15:8; cf. 1:24; 2:4; 10:47; 11:15, 17). Again, the experience of the Gentile believers is likened to that of the apostles at Pentecost. The Holy Spirit is a trustworthy indicator of the spiritual status of the new believers. Peter's audience, as well as the reader, is assured that God is at work. Note that the Spirit's testimony, as experienced by Peter, is offered as evidence to resolve a conflict within the church.

The testimony of Paul and Barnabas moves along the same prophetic lines as that of Peter. By speaking of "signs and wonders" (σημεῖα καὶ τέρατα, Acts 15:12), they invoke the traditional language of the prophetic Spirit (cf. Acts 2:19, 22, 43; 4:16, 22, 30;

---

science religieuse 69 (1981): 195-208; Tannehill, *Narrative Unity of Luke-Acts*, 2:190-93.

[201] Luke says that Judas and Silas were "prophets," and D adds that they were "filled with the Spirit" (Acts 15:32)—a significant note, since Silas will soon become Paul's new partner (v. 40). See B. N. Kaye, "Acts' Portrait of Silas," *Novum Testamentum* 21 (1979): 13-26.

[202] Texts following the Western tradition enhance the prophetic character of Peter's speech by adding "in the Spirit" or "in the Holy Spirit" (ἐν [ἁγίῳ] πνεύματι) before or after Πέτρος (Acts 15:7). See Bruce, *Acts*, 335; Johnson, *Acts*, 260; Metzger, *Textual Commentary*, 428.

[203] Cf. Tannehill (*Narrative Unity of Luke-Acts*, 2:184-85): "Peter is drawing emphatic theological conclusions from specific aspects of his past experience."

5:12; 6:8; 8:6, 13; 14:3).[204] The work of the Holy Spirit with and through Paul and Barnabas, as it has already been related to the reader since Acts 13, is presented as evidence confirming Peter's initial testimony.

James,[205] too, invokes the Holy Spirit in his letter to the church in Antioch. He characterizes the Spirit as a direct actor in the decision-making process of the church: "For it has seemed good to the Holy Spirit and to us to impose on you no further burden..." (Acts 15:28). Here Luke presents both the Spirit and the church jointly as direct actors; the Spirit is directly involved in this conflict, and takes a side. James is certainly correct to invoke the Holy Spirit in his decision, for it is precisely the direct action of that Spirit which has brought the church to this decision. The Spirit picked up (literally!) and moved the community outside the boundaries of Jerusalem and Judea in the person of Philip (Acts 8:29, 39). The Spirit personally directed Peter (10:20; 11:12) and fell directly on Cornelius (10:44; 11:15). The Spirit was directly responsible for the missionary journey of Barnabas and Saul (13:1-3). Everything about this story points to its origin in God, who works through the Spirit.[206]

The Apostolic Council forms the watershed of the book of Acts. Luke will now focus on the acts of Paul and the development of the Gentile mission. Only towards the end does he return to the church at Jerusalem, and then only by virtue of its pull on Paul. Luke has

---

[204]Cf. Johnson, *Acts*, 263.

[205]James appears for the first time as the leader of the Jerusalem church (Peter seems to have stepped down at 12:17). Cf. 21:18-24; also 1 Cor 15:7; Gal 1:19; 2:9, 12. See Bruce, *Acts*, 339; Johnson, *Acts*, 264. On James's speech, see Nils Alstrup Dahl, "'A People for His Name' (Acts xv. 14)," *New Testament Studies* 4 (1958): 319-27; Jacques Dupont, "ΛΑΟΣ 'ΕΞ 'ΕΘΝΩΝ (Ac 15, 14)," in *Etudes*, 361-65; idem, "Un peuple d'entre les nations (Actes 15:14)," *New Testament Studies* 31 (1985): 321-35; Jervell, *Luke and the People of God*, 185-207; Tannehill, *Narrative Unity of Luke-Acts*, 2:186-90.

[206]"The invocation of the Holy Spirit as a partner to the decision has an odd sound to contemporary ears, but it nicely captures the dynamics of the process as portrayed by Luke" (Johnson, *Acts*, 277). Cf. Isaacs, *Concept of Spirit*, 89.

shown that the church has followed the guidance of the Holy Spirit in opening membership to the Gentiles; the Jerusalem community has officially moved to follow God's lead: the salvation of all humanity is given on the basis of faith, and not through any local custom. Luke has also shown that the great missionary to the Gentiles is above all a man of the Spirit. To that mission, in detail, the narrative will now turn.

Conclusion: The Spirit and the Gentile Mission

Luke characterizes the Spirit consistently, very much along the lines he has established already in Luke-Acts. The Spirit acts directly and is involved in conflict with other characters. The Spirit's character is highly coherent and simple, as it seems to be interested mainly in the progress of the mission. This tends to make the character fragmentary as well, even though it has expanded its interests to include a Gentile mission, and has been very active in this mission. The Spirit retains its stylized and symbolic function as the Spirit of prophecy, clearly active among the assembled group of prophets, who can speak of the Spirit as a co-actor. The transparency of the Spirit enables the church to come to a firm decision in the knotty problem of the Gentiles' status as part of the new people of God; it is clear that the Spirit is at work among the Gentiles, a plain indication that God has granted them grace on a par with that given to Jews. And finally, the character of the Spirit demonstrates dynamism and openness, as the actions of the Spirit, being the sovereign actions of God, are unpredictable.

There are relatively few references to the Holy Spirit in the remaining sections of Acts. The most likely reason for this is that Luke has in essence accomplished his literary purpose: the reliability of God's promise has been established as soon as salvation is truly offered to all people. The rest of the narrative demonstrates this truth, as Luke shows how the mission grew among the Gentiles. If the Spirit is mentioned rarely, it is because the character has largely fulfilled its function; as promised to Theophilus in the prologue (Luke 1:1-4), Luke has provided certainty that God's promises are sure. The Holy Spirit has functioned as a sign and a guarantee of that certainty; through the Spirit, God's promises to Israel were fulfilled. And through the Spirit, the gospel has now been preached to the Gentiles. The character of the Spirit, being an extension of the character of God, functions to assure that Luke's narrative of God's action is reliable and trustworthy.

The European Mission (Acts 15:36-16:10)

Having received the official approval of the Jerusalem church, Paul returns to the churches he has founded (Acts 15:36), parting ways with Barnabas (Acts 15:37-39)[207] and taking with him Silas (Acts 15:40, cf. v. 32) and Timothy (16:1-5).[208] Through a series

---

[207]The "sharp disagreement" (Acts 15:39) between the two apostles was not permanent, if 1 Cor 9:6 and Col 4:10 are trustworthy; John Mark, too, may have recovered in Paul's eyes (Phlm 24; 2 Tim 4:11). However, it is not clear from the epistles that Barnabas and Paul were ever as close as Luke implies. According to Col 4:10, John Mark was Barnabas' nephew, so Luke may be giving us an understated picture of the conflict between ministry and family loyalty. See Bruce, *Acts,* 349-50; Johnson, *Acts,* 282-83, 287-88; Haenchen, *Acts,* 474-77.

[208]Timothy figures prominently in both Luke's account of Paul's ministry (Acts 17:14-15; 18:5; 19:22; 20:4) and Paul's own letters (Rom 16:21; 1 Cor 4:17; 16:10; Phil 2:19; 1 Thess 3:2, 6). He is also involved in the writing of Paul's letters (2 Cor 1:1; Phil 1:1; Col 1:1; 1 Thess 1:1; 2 Thess 1:1; Phlm 1) as well as a major recipient of two letters. See Johnson, *Acts,* 283; Haenchen, *Acts,* 476.

Paul's circumcision of Timothy (Acts 16:3) is inconsistent with his previous actions only if Timothy were to be considered a Greek. But apparently "the Jews who were in those places" would have considered him a Jew because of his mother (this seems to be Luke's intent, despite the lack of evidence that matrilineal descent was recognized in the first century; see Shaye J. D. Cohen, "Was Timothy Jewish (Acts 16:1-3)? Patristic Exegesis, Rabbinic Law, and Matrilineal Descent," *Journal of Biblical Literature* 105 (1986): 251-68, and the critique of Christopher Bryan, "A Further Look at Acts 16:1-3," *Journal of Biblical Literature* 107 (1988): 292-94). Timothy would have been impeded in spiritual progress because "his father was a Greek" who had prevented him from carrying out the customs of his true heritage. Unfortunately, Luke is not entirely clear here. The episode does, however, pave the way for the controversy in Acts 21: the reader knows that Paul does indeed follow Jewish customs. See Bruce, *Acts,* 352; Johnson, *Acts,* 284, 288-90; Haenchen, *Acts,* 479-82; Wilson, *Luke and the Law,* 64.

of divine interventions, he ends up preaching the gospel for the first time in Europe.[209]

Luke makes it clear that the European mission is divinely prompted and works against human resistance. Paul travels through Phrygia and Galatia,[210] skirting the province of Asia,[211] "having been forbidden[212] by the Holy Spirit to speak the word in Asia" (Acts 16:6). At one point he attempts to enter Bithynia,[213] "but the Spirit of Jesus did not allow them" (Acts 16:7). Finally, God provides positive instruction to Paul through a vision, and he crosses over to Macedonia (Acts 16:10).[214] Luke gives no human motiva-

---

[209]On this section, see Bauernfeind, *Apostelgeschichte*, 201-6; Bruce, *Acts*, 349-56; Conzelmann, *Acts*, 123-27; Haenchen, *Acts*, 473-91; Johnson, *Acts*, 281-90; Lake and Cadbury, *Beginnings*, 4:183-86; Pesch, *Apostelgeschichte*, 2:91-103; Schneider, *Apostelgeschichte*, 2:193-208; Stählin, "Tò πνεῦμα 'Ιησοῦ"; Tannehill, *Narrative Unity*, 2:194-96.

[210]The precise borders of "Phrygia" and "Galatia" are unclear, and manuscript variants reflect this confusion (cf. Strabo, *Geography* 12.7.1-5). See W. P. Bowers, "Paul's Route through Mysia: A Note on Acts 16:8," *Journal of Theological Studies*, n.s. 30 (1979): 507-11; Bruce, *Acts*, 353-54; Johnson, *Acts*, 285; Haenchen, *Acts*, 483-84; Kirsopp Lake, "Paul's Route in Asia Minor," in *Beginnings*, 5:224-40; Metzger, *Textual Commentary*, 441.

[211]"Asia" perhaps designates the coastal region (cf. Acts 18:19; 19:1-10) rather than the entire province of Asia, which would have included Phrygia. There is no firm evidence to determine Paul's route exactly. See Bowers, "Paul's Route"; Bruce, *Acts*, 354; Johnson, *Acts*, 285; Lake, "Paul's Route."

[212]κωλύω is a favorite Lukan word, cf. Luke 6:29; 9:49-50; 11:52; 18:16; 23:2; Acts 8:36; 10:47; 11:17; 16:6; 24:23; 27:43. Luke makes no allusion whatsoever to a prophetic intermediary, despite Bruce, *Acts*, 354-55; G. B. Caird, *The Apostolic Age*, 64; Stählin, "Tò πνεῦμα 'Ιησοῦ," 251.

[213]Bithynia lay northeast of Asia (Strabo, *Geography* 12.4.5), and was quickly populated by Christians (1 Pet 1:1; Pliny the Younger, *Letter* 10.96). See Bruce, *Acts*, 355; Johnson, *Acts*, 285.

[214]"Many words have been wasted on the attempt to explain how Paul knew that the man was a Macedonian. The man's words were a sufficient indication" (Bruce, *Acts*, 356). Macedonia lay north of Achaia, between the Adriatic and Aegean Seas. See Haenchen, *Acts*, 488-89; Johnson, *Acts*, 286.

This begins the first "we-section" in (the best texts of) Acts ("we-sections" are Acts 16:10-17; 20:5-15; 21:8-18; 27:1-28:16). As a source-critical problem, the

tion for Paul's itinerary, no reference to the goals of the human missionaries; the direction is strictly divine.

Luke tinges what has become a common characterization of the Spirit with irony. The Spirit is again presented as a direct actor, again in conflict with human characters. But against type, the Spirit at first seems to forbid that which it usually empowers: the

---

"we-sections" present insoluble dilemmas—do they represent first-hand testimony of the author, the uncritical use of a travel diary or eyewitness account, or a literary fiction? Literarily, the "we-sections" change the relation between narrator and reader: as in the prologues (Luke 1:1-4; Acts 1:1-2), the narrator of the "we-sections" is now first person (now plural, rather than the "I" of the prologues). Thus the "we-sections" introduce the same kind of narrative gap encountered in the earlier prologues, as there is a shift from a first-person narrator to a third-person narrator, and back again, now not once but several times. What the reader is to make of this confusing narrative transition is not entirely clear. The first person narrator provides more intimacy with the reader; the reader seems to be there, observing from a distance, but not too far away. But the change in narrative point of view raises the issue of reliability. The shift to this new narrative voice involves a change from "showing" to "telling," and it is generally true that telling is a less effective form of persuasion than showing (cf. the negative reaction of Sternberg to the change from first-person participatory to omniscient narration in Luke 1 (*Poetics of Biblical Narrative,* 86)). The shift back and forth to a less reliable form of narration results in the inevitable bewilderment of the reader, which in turn exacerbates the loss of reliability. Thus Luke's alternation between third-person and first-person narration in these "we-sections" hardly seems a competent literary move, as the increase in intimacy which is gained by this shift hardly seems worth the resulting loss of clarity, relability, and trust. While the first-person narration of the prologues have a clear literary purpose, the same cannot be said of the "we-sections."

Note, however, that Luke does not introduce "we" narration until after he has established his main point, the "certainty of what you have been taught" (Luke 1:4) about God's faithfulness to all people, and after he has depicted the direct guidance of the Spirit in the mission (Acts 16:6-7). And where they can be tested in matters of fact and detail, the "we-sections" prove to be as reliable as any other part of Luke-Acts. See Bruce, *Acts,* 356; Henry J. Cadbury, "'We' and 'I' Passages in Luke-Acts," *New Testament Studies* 3 (1957): 128-32; Joseph A. Fitzmyer, *Luke the Theologian: Aspects of His Teaching* (New York: Paulist Press, 1989), 16-44; Haenchen, *Acts,* 489-91; Johnson, *Acts,* 296-97; Kurz, "Narrative Approaches to Luke-Acts," 204-8, 215-19; Susan Marie Praeder, "The Problem of First-Person Narration in Acts," *Novum Testamentum* 29 (1987): 193-218.

proclamation of the gospel. Only at the end of the story do we see the purpose of this seemingly contradictory action: the Spirit is guiding the mission towards Europe by forbidding it to go elsewhere.[215] The actions of the Spirit are unexpected, providing suspense and surprise for the reader, while eventually proving consistent with the portrait Luke has been painting all along. Thus Luke momentarily introduces some incoherence into his characterization of the Spirit, only to establish more fully its coherence.

The unique expression τὸ πνεῦμα Ἰησοῦ (Acts 16:7), used only here in the entire New Testament, marks an important development in Lukan plot as well as characterization.[216] Luke has already noted that the Spirit comes from Jesus (cf. Luke 24:49; Acts 2:33) and that Jesus has taken an active role in the story (Acts 1:1, 2-9; 2:33; 7:56; 9:5). The latter half of Acts brings a greater emphasis on Jesus as the subject of both preaching and belief (Acts 16:31; 17:3, 7, 18; 18:5, 25, 28; 19:4, 5, 13, 15, 17; 2021, 24, 35; 21:13; 24:24; 28:23, 31); Luke takes on a more distinctively Pauline ethos as he tells the story of Paul's mission. The expression "Spirit of Jesus" implies not only that Jesus bestows the Spirit, but that Jesus has worked and will continue to work in the power and actions of the Spirit. Again, one can detect a Pauline emphasis, in that the Spirit functions as a transformative power, molding its recipients in the image of its giver. The actions of the disciples working in the power of the prophetic Spirit are interpreted as actions of Jesus. Luke continues his characterization of the Spirit as closely linked with the risen Jesus; the "Spirit of Jesus" is that which empowers Jesus himself, and then is given by Jesus in order to enable his will to be done by his servants the prophets.

---

[215]Cf. Haenchen *(Acts,* 489): "The positive summons to Paul to go to Macedonia shows the reader that the proscriptions of the mission in vv. 6 and 7 are now revealed to have been the gracious guidance of the Lord." See also Tannehill, *Narrative Unity of Luke-Acts,* 2:195.

[216]The reading is well-attested, despite scribal attempts to substitute a more familiar expression. See Bruce, *Acts,* 355; Johnson, *Acts,* 285; Metzger, *Textual Commentary,* 442; Stählin, "Τὸ πνεῦμα Ἰησοῦ."

Apollos and the Ephesian Disciples (Acts 18:24-19:7)

Luke includes two parallel stories about disciples of John the Baptist in Ephesus.[217] First, Apollos appears (Acts 18:24-28), preaching eloquently and accurately but incompletely about Jesus, since "he knew only the baptism of John" (Acts 18:25). Paul's astonished colleagues Priscilla and Aquila "took him aside and explained the Way of God to him more accurately" (v. 26), and Apollos goes on to preach more powerfully. Next (19:1-7), Paul finds "some disciples" (v. 1),[218] twelve in number (v. 7), who know nothing of the Holy Spirit (v. 3), because they like Apollos were baptized "into John's baptism" (v. 3). Paul, like his colleagues, provides more complete instruction, and baptizes the Johannine disciples "in the name of the Lord Jesus" (v. 5). Now, as at Pentecost and the household of Cornelius (2:4; 10:44), "the Holy Spirit came upon them, and they spoke in tongues and prophesied" (v. 6).[219] The two stories roughly parallel each other: missioner(s)

---

[217] On this section, see C. K. Barrett, "Apollos and the Twelve Disciples of Ephesus," in *The New Testament Age*, ed. William C. Weinrich (Mercer, Ga.: Mercer University Press, 1984), 1:29-39; Bauernfeind, *Apostelgeschichte*, 227-29; Bruce, *Acts*, 401-7; Conzelmann, *Acts*, 157-60; Dunn, *Baptism in the Holy Spirit*, 83-89; Haenchen, *Acts*, 549-57; Johnson, *Acts*, 327-45; Ernst Käsemann, "The Disciples of John the Baptist in Ephesus," in *Essays on New Testament Themes* (Philadelphia: Fortress Press, 1982), 136-48; Lake and Cadbury, *Beginnings*, 4:231-38; Lampe, "Holy Spirit in Writings of Luke," 196-99; Menzies, *Development of Early Christian Pneumatology*, 268-77; Pesch, *Apostelgeschichte*, 2:159-67; Schneider, *Apostelgeschichte*, 2:258-65; Eduard Schweizer, "Die Bekehrung des Apollos, Ag. 18, 24-26," *Evangelische Theologie* 15 (1955): 247-54; Tannehill, *Narrative Unity*, 2:230-51; Michael Wolter, "Apollos und die ephesinischen Johannesjünger (Act 18:24-19:7)" *Zeitschrift für die neutestamentliche Wissenschaft* 78 (1987): 49-73.

[218] The Western text of Acts 19:1 reads "And although Paul wished, according to his own plan, to go to Jerusalem, the Spirit told him to return to Asia." The expansion reinforces the role of the Holy Spirit in this episode. See Bruce, *Acts*, 405; Johnson, *Acts*, 337; Metzger, *Textual Commentary*, 468-69.

[219] The Western text of Acts 19:6 reads "they spoke in other tongues, and they themselves knew them, which they also interpreted for themselves, and certain ones also prophesied." This reading seems to be influenced by 1 Corinthians 14. See Johnson, *Acts*, 338; Metzger, *Textual Commentary*, 470.

meet(s) disciple(s), is astonished to find disciple(s) accurately but incompletely informed by virtue of John's baptism, and then corrects the problem; the story concludes with inspired speech by the disciple(s).

The interpretive issues raised by these stories are complex, and there has been little consensus about why Luke has included them, what their historical background is, and how they fit into the Lukan theology of the Spirit.[220] Who were these disciples?[221] Were they non-Christians, or simply deficient Christians?[222] Are these stories intended to show how a fringe group was included in the church (and was this group still active in Luke's own day)?[223] Was Apollos empowered by the Spirit, and how can the reception of the Spirit by the Ephesians be fit into Luke's overall pattern?[224] In short, this passage is a fine example of how the reader must fill in the interpre-

---

[220]See Käsemann, "Disciples," for an overview of the problems.

[221]Apollos appears in quite a different guise in the Pauline epistles as Paul's co-worker, sometimes taken as a rival (mistakenly, according to Paul, though some modern scholars would challenge him on this point; see Haenchen, *Acts*, 555-56). See 1 Cor 1:12; 3:4-6, 22; 4:6; 16:12; Tit 3:13. Though Apollos is well known outside Acts, the others are given a symbolic number, no names, and no further role in the story.

[222]See e.g., Bruce, *Acts*, 406; Dunn, *Baptism in the Holy Spirit*, 88, 176; Haenchen, *Acts*, 554-57; Hull, *Holy Spirit in Acts*, 109-15; Opsahl, *Holy Spirit in Life of Church*, 35. The answer to this question depends largely on whether the interpreter believes that Luke ties the Holy Spirit to salvation; see Menzies, *Development of Early Christian Pneumatology*, 268-77.

[223]See Barrett, "Apollos," 37; See Johnson, *Acts*, 338; Käsemann, "Disciples," 141-42. For the possibility that John the Baptist's influence continued in parallel with early Christianity, cf. John 3:23-30; Josephus, *Antiquities* 18.116-19.

[224]See e.g., Dunn, *Baptism in the Holy Spirit*, 83-89; Hull, *Holy Spirit in Acts*, 109-15; Menzies, *Development of Early Christian Pneumatology*, 268-77. As with the Samaritans (8:17), the reception of the Holy Spirit by the Ephesian disciples follows the laying-on-of-hands; unlike that story, and like that of Pentecost (2:4) and the household of Cornelius (10:46), glossolalia is mentioned.

tive "gaps." While the ambiguity of Luke's narrative precludes any conclusive answers to all these questions, a literary analysis of the passage can clarify what the text says, and how it fits into Luke's overall narrative. The interpretive clue left by the implied author is the parallel structure between the two stories: the reader is invited to re-read the Apollos story in light of that of the twelve Ephesian disciples. The parallelism encourages the reader to fill in the gaps of one story in light of the other.

Apollos is described in positive terms, but not quite as a prophet. He is "eloquent" as well as "learned" (two possible translations of λόγιος), being well-versed in the scriptures (Acts 18:24; cf. v. 28).[225] He has been "instructed in the Way of the Lord" (cf. Luke 1:4), and he speaks "boldly,"[226] "with burning enthusiasm"[227] and "taught accurately the things concerning Jesus" (Acts 18:25-26; cf. Luke 1:3; Acts 1:3). Yet he is not said to be "full of the Spirit," nor does he speak "God's Word" nor do "signs and wonders"; thus his characterization differs from that Luke affords his prophetic figures.[228] Apollos stands as a positive figure, but with obvious

---

[225]See Bruce, *Acts*, 401; Haenchen, *Acts*, 550; Johnson, *Acts*, 331; Tannehill, *Narrative Unity of Luke-Acts*, 2:232.

[226]Boldness is Apollos' one truly prophetic attribute, cf. Acts 2:29; 4:13, 29-31; 9:27-28; 13:46; 14:3; 19:8; 26:26; 28:31—a point which Johnson misses when he says "although Apollos is described in highly favorable terms, Luke refrains from portraying him in the stereotypically prophetic terms that he has used for all his major protagonists" (*Acts*, 335). Since Johnson admits that παρρησία/παρρησιάζομαι "is part of Luke's prophetic/philosophical presentation of the apostles" (338), Apollos might be best described as a deficient prophet, lacking some but not all of the features of the Lukan prophetic stereotype.

[227]Or "Being fervent in spirit/Spirit" (ζέων τῷ πνεύματι); it is unclear whether the Holy Spirit is meant. Käsemann ("Disciples," 143) cites Rom 12:11 (τῷ πνεύματι ζέοντες) as justification for seeing Apollos as "fervent in the Holy Spirit," but it is not at all clear that Rom 12:11 has this meaning, nor that Paul's usage influenced Luke. At best, the passage is ambiguous, probably deliberately so. See Barrett, "Apollos," 36 n. 26; Bruce, *Acts*, 402; Haenchen, *Acts*, 550; Johnson, *Acts*, 332; Menzies, *Development of Early Christian Pneumatology*, 271-72; Tannehill, *Narrative Unity of Luke-Acts*, 2:232-33.

[228]See Johnson, *Acts*, 332-36.

deficiency: knowing only the baptism of John, he knows only that which is preparatory (cf. Luke 3:16; Acts 1:5; 11:16); he must be taught "more accurately" (18:26; cf. v. 25). But what Luke does not say is as interesting as what he does say. He leaves the reader in the dark—was Apollos rebaptized? Did he then receive the Spirit? The implicit invitation to the reader is to fill the gaps in light of the following story.

That gap-filling is in order here is indicated by the ambiguity Luke has left in the text of the second story. He speaks of "disciples" ($\mu\alpha\theta\eta\tau\acute{\alpha}\varsigma$), an absolute term which would normally refer to Christians; only as the narrative proceeds does the reader learn that it must refer to disciples of John the Baptist.[229] And even this detail is ambiguous, as the reader is left to discern it on the basis of the strange phrase "into the baptism of John."[230] The strange question of Paul, and the Ephesians' strange answer, only serve to complicate the matter.[231] The strange, ambiguous text demands of the reader a concerted effort to creative coherency by filling in the gaps.

The reader's struggle for clarity is resolved by attention to form. The story of the twelve disciples at Ephesus parallels that of Apollos in structure—Paul happens upon some stray disciples, and is

---

[229]Luke's ambiguity has frustrated a good number of exegetes. See Bauernfeind, *Apostelgeschichte*, 228-29; Bruce, *Acts*, 406; Haenchen, *Acts*, 553; Käsemann, "Disciples," 136; Menzies, *Development of Early Christian Pneumatology*, 272-76.

[230]See Käsemann, "Disciples," 137. The expression $\varepsilon\iota\varsigma$ $\tau\grave{o}$ Ἰωάννου $\beta\acute{\alpha}\pi\tau\iota\sigma\mu\alpha$ probably means "with the baptism proclaimed by John." On the construction cf. Rom 6:3; 1 Cor 1:13, 15; 10:2; 12:13; Gal 3:27. See Barrett, "Apollos," 37 n. 27; Bruce, *Acts*, 406-7; Haenchen, *Acts*, 553.

[231]The question Paul puts would only make sense if he thought they were Christian believers—but if so, why would he ask the question? The answer the disciples give is incomprehensible if they had listened to John's preaching (cf. Luke 3:16). Indeed, the thought of a observant Hellenistic Jew who did not know of the Holy Spirit is ludicrous; the Western text resolves this issue by emendation to "We have never heard that anyone has received the Holy Spirit." See Barrett, "Apollos," 38; Bruce, *Acts*, 406-7; Johnson, *Acts*, 337; Käsemann, "Disciples," 136-38; Metzger, *Textual Commentary*, 469.

astonished to find that they have insufficient knowledge of the Way; he instructs them more completely, and they respond with inspired speech. The parallel structure is an encouragement to read the two stories in tandem. Here, however, the gaps so evident in the Apollos story are filled in for the reader in the second story. The Ephesian disciples know nothing of the Holy Spirit (Acts 19:2). John's baptism is thus shown to be deficient in regards to the Spirit—Luke would seem to be pushing the reader to resolve the ambiguous ζέων τῷ πνεύματι in the Apollos story (18:25) towards "burning enthusiasm" rather than "fervent in the Holy Spirit."[232] On being properly instructed, the disciples are baptized; again, Luke invites the reader to fill in the blank for Apollos as well—Priscilla and Aquila probably would have baptized him. Following the baptism, the disciples become prophetic figures: "the Holy Spirit came upon them,[233] and they spoke in tongues and prophesied" (19:6); only at the end does Luke tell the reader that the number of the disciples was a symbolic twelve, turning the scene into yet another replication of Pentecost (cf. Acts 1:15-2:13).[234] The parallel with Apollos implies that he would have had a similar experience, and though again Luke does not spell it out, he provides a hint in that direction when he describes Apollos in language reminiscent of the work of Stephen, Philip, and Paul: "he powerfully refuted the Jews in public, showing by the scriptures that the Messiah is Jesus" (18:28; cf. 6:8-10; 8:35; 9:22; 17:3; 18:5; 20:20).

It is intriguing that Luke subtly downplays the prophetic side of Apollos' character, gently implies that he was without baptism and

---

[232]Contra Bruce, *Acts,* 402; Dunn, *Baptism in the Holy Spirit,* 88; Käsemann, "Disciples," 143; Tannehill, *Narrative Unity of Luke-Acts,* 2:232-33.

[233]Again, Luke depicts this as a direct action of the Holy Spirit; Paul plays his human role as he instructs, baptizes, and lays his hands on their heads, but the Spirit acts sovereignly.

[234]Cf. Johnson, *Acts,* 338; Richard, "Pentecost as a Recurrent Theme," 139-40. Luke is accustomed to cite his numbers with ὡς or ὡσεί (Acts 2:41; 4:4; 5:7, 36; 10:3; 13:18, 20; 19:7, 34). See Haenchen, *Acts,* 554; Johnson, *Acts,* 338.

the Spirit, and yet still gives him a positive portrayal.[235] Perhaps Luke was concerned to show how this segment of the early Christian movement was subordinated to the mainstream of the apostolic ministry (the parallels with the story of the Samaritans in chap. 8 are obvious); there was perhaps still the remnant of a Baptist sect within or on the fringes of Luke's church.[236] However, any reconstruction of the historical author's intentions here remains purely speculative.[237]

Literarily, these stories serve several functions. Luke gives closure to one of his major sub-plots: John the Baptist, one of the main figures of Luke's Gospel, looked forward to the coming of Messiah Jesus, and now the disciples taught by him have come into the community established by Jesus and his disciples through the Spirit.[238] Also, the two stories function in the immediate context

---

[235]Wolter ("Apollos," 49-73) contends that Acts here reflects the Corinthian controversy (1 Corinthians 1-4) and subordinates Apollos to Paul while denying that Paul transmitted the Spirit to Apollos. But as Tannehill (*Narrative Unity of Luke-Acts*, 2:232) notes, Wolter fails to account for the general positive tone which Luke takes towards Apollos. While Luke does not put Apollos on the same level with Paul, he does not denigrate him either, at least not explicitly.

[236]See above, n. 223.

[237]Käsemann's solution ("Disciples," 144-48)—that the Spirit is the seal of the Ephesian disciples' sacramental incorporation into the *Una sancta apostolica* through baptism and laying-on-of-hands—is too facile: Luke is not so consistently sacramental in his depiction of baptism, laying-on-of-hands, and the reception of the Spirit. Cf. Conzelmann, *Acts* 157-60; Haenchen, *Acts*, 556-57; Pesch, *Apostelgeschichte*. See the critiques of Barrett, "Apollos," 35-36; Coppens, "L'imposition des mains," 426-27; Marshall, *Luke: Historian and Theologian*, 212-15; Menzies, *Development of Early Christian Pneumatology*, 268-69; Schweizer, "Bekehrung," 71-79.

[238]Cf. Darr, *On Character Building*, 82-83. Darr finds in Apollos and the Ephesian disciples a perfect contrast with the unbelieving Jews so prominently featured in this section of Acts: "In the midst of reading about the overwhelming rejection of the gospel by Jews in Asia and Greece, the reader is given a contrasting report of a group of properly-prepared Jews, that is, of Baptist Jews, who grasp the true significance of the gospel message and embrace it" (83). Cf. Johnson, *Acts*, 355-36.

(18:18-19:20) as part of a "foundation account," describing the origin of the Christian community in Ephesus in terms of conversion, baptism, laying-on-of-hands, and reception of the Holy Spirit as manifested in inspired speech.[239] Further, Luke reinforces his portrait of Paul as apostle and prophet; like Peter (8:17), Paul's hands bring on the Holy Spirit and help legitimate the presence of a new group within the community.[240] Ephesus will prove to be an important center of Paul's activity in the narrative which follows.[241]

Despite the complexities and ambiguities of these stories, Luke remains consistent in his portrayal of the Spirit. The Spirit is the Spirit of prophecy, and produces inspired speech. Again, Luke depicts a direct action of the Holy Spirit; Paul plays his human role as he instructs, baptizes, and lays his hands on their heads, but the Spirit acts sovereignly. Here the Spirit comes after baptism and the laying-on-of-hands by Paul (cf. 8:17); again, Luke does not depict a sole relationship among baptism, laying-on-of-hands, and the reception of the Spirit. The presence of the Spirit, however, indicates both to the characters in the narrative and to the reader outside it that God is at work here. The coming of the prophetic Spirit ensures that these Christians, like the Samaritans and Cornelius, have been fully incorporated into the community by God's action.

Paul's Resolve to Go to Jerusalem (Acts 19:21-22)

In a brief preview statement, Luke records Paul's determination to go through Macedonia, Achaia, to Jerusalem, and then on to Rome (cf. Rom 15:25-32; 1 Cor 16:1-4; 2 Cor 8-9).[242] Luke sets

---

[239]See Johnson, *Acts*, 343; Menzies, *Development of Early Christian Pneumatology*, 276-77.

[240]See Johnson, *Acts*, 338.

[241]See Tannehill, *Narrative Unity of Luke-Acts*, 2:231.

[242]On these verses, see Bauernfeind, *Apostelgeschichte*, 232-33; Bruce, *Acts*, 413-44; Conzelmann, *Acts*, 164; Haenchen, *Acts*, 568-70; Johnson, *Acts*, 345-53; Lake and Cadbury, *Beginnings*, 4:243-44; Pesch, *Apostelgeschichte*, 2:175-77; Schneider, *Apostelgeschichte*, 2:271-79; Tannehill, *Narrative Unity*, 2:239-40.

the tone for the narrative to follow[243] by solemnly noting that "Paul resolved in the Spirit"[244] to make this trip (Acts 19:21). Here is a subtle signal to the reader on how to fill in the gaps of the rest of the narrative, for the question will be raised more than once: should Paul go to Jerusalem, only to end up in chains in Rome (cf. Acts 21:4; 21:11-14; 26:30-32)? The reader who reads in light of Acts 19:21 will conclude that God is at work in Paul's trials and tribulations, because it is God through the Spirit who has led him to

---

[243]"Luke provides the first signal for the turning point to be taken by the narrative....Paul's announcement of his intention begins the process and functions as a programmatic prophecy for the narrative to follow" (Johnson, *Acts*, 346, 351). Johnson (351) also notes the formal parallel to Jesus' decision to go to Jerusalem in Luke 9:51—Paul has been established as a prophetic figure, and now like Jesus will travel to the city which kills prophets (Luke 13:34). Cf. Tannehill, *Narrative Unity of Luke-Acts*, 2:239-40: the parallels extend even to the sending of messengers ahead (Luke 9:51-52). Though Jerusalem is the symbolic center of Luke's narrative, and he keeps returning to it, it is a deadly place for the prophets.

[244]The expression ἔθετο ὁ Παῦλος ἐν τῷ πνεύματι is ambiguous: does it mean that "Paul was inspired by the Holy Spirit to propose" or "Paul decided within himself"? (see Bruce, *Acts*, 413; Haenchen, *Acts*, 568; Johnson, *Acts*, 346; Lake and Cadbury, *Beginnings*, 4:244; Tannehill, *Narrative Unity of Luke-Acts*, 2:239). It is unclear whether the expression refers to the Holy Spirit or the human spirit. I contend (with Bruce and Tannehill) that this is a reference to the Holy Spirit, in light of Acts 20:22-23. Further, "a reference to the Holy Spirit in 19:21 would also attribute this new journey to the same divine initiative as Paul's first journey from Antioch (13:2, 4)" (Tannehill).

Luke does not give any reasons other than inspiration for Paul's trip. The reference to οἱ διακονοῦντες αὐτῷ may hint at his purpose, for Luke refers to the monetary collection in Acts 11:29 and 12:25 as a διακονία (cf. Rom 15:31; 2 Cor 8:4; 9:1). Since Paul was known to collect money in Macedonia (2 Cor 8:1-2; 9:2-4; Rom 15:26; Phil 4:10-20), it would make sense for him to send his helpers there. Why Luke is so coy on this point is a matter of speculation: was the money refused by the Jerusalem church, and so Luke is downplaying an embarrassment? Or does Luke merely shape the incident to fit his literary purpose? See Bauernfeind, *Apostelgeschichte*, 232; Bruce, *Acts*, 413-14; Conzelmann, *Acts*, 164; Haenchen, *Acts*, 569-70; Johnson, *Acts*, 351, 377-79; Schneider, *Apostelgeschichte*, 2:273-74.

Jerusalem and Rome.[245] Here mention of the Spirit serves as an indication of how to read what follows: the story of Paul's journey to Jerusalem, his arrest and imprisonment, and his appeal to Rome are part of the divine plan, inspired by the Spirit. The Spirit once again functions as a sign of the reliability of the apostle.

Paul's Farewell Discourse (Acts 20:17-38)

Luke presents Paul's final words to the Ephesian elders, spoken immediately before his departure for Jerusalem.[246] As in the Last Supper account (Luke 22:24-38), Luke follows the conventions of the farewell discourse, found in both Hellenistic and Jewish litera-

---

[245]Note Paul's expression δεῖ με καὶ 'Ρώμην ἰδεῖν (Acts 19:21). The wording (with δεῖ) reflects divine direction; see Bruce, *Acts*, 414; Cosgrove, "Divine ΔΕΙ"; Tannehill, *Narrative Unity of Luke-Acts*, 2:239.

[246]On Paul's farewell speech, see C. K. Barrett, "Paul's Address to the Ephesian Elders," in *God's Christ and His People*, ed. Jacob Jervell and Wayne A. Meeks (Oslo: Universitetsforlaget, 1977), 107-21; Bauernfeind, *Apostelgeschichte*, 237-39; Bruce, *Acts*, 429-37; Conzelmann, *Acts*, 172-76; Jacques Dupont, *Le discours de Milet. Testament pastoral de Paul Actes 20, 18-36* (Paris: Editions du Cerf, 1962); Haenchen, *Acts*, 589-98; Johnson, *Acts*, 359-68; Lake and Cadbury, *Beginnings*, 4:259-64; J. Lambrecht, "Paul's Farewell-Address at Miletus (Acts 20:17-38)," in *Les Actes des Apôtres: traditions, rédaction, théologie*, 307-37; Hans-Joachim Michel, *Die Abschiedsrede des Paulus an die Kirche Apg 20, 17-38: Motivgeschichte und theologische Bedeutung* (Munich: Kösel-Verlag, 1973); Johannes Munck, "Discours d'adieu dans le Nouveau Testament et dans la littérature biblique," in *Aux sources de la tradition chrétienne*, 155-70; Pesch, *Apostelgeschichte*, 2:196-208; Franz Prast, *Presbyter und Evangelium im nachapostolischer Zeit: Die Abschiedsrede des Paulus in Milet (Apg 20, 17-38)*, Forschung zur Bible, vol. 29 (Stuttgart: Verlag Katholisches Bibelwerk, 1979); Schneider, *Apostelgeschichte*, 2:290-300; Tannehill, *Narrative Unity*, 2:252-61.

The speech is a clear example of Lukan προσωποποιία, the writing of a speech in the style appropriate a character (for the historical problems attendant to both the meeting and the speech, see Haenchen, *Acts*, 590-98). Luke here presents Paul as he conceived him. See Johnson, *Acts*, 367.

ture.[247] Paul's final words to the church sum up the meaning of his ministry among them, in fact his entire ministry, while giving the reader guidance on how to interpret what follows.[248] Paul once again sets forth the prophetic pattern of service and suffering, which his audience within the story, and readers without, can expect to emulate.

Of interest to this study are Paul's claims that the Holy Spirit has inspired his present plans. Paul articulates for himself what the narrator has already told the reader: his decision to go to Jerusalem was made in the Spirit (cf. Acts 19:21). But Paul is much more graphic than the narrator: he is "bound in the Spirit" (20:22),[249] and the Spirit prophesies that constant imprisonment and persecution are in store for him (v. 23).[250] Luke's metaphor δεδεμένος ἐγὼ τῷ πνεύματι is striking. The verb δέω is usually used literally by Luke (cf. Luke 19:30; Acts 12:6) but can be used of physical illness attributed to spiritual forces ("bound by Satan," Luke 13:16). Ironically, Paul once chained Christians together (Acts 9:2, 14, 21; 22:5), but now will find himself in chains as a Christian (21:11, 13,

---

[247]E.g., Plato, *Phaedo;* Diogenes Laertius, *Life of Epicurus* 10.16-22; Gen 49:1-28; Deut 31; Philo, *Life of Moses* 2.290-92; *Testaments of the Twelve Patriarchs.* Elements of the common farewell address present here are the summary of one's life (Acts 20:18-21), prediction of destiny both of the speaker and the audience (20:22-25, 28-30), and exhortation (20:28-31). As Johnson (*Acts,* 367) notes, the farewell discourse makes use of the speaker as a model for "a kind of paraenetic discourse, in which the main point is the instruction of the listener in certain moral values." See Johnson, *Acts,* 366-67; idem, *Luke,* 347-49; Munck, "Discours d'adieu"; Tannehill, *Narrative Unity,* 2:252-61.

[248]Cf. Tannehill, *Narrative Unity of Luke-Acts,* 2:258-61.

[249]As in 19:21 the expression τῷ πνεύματι is ambiguous, and may refer to the human or divine Spirit; in light of 20:23, the latter is more probable. See above, n. 244, and Barrett, "Paul's Address," 112; Bruce, *Acts,* 432; Johnson, *Acts,* 361.

[250]Bruce (*Acts,* 432) sees references to the warnings of 21:4, 11 here (cf. Haenchen, *Acts,* 591), but this does not make narrative sense except as a programmatic prophecy, since these warnings have not yet been made. Here is another example of the Holy Spirit speaking directly to another character (this time presented in indirect discourse, cf 11:12; 16:6-7), with intermediary at best implied.

33; 22:29; 24:27).[251] Paul's statement of faith that he is a prisoner of the Spirit is an indication to the reader that the trials and tribulations he is about to face are part of the divine plan, in line with the pattern followed by all the prophets in Luke's narrative.[252] Again, Luke characterizes the Spirit indirectly, through the description of the Spirit's action ("binding," "testifying") by another character.

The other statement of interest here is Paul's claim that the Holy Spirit was responsible for the leadership positions held by his audience: "Keep watch over yourselves and over all the flock, of which the Holy Spirit has made you overseers, to shepherd the church of God that he obtained with the blood of his own Son" (Acts 20:28). Luke indicates that it was the common practice of Paul and his colleagues to appoint elders in each church they established (Acts 14:23; cf. 11:30; 15:2, 4, 6, 22, 23; 16:4; 21:18; also 1 Tim 5:17, 19; Tit 1:5; Jas 5:14; 1 Pet 5:1; 2 John 1; 3 John 1); now Paul clearly attributes this action to the Holy Spirit. This is the only time Luke refers to ἐπίσκοποι, though it is provocative that the related term ἐπισκοπή is used of the apostolic ministry in Acts 1:20.[253] Luke has already given the reader a narrative picture of this

---

[251] "The participle 'being bound' initiates a theme that is an ironic reversal of Paul's initial trip to Damascus to deliver back to Jerusalem 'bound' disciples" (Johnson, *Acts,* 361).

[252] Cf. Paul's self-description as a "slave" (δοῦλος) of Jesus (Rom 1:1; Gal 1:10; Phil 1:1; Tit 1:1); the terminology was not restricted to Paul, however (see Jas 1:1; 2 Pet 1:1; Rev 1:1).

Johnson (*Acts,* 361) notes the parallel between Acts 20:22-23 and Jesus' passion predictions: "Luke makes every effort to assure the reader that what awaits Paul is part of God's plan, in conformity with the pattern of the rejected prophet Jesus." Cf. Tannehill, *Narrative Unity of Luke-Acts,* 2:252, 259-60.

[253] The term ἐπίσκοπος was used for a number of offices in Hellenistic literature. It has strong echoes of the Greek Bible as well (the verb ἐπισκέπτομαι is used of Israel's leadership in Jer 23:2; Ezek 34:11; Zech 10:3; 11:16). In the Pauline corpus it is used in relation with διάκονος and, as here (cf. 20:17), seems to be synonymous with πρεσβύτερος (Phil 1:1; 1 Tim 3:2; Tit 1:7). Despite accusations of "incipient catholicism," there is no intimation in Luke-Acts of later hierarchical structure (as in Ignatius, *Ephesians* 4.1-2; 6.1; *Trallians* 3.1). See Bauernfeind, *Apostelgeschichte,* 239; Bruce, *Acts,* 433; Johnson, *Acts,* 362-63; Pesch, *Apostelgeschichte,* 2:204; Schneider, *Apostelgeschichte,* 2:296-97; Tannehill, *Narrative Unity of Luke-Acts,* 2:258-59.

kind of action by the Holy Spirit, in the story of the sending of Barnabas and Paul (Acts 13:1-4). Again Paul reiterates what the narrator has previously shown. Ascribing ecclesiastical appointment to the work of the Holy Spirit provides strong legitimation to Paul's work in the Ephesian church. It also assures the church that the leadership Paul left in place is competent to carry on his work.[254] Once again, the Spirit is indirectly characterized by description of its actions: the Spirit is responsible for the continued prophetic leadership of the community.

Prophetic Warnings (Acts 21:1-14)

Paul has already noted that the Holy Spirit has warned him about what he is to face; now his statement becomes a programmatic prophecy, as Christian prophets speak against Paul's plan.[255] Luke continues to foreshadow the events to come, and in the process demonstrates once again the church's struggle to understand the leading of the Spirit. Paul and his companions travel to Tyre and stay with the disciples there seven days (cf. Luke 6:17; Acts 11:19; 15:3). Luke says, "Through the Spirit[256] they told Paul not to go on

---

[254]Paul's warning against wolves that would savage the flock (Acts 20:28-31) is often taken as a reference to problems with Gnostics in Luke's own day (e.g., Haenchen, *Acts*, 596-97; Walter Bauer, *Orthodoxy and Heresy in Earliest Christianity*, ed. Robert A. Kraft and Gerhard Krodel (Philadelphia: Fortress Press, 1971); Charles H. Talbert, *Luke and the Gnostics: An Examination of the Lucan Purpose* (Nashville: Abingdon, 1966)). But such warnings are part of the stock features of the farewell discourse and should not be over-read. See Johnson, *Acts*, 362-63.

[255]On this section, see Bauernfeind, *Apostelgeschichte*, 239-42; Bruce, *Acts*, 438-42; Conzelmann, *Acts*, 177-78; Ellis, "Role of Christian Prophet"; Haenchen, *Acts*, 599-605; Johnson, *Acts*, 368-72; Lake and Cadbury, *Beginnings*, 4:264-69; Pesch, *Apostelgeschichte*, 2:208-16; Schneider, *Apostelgeschichte*, 2:300-305; Tannehill, *Narrative Unity*, 2:262-67.

[256]Here διὰ τοῦ πνεύματος clearly refers to the Holy Spirit (Haenchen, *Acts*, 600).

to Jerusalem" (Acts 21:4). Here Luke is clear that the Spirit is an indirect actor, working through the Christian prophets of Tyre. The prophets, however, are not clear about why Paul should forego Jerusalem; the reader will fill in the gaps in light of Acts 20:22-23 and 21:11, and conclude that the prophets wish Paul to avoid the danger he will face there. The prophets' statement is on the face of it, however, a contradiction of what the narrator has said in 19:21: that Paul's decision to go to Jerusalem was made under the influence of the Spirit. Here the Spirit seems to be saying the opposite.

When Paul reaches Caesarea, he goes to the home of Philip the evangelist (Acts 21:8), whom Luke has already shown to be a prophetic figure (Acts 6:5; 8:4-40).[257] Luke reinforces this picture by saying that Philip "had four unmarried daughters who had the gift of prophecy" (21:9).[258] Philip and his daughters are joined by the prophet Agabus from Jerusalem, one of the few Christian prophets directly so characterized by the narrator (cf. 11:27-28). In a striking scene reminiscent of the Old Testament prophets (cf. Isa 20:2-6; Jer 19:1-13; Ezek 4:1-17),[259] Agabus binds himself in Paul's belt to demonstrate Paul's impending bondage (21:11), repeating the message Paul himself has already given (20:22-23). Agabus' announcement that Paul will be handed over to the Gentiles

---

[257]Luke places Philip where he left him, at Caesarea (Acts 8:40). Similarly, Agabus "comes down from Jerusalem" again (cf. Acts 11:27). "Luke reminds the reader that Paul and the narrative are completing a full circle. The trip to Jerusalem is not simply a trip to a geographical location, but a return to a narrative 'place' that is, for Paul, filled with the memories and possibilities of conflict" (Johnson, *Acts*, 371). On Philip, see Spencer, *Portrait of Philip*.

[258]Luke describes the daughters as παρθένοι, invoking images of prophetesses in Hellenistic religion (Plutarch, *The Oracles at Delphi* 22; Pausanias, *Description of Greece* 10.12.6) and later Christianity (*Acts of Paul and Thecla* 7). See Johnson, *Acts*, 369-70. There is rampant speculation about Philip's daughters; see Bruce, *Acts*, 441.

[259]Even Agabus' language has Old Testament overtones, e.g., τάδε λέγει (used quite often in LXX; see e.g., Amos 1:6; Obad 1:1; Nah 1:12; Hag 1:2; Zech 1:16; Isa 1:24; Jer 2:31; Ezek 2:4. Cf. Rev 2:1, 8, 12, 18; 3:1, 7, 14). The use of "Holy Spirit" with the formula is unique to this passage. See Haenchen, *Acts*, 602; Johnson, *Acts*, 370.

echoes Jesus' passion predictions (cf. Luke 9:44; 18:32).[260] Those who hear the message, presumably including the Spirit-filled prophets present, urge Paul to cancel his trip (21:12). Paul, however, is adamant that he will follow the prophetic pattern, and die in Jerusalem, if it is the will of the Lord (21:13-14, cf. Acts 20:24; Rom 15:31-32). Again, the prophet Agabus reports the Spirit's words in indirect discourse as well as symbolic action; the conclusions drawn from this action differ from one prophet to the next, however—Paul wishes to go, while the rest of the community is resistant.

These episodes raise the question of what it means for Spirit-filled, prophetic figures to disagree and be in conflict. Luke clearly pictures Paul and the other prophets in disagreement; there is no reason to think that either party is defective in faith or understanding.[261] Rather, Luke again pictures the church as involved in a discernment process.[262] Two groups claim the inspiration of the Spirit for differing courses of action: should Paul go or not go to Jerusalem? Luke subtly builds suspense in this passage by constantly referring to prophetic figures (21:4, 8, 9, 10), but having Paul give

---

[260]Both Bruce (*Acts,* 442; also "Holy Spirit in Acts, 181-82) and Johnson *(Acts,* 370) object that it is not actually the Jews who do the binding of Paul (in 21:33), but certainly it was instigated by "the Jews from Asia" (v. 27), so Agabus' reliability is hardly suspect.

[261]Contra Lake and Cadbury, *Beginnings,* 4:266, who imply that Paul doubted their inspiration; the reliable narrator belies that notion for both Paul and the disciples. For the confusion this passage has caused to commentators, see Haenchen, *Acts,* 602 n. 1.

[262]Cf. Bovon, "Le Saint-Esprit, l'Eglise et les relations humaines selon Actes 20,36-21,16," in *Les Actes des Apôtres: traditions, rédaction, théologie,* 339-58; Tannehill, *Narrative Unity of Luke-Acts,* 2:262. "It is interesting that the narrator has allowed to surface at least a superficial contradiction in the divine guidance that Paul is receiving, an indication that it is seldom easy to separate divine revelation from human interpretation. Appeal to divine guidance is not an easy escape from the ambiguities of human life" (Tannehill, *Narrative Unity of Luke-Acts,* 2:263).

his answer only after the dramatic speech of Agabus.[263] Luke takes the narrative to an extremely high emotional level ("weeping and breaking my heart," v. 13), which is compounded by the vivacity of the "we" language of 21:12-14.[264] The issue is finally resolved by appeal to the prophetic pattern Luke has set forth throughout his narrative. Paul appeals to the example of Jesus and all the prophets, who go to Jerusalem only to suffer and die (cf. Luke 11:49-51; 13:33-34).[265] He will suffer "for the name of the Lord Jesus" (21:13), as Jesus himself predicted (Luke 6:22-23; 21:12, 17). His answer silences the opposition, except for prayer (cf. 11:18).

Luke thus pictures the Spirit working on both sides of this inter-community conflict, bringing the community together once again through the powerful example of the prophetic pattern. Paul convinces his companions by the implicit appeal to the story of Jesus. The resolution of the conflict helps to reassure the reader that Paul is still working according to the divine plan; the Spirit at work once again functions as a sign of Paul's reliability.

Paul and the Sanhedrin (Acts 22:30-23:11)

Paul, now in the bonds he had predicted, finally gains a hearing before the Sanhedrin.[266] After a brutal encounter with the high

---

[263]As Haenchen (*Acts*, 604) notes; cf. Tannehill, *Narrative Unity of Luke-Acts*, 2:263-64.

[264]Johnson (*Acts*, 370-72) comments on the high emotional tone; while Haenchen (*Acts*, 605) notes the impact of the "we" language.

[265]Cf. Haenchen, *Acts*, 602; Johnson, *Acts*, 372; Tannehill, *Narrative Unity of Luke-Acts*, 2:264-65.

[266]On this passage, see Bauernfeind, *Apostelgeschichte*, 254-58; Bruce, *Acts*, 461-67; Conzelmann, *Acts*, 191-92; Gowler, *Host, Guest, Enemy and Friend*, 285-92; Haenchen, *Acts*, 636-43; Jervell, "Paul the Teacher of Israel: the Apologetic Speeches of Paul in Acts," in *Luke and the People of God*, 153-83; Johnson, *Acts*, 395-402; Lake and Cadbury, *Beginnings*, 4:285-90; Pesch, *Apostelgeschichte*, 2:239-45; Schneider, *Apostelgeschichte*, 2:328-34; Paul Schubert, "The Final Cycle of Speeches in the Book of Acts," *Journal of Biblical Literature* 87 (1968): 1-16; Gedaliahu G. Strousma, "Le couple de l'ange et de l'esprit: traditions juives et chrétiennes," *Revue biblique* 88 (1981): 42-61; Tan-

priest (which shows Paul to be an obedient Jew, the high priest to be vile, Acts 23:1-5),[267] Paul craftily plays on the division between Pharisees and Sadducees when he defends himself on the basis of his belief in resurrection (v. 6).[268] This causes no little controversy in the assembly (v. 7) since, as Luke offers in an aside, "the Sadducees say that there is no resurrection, or angel, or spirit; but the Pharisees acknowledge all three" (v. 8; cf. Luke 20:27).[269] Sure enough, certain Pharisees defend Paul on the basis that a spirit or angel might have spoken to him (v. 9). In the commotion, Paul is saved by the intervention of the Roman tribune (v. 10). Luke concludes the episode by picturing the very sort of incident in question, a divine visitation (v. 11; cf. 9:4; 16:9; 18:9-10; 22:17), which will

---

nehill, *Narrative Unity,* 2:285-92.

[267]On the historical problems attendant here, see Haenchen, *Acts,* 639-43. Luke has already shown the violent, abusive nature of the Sanhedrin (Luke 22:66-71; Acts 4:5-22; 5:21-42; 6:12-7:60), in line with the prophecy of Jesus (Luke 21:12). The high priest Ananias, widely reputed to be corrupt (Josephus, *Antiquities* 20.213-14; *b. Pesah.* 57a; see Bruce, *Acts,* 464; Haenchen, *Acts,* 637 n. 6), violates Torah by denying Paul due process (*m. Sanh.* 3:6-8; cf. Acts 7:53). Paul as the good Jew who has a "clear conscience" (Acts 23:1) apologizes for his harsh words in light of Exod 22:28 (Haenchen, *Acts,* 638; cf. Tannehill, *Narrative Unity of Luke-Acts,* 2:285-86, 291). See Johnson, *Acts,* 396-97, who considers Paul's "disingenuous statement" to be "another prophetic criticism of the chief priest, whose behavior makes him 'unrecognizable'" (397). Cf. Gowler, *Host, Guest, Enemy and Friend,* 287.

[268]On Paul himself as a Pharisee, cf. Phil 3:5 (see Bruce, *Acts,* 465-66; Lührmann, "Paul"). As Johnson (*Acts,* 400-402) notes, the issue of the possibility of resurrection provides the common ground on which Luke can argue the fact of Jesus' resurrection with the Judaism of his day. The high priest has proven unworthy, the Sadduccees are extinct, but the descendents of the Pharisees are still very much active in Luke's own time. Paul is presented as the authentic Pharisee, who not only admits the possibility of resurrection, spirit, and angel in the abstract, but recognizes Jesus' resurrection, the Holy Spirit, and the angelic messengers of God. See also Darr, *On Character Building,* 122-25; Schubert, "Final Cycle," 11-12.

[269]Corroboration of Luke's statement comes from Josephus, *Jewish War* 2.163-65; *Antiquities* 18:14-16. See Bruce, *Acts,* 466; Johnson, *Acts,* 398.

serve as a programmatic prophecy for the rest of the narrative: Paul will indeed bear witness in Rome (cf. 19:21).[270]

The irony in this sequence is palpable. Paul, like Jesus, must face the Sanhedrin (cf. Luke 22:66-71).[271] The reader knows not only that there is a resurrection, but that both angel and Spirit have spoken to Paul; Paul's prophetic boldness is given narrative enactment as he confronts both high priest and council (cf. 4:13; 5:29). The subsequent plot within the Sanhedrin to kill Paul (23:12-15) thus appears all the more venal. And while Paul's Pharisaic defenders offer some support, they fall far short of recognizing Jesus as resurrected Messiah.

Luke skillfully uses irony to reinforce his characterization of both Paul and the Spirit. The Spirit has indeed spoken to Paul, and shown Paul to be a reliable prophetic figure. Now even his enemies have unwittingly acknowledged him so.

Paul at Rome (Acts 28:16-31)

In Luke's climactic final scene,[272] Paul arrives in Rome and

---

[270]See Haenchen, *Acts,* 639; Johnson, *Acts,* 399-400.

[271]"Paul's *imitatio Christi* serves to show how the prophetic Spirit continues to work in Jesus' witnesses, and also thereby certifies Paul as a trustworthy bearer of that witness" (Johnson, *Acts,* 400).

[272]On Luke's final scene, see Bauernfeind, *Apostelgeschichte,* 278-80; François Bovon, "»Schön hat her heilige Geist durch den Propheten Jesaja zu euren Vätern gesprochenen« (Acts 28:25)," *Zeitschrift für die neutestamentliche Wissenschaft* 75 (1984): 226-32; Bruce, *Acts,* 536-43; Conzelmann, *Acts,* 226-28; Philip Davies, "The Ending of Acts," *Expository Times* 94 (1983): 334-35; Gerhard Delling, "Das lezte Wort der Apostelgeschichte," *Novum Testamentum* 15 (1973): 193-204; J. Dupont, "La conclusion des Actes et son rapport a l'ensemble de l'ouvrage," in *Les Actes des Apôtres: traditions, rédaction, théologie,* 359-404; Haenchen, *Acts,* 721-32; Herman J. Hauser, *Strukturen der Abschlusserzählung der Apostelgeschichte (Apg 28, 16-31),* Analecta Biblica, vol. 86 (Rome: Biblical Institute Press, 1986); Johnson, *Acts,* 468-77; Lake and Cadbury, *Beginnings,* 4:345-50; D. L. Mealand, "The Close of Acts and its Hellenistic Greek Vocabulary," *New Testament Studies* 36 (1990): 583-97; David P. Moessner, "Paul in Acts: Preacher of Eschatological Repentance to Israel," *New Testament Studies* 34 (1988): 96-104; Pesch, *Apostelgeschichte,* 2:305-12; C. B. Puskas, "The Conclusion of Luke-Acts: An Investigation of the Literary Function and

meets with the Jewish leaders there.[273] Their encounter follows Luke's usual pattern: some believe, while others disagree (Acts 28:24-25), and so the people of God prove once again to be divided. Thus Paul announces God's plan to bring the good news of salvation to the Gentiles, now that it has been proclaimed to the Jews (vv. 25-28).[274] Luke leaves his second volume open-ended, with Paul free to preach for two years in Rome, presumably to Gentiles, with no further word of his eventual fate.[275]

So too, the reader may surmise, the success of the gospel among both Jew and Gentile is left open. Luke's open ending is a final example of a gap left to the reader to fill in. Although many flesh-and-blood readers see in this passage a third and final dismissal of

---

Theological Significance of Acts 28:16-31," Ph.D. diss., St. Louis University, 1980; Schneider, *Apostelgeschichte*, 2:409-21; Tannehill, *Narrative Unity*, 2:344-57.

[273]On the Jewish presence in Rome, see 1 Macc 14:16-18; 15:15-24; Josephus, *Life* 13; *Jewish War* 2.80-92; *Antiquities* 17.300; 18.81-83; Philo, *Embassy to Gaius* 155-58; Dio Cassius, *History* 60.6.6. See Raymond E. Brown and John P. Meier, *Antioch and Rome: New Testament Cradles of Catholic Christianity* (New York: Paulist Press, 1982), 89-127; Bruce, *Acts*, 535-36; Haenchen, *Acts*, 722; Johnson, *Acts*, 468.

[274]See Johnson, *Acts*, 471-72.

[275]On Paul's legal status in Rome, see Mealand, "Close of Acts"; on Luke's open ending, see Delling, "Letzte Wort"; Haenchen, *Acts*, 724-32; Johnson, *Acts*, 474-76; Tannehill, *Narrative Unity of Luke-Acts*, 2:353-57. Open endings were not uncommon in ancient literature; see Davies, "Ending of Acts," and more comprehensively, J. Lee Magness, *Sense and Absence: Structure and Suspension in the Ending of Mark's Gospel*, Semeia Studies (Atlanta: Scholars Press, 1986), 25-86. Luke does provide some closure to his story, e.g., Paul's fate has been predicted already (20:22-24, 29, 38; 21:10-14; 27:24). The ending also closes off a major plot line: Paul has arrived at Rome for his trial, in keeping with the prophetic pattern established by Jesus; see Tannehill, *Narrative Unity of Luke-Acts*, 2:354-56.

the Jews,[276] another reading is possible. The pattern which Luke has set for the reader in the previous narrative is clear: Paul preaches to the Jews, receives a mixed response, is rejected, and then announces that he will turn to the Gentiles (cf. 13:46; 18:6); however, the turn to the Gentiles is local rather than global, for Paul will preach in the synagogue in the next town. This pattern forms a paradigm for reading the last chapter in Acts: the first elements of the pattern are here, the later elements may be assumed.[277] Having seen that Paul has preached to the Jews, received a mixed response, pronounced judgment on the Jews, and turned to the Gentiles in Rome, the reader may safely infer that the rest of the pattern would follow were the narrative to continue; until the gospel has been preached literally "to the ends of the earth," there is still hope for the Jewish mission. The work of the Spirit will continue among both Jews and Gentiles. And since the Spirit is responsible for the faithful transmission of the gospel message, the character of the Spirit is ultimately left open. For Luke, there can be no closure of the activities of this character, as long as there is gospel left to preach.

Luke's final reference to the Holy Spirit recapitulates the Spirit's prophetic function in the inspiration of scripture (Acts 28:25; cf.

---

[276]See Bruce, *Acts,* 541; Johnson, *Acts,* 475-76; Moessner, "Paul in Acts"; Tannehill, *Narrative Unity of Luke-Acts,* 2:346-52; and above, chap. 3, on Luke 1:1-4.

[277]Johnson (*Acts,* 475-76) argues that Luke has varied his pattern in order to create a different expectation in the reader: this is the final announcement to the Jews. But are these variations really that significant? Johnson makes too much of "the fact that they *all* leave 'disagreeing with each other' (28:25)" (475), since Luke says clearly that "some were convinced by what he had said" (v. 24). A more challenging argument involves Paul's damning quotation of Isa 6:9-10 (vv. 26-27), which blames a stubborn and obtuse people for their own rejection: "Luke had not made full use of the Isaiah 6:9-10 passage in his Gospel....Only now after so many attempts at persuading this people, is it time to employ this most chilling prophecy, spoken first of the ancient people but now 'fulfilled' in the events of Luke's story" (476). Johnson fails to note that the previous rejections of the Jews contain equally damning statements: "You reject it [the word of God] and judge yourselves to be unworthy of eternal life" (Acts 13:46); "Your blood be on your own heads!" (18:6). The quotation of Isa 6:9-10, rather than being a variation in the pattern, merely confirms it.

Acts 1:16; 4:25). Luke concludes his portrait of the Spirit with a reference to the Spirit's direct action as the power behind the prophets. The Spirit spoke to ancient Israel through the mediation of Isaiah. If the message is a negative one, it is because Israel has always been a stubborn people who refused to listen to the prophets. Why then does God continue to talk to them through the Spirit? Not on the basis of their own merit, but because God is a faithful God. The faithfulness of God is signaled to the people by the continued presence of the prophetic Spirit, always pushing, prodding, calling for repentance. And the continued presence of the prophetic Spirit in the narrative of Luke-Acts is testimony to the continued faithfulness of God.

Chapter 5

Conclusion

Traditional approaches to the study of the Holy Spirit in Luke-Acts have asked theological questions: about Luke's doctrine of the Spirit, the beliefs he held in common with his contemporaries, where he and they acquired such beliefs, and so on. Some of these questions admit answers, others do not, still others are debatable. Wringing theological statements out of a narrative text is difficult at best.

An approach informed by recent theories of narrative confirms and supports the most solid conclusion of earlier studies: the Holy Spirit is for Luke the biblical Spirit of prophecy. A literary analysis of Luke-Acts further shows how pervasive the prophetic motif is. In both form and content, the Lukan narrative is structured by a pattern of prophetic fulfillment. Using the device of literary prophecy, Luke builds the motif of divine promise and fulfillment into the narrative. He portrays the main protagonists of the narrative, especially Jesus and the apostles, as prophets; predictions made by these prophetic characters will surely come true. Speeches are positioned so that what is said within them comes to pass in the following narrative (e.g., Acts 1:5, 8 and 2:1-4). At critical points, a character's prophecies provide structural indicators of the plot which follows (e.g., Acts 1:8). At the heart of Luke's prophetic structure stands the Holy Spirit, for no character in Luke-Acts functions as a prophet without clear indication of the Spirit's presence.

To study the character of the Spirit in Luke-Acts is to confirm the inevitable entanglement of plot and character. At the most basic level, the Spirit is the narrative symbol of human reliability: the epithet "filled with the Spirit" functions to signal the reader that what follows is reliable, prophetic human speech and action. The divine Spirit assures the reliability of the human characters (Luke 1:35, 41-44, 67; 2:25-27, 36; 3:16; 10:21; Acts 2:1-4; 4:8, 31: 5:32; 6:3, 5; 7:55; 8:29, 39; 9:17; 10:20, 44-46; 11:15, 24, 28; 13:1-3, 9, 52; 15:8, 28; 16:6-7; 19:6, 21; 20:22-23, 28; 21:4). In an example of Lukan literary prophecy, Jesus himself informs the reader that this will be the case: "the Holy Spirit will teach you at that very hour what you ought to say" (Luke 12:12; cf. 24:49; Acts 1:8). The perceptive reader sees more than one layer of meaning in this promise; it is a note of assurance not only to the disciples in the narrative, but to the one who reads the narrative as well.

And assurance is the avowed intention of the implied author of Luke-Acts. Luke, like any author, must convince the reader of his truthfulness. Yet Luke's concern with reliability goes beyond normal authorial interests, because his work is an apology for the reliability of God: has God indeed been true to the promise given to Israel? What better way to prove his point than to show a God who inspires and fulfills prophecy? The Lukan God, however, never appears directly on stage. The Spirit is above all a divine figure that represents God in the discourse. Through the actions of the Spirit— who not only inspires human prophets, but acts directly in the discourse itself—Luke shows a God who is reliable. The prophecies uttered in the power of the Spirit are fulfilled. When the human characters are slow or obtuse, the Spirit intervenes directly to bring to pass what God has ordained (see especially Acts 10-15). The one who reads cannot help but be impressed that here is a God who cares, who is at work in the world, and can be trusted. The Spirit functions onstage to prove the reliability of the offstage God. Thus plot and characterization go hand-in-hand, the main concern of the narrative becoming the main function of the character. The Spirit's words and deeds contribute to the "certainty" promised to the implied reader (Luke 1:4). In short, the Spirit does what the narrative does: assures reliability.

It has been the contention of this study that the Holy Spirit is best understood as a character in the narrative of Luke-Acts, and that the function of that character is to signal narrative reliability. I have used categories drawn from recent theories of character and characterization in narrative to draw a portrait of this character and explain how the characterization is made. It remains to summarize Luke's characterization of the Spirit, and to explore the implications of Luke's work for subsequent generations of readers.

Presentation of Character

Using the categories developed by a number of narrative theorists and conveniently summarized by David Gowler, I have analyzed Luke's presentation of the character of the Holy Spirit.[1] To review, there are two basic ways characterization may be made: through direct definition, and through indirect presentation. For each instance of characterization, varying degrees of reliability must be taken into account. In almost every instance, Luke characterizes the Spirit indirectly, using a reliable figure such as the narrator or Jesus to make the characterization.

Direct Definition. Luke does not often define the character of the Spirit directly, but in each case the definition is made by a highly reliable source. The Spirit is defined directly in the Gospel only once, when Jesus speaks of the "promise of the Father" (Luke 24:49). Jesus reiterates this characterization in Acts (1:4), as does Peter (Acts 2:33). Peter also directly characterizes the Spirit as a "witness" (Acts 5:32) and a "gift" (Acts 11:17; this characterization was first made by the narrator in Acts 10:45). In each case, the defined attribute is a highly significant factor in Luke's characterization: that the Spirit is the promised gift from the Father is central to Luke's prophetic scheme, and the attribute "witness" well-

---

[1] See above, chap. 2, "Character: Presentation and Reception."

summarizes the Spirit's role in the narrative. Luke uses direct characterization of the Spirit sparingly, but tellingly.

Indirect Presentation. Indirect presentation is made through
speech, action, appearance, description of environment, and comparison or contrast.

Speech. The characterization of the Spirit is often presented
indirectly through speech, whether that of the reliable narrator (e.g.,
Luke 1:67; 10:21; Acts 4:8, 31), Jesus (Luke 4:18-19; 11:13; 12:8-
12; 24:29; Acts 1:4-5, 8), Peter (Acts 2:17, 33, 28; 5:32), or
another reliable figure (Luke 1:15; 3:16). Again, a high degree of
reliability is implicit in each instance, though indirect characterization is inherently less reliable than direct presentation. Most stun-
ning are the instances when the Spirit itself speaks (Acts 8:29;
10:19; 11:12; 13:2; 15:28; cf. 1:16; 4:25; 28:25). Again, form and
function work together for Luke, as the Spirit who inspires divine
speech is reliably characterized by that speech.

Action. The Spirit frequently does things in Luke-Acts. The narrator frequently shows the Spirit as inspiring prophetic speech (e.g.,
Luke 1:67). In Acts this attribute is explicitly stated: the Spirit
"gave utterance" (Acts 2:4; cf. 11:28; 21:4, 9) or functioned as a
"witness" (Acts 5:32). The narrator uses a number of action verbs
to describe this function: the Spirit "leads" (Luke 4:1), "teaches"
(12:12), "forbids" (16:6-7), and "makes overseers" (Acts 20:28).
All of these verbs describe some aspect of the Spirit's prophetic
inspiration. Further, Luke uses metaphorical language to describe
the Spirit's inspiration: the Spirit "descends" or "falls upon" (Luke
3:21-22; Acts 10:44; 11:15), and "binds" (20:22-23). Sometimes
the Spirit is said to have "sent" someone to the next place of missionary activity (Acts 10:20; 13:4), and once the Spirit moves the
missioner bodily (8:39). The actions of this character show it to be
primarily concerned with the expansion of the Christian mission.

Appearance. Interestingly, Luke's reliable narrator gives a physical description of the Spirit twice, once as a "dove," once as "fire"
(Luke 3:22; Acts 2:3). Both descriptions are metaphorical and
highly allusive, and as such, slippery at best.

Environment. Luke consistently locates the Spirit's activity
among the people of God. In the Gospel, the Spirit's activity centers
on Jesus, though the faithful prophetic figures of the infancy narrative also act in the Spirit, as does John the Baptist, and to some

extent, Jesus' disciples. In Acts, the Spirit is at work exclusively among the followers of Jesus; now even disciples of the Baptist must bow to Jesus in order to receive the Spirit (Acts 19:1-7). That faithfulness and not mere affiliation is in view is shown by the episode of Ananias and Sapphira, who "lied to the Holy Spirit" and were punished severely (Acts 5:1-12).

Comparison and Contrast. The Spirit is most frequently associated with the work of the prophetic figures in the narrative (Luke 1:15, 35, 41-45; 2:25-27, 36; 3:22, 4:1-14, 16-30; 10:21; 11:13; 12:10-12; 24:48-49; Acts 1:2; 2:1-4, 17-18, 33; 4:8, 31, 32-37; 5:9, 32; 6:1-8; 7:55; 8:29, 39; 9:17; 10:20, 44-46; 11:15, 24, 28; 13:1-3; 15:8, 28; 16:6-7; 19:6, 21; 20:22-23, 28; 21:4, 9). But Luke also makes a sharp contrast between the work of the Spirit and the work of the devil; it is clear that behind many a human conflict there stands a cosmic battle (Luke 4:1-14; Acts 5:1-11; 6:1-7:55; 8:4-25; 13:4-12). The Spirit is characterized by contrast with the forces which work against the fulfillment of God's purposes.

Why does Luke favor indirect presentation as a means of characterizing the Spirit? A number of possibilities spring to mind. Luke may simply be following the rule that showing is better than telling—in Luke, as in many other writers, indirect presentation of character is the preferred method for every characterization. To let a character be presented by speech and action is a favorite authorial device, common to all kinds of narrative.

Indirect presentation also fits Luke's literary purpose, in light of the simple rule that showing is more persuasive than telling. While indirect characterization by nature raises more issues of reliability than direct presentation, in the end a reader who must piece together a character from its component parts will be of a more firm persuasion about that character than one who did no such work. Direct presentation by highly reliable narrative voices requires only the assent of the reader, direct characterization by voices of questionable reliability asks the reader's judgment—but indirect characterization means hard work. And one who works hard concludes resolutely. The reader who puzzles through Luke's presentation of the Spirit as the reliable inspiration of prophetic speech will arrive exactly where Luke wants that reader to be: convinced of the faithfulness of God.

The indirect method of characterization is appropriate in at least one other respect: in a way, Luke-Acts is one big indirect characterization of God. Luke seeks to answer the eternal question: who is God, and what is that God like? Luke's answer is that God is the God of Abraham, Isaac, and Jacob, proclaimed by the prophets, revealed by Jesus. It is this God, and no other, who is the subject of Luke's proclamation. Yet Luke's God is proclaimed indirectly, through a narrative, rather than through a sermon or systematic treatise. The indirect characterization of the Spirit, Luke's preferred divine representative within the narrative, fits well with the indirect presentation of God which constitutes that narrative as a whole.

Type of Character

I have used Baruch Hochman's method for describing the various facets of a character, a system of eight categories delineating various aspects of a character's existence. These categories embrace their polar opposites, and characters may be placed somewhere along a continuum between the opposites in each of the eight categories.[2] The system is by no means exact, but I have attempted to place the Spirit within each category. I have also noted, in accordance with the insight that characters change and develop as the reading process continues, where and how the characterization of the Spirit changes.

Stylization/Naturalism. I have defined stylization largely in terms of the degree to which Luke conforms to the portrait of the Spirit inherited from the Septuagint. It is clear beginning with the infancy narrative that Luke's characterization of the Spirit is in this respect highly stylized: Luke's Spirit stands in continuity with the ancient prophetic Spirit. The Spirit rests on prophetic figures such as Jesus, who are portrayed in terms reminiscent of Old Testament prophets such as Moses, Elijah, and Ezekiel (e.g., Luke 4:16-30; Acts 1:1-11; 7:1-55; 8:39). The Spirit is the gift of God (Luke 11:13; cf. Num 11:24-30; 24:2; Ps 51:11 (50:13 LXX); Isa 63:10f; Sir 48:12 (Codex A); Sus 45 (Theod.)) and is promised by God (Luke 24:49; Acts 2:17-21; cf. Joel 3:1-5 LXX; Isa 32:15). It is given in response

---

[2]See above, chap. 2, "Types of Characters."

to prayer (Luke 10:21; 11:13; Num 11:29; Ps 51:11). It brings joy (Luke 10:21; Acts 13:52; cf. Ps 51:11-12).

This stylization diminishes as the narrative moves toward its second volume. At the end of the Gospel, Luke attributes the dispensation of the Spirit to Jesus; this is certainly a new idea (Luke 24:49). In Acts, the stylization diminishes markedly in several respects. The Spirit is to be given universally, making all believers prophets—something promised in the Old Testament, but fulfilled only at Pentecost (Acts 2:17-18, 38; cf. Joel 3:1-5 LXX); here Luke does not invent as much as bring forward the implications of the traditional view. The Spirit becomes responsible for forming a community of friendship and commonality (Acts 2:44-46; 4:32-5:11). Most importantly, the Spirit becomes directly responsible for turning the mission outward towards the Gentiles, in fulfillment of God's promise that salvation will be opened to all peoples (Acts 10:44-46).

We have in Luke-Acts continuity and discontinuity with tradition, and thus varying degrees of stylization. Certainly Luke stands close to the traditional prophetic portrait of the Spirit; overall, his portrait of the Spirit is fairly stylized. But his belief that Jesus sends the Spirit puts him in this respect in the company of the Gospel of John. And his emphasis on the power of the Spirit in forming a community, and in the universality of that community, places him next to Paul. To the extent that Luke anticipates later developments in Christian pneumatology, he breaks from the stylistic portrait he has inherited.

Coherence/Incoherence. Luke begins his portrait of the Spirit with a high degree of coherence. From the infancy narrative on, the Spirit seems to have one primary function: it inspires prophetic speech. This one-dimensional portrait becomes less coherent in Acts, with its confusing inconsistency about which comes first: baptism, laying-on-of-hands, faith, or the coming of the Spirit (see esp. Acts 2:38, 8:4-25; 19:1-7). However, other functions of the Spirit, such as the formation of the community, tend to increase coherency by reinforcing and expanding the initial characterization. On the whole, Luke's picture of the prophetic Spirit is highly coherent.

An example of a momentary introduction of incoherence used to produce narrative suspense is found in Acts 16:6-7, where the Spirit forbids Paul and his company to preach in Asia or Bithynia. The Spirit seems to be obstructing that which it is supposed to promote, the spread of the gospel to new areas. But it becomes apparent in the subsequent narrative that the Spirit is not so much leading Paul away from Asia or Bithynia as leading him towards Europe. So momentary incoherence gives way to greater coherence, as the Spirit pushes the missionary beyond the sea to important new territory.

Wholeness/Fragmentariness. The single-mindedness of the Spirit as the inspiration of prophecy lends it a fragmentary feeling. The fragmentariness is gradually diminished as the narrative proceeds, however: the Spirit not only inspires speech, but produces joy (Luke 10:21) and courage (12:10-12). It forms a community (Acts 2:44-46; 4:32-5:11). And it does not stop at inspiring others, but speaks and acts itself (e.g., 8:1-40; 10:1-41).

Literalism/Symbolism. The Spirit is both highly symbolic and highly literal. "Spirit" is in some respect an epithet for "God," and thus symbolic in function; as a symbol, it resonates mightily with those who have read the Old Testament. Yet Luke is describing what he obviously believes to be a literal, specific God, who is acting in a specific way.

The Spirit's characterization is at times both enhanced and complicated by symbolism, especially that of the dove, the tongues of fire, and the contrast between light and darkness (Luke 3:22; Acts 2:1-4; 9:1-31).

Complexity/Simplicity. As with fragmentariness, the simplicity of Luke's characterization begins strong and lessens as the narrative proceeds, and for the same reasons. A Spirit whose only function is to inspire prophetic speech is a simple character. The simplicity is diminished when the Spirit is pictured as a generative force (Luke 1:35), and when it takes on new functions as the source of joy (Luke 10:21) and the builder of a community (Acts 2:44-46; 4:32-5:11). The duality between the Spirit as a life-giving and a death-dealing force adds further complexity; the Spirit is responsible for harsh punishments (Acts 5:1-11; 8:20; 13:4-12), but also for comfort and consolation (Luke 2:25; Acts 9:31; 13:15; 15:31), as well as "all the words of this life" (Acts 5:20). Some complexity is also introduced by Luke's theological inconsistency concerning baptism, laying-on-of-hands, faith, and the coming of the Spirit. Also, the odd geographical references in Acts 8 make the Spirit's character seem more complex as it moves Philip back and forth at will but without apparent logic.

Transparency/Opacity. In general, the Spirit is a transparent character in Luke-Acts. The motives of this character are clear to the reader: the purpose of the Spirit's work is to further the divine mission. This is most clear in those sections where the Spirit acts directly to further that mission (e.g., Acts 8:1-40). But there are several strange notes of opacity. The reader never sees into the mind of the Spirit, and rarely knows more about what the Spirit is doing than the characters in the story (an exception is the formation of the Gentile mission in Acts 10-15, long foreshadowed by the narrator and Jesus, but only slowly perceived by the human characters in the narrative). The symbolism of fire, opaque on the lips of John the Baptist (Luke 3:16), becomes more transparent in Acts 2:1-4. However, the symbolism of the Spirit as a dove is quite opaque, as are the geographical references in Acts 8 and Luke's theological inconsistency about baptism, laying-on-of-hands, faith, and the coming of the Spirit. In short, while the overall movement of the Spirit is quite transparent, the reader may hunger for more.

Dynamism/Staticism. As we have already seen, the activities of the Spirit change and develop somewhat as the narrative proceeds. The portrait of a prophetic Spirit established in the infancy narrative takes on new features as the story progresses; there are enough surprises as the narrative moves along that the characterization avoids the staticism inherent in a portrait based on ancient tradition. The direct actions of the Spirit indicate occasions of great dynamism; note that many of these actions are clustered in the narrative concerning the foundation of the Gentile mission (Acts 8:29, 39; 10:19-20, 44-46; 11:12; 13:2; 15:28). Another section contributing to dynamism comes as Paul journeys toward Jerusalem in the power of the Spirit (Acts 20:22-23; 21:4, 9).

Closure/Openness. Luke's portrait of the Spirit remains largely open-ended. There can be no closure as long as there is gospel left to preach. Luke's ending is itself open-ended, since Luke and his readers know that the gospel was and will yet be preached.

Conclusion: The Spirit and Its Readers

Narrative criticism has shown that texts and readers react and interact—it is not just a text which produces a characterization, but a text and a reader working together. Thus the value of narrative criticism does not end with the analysis of Luke's text, for the same tools help us understand Luke's readers—not only the implied reader posited by the text, but also the flesh-and-blood readers who have read Luke-Acts through the ages. Traditionally, most flesh-and-blood readers have interacted with Luke's text on a theological level. Narrative criticism helps account for this interaction as an example of the power of a community over the interpretation of texts. In light of the particular form into which Luke cast his material, and the particular community which preserved Luke's work, attempts to fit Luke's Holy Spirit into theological categories were understandable if not inevitable. I close this study with a brief example of how the study of narrative theory can clarify the development between Luke's narrative and the later theological reading of his text. The theories I have used to explain the Lukan characterization of the Holy Spirit elucidate the step between the character of the Holy Spirit in Luke-Acts and the hypostatic entity of later Trinitarian theology—a theology that proves, to some extent, to be a matter of reading and re-reading.

My assessment of Luke's place in the developing pneumatology of the early church begins with an understanding of Luke's own appropriation of tradition. Luke's deep indebtedness to Septuagintal tradition has been shown time and time again in this study. One strain of that tradition included dynamic depictions of the Spirit's activities. For one steeped in the prophetic literature, to write of a Spirit who speaks to Philip and then whisks him away is to do no more than echo Ezekiel; the seeds of the personification of the Spirit are found in the Old Testament. Luke took this personified Spirit and placed it inside a narrative, thus making it a character. Once Luke had chosen a genre, the issue was virtually decided: the Spirit became a character because Luke wrote a narrative.

Luke's unique contribution to subsequent tradition was that he wrote such a narrative with such a character. The unmediated presentation of the Spirit, not through a sermon or treatise but through narrative, allows Luke to engage the reader in a manner more compelling than the alternatives. The complex acts of character-building that take place in the (largely indirect) characterization of Luke's Spirit help Luke achieve his apologetic purpose. The reader assembles a view of the prophetic Spirit, and thus of the faithful God, by virtue of narrative's uncanny ability to touch the human psyche in ways other genres do not.

Luke's discourse is theological in that it ultimately speaks about God. Yet a good deal of Luke's speech about God is indirect; God acts within the story but not in the discourse—there are summaries which present events retrospectively as acts of God (e.g., Acts 10:34-43), but God never appears onstage as an actor. Luke presents God's actions in indirect ways, one of which is to speak of the Holy Spirit. One scholar has suggested that "the Holy Spirit" is a "seme" which repeatedly traverses and stands in for another seme, "God"; that is, to say "Holy Spirit" is just another way of saying "God."[3] Luke's Holy Spirit is a character where God cannot be. The mysterious, ineffable God acts offstage. But the actions of that God can be known, because they take place under the aegis of the Spirit. And the Spirit can be detected by careful examination of the prophetic tradition—prophets, after all, have easily recognized features. To recognize the prophetic Spirit is indirectly to recognize God. The reader in effect looks over Luke's shoulder as Luke looks over the Spirit's shoulder at the hand of God. The characterization of the Holy Spirit in Luke-Acts is an indirect characterization of God.

Luke's presentation of a (generally-speaking) stylized, coherent, fragmentary, symbolic, simple, transparent, dynamic, open-ended Spirit influenced the theology of later generations. Reading and rereading inevitably has its effects, especially when Luke is read (as it was by the early church) alongside the more developed pneumatologies of John and Paul. Is it a surprise that a Holy Spirit presented as a character who is virtually a stand-in for God would eventually be absorbed into the Godhead? The step between Luke's character and the Third Person of the Trinity proves to be small indeed.

---

[3]Brawley, *Centering on God*, 111. See above, chap. 1, "The Holy Spirit and the Literary Critics."

As an example of the power the reading of Luke-Acts exerted over the development of Christian pneumatology, take the following argument by Gregory of Nazianzus (c. 380 C.E.). Gregory seeks to prove that the Holy Spirit cannot be conceived of as merely the impersonal power of God, but must be a spiritual being, and certainly cannot be a created being:

> The Holy Spirit must certainly be conceived of either in the category of the self-existent or in that of the things which are contemplated in another: those skilled in such matters call the one substance and the other accident. Now if he were an accident, he would be an activity of God. For what else, or of whom else, could he be, since this is what most avoids composition? If he is an activity, he will be effected, but will not effect and will cease to exist as soon as he has been effected, for this is the nature of an activity. How is it, then that he acts and says such and such things, and defines, and is grieved, and is angered, and has all the qualities which belong clearly to one that moves, but not to movement itself? If he is, on the other hand, a substance and not an attribute of substance, he will be conceived of either as a creature of God or as God. For anything between these two, whether having nothing in common with either or a compound of both, not even those who invented the goat-stag could imagine. Now, if he is a creature, how do we believe in him, how are we made perfect in him? (Gregory of Nazianzus, *Fifth Theological Oration* 31.6).[4]

Gregory's logic is based in part on his reading of Luke-Acts, where the Spirit "acts and says such and such things," i.e., in the terms of narrative criticism, the Spirit is portrayed as a character. The Spirit, in Gregory's theological terms, cannot be merely the activity of God, for Luke shows the Spirit acting, speaking, and doing. From there it is a short step through Paul's doctrine of sanctification, in which Christians are "made perfect" through the Spirit, to Gregory's conclusion that the Spirit cannot be a creature, but must be God.[5]

This is not to argue, with traditional theological studies, that Luke anticipated later Trinitarian theology—far from it. It is rather

---

[4]Cited Burns and Fagin, *Holy Spirit,* 128-29; see also Swete, *Holy Spirit in Ancient Church,* 241-42.

[5]On the role of Luke-Acts in the development of Trinitarian theology, see also Bovon, *De Vocatione Gentium,* 195-98.

to demonstrate that the complex process of reading and re-reading texts within interpretive communities is open-ended and unpredictable, and that narrative criticism can further our understanding of how readers and texts work together to beget something new. The flesh-and-blood Luke could have had no idea what forces this text would unleash among those who read it, just as his predecessors had no control over how Luke used their material. By placing the personified biblical Spirit within a narrative, Luke transformed traditional material into a new literary construct which served to designate a faithful God. Gregory transformed Luke's literary construct into a theological one; in the hands of Gregory, reading years later in a different time and place, the Spirit breathed life as a distinct entity within the Godhead. Gregory, like any reader, engaged in the process of consistency building, filling in gaps from within and without, reading and re-reading to make sense of the puzzle which was handed down to him in certain terms and within certain limits. What the community of modern narrative critics would designate a character, Gregory and his church saw simply as God. Here the power of the tools I have employed in this study becomes clear. Narrative criticism not only elucidates the dynamics of the biblical text, but also provides a way of understanding how that text came to be read.

In a community formed by narrative criticism, the Spirit as character may well be said (without insult to orthodox theology) to be a creature—jointly created by reader, text, and context in the act of reading. That the characterization found in this intersection has proved so powerful is testimony not only to the flesh-and-blood author's skill, but to the collective skills of the many flesh-and-blood readers who have tried to make sense of Luke's text over the years. When they do their job, the various threads Luke has left in the narrative are woven into glorious tapestry. If Luke has done his job, the Spirit sighted in those threads will assure his readers of the faithfulness of the God he proclaimed.

Works Cited

Abri, J. "The Theological Meaning of Pentecost." *Kator Shin* 4 (1965): 133-51.

Ades, John I. "Literary Aspects of Luke." *Papers on Language and Literature* 15 (1979): 193-99.

Adler, N. *Das erste christliche Pfingstfest. Sinn und Bedeutung des Pfingsberichtes, Apg. 2, 1-13.* Münster: Aschendorff'sche Verlagsbuchhandlung, 1938.

_____. *Taufe und Handauflegung. Eine exegetisch-theologische Untersuchung von Apg. 8, 14-17.* Münster: Aschendorff'sche Verlagsbuchhandlung, 1951.

Alexander, Loveday. "Luke's Preface in the Context of Greek Preface-Writing." *Novum Testamentum* 28 (1986): 48-74.

_____. *The Preface to Luke's Gospel: Literary Conventions and Social Context in Luke 1.1-4 and Acts 1.1.* Society for New Testament Studies Monograph Series. Cambridge: Cambridge University Press, 1993.

Alter, Robert. *The Art of Biblical Narrative.* New York: Basic Books, 1981.

_____. *The Pleasures of Reading in an Ideological Age.* New York: Simon and Schuster, Inc., 1989.

_____. *The World of Biblical Literature.* New York: Basic Books, 1992.

Anderson, Hugh. "The Rejection at Nazareth Pericope of Luke 4:16-30 in Light of Recent Critical Trends." *Interpretation* 18 (1964): 259-75.

Aristotle. "On the Art of Poetry." In *Classical Literary Criticism*, translated with an introduction by T. S. Dorsch. New York: Penguin Books, 1965.

Aune, David E. *Prophecy in Early Christianity and the Ancient Mediterranean World*. Grand Rapids: Eerdmans, 1983.

Baer, Heinrich von. *Der Heilige Geist in den Lukasschriften*. Beiträge zur Wissenschaft vom Alten und Neuen Testament, Ditte Folge Heft 3. Stuttgart: W. Kohlhammer, 1926.

Bajard, J. "La structure de la pericope de Nazareth en Lc iv. 16-30." *Ephemerides Theologicae Lovanienses* 45 (1969): 165-71.

Bakhtin, M. M. *The Dialogic Imagination: Four Essays*. Edited by Michael Holquist. Translated by Michael Holquist and Caryl Emerson. University of Texas Press Slavic Series, vol. 1. Austin: University of Texas, 1981.

Bal, Mieke. *Narratology: Introduction to the Theory of Narrative*. Translated by Christine von Boheemen. Toronto: University of Toronto Press, 1985.

Barr, D. L., and J. L. Wentling. "The Conventions of Classical Biography and the Genre of Luke-Acts." In *Luke-Acts: New Perspectives from the Society of Biblical Literature Seminar*, edited by Charles H. Talbert, 63-88. New York: Crossroad, 1984.

Barrett, C. K. "Apollos and the Twelve Disciples of Ephesus." In *The New Testament Age*, edited by William C. Weinrich, 1:29-39. Mercer, Ga.: Mercer University Press, 1984.

_____. *The Holy Spirit and the Gospel Tradition*. London: SPCK, 1947.

_____. "Light on the Holy Spirit from Simon Magus (Acts 8, 4-25)." In *Les Actes des Apôtres: traditions, rédaction, théologie*, edited by J. Kremer, 281-95. Bibliotheca Ephemeridum Theologicarum Lovaniensium, vol. 48. Gembloux: Leuven University Press, 1979.

_____. "Paul's Address to the Ephesian Elders." In *God's Christ and His People*, edited by Jacob Jervell and Wayne A. Meeks, 107-21. Oslo: Universitetsforlaget, 1977.

Barthes, Roland. "L'Analyse structurale du récit a propos d'Actes X-XI." *Recherches de science religieuse* 58 (1970): 17-37.

_____. *S/Z*. Translated by Richard Miller, with a preface by Richard Howard. New York: Hill and Wang, 1974.

Bassler, Jouette M. "Luke and Paul on Impartiality." *Biblica* 66 (1985): 546-52.

Bauer, Walter. *Orthodoxy and Heresy in Earliest Christianity*. Translated by Philadelphia Seminar on Christian Origins. Appendices by Georg Strecker. Edited by Robert A. Kraft and Gerhard Krodel. Philadelphia: Fortress Press, 1971.

Bauer, Walter, William F. Arndt, F. Wilbur Gingrich, and Frederick W. Danker. *A Greek-English Lexicon of the New Testament and Other Early Christian Literature*. Chicago: University of Chicago Press, 1979.

Bauernfeind, Otto, and Volker Metelmann. *Kommentar und Studien zur Apostelgeschichte*. Wissenschaftliche Untersuchungen zum Neuen Testament, vol. 22. Tübingen: J. C. B. Mohr (Paul Siebeck), 1980.

Benoit, A. "Le Saint-Esprit et l'église, dans la théologie patristique greque des quatre premiers siècles." In *L'Esprit Saint et L'Eglise*, edited by S. Dockx, 125-41. Paris: Fayard, 1969.

Benoit, Pierre. "La deuxième visite de Saint Paul à Jerusalem." *Biblica* 40 (1959): 778-92.

Best, Ernest. "Acts XIII. 1-3." *Journal of Theological Studies* n.s. 11 (1960): 344-48.

Black, Max. *Models and Metaphors: Studies in Language and Philosophy*. Ithaca: Cornell University Press, 1962.

Blomberg, Craig L. "The Law in Luke-Acts." *Journal for the Study of the New Testament* 22 (1984): 53-80.

Bock, Darrell L. *Proclamation from Prophecy and Pattern: Lucan Old Testament Christology*. Journal for the Study of the New Testament Supplement Series, vol. 12. Sheffield: Sheffield Academic Press, 1987.

Boismard, M. -E. "Le Martyre d'Etienne (Acts 6, 8-8,2)." *Recherches de science religieuse* 69 (1981): 181-94.

Booth, Wayne C. *The Rhetoric of Fiction*. 2nd Ed. Chicago: University of Chicago Press, 1983.

_____. *A Rhetoric of Irony*. Chicago: University of Chicago Press, 1974.

Boring, M. Eugene. *The Continuing Voice of Jesus: Christian Prophecy and the Gospel Tradition.* Louisville: Westminster/John Knox Press, 1991.

_____. "The Unforgivable Sin Logion, Mark III 28-29/Matt XII 31-32/Luke XII 10: Formal Analysis and History of the Tradition." *Novum Testamentum* 18 (1976): 258-79.

Borremans, John. "The Holy Spirit in Luke's Evangelical Catechesis. A Guide to Proclaiming Jesus Christ in a Secular World." *Lumen Vitae* 25 (1970): 279-98.

Bovon, François. *Das Evangelium Nach Lukas.* Evangelisch-Katholischer Kommentar zum Neuen Testament Band 3. Zürich: Benziger Verlag, 1989.

_____. *Luke the Theologian: Thirty-Three Years of Research (1950-1983).* Translated by Ken McKinney. Princeton Theological Monograph Series, no. 12. Allison Park, Penn.: Pickwick Publications, 1987.

_____. "Le Saint-Esprit, L'Eglise et les relations humaines selon Actes 20,36-21,16." In *Les Actes Des Apôtres: Traditions, Rédaction, Théologie,* edited by J. Kremer, 339-58. Bibliotheca Ephemeridum Theologicarum Lovaniensium, vol. 48. Gembloux: Leuven University Press, 1979.

_____. "»Schön hat her heilige Geist durch den Propheten Jesaja zu euren Vätern gesprochenen« (Acts 28:25)." *Zeitschrift für die neutestamentliche Wissenschaft* 75 (1984): 226-32.

_____. "Tradition et rédaction en Actes 10, 1-11, 18." *Theologische Zeitschrift* 26 (1970): 22-45.

_____. *De Vocatione Gentium: histoire de l'interprétation d'Act 10, 1 - 11, 18 dans les six premiers siècles.* Beiträge zur Geschichte der biblischen Exegese, vol. 8. Tübingen: J. C. B. Mohr (Paul Siebeck), 1967.

Bowers, W. P. "Paul's Route Through Mysia: A Note on Acts 16:8." *Journal of Theological Studies* n.s. 30 (1979): 507-11.

Brawley, Robert L. *Centering on God: Method and Message in Luke-Acts.* Literary Currents in Biblical Interpretation. Louisville: Westminster/John Knox Press, 1990.

_____. *Luke-Acts and the Jews: Conflict, Apology, and Conciliation.* Society of Biblical Literature Monograph Series, no. 33. Atlanta: Scholars Press, 1987.

Bredin, Hugh. "The Displacement of Character in Narrative Theory." *British Journal of Aesthetics* 22 (1982): 291-300.

Bremond, Claude. *Logique du récit.* Paris: Seuil, 1973.

Briggs, Charles A. "The Use of רוח in the Old Testament." *Journal of Biblical Literature* 19 (1900): 132-45.

Brooks, Cleanth. *The Well Wrought Urn: Studies in the Structure of Poetry.* New York: Harcourt Brace and World, 1947.

Brown, Raymond E. *The Birth of the Messiah: A Commentary on the Infancy Narratives in Matthew and Luke.* Garden City: Doubleday, Inc., 1979.

_____. "The Pater Noster as Eschatological Prayer." In *New Testament Essays,* 217-53. Milwaukee: Bruce, 1965.

_____, and John P. Meier. *Antioch and Rome: New Testament Cradles of Catholic Christianity.* New York: Paulist Press, 1982.

Brown, Schuyler. *Apostasy and Perseverance in the Theology of Luke.* Analecta Biblica. Rome: Biblical Institute, 1969.

_____. "The Role of the Prologues in Determining the Purpose of Luke-Acts." In *Perspectives on Luke-Acts,* edited by Charles H. Talbert, 99-111. Danville, Va.: Association of Baptist Professors of Religion, 1978.

_____. "'Water-Baptism' and 'Spirit-Baptism' in Luke-Acts." *Anglican Theological Review* 59 (1977): 135-51.

Bruce, F. F. *The Acts of the Apostles: The Greek Text with Introduction and Commentary.* 3d ed. Grand Rapids: Eerdmans, 1990.

_____. "The Apostolic Decree of Acts 15." In *Studien zum Text und zur Ethik des Neuen Testaments,* edited by Wolfgang Schrage, 115-24. Berlin: Walter de Gruyter, 1986.

_____. "The Holy Spirit in the Acts of the Apostles." *Interpretation* 27 (1973): 166-83.

Brunner, Peter. "Das Pfingstereignis: eine dogmatische Beleuchtung seiner historischen Problematik." In *Volk Gottes: zum Kirchenverständis der katholischen, evangelischen und anglikanischen Theologie,* edited by Remigius Bäumer and Heimo Dolch, 230-42. Freiburg: Herder, 1967.

Bryan, Christopher. "A Further Look at Acts 16:1-3." *Journal of Biblical Literature* 107 (1988): 292-94.

Bultmann, Rudolf. *Theology of the New Testament.* Translated by Kendrick Grobel. Scribner Studies in Contemporary Theology. New York: Scribner's, 1951-55.

Burleigh, J. H. S. "The Doctrine of the Holy Spirit in the Latin Fathers." *Scottish Journal of Theology* 7 (1954): 113-32.

Burns, Edward. *Character: Acting and Being on the Pre-Modern Stage.* New York: St. Martin's Press, 1990.

Burns, J. Patout, and Gerald M. Fagin. *The Holy Spirit.* Message of the Fathers of the Church, vol. 3. Wilmington: Michael Glazier, 1984.

Burton, Ernest DeWitt. *Spirit, Soul, and Flesh: The Usage of Πνεῦμα, Ψυχή, and Σάρξ in Greek Writings and Translated Works from the Earliest Period to 180 A.D.; and of Their Equivalents רוּחַ, נֶפֶשׁ, and בָּשָׂר in the Hebrew Old Testament.* Reprinted, with additions and revisions, from the *American Journal of Theology,* 1913-1916. Historical and Linguistic Studies. Chicago: University of Chicago Press, 1918.

Buss, Matthäus Franz-Josef. *Die Missionspredigt des Paulus im Pisidischen Antiochien: Analyse von Apg 13, 16-41 im Hinblick auf die literarische und thematische Einheit der Paulusrede.* Stuttgart: Verlag Katholisches Bibelwerk, 1980.

Cadbury, Henry J. *The Book of Acts in History.* New York: Harper and Brothers, 1955.

_____. "Commentary on the Preface of Luke." In *The Beginnings of Christianity: Part I, the Acts of the Apostles,* edited by Kirsopp Lake and Henry J. Cadbury, 2:489-510. London: Macmillan and Co., Ltd., 1933.

_____. "The Hellenists." In *The Beginnings of Christianity: Part I, the Acts of the Apostles,* edited by Kirsopp Lake and Henry J. Cadbury, 5:59-74. London: Macmillan and Co., Ltd., 1933.

_____. *The Making of Luke-Acts.* New York: Macmillan Co., 1927.

_____. *The Style and Literary Method of Luke.* Harvard Theological Studies, vol. 6. Cambridge: Harvard University Press, 1920.

_____. "'We' and 'I' Passages in Luke/Acts." *New Testament Studies* 3 (1957): 128-32.

Caird, G. B. *The Apostolic Age*, 57-72. London: Gerald Duckworth & Co., Ltd., 1955.

_____. *The Language and Imagery of the Bible*. London: Duckworth, 1981.

Carroll, John T. "Luke's Portrayal of the Pharisees." *Catholic Biblical Quarterly* 50 (1988): 604-21.

Casey, R. P. "Simon Magus." In *The Beginnings of Christianity: Part I, the Acts of the Apostles*, edited by Kirsopp Lake and Henry J. Cadbury, 5:151-63. London: Macmillan and Co., Ltd., 1933.

Chance, J. Bradley. *Jerusalem, the Temple, and the New Age in Luke-Acts*. Macon: Mercer University Press, 1988.

Chatman, Seymour. *Story and Discourse: Narrative Structure in Function and Film*. Ithaca: Cornell University Press, 1978.

Chevallier, Max-Alain. "Luc et l'Esprit Saint." A la Mémoire Du P. Augustin George (1915-1977). *Revue des sciences religieuses* 56 (1982): 1-16.

_____. *Souffle de Dieu. Le Saint-Esprit dans le Nouveau Testament*, 160-225. Le Point Théologique, no. 26. Paris: Editions Beauchesne, 1978.

Childs, Brevard S. *The New Testament as Canon: An Introduction*. Philadelphia: Fortress Press, 1984.

Ciardi, John. *How Does a Poem Mean?* Part 3 of *An Introduction to Literature*, by Herbert Barrows, Hubert Heffner, John Ciardi, and Wallace Douglas. Boston: Houghton Mifflin Co., 1959.

Cohen, Shaye J. D. "Was Timothy Jewish (Acts 16:1-3)? Patristic Exegesis, Rabbinic Law, and Matrilineal Descent." *Journal of Biblical Literature* 105 (1986): 251-68.

Congar, Yves M. J. *I Believe in the Holy Spirit*. Translated by David Smith. New York: Seabury Press, 1983.

Conzelmann, Hans. *Acts of the Apostles*. Translated by James Limburg, A. Thomas Kraabel, and Donald H. Juel. Edited by Eldon Jay Epp and Christopher R. Matthews. Hermeneia. Philadelphia: Fortress Press, 1987.

_____. *The Theology of St. Luke*. Translated by Geoffrey Buswell. New York: Harper & Row, 1961.

Coppens, J. "L'imposition des mains dans les Actes des Apôtres." In *Les Acts des Apôtres: traditions, rédaction, théologie*, edited by J. Kremer, 405-38. Bibliotheca Ephemeridum Theologicarum Lovaniensium, vol. 48. Gembloux: Leuven University Press, 1979.

Cosgrove, Charles H. "The Divine ΔEI in Luke-Acts: Investigations Into the Lukan Understanding of God's Providence." *Novum Testamentum* 26 (1984): 168-90.

Craddock, Fred B. *Luke*. Interpretation. Louisville: John Knox Press, 1990.

Culler, Jonathan. *Structuralist Poetics: Structuralism, Linguistics and the Study of Literature*. Ithaca: Cornell University Press, 1976.

Dahl, Nils Alstrup. "'A People for His Name' (Acts xv. 14)." *New Testament Studies* 4 (1958): 319-27.

_____. "The Purpose of Luke-Acts." In *Jesus in the Memory of the Early Church*, 87-98. Minneapolis: Augsburg Publishing House, 1976.

_____. "The Story of Abraham in Luke-Acts." Reprinted from *Studies in Luke-Acts*, ed. Leander Keck and J. Louis Martyn. Nashville: Abingdon, 1966. In *Jesus in the Memory of the Early Church*, 66-86. Minneapolis: Augsburg Publishing House, 1976.

Danto, Arthur C. *Narration and Knowledge (including the Integral Text of "Analytical Philosophy of History")*. New York: Columbia University Press, 1985.

Darr, John A. *On Character Building: The Reader and the Rhetoric of Characterization in Luke-Acts*. Literary Currents in Biblical Interpretation. Louisville: Westminster/John Knox Press, 1992.

_____. Review of *Host, Guest, Enemy and Friend*, by David B. Gowler. In *Journal of Biblical Literature* 112 (1993): 152-54.

Davies, J. G. "Pentecost and Glossolalia." *Journal of Theological Studies* n.s. 3 (1952): 228-31.

Davies, Philip. "The Ending of Acts." *Expository Times* 94 (1983): 334-35.

Dawsey, James M. "The Literary Function of Point of View in Controlling Confusion and Irony in the Gospel of Luke." Ph.D. Diss., Emory University, 1983.

_____. "The Literary Unity of Luke-Acts: Questions of Style—a Task for Literary Critics." *New Testament Studies* 35 (1989): 48-66.

_____. *The Lukan Voice: Confusion and Irony in the Gospel of Luke.* Macon: Mercer University Press, 1986.

_____. "What's in a Name? Characterization in Luke." *Biblical Theology Bulletin* 16 (1986): 143-47.

Degenhardt, H. -J. *Lukas Evangelist der Armen.* Stuttgart: Katholisches Bibelwerk, 1965.

Delling, Gerhard. "Das lezte Wort der Apostelgeschichte." *Novum Testamentum* 15 (1973): 193-204.

Derrett, J. Duncan M. "Ananias, Sapphira, and the Right of Property." *Downside Review* 89 (1971): 225-32.

_____. "Simon Magus (Act 8^{9-24})." *Zeitschrift Für die Neutestamentliche Wissenschaft* 73 (1982): 52-68.

Dibelius, Martin. "Judentum Quellenanalyze und Kompositionanalyze in Acts 15," In *Judentum, Urchristentum, Kirche,* edited by Walther Eltester, 153-64. Berlin: A. Töpelmann, 1960.

_____. *Studies in the Acts of the Apostles.* Translated by M. Ling. Edited by Heinrich Greeven. London: SCM, 1956.

Dillon, Richard J. *From Eye-Witnesses to Ministers of the Word: Tradition and Composition in Luke 24.* Analecta Biblica: Investigationes Scientificae in Res Biblicas, vol. 82. Rome: Biblical Institute Press, 1978.

_____. "Previewing Luke's Project from His Prologue (Luke 1:1-4)." *Catholic Biblical Quarterly* 43 (1981): 205-27.

Dinkler, Erich. "Philippus und der ANHP AIΘIOΨ (Apg. 8, 26-40)." In *Jesus und Paulus,* edited by E. Earle Ellis and Erich Grässer, 85-95. Göttingen: Vandenhoeck & Ruprecht, 1975.

Docherty, Thomas. *Reading (Absent) Character: Towards a Theory of Characterization in Fiction.* Oxford: Clarendon Press, 1983.

Drury, John. *Tradition and Design in Luke's Gospel: A Study in Early Christian Historiography.* Atlanta: John Knox Press, 1977.

Dunn, James D. G. *Baptism in the Holy Spirit: A Re-Examination of the New Testament Teaching on the Gift of the Spirit in Relation to Pentecostalism Today.* Studies in Biblical Theology: Second Series, no. 15. London: SCM Press Ltd., 1970.

_____. *Jesus and the Spirit: A Study of the Religious and Charismatic Experience of Jesus and the First Christians as Reflected in the New Testament.* Philadelphia: Westminster Press, 1975.

Dupont, J. "La conclusion des Actes et son rapport a l'ensemble de l'ouvrage." In *Les Actes des Apôtres: traditions, rédaction, théologie,* edited by J. Kremer, 359-404. Bibliotheca Ephemeridum Theologicarum Lovaniensium, vol. 48. Gembloux: Leuven University Press, 1979.

_____. *Le discours de Milet. Testament pastoral de Paul Actes 20, 18-36.* Paris: Editions du Cerf, 1962.

_____. *Etudes sur les Actes Des Apôtres.* Lectio Divina, vol. 45. Paris: Editions du Cerf, 1967.

_____. "ΛΑΟΣ 'ΕΞ 'ΕΘΝΩΝ (Ac 15, 14)." In *Etudes sur les Actes des Apôtres,* 361-65. Lectio Divina, vol. 45. Paris: Editions du Cerf, 1967.

_____. "Un peuple d'entre les nations (Actes 15:14)." *New Testament Studies* 31 (1985): 321-35.

_____. *The Salvation of the Gentiles: Essays on the Acts of the Apostles.* Translated by John R. Keating. New York: Paulist Press, 1979.

Eagleton, Terry. *Literary Theory: An Introduction.* Minneapolis: University of Minnesota Press, 1983.

Edmonds, Peter. "The Lucan Our Father: A Summary of Lucan Teaching on Prayer?" *Expository Times* 91 (1979-80): 140-43.

Ellis, E. Earle. "The Role of the Christian Prophet in Acts." In *Apostolic History and the Gospel,* edited by W. Ward Gasque and Ralph P. Martin, 129-44. Grand Rapids: Eerdmans, 1970.

Evans, Craig A. "The Prophetic Setting of the Pentecost Sermon." *Zeitschrift für die Neutestamentliche Wissenschaft* 74 (1983): 148-50.

Ewen, Yosef. *Character in Narrative*. In Hebrew. Tel Aviv: Sifriyat Hapoalim, 1980.

_____. "The Theory of Character in Narrative Fiction." In Hebrew with English Synopsis. *Hasifrut* 3 (1971): 1-30.

Feuillet, A. "Le Baptême de Jésus." *Revue biblique* 71 (1964): 321-52.

_____. "Le récit lucanien de la tentation (Lc 4, 1-13)." *Biblica* 40 (1959): 613-31.

Fish, Stanley. *Is There a Text in This Class? The Authority of Interpretive Communities*. Cambridge: Harvard University Press, 1980.

Fitzmyer, Joseph A. "The Ascension of Christ and Pentecost." *Theological Studies* 45 (1984): 409-40.

_____. *The Gospel According to Luke*. Anchor Bible, vol. 28. 2 vols. Garden City: Doubleday, 1981-5.

_____. *Luke the Theologian: Aspects of His Teaching*. New York: Paulist Press, 1989.

Foakes-Jackson, F. J., and Kirsopp Lake, eds. *The Beginnings of Christianity: Part I, the Acts of the Apostles*. 5 vols. London: Macmillan and Co., Ltd., 1920-33.

Forster, E. M. *Aspects of the Novel*. New York: Harcourt, Brace & World, 1927.

Fowler, Robert M. *Let the Reader Understand: Reader-Response Criticism and the Gospel of Mark*. Minneapolis: Fortress Press, 1991.

_____. *Loaves and Fishes: The Function of the Feeding Stories in the Gospel of Mark*. Society of Biblical Literature Dissertation Series, vol. 54. Chico, Cal.: Scholars Press, 1981.

_____. "Who is 'the Reader' in Reader Response Criticism?" *Semeia* 31 (1985): 5-23.

Freedman, David Noel, ed. *Anchor Bible Dictionary*. New York: Doubleday, 1992.

Freund, Elizabeth. *The Return of the Reader: Reader-Response Criticism*. New York: Methuen, 1987.

Frye, Northrop. *Anatomy of Criticism: Four Essays.* Princeton: Princeton University Press, 1957.

Funk, Robert W. "The Enigma of the Famine Visit." *Journal of Biblical Literature* 75 (1956): 130-36.

Garnsey, Peter. *Famine and Food Supply in the Graeco-Roman World: Responses to Risk and Crisis.* New York: Cambridge University Press, 1988.

Garrett, Susan R. *The Demise of the Devil: Magic and the Demonic in Luke's Writings.* Minneapolis: Fortress Press, 1989.

Garvey, James. "Characterization in Narrative." *Poetics* 7 (1978): 63-78.

Gasque, W. Ward. *A History of the Interpretation of the Acts of the Apostles.* Peabody, Mass.: Hendrickson Publishers, 1989.

Gaventa, Beverly Roberts. *From Darkness to Light: Aspects of Conversion in the New Testament.* Philadelphia: Fortress Press, 1986.

_____. "Toward a Theology of Acts: Reading and Rereading." *Interpretation* 42 (1988): 146-57.

Genette, Gérard. *Narrative Discourse: An Essay in Method.* Translated by Jane E. Lewin, with a foreword by Jonathan Culler. Ithaca: Cornell University Press, 1980.

George, A. "L'Esprit Saint dans l'oeuvre de Luc." *Revue biblique* 85 (1978): 500-42.

Gero, Stephen. "The Spirit as a Dove at the Baptism of Jesus." *Novum Testamentum* 18 (1976): 17-35.

Giblet, J. "Baptism in the Spirit in the Acts of the Apostles." *One in Christ* 10 (1974): 162-71.

Giles, Kevin. "Present-Future Eschatology in the Book of Acts (1)." *The Reformed Theological Review* 40 (1981): 65-71.

_____. "Present-Future Eschatology in the Book of Acts (II)." *The Reformed Theological Review* 41 (1982): 11-18.

Gill, David. "The Structure of Acts 9." *Biblica* 55 (1974): 546-48.

Gils, F. *Jésus prophète d'apres les évangiles synoptiques.* Orientalia et Biblica Lovaniensia. Louvain: Publications Universitaires, 1957.

Ginsberg, Warren. *The Cast of Character: The Representation of Personality in Ancient and Medieval Literature.* Toronto: University of Toronto Press, 1983.

Gowler, David B. "Characterization in Luke: A Socio-Narratological Approach." *Biblical Theology Bulletin* 19 (1989): 54-62.

_____. *Host, Guest, Enemy and Friend: Portraits of the Pharisees in Luke and Acts.* Emory Studies in Early Christianity, vol. 2. New York: Peter Lang, 1991.

Greimas, A. -J. "Les actants, les acteurs, et les figures." In *Sémiotique narrative et textuelle,* edited by Claude Chabrol, 161-76. Paris: Librairie Larousse, 1973.

Grelot, Pierre. "La cantique de Siméon (Luc II, 29-32)." *Revue biblique* 93 (1986): 481-509.

Grundmann, W. "Der Pfingstbericht der Apostelgeschichte in seinem theologischen Sinn." In *Studia Evangelica.* Papers Presented to the Second International Congress on New Testament Studies Held at Christ Church, Oxford, 1961. Part I The New Testament Scriptures, edited by F. L. Cross, vol. II, 584-94. Texte und Untersuchungen zur Geschichte der altchristlichen Literatur, vol. 87. Berlin: Akademie-Verlag, 1964.

Gunkel, Hermann. *The Influence of the Holy Spirit: The Popular View of the Apostolic Age and the Teaching of the Apostle Paul.* Translation of *Die Wirkungen Des Heiligen Geistes Nach der Populären Anschauung der Apostolischen Zeit und der Lehre Des Apostels Paulus* (Göttingen: Vandenhoeck & Ruprecht, 1888). Translated by Roy A. Harrisville and Philip A. Quanbeck, II. Philadelphia: Fortress Press, 1979.

Haacker, Klaus. "Das Pfingstwunder als exegetisches Problem." In *Verborum Veritas,* edited by Otto Böcher and Klaus Haacker, 125-31. Wuppertal: Theologischer Verlag Rolf Brockhaus, 1970.

Haenchen, Ernst. *The Acts of the Apostles: A Commentary.* Translated by Bernard Noble, Gerald Shinn, Hugh Anderson, and R. McL. Wilson. Philadelphia: Westminster Press, 1971.

_____. "Quellenanalyze und Kompositionanalyze in Act 15." In *Judentum, Urchristentum, Kirche,* edited by Walther Eltester, 153-64. Berlin: A. Töpelmann, 1960.

Halliwell, Stephen. "Traditional Greek Conceptions of Character." In *Character-ization and Individuality in Greek Literature*, edited by Christopher Pelling, 32-59. Oxford: Clarendon Press, 1990.

Hamm, Dennis. "Sight to the Blind: Vision as Metaphor in Luke." *Biblica* 67 (1986): 457-77.

Harm, Frederick. "Structural Elements Related to the Gift of the Holy Spirit in Acts." *Concordia Journal* 14 (1988): 28-41.

Harnack, Adolph von. *Luke the Physician: The Author of the Third Gospel and the Acts of the Apostles*. Translated by J. R. Wilkinson. New York: G. P. Putnam's Sons, 1907.

Harvey, W. J. *Character and the Novel*. Ithaca: Cornell University Press, 1965.

Hastings, Adrian. *Prophet and Witness in Jerusalem: A Study of the Teaching of St. Luke*. London: Longmans, Green, 1958.

Haulotte, Edgar. "Fondation d'une communauté de type universel: Acts 10, 1 - 11, 18. Etude critique sur la rédaction, la «structure» et la «tradition» du récit." *Recherches de science religieuse* 58 (1970): 63-100.

Hauser, Herman J. *Strukturen der Abschlusserzählung der Apostelgeschichte (Apg 28, 16-31)*. Analecta Biblica, vol. 86. Rome: Biblical Institute Press, 1986.

Hawkes, Terence. *Structuralism and Semiotics*. Berkeley: University of California Press, 1977.

Haya-Prats, Gonzalo. *L'Esprit, force de l'Eglise. Sa nature et son activité d'apres les Actes des apôtres*. Translated from the Spanish by José J. Romero and Hubert Faes. Paris: Éditions de Cerf, 1975.

Hedrick, Charles W. "Paul's Conversion/Call: A Comparative Analysis of the Three Reports in Acts." *Journal of Biblical Literature* 100 (1981): 415-32.

Higbie, Robert. *Character and Structure in the English Novel*. Gainesville: University of Florida Press, 1984.

Hill, Craig C. *Hellenists and Hebrews: Reappraising Division Within the Earliest Church*. Minneapolis: Fortress Press, 1992.

Hill, David. *New Testament Prophecy*. London: Marshall, Morgan & Scott, 1979.

_____. "The Spirit and the Church's Witness: Observations on Acts 1:6-8." *Irish Biblical Studies* 6 (1984): 16-26.

Hirsch, E. D., Jr. *Validity in Interpretation*. New Haven: Yale University Press, 1967.

Hochman, Baruch. *Character in Literature*. Ithaca: Cornell University Press, 1985.

Holtzmann, Oscar. "Die Jerusalemreisen des Paulus und die Kollekte." *Zeitschrift für die neutestamentliche Wissenschaft* 6 (1905): 102-04.

Hull, J. H. E. *The Holy Spirit in the Acts of the Apostles*. London: Lutterworth Press, 1967.

Ingarden, Roman. *The Literary Work of Art; an Investigation on the Borderlines of Ontology, Logic, and Theory of Literature*. Northwestern University Studies in Phenomenology & Existential Philosophy. Evanston: Northwestern University Press, 1973.

Isaacs, Marie E. *The Concept of Spirit: A Study of Pneuma in Hellenistic Judaism and Its Bearing on the New Testament*. Heythrop Monographs, vol. 1. London: Heythrop College (University of London), 1976.

Iser, Wolfgang. *The Act of Reading: A Theory of Aesthetic Response*. Baltimore: Johns Hopkins University Press, 1978.

James, Henry. *The Art of Criticism: Henry James on the Theory and Practice of Fiction*. Edited by William Veeder and Susan M. Griffin. Chicago: University of Chicago Press, 1986.

Jervell, Jacob. *Luke and the People of God*. Minneapolis: Augsburg Publishing House, 1972.

_____. *The Unknown Paul: Essays on Luke-Acts and Early Christian History*. Minneapolis: Augsburg Publishing House, 1984.

Johnson, Luke T. *The Acts of the Apostles*. Sacra Pagina Series. Collegeville, Minn.: The Liturgical Press, 1992.

_____. *Decision Making in the Church: A Biblical Model*. Philadelphia: Fortress Press, 1983.

_____. *The Gospel of Luke*. Sacra Pagina Series. Collegeville, Minn.: The Liturgical Press, 1991.

_____. *The Literary Function of Possessions in Luke-Acts.* Society of Biblical Literature Dissertation Series, no. 39. Missoula, Mont.: Scholars Press, 1977.

_____. "The New Testament's Anti-Jewish Slander and the Conventions of Ancient Polemic." *Journal of Biblical Literature* 108 (1989): 419-41.

_____. "Tongues, Gift of." S.v. in *Anchor Bible Dictionary,* edited by David Noel Freedman. New York: Doubleday, 1992.

_____. *The Writings of the New Testament.* Philadelphia: Fortress Press, 1986.

Kaiser, Walter C., Jr. "The Promise of God and the Outpouring of the Holy Spirit: Joel 2:28-32 and Acts 2:16-21." In *The Living and Active Word of God: Studies in Honor of Samuel J. Schultz,* edited by Morris Inch and Ronald Youngblood, 109-22. Winona Lake, Ind.: Eisenbrauns, 1983.

Karris, Robert J. "Windows and Mirrors: Literary Criticism and Luke's Sitz Im Leben." In *Society of Biblical Literature 1979 Seminar Papers,* edited by Paul J. Achtemeier, 1:47-58. Society of Biblical Literature Seminar Papers Series, no. 16. Missoula, Mont.: Scholars Press, 1979.

Käsemann, Ernst. "The Disciples of John the Baptist in Ephesus." In *Essays on New Testament Themes,* 136-48. Philadelphia: Fortress Press, 1982.

_____. "Das Problem des historischen Jesus." *Zeitschrift für Theologie und Kirche* 51 (1951): 123-53.

Kaye, B. N. "Acts' Portrait of Silas." *Novum Testamentum* 21 (1979): 13-26.

Keck, Leander E. "The Spirit and the Dove." *New Testament Studies* 17 (1970-71): 41-67.

_____, and J. Louis Martyn, eds. *Studies in Luke-Acts.* Nashville: Abingdon Press, 1966; reprint, Philadelphia: Fortress Press, 1980.

Kelber, Werner H. *The Oral and Written Gospel: The Hermeneutics of Speaking and Writing in the Synoptic Tradition, Mark, Paul, and Q.* Philadelphia: Fortress Press, 1983.

Kennedy, George A. *New Testament Interpretation Through Rhetorical Criticism.* Chapel Hill: University of North Carolina Press, 1984.

Kilgallen, John J. "Did Peter Actually Fail to Get a Word In? (Acts 11, 15)." *Biblica* 71 (1990): 405-10.

_____. "The Function of Stephen's Speech (Acts 7, 2-53)." *Biblica* 70 (1989): 173-93.

_____. *The Stephen Speech: A Literary and Redactional Study of Acts 7, 2-53.* Analecta Biblica. Rome: Biblical Institute Press, 1976.

Kingsbury, Jack Dean. *Conflict in Luke.* Philadelphia: Fortress Press, 1991.

_____. "The Pharisees in Luke-Acts." In *The Four Gospels: Festschrift Frans Neirynck,* edited by F. Van Segroeck, C. M. Tuckett, G. Van Belle, and J. Verheyden, 2:1497-512. Leuven: Leuven University Press, 1992.

Kirk, J. Andrew. "The Messianic Role of Jesus and the Temptation Narrative: A Contemporary Perspective." *Evangelical Quarterly* 44 (1972): 11-29, 91-102.

Klein, Günter. "Lukas 1,1-4 als theologisches Programm." In *Zeit und Geschichte: Dankesgabe an Rudolf Bultmann Zum 80. Geburtstag,* edited by Erich Dinkler, 193-216. Tübingen: J. C. B. Mohr (Paul Siebeck), 1964.

Knights, L. C. "How Many Children Had Lady Macbeth?" In *Explorations,* 15-54. New York: New York University Press, 1933, reprint 1964.

Knox, Wilfred L. *The Acts of the Apostles.* Cambridge: Cambridge University Press, 1948.

Köberle, J. *Natur und Geist nach dem Auffassung des Alten Testaments.* München: C. H. Beck, 1901.

Koch, Robert. *Geist und Messias: Beitrag zur biblischen Theologie des Alten Testaments.* Vienna: Verlag Herder, 1950.

_____. "Spirit." In *Encyclopedia of Biblical Theology,* 3:869-89. Originally published as *Bibeltheologisches Wörterbuch,* 3rd ed., 1967, edited by Johannes B. Bauer. London: Sheed and Ward, 1970.

Kremer, Jacob. *Pfingstbericht und Pfingstgeschehen: eine exegetische Untersuchung zu Apg 2, 1-13.* Stuttgarter Bibelstudien. Stuttgart: KBW Verlag, 1973.

_____. "Die Voraussagen des Pfingstgeschehens in Apg 1, 4-5 und 8: ein Beitrag zur Deutung des Pfingstberichts." In *Die Zeit Jesu,* edited by Günther Bornkamm and Karl Rahner, 145-68. Freiburg: Herder, 1970.

Kretschmar, Georg. "Himmelfahrt und Pfingsten." *Zeitschrift für Kirchengeschichte* 16 (1954-5): 209-53.

Kurz, William S. "Narrative Approaches to Luke-Acts." *Biblica* 68 (1987): 195-220.

Lake, Kirsopp. "The Apostolic Council in Jerusalem." In *The Beginnings of Christianity: Part I, the Acts of the Apostles*, edited by Kirsopp Lake and Henry J. Cadbury, 5:195-212. London: Macmillan and Co., Ltd., 1933.

_____. "The Gift of the Spirit on the Day of Pentecost." In *The Beginnings of Christianity: Part I, the Acts of the Apostles*, edited by Kirsopp Lake and Henry J. Cadbury, 5:111-21. London: Macmillan and Co., Ltd., 1933.

_____. "The Holy Spirit." In *The Beginnings of Christianity: Part I, the Acts of the Apostles*, edited by Kirsopp Lake and Henry J. Cadbury, 5:96-111. London: Macmillan and Co., Ltd., 1933.

_____. "Paul's Route in Asia Minor." In *The Beginnings of Christianity: Part I, the Acts of the Apostles*, edited by Kirsopp Lake and Henry J. Cadbury, 5:224-40. London: Macmillan and Co., Ltd., 1933.

_____. "Proselytes and God-Fearers." In *The Beginnings of Christianity: Part I, the Acts of the Apostles*, edited by Kirsopp Lake and Henry J. Cadbury, 5:74-96. London: Macmillan and Co., Ltd., 1933.

Lambrecht, J. "Paul's Farewell-Address at Miletus (Acts 20:17-38)." In *Les Actes des Apôtres: traditions, rédaction, théologie*, edited by J. Kremer, 307-37. Bibliotheca Ephemeridum Theologicarum Lovaniensium, vol. 48. Gembloux: Leuven University Press, 1979.

Lampe, G. W. H. *God as Spirit*. The Bampton Lectures, 1976. Oxford: Clarendon Press, 1977.

_____. "The Holy Spirit in the Writings of St. Luke." In *Studies in the Gospels: Essays in Memory of R. H. Lightfoot*, edited by D. E. Nineham, 159-200. Oxford: Basil Blackwell, 1955.

_____. *The Seal of the Spirit: A Study in the Doctrine of Baptism and Confirmation in the New Testament and the Fathers*. London: Longmans, Green and Co., 1951.

Laurentin, Rene. *Structure et théologie de Luc 1-2*. Paris: Gabalda, 1957.

Leavis, F. R., ed. *Towards Standards of Criticism: Selections from "The Calendar of Modern Letters," 1925-7*. London: Lawrence and Wishart, 1976.

Leisegang, Hans. *Pneuma Hagion: der Ursprung des Geistbegriffs der synoptischen Evangelien aus der grieschischen Mystik.* Leipzig: Hinrichs, 1922.

Lentricchia, Frank. *After the New Criticism.* Chicago: University of Chicago Press, 1980.

Lévi-Strauss, Claude. *Structural Anthropology.* Translated by Claire Jacobsson and Brooke Grundfest Schoepf. Garden City: Doubleday, 1967.

_____. *Structural Anthropology.* Translated by Monique Layton. Vol. 2. Chicago: University of Chicago Press, 1976.

Liddell, Henry George, Robert Scott, and Henry Stuart Jones. *A Greek-English Lexicon.* New York: Oxford University Press, 1968.

Lohfink, Gerhard. *The Conversion of St. Paul: Narrative and History in Acts.* Translated by Bruce Malina. Chicago: Franciscan Herald Press, 1976.

_____. *Die Himmelfahrt Jesu: Untersuchungen zu den Himmelfahrts- und Erhöhungstexten bei Lukas.* München: Kösel-Verlag, 1971.

Lohse, Eduard. "Die Bedeutung des Pfingstberichtes im Rahmen des lukanischen Geschichtswerkes." *Evangelische Theologie* 13 (1953): 422-36.

Loning, Karl. "Die Korneliustradition." *Biblische Zeitschrift* 18 (1974): 1-19.

Louw, Johannes P., and Eugene A. Nida, eds. *Greek-English Lexicon of the New Testament Based on Semantic Domains.* New York: United Bible Societies, 1988.

Lukács, Georg. *Studies in European Realism.* With an introduction by Alfred Kazin. New York: Grosset and Dunlap, The Universal Library, 1964.

Lundgren, Sten. "Ananias and the Calling of Paul in Acts." *Studia Theologica* 25 (1971): 117-22.

Lys, Daniel. *"RUACH": Le Souffle dans l'Ancien Testament: enquête anthropologie a travers l'histoire theologique d'Israel.* Paris: Presses Universitaires de France, 1962.

McIntyre, John. "The Holy Spirit in Greek Patristic Thought." *Scottish Journal of Theology* 7 (1954): 353-75.

Mack, Burton L. *Rhetoric and the New Testament.* Guides to Biblical Scholarship. Minneapolis: Fortress Press, 1990.

_____, and Vernon K. Robbins. *Patterns of Persuasion in the Gospels.* Foundations & Facets. Literary Facets. Sonoma, Calif.: Polebridge Press, 1989.

Magne, Jean. "La réception de la variante «Vienne ton esprit sur nous et qu'il nous purifie» (Lc 11, 2) et l'origine des épiclèses, du baptéme et du «Notre Pere»." *Ephemerides Liturgicae* 102 (1988): 81-106.

Magness, J. Lee. *Sense and Absence: Structure and Suspension in the Ending of Mark's Gospel.* Semeia Studies. Atlanta: Scholars Press, 1986.

Malherbe, Abraham J. *Paul and the Popular Philosophers.* Minneapolis: Fortress Press, 1989.

Marin, Louis. "Essai d'analyse structurale d'Actes 10, 1 - 11, 18." *Recherches de science religieuse* 58 (1970): 39-61.

Marrow, Stanley B. "*Parrhēsia* and the New Testament." *Catholic Biblical Quarterly* 44 (1982): 431-46.

Marsh, Thomas. "Holy Spirit in Early Christian Teaching." *Irish Theological Quarterly* 45 (1978): 101-16.

Marshall, I. Howard. *The Gospel of Luke: A Commentary on the Greek Text.* New International Greek Testament Commentary. Grand Rapids: Eerdmans, 1978.

_____. *Luke: Historian and Theologian.* Grand Rapids: Zondervan Publishing House, 1970.

_____. "The Significance of Pentecost." *Scottish Journal of Theology* 30 (1977): 347-69.

Martin, Clarice J. "A Chamberlain's Journey and the Challenge of Interpretation for Liberation." *Semeia* 47 (1989): 105-35.

Martin, Wallace. *Recent Theories of Narrative.* Ithaca: Cornell University Press, 1986.

Mealand, D. L. "The Close of Acts and Its Hellenistic Greek Vocabulary." *New Testament Studies* 36 (1990): 583-97.

Meeks, Wayne A. "Simon Magus in Recent Research." *Religious Studies Review* 3 (1977): 137-42.

Menoud, Phillipe -H. "La mort d'Ananias et de Sapphira (Actes 5:1-11)." In *Aux sources de la tradition chrétienne,* 146-54. Biblioteque Théologique. Neuchatel: Delachaux & Niestlé, 1950.

Menzies, Robert P. *The Development of Early Christian Pneumatology with Special Reference to Luke-Acts.* Journal for the Study of the New Testament Supplement Series, no. 54. Sheffield: JSOT Press, 1991.

Metahistory: Six Critiques. History and Theory 19 (1980). Middletown, Conn.: Wesleyan University Press, 1980.

Metzger, Bruce M. "Seventy or Seventy-Two Disciples?" *New Testament Studies* 5 (1958-9): 299-306.

_____. *A Textual Commentary on the Greek New Testament.* New York: United Bible Societies, 1971.

Michel, Hans-Joachim. *Die Abschiedsrede des Paulus an die Kirche Apg 20, 17-38: Motivgeschichte und theologische Bedeutung.* Munich: Kösel-Verlag, 1973.

Minear, Paul S. "Luke's Use of the Birth Stories." In *Studies in Luke-Acts,* edited by Leander E. Keck and J. Louis Martyn, 111-30. Philadelphia: Fortress Press, 1980.

_____. *To Heal and to Reveal: The Prophetic Vocation According to Luke.* New York: The Seabury Press, 1976.

Moessner, David P. "The Christ Must Suffer: New Light on the Jesus-Peter, Stephen, Paul Parallels in Luke-Acts." *Novum Testamentum* 28 (1986): 220-56.

_____. "The Ironic Fulfillment of Israel's Glory." Chapter 3 in *Luke-Acts and the Jewish People: Eight Critical Perspectives,* edited by Joseph B. Tyson, 35-50. Minneapolis: Augsburg Publishing House, 1988.

_____. *Lord of the Banquet: The Literary and Theological Significance of the Lukan Travel Narrative.* Minneapolis: Fortress Press, 1989.

_____. "Luke 9:1-50: Luke's Preview of the Journey of the Prophet Like Moses of Deuteronomy." *Journal of Biblical Literature* 102 (1983): 575-605.

_____. "The Meaning of ΚΑΘΕΞΗΣ in the Lukan Prologue as a Key to the Distinctive Contribution of Luke's Narrative Among the 'Many.'" In *The Four Gospels: Festschrift Frans Neirynck,* edited by F. Van Segroeck, C. M. Tuckett, G. Van Belle, and J. Verheyden, 2:1513-28. Leuven: Leuven University Press, 1992.

_____. "Paul in Acts: Preacher of Eschatological Repentance to Israel." *New Testament Studies* 34 (1988): 96-104.

Montague, George T. *The Holy Spirit: Growth of a Biblical Tradition.* Exploration. New York: Paulist Press, 1976.

Moore, Stephen D. *Literary Criticism and the Gospels: The Theoretical Challenge.* New Haven: Yale University Press, 1989.

_____. *Mark and Luke in Poststructural Perspectives: Jesus Begins to Write.* New Haven: Yale University Press, 1992.

_____. "Narrative Homiletics: Lucan Rhetoric and the Making of the Reader." Ph.D. Diss., University of Dublin (Trinity College), 1986.

Moule, C. F. D. "Once More, Who Were the Hellenists?" *Expository Times* 70 (1958-9): 100-02.

Moulton, James Hope, and George Milligan. *The Vocabulary of the Greek Testament Illustrated from the Papyrii and Other Non-Literary Sources.* Grand Rapids: Eerdmans, 1930.

Munck, Johannes. "Discours d'adieu dans le Nouveau Testament et dans la littérature biblique." In *Aux sources de la tradition chrétienne,* 155-70. Biblioteque Théologique. Neuchatel: Delachaux & Niestlé, 1950.

Nebe, Gottfried. *Prophetische Züge im Bilde Jesu bei Lukas.* Beiträge zur Wissenschaft vom Alten und Neuen Testament, vol. 127. Stuttgart: Verlag W. Kohlhammer, 1989.

Nelson, Edwin S. "Paul's First Missionary Journey as Paradigm: A Literary-Critical Assessment of Acts 13-14." Ph.D. Diss., Boston University, 1982.

Neve, Lloyd. *The Spirit of God in the Old Testament.* Tokyo: Seibunsha, 1972.

Niehoff, M. "Do Biblical Characters Talk to Themselves? Narrative Modes of Representing Inner Speech in Early Biblical Fiction." *Journal of Biblical Literature* 111 (1992): 577-95.

Noack, B. "The Day of Pentecost in Jubilees, Qumran and Acts." *Annual of the Swedish Theological Institute* 1 (1962): 73-95.

Nock, Arther Darby. "Paul and the Magus." In *The Beginnings of Christianity: Part I, the Acts of the Apostles,* edited by Kirsopp Lake and Henry J. Cadbury, 5:164-88. London: Macmillan and Co., Ltd., 1933.

Nuttall, Geoffrey F. *The Moment of Recognition: Luke as Storyteller.* London: Athlone Press, 1978.

O'Reilly, Leo. *Word and Sign in the Acts of the Apostles: A Study in Lucan Theology.* Rome: Editrice Pontificia Università Gregoriana, 1987.

O'Toole, R. F. "Activity of the Risen Jesus in Luke-Acts." *Biblica* 62 (1981): 471-98.

_____. "Philip and the Ethiopian Eunuch (Acts viii, 25-40)." *Journal for the Study of the New Testament* 17 (1983): 25-34.

Ong, Walter J. *Orality and Literacy: The Technologizing of the Word.* New Accents. New York: Methuen, 1982.

Opsahl, Paul D., ed. *The Holy Spirit in the Life of the Church from Biblical Times to the Present.* Minneapolis: Augsburg Publishing House, 1978.

Oulton, J. E. L. "The Holy Spirit, Baptism, and Laying on of Hands in Acts." *Expository Times* 66 (1954-5): 236-40.

Palmer, D. W. "The Literary Background of Acts 1:1-14." *New Testament Studies* 33 (1987): 427-38.

Parsons, Mikeal C. *The Departure of Jesus in Luke-Acts: The Ascension Narratives in Context.* Journal for the Study of the New Testament Supplement Series, vol. 21. Sheffield: Sheffield Academic Press, 1987.

Parsons, Mikeal C., and Joseph B. Tyson, eds. *Cadbury, Knox and Talbert: American Contributions to the Study of Acts.* Biblical Scholarship in North America. Atlanta: Scholars Press, 1992.

Peirce, Charles S. *Collected Papers.* Edited by Charles Hartshorne and Paul Weiss. Cambridge: Harvard University Press, 1958-60.

Pelling, Christopher, ed. *Characterization and Individuality in Greek Literature.* Oxford: Clarendon Press, 1990.

Perrot, Charles. "Les Decisions de L'assemblée de Jérusalem." *Recherches des science religieuse* 69 (1981): 195-208.

Pervo, Richard I. *Profit with Delight: The Literary Genre of the Acts of the Apostles.* Philadelphia: Fortress Press, 1987.

Pesch, Rudolf. *Die Apostelgeschichte.* Evangelisch-Katholischer Kommentar zum Neuen Testament, vol. 5. Zürich: Benziger, 1986.

Plunkett, Mark A. "Ethnocentricity and Salvation History in the Cornelius Episode." In *Society of Biblical Literature 1985 Seminar Papers,* edited by Kent Harold Richards, 465-79. Atlanta: Scholars Press, 1985.

Pokorný, Petr. "The Temptation Stories and Their Intention." *New Testament Studies* 20 (1973-4): 115-27.

Poland, Lynn M. *Literary Criticism and Biblical Hermeneutics: A Critique of Formalist Approaches.* Chico: Scholars Press, 1985.

Potin, J. *La fête juive de la Pentecôte.* Paris: Editions du Cerf, 1971.

Powell, Mark Allan. "The Religious Leaders in Luke: A Literary-Critical Study." *Journal of Biblical Literature* 109 (1990): 93-110.

_____. *What Are They Saying About Acts?* New York: Paulist Press, 1991.

_____. *What Are They Saying About Luke?* New York: Paulist Press, 1989.

Praeder, Susan Marie. "The Problem of First-Person Narration in Acts." *Novum Testamentum* 29 (1987): 193-218.

Prast, Franz. *Presbyter und Evangelium im nachapostolischer Zeit: Die Abschiedsrede des Paulus in Milet (Apg 20, 17-38).* Forschung zur Bible, vol. 29. Stüttgart: Verlag Katholisches Bibelwerk, 1979.

Prince, Gerald. *Narratology: The Form and Functioning of Narrative.* New York: Mouton, 1982.

Propp, Vladímir. *Morphology of the Folktale.* 2nd Ed. Translated by Laurence Scott. With an introduction by Svatava Pirkova-Jakobson. Edited with a preface by Louis A. Wagner. New introduction by Alan Dundes. Publications of the American Folklore Society. Bibliographical and special series, vol. 9. Austin: University of Texas Press, 1968.

Puskas, C. B. "The Conclusion of Luke-Acts: An Investigation of the Literary Function and Theological Significance of Acts 28:16-31." Ph.D. Diss., St. Louis University, 1980.

Quesnel, Michael. *Baptisés dans L'Esprit: Baptême et Esprit dans les Actes des Apôtres.* Lectio Divina, vol. 120. Paris: Editions du Cerf, 1985.

Radl, W. *Das Lukas-Evangelium.* Erträge der Forschung, vol. 261. Darmstadt: Wissenschaftliche Buchgesellschaft, 1988.

Ransom, John Crowe. *The New Criticism.* New York: New Directions, 1941.

Resseguie, James L. "Point of View in the Central Section of Luke (9:51-19:44)." *Journal of the Evangelical Theological Society* 25 (1982): 41-47.

Rhoads, David, and Donald Michie. *Mark as Story: An Introduction to the Narrative of a Gospel.* Philadelphia: Fortress Press, 1982.

Richard, Earl. *Acts 6:1-8:4: The Author's Method of Composition.* Society of Biblical Literature Dissertation Series, no. 41. Missoula, Mont.: Scholars Press, 1978.

_____. "The Divine Purpose: The Jews and the Gentile Mission (Acts 15)." In *Luke-Acts: New Perspectives from the Society of Biblical Literature Seminar,* edited by Charles H. Talbert, 188-209. New York: Crossroad, 1984.

_____. "Pentecost as a Recurrent Theme in Luke-Acts." In *New Views on Luke and Acts,* edited by Earl Richard, 133-49. Collegeville: The Liturgical Press, 1990.

Ricoeur, Paul. *The Rule of Metaphor: Multi-Disciplinary Studies of the Creation of Meaning in Language.* Translated by Robert Czerny, Kathleen McLaughlin, and John Costello. Toronto: University of Toronto Press, 1977.

_____. *Time and Narrative.* Translated by Kathleen McLaughlin and David Pellauer. 3 vols. Chicago: University of Chicago Press, 1984-8.

Rimmon-Kenan, Shlomith. *Narrative Fiction: Contemporary Poetics.* New York: Methuen, 1983.

Robbins, Vernon K. *Jesus the Teacher: A Socio-Rhetorical Interpretation of Mark.* Philadelphia: Fortress Press, 1984.

Sabourin, Leopold. *L'Evangile de Luc: introduction et commentaire.* Rome: Editrice Pontificia Universita Gregoriana, 1987.

Sacks, S., ed. *On Metaphor.* Chicago: University of Chicago Press, 1979.

Sanders, Jack T. *The Jews in Luke-Acts.* Philadelphia: Fortress Press, 1987.

_____. "The Salvation of the Jews in Luke-Acts." In *Luke-Acts: New Perspectives from the Society of Biblical Literature Seminar*, edited by Charles H. Talbert, 104-28. New York: Crossroad, 1984.

Saussure, Ferdinand de. *Course in General Linguistics*. Edited by Charles Bally, Albert Sechehaye, and Albert Riedlinger. Translated by Roy Harris. LaSalle, Ill.: Open Court, 1983.

Schaberg, Jane. *The Illegitimacy of Jesus: A Feminist Theological Interpretation of the Infancy Narratives*. San Francisco: Harper & Row, 1987.

Schäfer, Peter. *Die Vorstellung vom Heiligen Geist in der rabbinischen Literature*. Studien zum Alten und Neuen Testament, vol. 28. Munich: Kösel-Verlag, 1972.

Scharlemann, Martin H. *Stephen: A Singular Saint*. Analecta Biblica. Rome: Pontifical Biblical Institute, 1968.

Schneider, Gerhard. *Die Apostelgeschichte*. Herders theologischer Kommentar zum Neuen Testament, vol. 5, pts. 1-2. Freiburg: Herder, 1980-2.

_____. "Die Bitte um das Kommen des Geistes im lukanischen Vaterunser (Lk 11, 2 v.l.)." In *Studien zum Text und zur Ethink des Neuen Testaments*. Festschrift Zum 80. Geburtstag von Heinrich Greeven, edited by Wolfgang Schrage, 344-73. Berlin: Walter de Gruyter, 1986.

_____. *Das Evangelium nach Lukas*. Ökumenischer Taschenbuchkommentar zum Neuen Testament, vol. 3. Gütersloh: Gütersloher Verlagshaus Mohn, 1977.

_____. "Zur Bedeutung von καθεξῆς im lukanischen Doppelwerk." *Zeitschrift Für die Neutestamentliche Wissenschaft* 68 (1977): 128-31.

Scholes, Robert, and Robert Kellogg. *The Nature of Narrative*. London: Oxford University Press, 1966.

Schubert, Paul. "The Final Cycle of Speeches in the Book of Acts." *Journal of Biblical Literature* 87 (1968): 1-16.

Schürmann, Heinz. *Das Lukasevangelium: Kommentar zu Kap. 1, 1-9, 50*. Herders Theologischer Kommentar zum Neuen Testament. Freiburg: Herder, 1969.

Schwartz, Daniel R. "The End of the ΓΗ (Acts 1:8): Beginning or End of the Christian Vision?" *Journal of Biblical Literature* 105 (1986): 669-76.

Schweizer, Eduard. "Die Bekehrung des Apollos, Ag. 18, 24-26." *Evangelische Theologie* 15 (1955): 247-54.

_____. *The Good News According to Luke.* Atlanta: John Knox Press, 1984.

_____. *The Holy Spirit.* Translation of *Heiliger Geist* (Stuttgart: Kreuz-Verlag, 1978). Translated by Reginald H. Fuller and Ilse Fuller. Philadelphia: Fortress Press, 1980.

_____. "πνεῦμα." (sections on Gnosticism and New Testament). In *Theological Dictionary of the New Testament,* edited by Gerhard Friedrich, edited and translated by Geoffrey W. Bromiley, 6:389-455. Grand Rapids: Eerdmans, 1968.

_____. "The Spirit of Power: The Uniformity and Diversity of the Concept of the Holy Spirit in the New Testament." Translated by John Bright and Eugene Debor. *Interpretation* 6 (1952): 259-78.

Scott, Ernest F. *The Spirit in the New Testament.* New York: George H. Doran Co., [1923].

Sheeley, Steven M. "Narrative Asides and Narrative Authority in Luke-Acts." *Biblical Theology Bulletin* 18 (1988): 102-07.

_____. *Narrative Asides in Luke-Acts.* Journal for the Study of the New Testament Supplement Series, no. 72. Sheffield: JSOT Press, 1992.

Shelton, James B. *Mighty in Word and Deed: The Role of the Holy Spirit in Luke-Acts.* Peabody, Mass.: Hendrickson Publishers, 1991.

Shklovsky, Viktor. "Art as Technique." Reprinted from *Russian Formalist Criticism: Four Essays,* edited by Lee T. Lemon and Marion J. Reis, 5-24. Lincoln: University of Nebraska Press, 1965. In *Contemporary Literary Criticism,* edited by Robert Con Davis, 51-63. New York: Longman, 1986.

Shoemaker, William Ross. "The Use of רוּחַ in the Old Testament and of πνεῦμα in the New Testament. A Lexicographical Study." *Journal of Biblical Literature* 23 (1904): 13-67.

Sieber, John H. "The Spirit as the 'Promise of My Father' in Luke 24:49." In *Sin, Salvation, and the Spirit.* Commemorating the Fiftieth Year of The Liturgical Press, edited by Daniel Durken, 271-78. Collegeville, Minn.: Liturgical Press, 1979.

Siker, Jeffrey S. *Disinheriting the Jews: Abraham in Early Christian Controversy.* Louisville: Westminster/John Knox Press, 1991.

_____. "'First to the Gentiles': A Literary Analysis of Luke 4:16-30." *Journal of Biblical Literature* 111 (1992): 73-90.

Simon, Marcel. *St. Stephen and the Hellenists in the Primitive Church.* London: Longmans, Green and Co., 1958.

Smalley, Stephen S. "Spirit, Kingdom and Prayer in Luke-Acts." *Novum Testamentum* 15 (1973): 59-71.

Smeed, J. W. *The Theophrastan "Character": The History of a Literary Genre.* Oxford: Clarendon Press, 1985.

Spencer, F. Scott. *The Portrait of Philip in Acts: A Study of Roles and Relations.* Journal for the Study of the New Testament Supplement Series, vol. 67. Sheffield: JSOT Press, 1992.

Squires, John T. *The Plan of God in Luke-Acts.* Society for New Testament Studies Monograph Series, vol. 76. Cambridge: Cambridge University Press, 1993.

Stählin, G. "Τὸ πνεῦμα Ἰησοῦ (Apostelgeschichte 16:7)." In *Christ and Spirit in the New Testament,* edited by Barnabas Lindars and Stephen S. Smalley, 229-52. Cambridge: Cambridge University Press, 1973.

Sternberg, Meir. *The Poetics of Biblical Narrative: Ideological Literature and the Drama of Reading.* Indiana Literary Biblical Series. Bloomington: Indiana University Press, 1985.

Stronstad, Roger. *The Charismatic Theology of St. Luke.* Peabody, Mass.: Hendrickson Publishers, 1984.

Strousma, Gedaliahu G. "Le couple de l'ange et de l'esprit: traditions juives et chrétiennes." *Revue biblique* 88 (1981): 42-61.

Suleiman, Susan, and Inge Karalus Crosman, eds. *The Reader in the Text: Essays on Audience and Interpretation.* Princeton: Princeton University Press, 1980.

Swanston, Hamish. "The Lukan Temptation Narrative." *Journal of Theological Studies* n.s. 17 (1966): 71.

Swete, Henry Barclay. *The Holy Spirit in the Ancient Church: A Study of Christian Teaching in the Age of the Fathers.* London: Macmillan and Co., Ltd., 1912.

_____. *The Holy Spirit in the New Testament: A Study of Primitive Christian Teaching.* London: Macmillan and Co., Ltd., 1909.

Talbert, Charles H. *Literary Patterns, Theological Themes and the Genre of Luke-Acts.* Society of Biblical Literature Monograph Series. Missoula, Mont.: Scholars Press, 1974.

_____, ed. *Luke-Acts: New Perspectives from the Society of Biblical Literature Seminar.* New York: Crossroad, 1984.

_____. *Luke and the Gnostics: An Examination of the Lucan Purpose.* Nashville: Abingdon, 1966.

_____. *Reading Luke: A Literary and Theological Commentary on the Third Gospel.* New York: Crossroad, 1982.

Tannehill, Robert C. "The Magnificat as Poem." *Journal of Biblical Literature* 93 (1974): 263-75.

_____. *The Narrative Unity of Luke-Acts: A Literary Interpretation.* Vol. 1 The Gospel According to Luke. Philadelphia: Fortress Press, 1986.

_____. *The Narrative Unity of Luke-Acts: A Literary Interpretation.* Vol. 2 The Acts of the Apostles. Minneapolis: Fortress Press, 1990.

Taylor, Arch. B., Jr. "Decision in the Desert: The Temptation of Jesus in the Light of Deuteronomy." *Interpretation* 14 (1960): 300-09.

Thornton, T. C. G. "To the End of the Earth: Acts 1[8]." *Expository Times* 89 (1978): 374-75.

Tiede, David L. "The Exaltation of Jesus and the Restoration of Israel in Acts 1." *Harvard Theological Review* 79 (1986): 278-86.

_____. *Prophecy and History in Luke-Acts.* Philadelphia: Fortress Press, 1980.

Todorov, Tzvetan. *The Fantastic: A Structural Approach to a Literary Genre.* Translated by Richard Howard, with a foreword by Robert Scholes. Ithaca: Cornell University Press, 1975.

Tompkins, Jane, ed. *Reader-Response Criticism.* Baltimore: Johns Hopkins University Press, 1980.

Turner, M. M. B. "Jesus and the Spirit in Lucan Perspective." *Tyndale Bulletin* 32 (1981): 3-42.

_____. "Luke and the Spirit. Studies in the Significance of Receiving the Spirit in Luke-Acts." Diss., Trinity Hall, Cambridge University. 1980.

_____. "The Significance of Receiving the Spirit in Luke-Acts: A Survey of Modern Scholarship." *Trinity Journal* n.s. 2 (1981): 131-58.

_____. "Spirit Endowment in Luke-Acts: Some Linguistic Considerations." *Vox Evangelica* 12 (1981): 45-63.

Turner, Nigel. "The Relation of Luke I and II to Hebraic Sources and to the Rest of Luke-Acts." *New Testament Studies* 2 (1955-6): 100-09.

Tyson, Joseph B. *Images of Judaism in Luke-Acts.* Columbia: University of South Carolina, 1992.

_____, ed. *Luke-Acts and the Jewish People: Eight Critical Perspectives.* Minneapolis: Augsburg Publishing House, 1988.

Van Stempvoort, P. A. "The Interpretation of the Ascension in Luke and Acts." *New Testament Studies* 5 (1958-9): 30-42.

van Unnik, W. C. "Der Ausdruck 'ΕΩΣ 'ΕΣΧΑΤΟΥ ΤΗΣ ΓΗΣ (Apostelgeschichte I 8) und sein alttestamentlicher Hintergrund." In *Sparsa Collecta,* 1:386-401. Leiden: E. J. Brill, 1973.

_____. "The Background and Signficance of Acts X 4 and 35." In *Sparsa Collecta,* 1:213-58. Leiden: Brill, 1973.

_____. "Der Befehl an Philippus." In *Sparsa Collecta,* 1:328-39. Leiden: Brill, 1973.

_____. "Once More St. Luke's Prologue." In *Essays on the Gospel of Luke and Acts,* 7-26. Neotestamentica 7 (1973). New Testament Society of South Africa, 1973.

Vielhauer, Philipp. "Zum 'Paulinismus' der Apostelgeschichte." *Evangelische Theologie* 10 (1950-51): 1-15.

Volz, Paul. *Der Geist Gottes und die verwandten Erscheinungen im Alten Testament und im anschliessenden Judentum.* Tübingen: J. C. B. Mohr (Paul Siebeck), 1910.

Vökel, Martin. "Exegetische Erwägungen Zum Verständnis Des Begriffs ΚΑΘΕΞΗΣ im Lukanischen Prolog." *New Testament Studies* 20 (1973-4): 289-99.

Wainwright, Arthur W. *The Trinity in the New Testament.* London: SPCK, 1962.

Walworth, Allen James. "The Narrator of Acts." Ph.D. Diss., Southern Baptist Theological Seminary, 1984.

Watkin-Jones, Howard. *The Holy Spirit from Arminius to Wesley: A Study of the Christian Teaching Concerning the Holy Spirit and His Place in the Trinity in the Seventeenth and Eighteenth Centuries.* London: Epworth, 1929.

_____. *The Holy Spirit in the Mediaeval Church: A Study of Christian Teaching Concerning the Holy Spirit and His Place in the Trinity from the Post-Patristic Age to the Counter-Reformation.* London: Epworth, 1922.

Weinsheimer, Joel. "Theory of Character: *Emma.*" *Poetics Today* 1, no. 1-2 (1979): 185-211.

Wellek, René, and Austin Warren. *Theory of Literature.* 3rd Ed. New York: Harcourt, Brace and World, Harvest, 1957.

White, Hayden. *The Content of the Form: Narrative Discourse and Historical Representation.* Baltimore: Johns Hopkins University Press, 1987.

_____. *Metahistory: The Historical Imagination in Nineteenth-Century Europe.* Baltimore: Johns Hopkins University Press, 1973.

Wiefel, Wolfgang, and Walter Grundmann. *Das Evangelium nach Lukas.* Theologischer Handkommentar zum Neuen Testament, vol. 3. Berlin: Evangelische Verlagsanstalt, 1988.

Williams, G. O. "The Baptism in Luke's Gospel." *Journal of Theological Studies* 45 (1944): 31-38.

Wills, Lawrence M. "The Depiction of the Jews in Acts." *Journal of Biblical Literature* 110 (1991): 631-54.

Wilson, Rawdon. "The Bright Chimera: Character as a Literary Term." *Critical Inquiry* 5 (1979): 725-49.

Wilson, Stephen G. *The Gentiles and the Gentile Mission in Luke-Acts*. Cambridge: Cambridge University Press, 1973.

_____. *Luke and the Law*. Society for New Testament Studies Monograph Series, vol. 50. Cambridge: Cambridge University Press, 1983.

Wimsatt, W. K., Jr. *The Verbal Icon: Studies in the Meaning of Poetry*. Lexington: University of Kentucky Press, 1954.

Wink, Walter. *John the Baptist in the Gospel Tradition*. Society for New Testament Studies Monograph Series. London: Cambridge University Press, 1968.

Winstanley, Edward William. *Spirit in the New Testament: An Enquiry Into the Use of the Word* ΠΝΕΥΜΑ *in All Passages, and a Survey of the Evidence Concerning the Holy Spirit*. Cambridge: Cambridge University Press, 1908.

Wojcik, Jan. *The Road to Emmaus: Reading Luke's Gospel*. West Lafayette, Ind.: Purdue University Press, 1989.

Wolter, Michael. "Apollos und die ephesinischen Johannesjünger (Act 18:24-19:7)." *Zeitschrift für die neutestamentliche Wissenschaft* 78 (1987): 49-73.

Wrege, Hans-Theo. "Zur Rolle des Geisteswortes in frühchristlichen Traditionen (LC 12, 10 parr.)." In *Logia: les paroles de Jésus—The Sayings of Jesus*. Mémorial Joseph Coppens, edited by Joël Delobel, 373-77. Bibliotheca Ephemeridum Theologicarum Lovaniensium, vol. 59. Leuven: Leuven University Press, 1982.

Zehnle, Richard F. *Peter's Pentecost Discourse: Tradition and Lukan Reinterpretation in Peter's Speeches of Acts 2 and 3*. Society of Biblical Literature Monograph Series, vol. 15. Nashville: Abingdon Press, 1971.

Ziesler, J. "Luke and the Pharisees." *New Testament Studies* 25 (1978-9): 146-57.